ASK FODOR'S

Great trips begin with great planning. You've seen your travel agent and read this guidebook, but what if you still have questions?

Visit us on the Web at
www.fodors.com

Our acclaimed Web site is an invaluable resource where you can:

- Swap stories with fellow travelers and get advice from our experts

- Search our database of hotels and restaurants worldwide for the ones that will suit you best

- Research everything from car rentals to how to take great travel photographs

- Find out about other Fodor's titles covering your destination (and others worldwide)

- Take a short course in French, German, Italian, and Spanish for travelers, complete with audio

Fodor's

Rome

The Complete Guide With Walking Tours of Classical Rome and the Vatican

Fodor's

FIRST 1st EDITION

Rome

The complete guide, thoroughly up-to-date

Packed with details that will make your trip

The must-see sights, off and on the beaten path

What to see, what to skip

Vacation itineraries, walking tours, day trips

Smart lodging and dining options

Essential local do's and taboos

Transportation tips

Key contacts, savvy travel advice

When to go, what to pack

Clear, accurate, easy-to-use maps

Books to read, videos to watch, background essays

Fodor's Travel Publications, Inc.
New York • Toronto • London • Sydney • Auckland
www.fodors.com

Fodor's Rome

EDITOR: Nancy van Itallie

Editorial Contributors: Barbara Angelillo, David Brown, Jon Eldan, Valerie Hamilton, Roger Jones, Jennifer Paull, Caragh Rockwood, Helayne Schiff, M. T. Schwartzman (Gold Guide editor), Lucy Villeneuve

Editorial Production: Melissa Klurman

Maps: David Lindroth, *cartographer*; Bob Blake and Steven Amsterdam, *map editors*

Design: Fabrizio La Rocca, *creative director*; Guido Caroti, *associate art director*; Jolie Novak, *photo editor*

Production/Manufacturing: Mike Costa

Cover Photograph: Kindra Clineff

Copyright

1st Edition

ISBN 0-679-00232-4

Special Sales

Fodor's Travel Publications are available at special discounts for bulk purchases for sales promotions or premiums. Special editions, including personalized covers, excerpts of existing guides, and corporate imprints, can be created in large quantities for special needs. For more information, contact your local bookseller or write to Special Markets, Fodor's Travel Publications, 201 East 50th Street, New York, NY 10022. Inquiries from Canada should be directed to your local Canadian bookseller or sent to Random House of Canada, Ltd., Marketing Department, 2775 Matheson Boulevard East, Mississauga, Ontario L4W 4P7. Inquiries from the United Kingdom should be sent to Fodor's Travel Publications, 20 Vauxhall Bridge Road, London SW1V 2SA, England.

PRINTED IN THE UNITED STATES OF AMERICA

10 9 8 7 6 5 4 3 2 1

CONTENTS

Maps

ON THE ROAD WITH FODOR'S

WHEN I PLAN A VACATION, the first thing I do is cast around among my friends and colleagues to find someone who's just been where I'm going. That's because there's no substitute for a recommendation from a good friend who knows your tastes, your budget, and your circumstances, someone who's just been there. Unfortunately, such friends are few and far between. So it's nice to know that there's Fodor's *Rome*.

In the first place, this book won't stay home when you hit the road. It will accompany you every step of the way, steering you away from wrong turns and wrong choices and never expecting a thing in return. Most important of all, it's written by the kind of people you *would* hit up for travel tips if you knew them. They're as choosy as your pickiest friend, except they've probably seen a lot more of Rome. In these pages, the writer doesn't send you chasing down every sight in Rome but has instead selected the best ones, the ones that are worthy of your time and money. To make it easy for you to put it all together in the time you have, she has created itineraries and neighborhood walks that you can mix and match in a snap. Will this be the vacation of your dreams? We hope so.

About Our Writers

Our success in helping to make your trip the best of all possible vacations is a credit to the hard work of our extraordinary writers.

The first time veteran Fodorite **Barbara Walsh Angelillo** arrived in Rome, she was traveling on a tight schedule; still, she had time to fall in love with both the city and a dark-eyed Italian—simultaneously. Within a year, Barbara said *arrivederci* to her native New York City to settle, marry, and raise three children in Italy. Barbara unwinds in what she calls "two of Italy's most special places," Umbria and the Amalfi Coast. For this book, she wrote the Exploring, Lodging, Nightlife and the Arts, Outdoor Activities and Sports, and Shopping chapters, as well as the essay on Rome dining in the Portraits chapter.

Jon Eldan, co-author of the Dining chapter, studied European history in Berkeley, California, before packing his bags in 1994 to see the real thing. He now lives and bakes bread in Rome and goes back to visit the old country from time to time. Eldan's colleague **Carla Lionello** grew up in Venice. Several years ago she traded Piazza San Marco for the Spanish Steps and moved to Rome. Although she still hasn't learned to drive, it doesn't stop her from traveling all over Italy in search of endangered pastry.

After a decade's long-distance love affair with Rome, **Valerie Hamilton,** who wrote the Closeups on Rome, recently settled in the city permanently, working in television—covering topics from wine-making to heli-rescue dogs—in between stints for Fodor's. While classic Italian specialties have charmed her since adolescence, it is Italy's subtle side that has captured her heart: the creative yet calculated twist of a *tortello,* or the gentle curve of an Italian shoe.

After studying classics at Oxford, **Roger Jones,** author of the essay on the arts in Rome in the Portraits chapter, lived in Rome for two years before taking an art history degree at the Courtauld Institute in London. He coauthored a widely acclaimed study of Raphael.

Lucy Villeneuve, a journalist who has lived in Italy for more than 10 years, wrote the Introduction.

Connections

We're pleased that the American Society of Travel Agents continues to endorse Fodor's as its guidebook of choice. ASTA is the world's largest and most influential travel trade association, operating in more than 170 countries, with 27,000 members pledged to adhere to a strict code of ethics reflecting the Society's motto, "Integrity in Travel." ASTA shares Fodor's devotion to providing smart, honest travel information and advice to travelers, and we've long recommended that our readers—even those who have guidebooks and traveling friends—consult ASTA member agents for the experience and professionalism they bring to your vacation planning.

On Fodor's Web site (www.fodors.com), check out the new Resource Center, an on-line companion to the Gold Guide section of this book, complete with useful hot links to related sites. In our forums, you can also get lively advice from other travelers and more great tips from Fodor's experts worldwide.

How to Use This Book

Organization

Up front is the **Gold Guide,** an easy-to-use section arranged alphabetically by topic. Under each listing you'll find tips and information that will help you accomplish what you need to in Rome. You'll also find addresses and telephone numbers of organizations and companies that offer destination-related services and detailed information and publications.

The first chapter in the guide, **Destination: Rome,** helps get you in the mood for your trip. New and Noteworthy cues you in on trends and happenings, What's Where gets you oriented, Pleasures and Pastimes describes the activities and sights that make Rome unique, Great Itineraries lays out a selection of complete trips, Fodor's Choice showcases our top picks, and Festivals and Seasonal Events alerts you to special events you'll want to seek out.

The **Exploring** chapter is divided into neighborhood sections; each recommends a walking or driving tour and lists neighborhood sights alphabetically, including sights that are off the beaten path. The remaining chapters are arranged in alphabetical order by subject (dining, lodging, nightlife and the arts, outdoor activities and sports, shopping, and side trips).

At the end of the book you'll find **Portraits:** a useful chronology of the eternal city followed by wonderful essays on the arts and on food in Rome followed by suggestions for pretrip research, from recommended reading to movies on tape that use Rome as a backdrop.

Icons and Symbols

★ Our special recommendations
✕ Restaurant
🏠 Lodging establishment
🐥 Good for kids (rubber duck)

☞ Sends you to another section of the guide for more information
✉ Address
☎ Telephone number
⊙ Opening and closing times
💷 Admission prices (those we give apply to adults; substantially reduced fees are almost always available for children, students, and senior citizens)

Numbers in white and black circles ③ ❸ that appear on the maps, in the margins, and within the tours correspond to one another.

Credit Cards

The following abbreviations are used: **AE,** American Express; **DC,** Diners Club; **MC,** MasterCard; and **V,** Visa.

Don't Forget to Write

You can use this book in the confidence that all prices and opening times are based on information supplied to us at press time; Fodor's cannot accept responsibility for any errors. Time inevitably brings changes, so always confirm information when it matters—especially if you're making a detour to visit a specific place.

Were the restaurants we recommended as described? Did our hotel picks exceed your expectations? Did you find a museum we recommended a waste of time? Keeping a travel guide fresh and up-to-date is a big job, and we welcome your feedback, positive *and* negative. If you have complaints, we'll look into them and revise our entries when the facts warrant it. If you've discovered a special place that we haven't included, we'll pass the information along to our correspondents and have them check it out. So send us your thoughts via e-mail at editors@fodors.com (specifying the name and year of the book on the subject line) or on paper in care of the Rome editor at Fodor's, 201 East 50th Street, New York, New York 10022. In the meantime, have a wonderful trip!

Karen Cure

Karen Cure
Editorial Director

Europe

FINLAND

Gulf
of
Bothnia

Oslo

SWEDEN

Helsinki

Gulf of Finland

St. Petersburg

Stockholm

Tallinn

ESTONIA

Göteborg

Riga

Kattegat

LATVIA

Moscow

Copenhagen

LITHUANIA

Baltic Sea

Kaunas

RUSSIA

RUSSIA

Vilnius

Kaliningrad

Minsk

Berlin

POLAND

BELARUS

NY

Warsaw

Prague

Kraków

Kiev

CZECH
REPUBLIC

UKRAINE

SLOVAKIA

Vienna

Bratislava

Salzburg

Budapest

MOLDOVA

AUSTRIA

HUNGARY

Chişinău

SLOVENIA

ROMANIA

bljana

Zagreb

CROATIA

Novi Sad

BOSNIA AND
HERZEGOVINA

Belgrade

Bucharest

Black Sea

Rome

Sarajevo

SERBIA

YUGOSLAVIA

BULGARIA

Adriatic Sea

MONTENEGRO

Priština

Sofia

Podgorica

Skopje

ITALY

Tiranë

MACEDONIA

Istanbul

Naples

ALBANIA

Ankara

GREECE

TURKEY

Aegean
Sea

ea

Ionian
Sea

Athens

Sicily

CYPRUS

MALTA

Crete

Mediterranean Sea

Rome

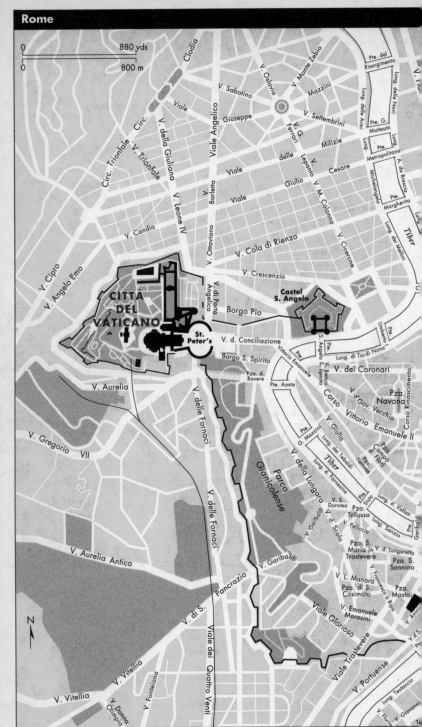

SMART TRAVEL TIPS A TO Z

Basic Information on Traveling to Rome, Savvy Tips to Make Your Trip a Breeze, and Companies and Organizations to Contact

AIR TRAVEL

BOOKING YOUR FLIGHT

Price is just one factor to consider when booking a flight: frequency of service and even a carrier's safety record are often just as important. Major airlines offer the greatest number of departures. Smaller airlines—including regional and no-frills airlines—usually have a limited number of flights daily. On the other hand, so-called low-cost airlines usually are cheaper, and their fares impose fewer restrictions, such as advance-purchase requirements. In terms of safety, low-cost carriers as a group have a good history—about equal to that of major carriers.

When you book, **look for nonstop flights** and **remember that "direct" flights stop at least once.** Try to **avoid connecting flights,** which require a change of plane. Two airlines may jointly operate a connecting flight, so ask if your airline operates every segment—you may find that your preferred carrier flies you only part of the way. International flights on a country's flag carrier are almost always nonstop; U.S. airlines often fly direct.

Ask your airline if it offers electronic ticketing, which eliminates all paperwork. There's no ticket to pick up or misplace. You go directly to the gate and give the agent your confirmation number. There's no worry about waiting on line at the airport while precious minutes tick by.

CARRIERS

When flying internationally, you must usually choose between a domestic carrier, the national flag carrier of the country you are visiting, and a foreign carrier from a third country. You may, for example, choose to fly Alitalia to Rome. National flag carriers have the greatest number of non-stops. Domestic carriers may have better connections to your home town and serve a greater number of gateway cities. Third-party carriers may have a price advantage.

➤ MAJOR AIRLINES: **Alitalia** (☎ 800/223–5730). **Continental** (☎ 800/231–0856). **Delta** (☎ 800/241–4141). **TWA** (☎ 800/892–4141). **US Airways** (☎ 800/428–4322).

➤ FROM THE U.K.: Direct service from Heathrow is provided by **Alitalia** (☎ 0171/602–7111 or 0990/448–259) and **British Airways** (☎ 0345/222–111). From Manchester there are least three flights weekly to Rome.

CHARTERS

Charters usually have the lowest fares but are the least dependable. Departures are infrequent and seldom on time, flights can be delayed for up to 48 hours or can be canceled for any reason up to 10 days before you're scheduled to leave. Itineraries and prices can change after you've booked your flight.

In the U.S., the Department of Transportation's Aviation Consumer Protection Division has jurisdiction over charters and provides a certain degree of protection. The DOT requires that money paid to charter operators be held in escrow, so if you can't pay with a credit card, **always make your check payable to a charter carrier's escrow account.** The name of the bank should be in the charter contract. If you have any problems with a charter operator, contact the DOT (☞ Airline Complaints, *below*). If you buy a charter package that includes both air and land arrangements, remember that the escrow requirement applies only to the air component.

➤ CHARTER CARRIERS: **Tower Air** (☎ 800/348–6937).

CONSOLIDATORS

Consolidators buy tickets for scheduled international flights at reduced rates from the airlines, then sell them at prices that beat the best fare available directly from the airlines, usually without restrictions. Sometimes you can even get your money back if you need to return the ticket. Carefully read the fine print detailing penalties for changes and cancellations, and **confirm your consolidator reservation with the airline.**

➤ CONSOLIDATORS: **Cheap Tickets** (☎ 800/377–1000). **Discount Travel Network** (☎ 800/576–1600). **Unitravel** (☎ 800/325–2222). **Up & Away Travel** (☎ 212/889–2345). **World Travel Network** (☎ 800/409–6753).

CUTTING COSTS

The least-expensive airfares to Rome are priced for round-trip travel and usually must be purchased in advance. It's smart to **call a number of airlines, and when you are quoted a good price, book it on the spot**—the same fare may not be available the next day. Airlines generally allow you to change your return date for a fee. If you don't use your ticket, you can apply the cost toward the purchase of a new ticket, again for a small charge. However, most low-fare tickets are nonrefundable. To get the lowest airfare, **check different routings.** Compare prices of flights to and from different airports if your destination or home city has more than one gateway. Also price off-peak flights, which may be significantly less expensive.

Travel agents, especially those who specialize in finding the lowest fares (☞ Discounts & Deals, *below*), can be especially helpful for booking a plane ticket. When you're quoted a price, **ask your agent if the price is likely to drop any lower.** Good agents know the seasonal fluctuations of airfares and can usually anticipate a sale or fare war. However, waiting can be risky: The fare could go *up* as seats become scarce, and you may wait so long that your preferred flight sells out. A wait-and-see strategy works best if your plans are flexible. If you must arrive and depart on certain dates, don't delay.

CHECK IN & BOARDING

Airlines routinely overbook planes, assuming that not everyone with a ticket will show up, but sometimes everyone does. When that happens, airlines ask for volunteers to give up their seats. In return these volunteers usually get a certificate for a free flight and are rebooked on the next flight out. If there are not enough volunteers, the airline must choose who will be denied boarding. The first to be bumped are passengers who checked in late and those flying on discounted tickets, so **get to the gate and check in as early as possible,** especially during peak periods.

Although the trend on international flights is to drop reconfirmation requirements, many airlines still ask you to reconfirm each leg of your international itinerary. Failure to do so may result in your reservation's being canceled.

Always **bring a government-issued photo ID to the airport.** You may be asked to show it before you are allowed to check in.

ENJOYING THE FLIGHT

For more legroom, **request an emergency-aisle seat.** Don't sit in the row in front of the emergency aisle or in front of a bulkhead, where seats may not recline.

If you don't like airline food, **ask for special meals when booking.** These can be vegetarian, low-cholesterol, or kosher, for example.

When flying internationally, try to maintain a normal routine, to help fight jet-lag. At night, **get some sleep.** By day, **eat light meals, drink water (not alcohol), and move around the cabin** to stretch your legs.

Many carriers have prohibited smoking on all of their international flights; others allow smoking only on certain routes or certain departures, so **contact your carrier regarding its smoking policy.**

FLYING TIMES

Flying time to Rome is 8½ hours from New York, 10–11 hours from Chicago, 12–13 hours from Los Angeles, and 2½ hours from London.

HOW TO COMPLAIN

If your baggage goes astray or your flight goes awry, complain right away. Most carriers require that you **file a claim immediately.**

➤ AIRLINE COMPLAINTS: U.S. Department of Transportation **Aviation Consumer Protection Division** (✉ C-75, Room 4107, Washington, DC 20590, ☎ 202/366–2220). **Federal Aviation Administration Consumer Hotline** (☎ 800/322–7873).

AIRPORTS & TRANSFERS

AIRPORTS

The principal airport is **Leonardo da Vinci Airport,** commonly known by the name of its location, **Fiumicino.** It's 30 km (18 mi) west of the city, on the coast. It has been enlarged and equipped with computerized baggage handling and has a direct train link with downtown Rome. Rome's other airport is **Ciampino,** on Via Appia Nuova, 15 km (9 mi) south of downtown Rome. Ciampino is a civil and military airport used by some international flights and most charter companies.

➤ AIRPORT INFORMATION: **Leonardo da Vinci Airport/Fiumicino** (☎ 06/659–53640). **Ciampino** (☎ 06/794–941).

TRANSFERS BETWEEN FIUMICINO AND DOWNTOWN

By car. Follow the signs from the airport for Rome and the GRA (the ring road that circles Rome). The direction you take on the GRA depends on where your hotel is located. If it is in the Via Veneto area, for instance, you would take the GRA in the direction of the Via Aurelia, turn off the GRA onto the Via Aurelia, and follow it into Rome. Get a map and directions from the car-rental people at the airport.

By taxi. A taxi ride from the airport to the center of Rome costs about 70,000 lire, including supplements, and takes about 30 to 40 minutes depending on the traffic. Private limousines can be booked at booths in the arrivals hall; they charge a little more than taxis but can carry more passengers. There is a taxi stand in front of the International Arrivals hall and a booth inside for taxi information. Use only licensed white or older yellow taxis. Avoid the gypsy drivers who may approach you in the arrivals hall; they charge exorbitant, unmetered rates.

By train. Two trains link downtown Rome with Fiumicino: inquire at the airport (EPT tourist information counter in the International Arrivals hall or train information counter near the tracks) to determine which takes you closest to your destination in Rome. The 30-minute non-stop Airport-Termini express (marked FS and run by the state railway) goes directly to Track 22 at Termini Station, Rome's main train station, well served by taxis and hub of Metro and bus lines. Departures are hourly, beginning at 7:35 AM from the airport, with a final departure at 10:05 PM. Tickets cost 13,000 lire. FM1, the other airport train, leaves from the same tracks and runs from the airport to Rome and beyond, serving commuters as well as air travelers. The main stops in Rome are at Trastevere, Ostiense, and Tiburtina (40 minutes) stations; at each you can find taxis and bus and/or Metro connections to other parts of Rome. FM1 trains run from Fiumicino between 6:15 AM and 12:15 AM, with departures every 20 minutes, a little less frequently in off-hours. Tickets cost 7,000 lire. For either train, buy your ticket at automatic vending machines (you need Italian currency) or at ticket counters at the airport and at some stations (Termini Track 22, Trastevere, Tiburtina). At the airport, stamp the ticket at the gate. Remember when using the train at other stations to stamp the ticket in the little yellow or red machine near the track before you board. During the night, COTRAL buses from the airport to Tiburtina Station in Rome (45 minutes) depart from in front of the International Arrivals hall at 1:15, 2:15, 3:30 and 5 AM. Tickets cost 7,000 lire.

➤ TRANSFER CONTACTS

FS and **Cotral** (☎ 167/431–784).

TRANSFERS BETWEEN CIAMPINO AND DOWNTOWN

By bus. A COTRAL bus connects the airport with the Anagnina Station of Metro Line A, which takes you into the center of the city. Buses depart from in front of the airport terminal every 30 minutes. The fare is 1,500 lire and your ticket is also good for the Metro; have change handy for the ticket machine.

By car. Go north on the Via Appia Nuova into downtown Rome.

By taxi. A taxi from Ciampino to the center of Rome costs about 45,000 lire, and the ride takes about 20 minutes.

BIKE TRAVEL

This is a pleasant way to get around when traffic is light. But remember: Rome was built on seven hills and has since incorporated several more. Rental rates for standard bikes are about 4,000 lire per hour, 18,000 lire for 24 hours; mountain bikes cost 7,000 per hour, 28,000 for 24 hours.

➤ RENTALS: **I Bike Rome** (✉ Underground parking lot at Villa Borghese, Via del Galoppatoio 33, ☎ 06/322–5240). **St. Peter Moto Rent** (✉ Via di Porta Castello 43, ☎ 06/687–5714), near St. Peter's. There are rental concessions at the Metro stations at **Piazza del Popolo** and **Piazza di Spagna** Metro stops, at **Viale del Bambino on the Pincio,** and at **Viale della Pineta in Villa Borghese park.**

➤ TOURS: **CTS** (✉ Via Genova 15, ☎ 06/46791) organizes guided bike tours of Rome. **Scala Reale** (✉ Via Varese 52, ☎ 06/447–00898) organizes bicycle and scooter tours of Rome for small groups.

BIKES IN FLIGHT

Most airlines will accommodate bikes as luggage, provided they are dismantled and put into a box. Call to see if your airline sells bike boxes (about $5; bike bags are at least $100) although you can often pick them up free at bike shops. International travelers can sometimes substitute a bike for a piece of checked luggage for free; otherwise, it will cost about $100. Domestic and Canadian airlines charge a $25–$50 fee.

BUS & TRAM TRAVEL

Rome's integrated Metrebus transportation system includes buses and trams (ATAC), Metro (subway) and suburban trains and buses (COTRAL), and some other suburban trains (FS) run by the state railways. A ticket (BIT) valid for 75 minutes on any combination of buses and trams and one entrance to the Metro costs 1,500 lire. Time-stamp your ticket when boarding the first vehicle, stamping it again when boarding for the last time within 75 minutes. You **stamp the ticket at Metro turnstiles and in the little machines near the entrances of buses and trams.** Tickets are sold at tobacconists, newsstands, some coffee bars, automatic ticket machines positioned in Metro stations, some bus stops, and ATAC and COTRAL ticket booths (in some Metro stations and at a few main bus stops). You can buy them singly or in quantity; it's always a good idea to **have a few handy** so you don't have to hunt for a vendor when you need one. A BIG tourist ticket, valid for one day (only for the day it is stamped, not 24 hours) on all public transport, costs 6,000 lire. A weekly ticket (Settimanale, also known as CIS) costs 24,000 lire and can be purchased only at ATAC and COTRAL booths.

Not as fast as the Metro, bus travel is more scenic. With reserved bus lanes and new tram lines, surface transportation has improved considerably in recent years, though is still crowded during rush hours. Orange or red-and-gray **ATAC** city buses and trams run from about 6 AM to midnight, with skeleton (notturno) services on main lines through the night. Remember to board at the rear and to exit at the middle; you must **buy your ticket before boarding.** A bus ticket costs 1,500 lire and is valid on all ATAC bus lines and for one Metro ride for a total of 75 minutes. **Time-stamp the ticket in the machine on the first bus you board.** With a valid ticket in hand, you can also board at the front of the bus, often less crowded. Tickets are sold at tobacconists, many newsstands, some coffee bars, and automatic ticket machines at some bus stops.

There is no central bus terminal in Rome. Long-distance and suburban COTRAL bus routes terminate either near Tiburtina Station or at outlying

Metro stops, such as Rebibbia (line B) and Anagnina (Line A).

Also see ☞ Subway Travel, *below.*

➤ INFORMATION: **COTRAL** (☎ 167/431784 weekdays 7 AM–6 PM, Saturday 7 AM–2 PM).

BUSINESS HOURS

Banks are open weekdays 8:30–1:30 and 2:45–3:45 or 3–4. Exchange offices are open all day, usually 8:30–8.

Most **churches** are open from early morning until noon or 12:30, when they close for two hours or more; they open again in the afternoon, closing about 7 PM or later. Major cathedrals and basilicas, such as St. Peter's, are open all day. Note that sightseeing in churches during religious rites is usually discouraged. **Be sure to have a fistful of coins handy for the luce (light) machines** that illuminate the works of art in the perpetual dusk of ecclesiastical interiors. A pair of binoculars will help you get a good look at painted ceilings and domes.

Museum hours vary and may change with the seasons. Many important national museums are closed one day a week, often on Monday. The Roman Forum, other sites, and some museums may be open until late in the evening during the summer. Always check locally.

Shop hours are flexible, and many shops in downtown Rome are open all day during the week and also on Sunday, as are some department stores and supermarkets. Alternating city neighborhoods also have general once-a-month Sunday opening days. Otherwise, most shops throughout the city are closed on Sunday. Shops that take a lengthy lunch break are open 9:30–1 and 3:30 or 4–7 or 7:30. All shops close one half-day during the week, either Monday morning in winter or Saturday afternoon in summer.

Food shops are open 8–2 and 5–7:30 and most are closed on Sunday. They also close one half-day during the week, usually Thursday afternoon from September to June and Saturday afternoon in July and August.

Post offices are open 8–2; central and main district post offices stay open until 8 or 9 PM for some operations. You can buy stamps at tobacconists.

Barbers and hairdressers, with some exceptions, are closed Sunday and Monday.

CAMERAS & COMPUTERS

EQUIPMENT PRECAUTIONS

Always **keep your film, tape, or computer disks out of the sun.** Carry an extra supply of batteries, and **be prepared to turn on your camera, camcorder, or laptop** to prove to security personnel that the device is real. Always **ask for hand inspection of film,** which becomes clouded after successive exposures to airport X-ray machines, and **keep videotapes and computer disks away from metal detectors.**

ONLINE ON THE ROAD

➤ INTERNET CAFÉS: **Internet Café** (✉ Via Marruccini 12, ☎ 06/445–4953). **Internet Centre** (✉ Via delle Fosse di Castello 8, ☎ 06/686–1464).

➤ PHOTO HELP: **Kodak Information Center** (☎ 800/242–2424). *Kodak Guide to Shooting Great Travel Pictures,* available in bookstores or from Fodor's Travel Publications (☎ 800/533–6478; $16.50 plus $4 shipping).

CAR RENTAL

Rates in Rome begin at $49 a day and $167 a week for an economy car with air-conditioning, a manual transmission, and unlimited mileage. This does not include the 19% tax on car rentals. Note that Italian legislation now permits certain rental wholesalers, such as Auto Europe, to drop the VAT (☞ Taxes, *below*). Many companies impose mandatory theft insurance on all rentals; coverage costs $12–$18 a day.

➤ MAJOR AGENCIES: **Avis** (☎ 800/331–1084; 01344/707070 in the U.K.). **Budget** (☎ 800/527–0700, 0800/181–181 in the U.K.). **Dollar** (☎ 800/800–4000; 0990/565–656 in the U.K., where it is known as Eurodollar). **Hertz** (☎ 800/654–3001, 800/263–0600 in Canada, 0345/555888 in the U.K., 03/9222–2523 in Australia, 03/358–6777 in New Zealand). **National InterRent** (☎ 800/227–3876; 0345/222–525 in the U.K., where it is known as Europcar InterRent).

CUTTING COSTS

To get the best deal, **book through a travel agent who is willing to shop around.**

Also **ask your travel agent about a company's customer-service record.** How has the company responded to late plane arrivals and vehicle mishaps? Are there often lines at the rental counter? If you're traveling during a holiday period, does a confirmed reservation guarantee you a car?

Be sure to **look into wholesalers,** companies that do not own fleets but rent in bulk from those that do and often offer better rates than traditional car-rental operations. Prices are best during off-peak periods. Rentals booked through wholesalers must be paid for before you leave the United States.

➤ RENTAL WHOLESALERS: **Auto Europe** (☎ 207/842–2000 or 800/223–5555, FAX 800–235–6321). **DER Travel Services** (✉ 9501 W. Devon Ave., Rosemont, IL 60018, ☎ 800/782–2424, FAX 800/282–7474 for information or 800/860–9944 for brochures). **Europe by Car** (☎ 212/581–3040 or 800/223–1516, FAX 212/246–1458). **Kemwel Holiday Autos** (☎ 914/835–5555 or 800/678–0678, FAX 914/835–5126).

INSURANCE

You are generally responsible for any damage to or loss of a vehicle you have rented. Before you rent, **see what coverage you already have** under the terms of your personal auto-insurance policy and credit cards.

All car-rental companies operating in Italy require that you buy theft-protection policies.

REQUIREMENTS

In Italy your own driver's license is acceptable. An International Driver's Permit is a good idea; it's available from the American or Canadian automobile association, and, in the United Kingdom, from the Auto-mobile Association or Royal Automobile Club. These international permits are universally recognized, and having one in your wallet may save you a problem with the local authorities.

SURCHARGES

Before you pick up a car in one city and leave it in another, **ask about drop-off charges or one-way service fees,** which can be substantial. Note, too, that some rental agencies charge extra if you return the car before the time specified in your contract. To avoid a hefty refueling fee, **fill the tank just before you turn in the car,** but be aware that gas stations near the rental outlet may overcharge.

CAR TRAVEL

AUTO CLUBS

➤ IN AUSTRALIA: **Australian Automobile Association** (☎ 06/247–7311).

➤ IN CANADA: **Canadian Automobile Association** (CAA, ☎ 613/247–0117).

➤ IN NEW ZEALAND: **New Zealand Automobile Association** (☎ 09/377–4660).

➤ IN THE U.K.: **Automobile Association** (AA, ☎ 0990/500–600), **Royal Automobile Club** (RAC, ☎ 0990/722–722 for membership, 0345/121–345 for insurance).

➤ IN THE U.S.: **American Automobile Association** (☎ 800/564–6222).

➤ BREAKDOWNS: **ACI Emergency Service** (✉ Servizio Soccorso Stradale, Via Solferino 32, 00185 Roma, ☎ 06/44595) offers 24-hour road service. Dial 116 from any phone, 24 hours a day, to reach the nearest ACI service station.

GASOLINE

Only a few gas stations are open on Sunday, and most close for a couple of hours at lunchtime and at 7 PM for the night. Gas stations on autostrade are open 24 hours. Gas costs about 2,500 lire per liter.

PARKING

Parking space is at a premium. Parking in an area signposted ZONA DISCO is allowed for limited periods (from 30 minutes to two hours or more—the limit is posted); if you don't have the cardboard disk to show what time you parked, you can use a piece of paper. The *parcometro,* the Italian version of metered parking, has been introduced in Rome. It's advisable to **leave your car only in guarded parking areas.** Unofficial parking attendants can help you find a space but offer no guarantees. Your car may be towed away if illegally parked.

ROAD CONDITIONS

Italians drive fast and are impatient with those who don't. Watch out for mopeds. Traffic is heaviest in morning and late afternoon commuter hours, and on weekends.

RULES OF THE ROAD

Driving is on the right, as in the United States. Regulations are largely as in Britain and the United States, except that the police have the power to levy on-the-spot fines. The use of the horn is forbidden in most areas; a large sign, ZONA DI SILENZIO, indicates where. Speed limits are 130 kph (80 mph) on autostrade and 110 kph (70 mph) on state and provincial roads, unless otherwise marked. Fines for driving after drinking are heavy, with the additional possibility of six months' imprisonment.

CHILDREN & TRAVEL

CHILDREN IN ROME

Although Italians love children and are generally very tolerant and patient with them, they provide few amenities for them. In restaurants and trattorias you may find a high chair or a cushion for the child to sit on, but rarely do they offer a children's menu. Order a *mezza porzione* (half-portion) of any dish, or ask the waiter for a *porzione da bambino* (child's portion).

Discounts do exist. Always ask about a *sconto-bambino* (child's discount) before purchasing tickets. Children under a certain height ride free on municipal buses and trams. Children under 18 who are EU citizens are admitted free to state-run museums and galleries, and there are similar privileges in many municipal or private museums. Discounts on concert tickets may be available for young people with student ID.

Be sure to plan ahead and **involve your youngsters** as you outline your trip. When packing, include things to keep them busy en route. On sightseeing days try to schedule activities of special interest to your children. If you are renting a car don't forget to **arrange for a car seat** when you reserve.

FLYING

If your children are two or older, **ask about children's airfares.** As a general rule, infants under two not occupying a seat fly at greatly reduced fares or even for free.

In general the adult baggage allowance applies to children paying half or more of the adult fare. When booking, **ask about carry-on allowances for those traveling with infants.** In general, for babies charged 10% of the adult fare you are allowed one carry-on bag and a collapsible stroller, which may have to be checked; you may be limited to less if the flight is full.

Experts agree that it's a good idea to use safety seats aloft for children weighing less than 40 pounds. Airlines, however, can set their own policies: U.S. carriers allow FAA-approved models but usually require that you buy a ticket, even if your child would otherwise ride free, since the seats must be strapped into regular seats. Airline rules vary, so it's important to **check your airline's policy about using safety seats during takeoff and landing.** Safety seats cannot obstruct the movement of other passengers in the row, so get an appropriate seat assignment as early as possible.

When making your reservation, **request children's meals or a free-standing bassinet** if you need them; the latter are available only for bulkhead seats, where there's enough legroom. Remember, however, that bulkhead seats may not have their own overhead bins, and there's no storage space in front of you—a major inconvenience.

GROUP TRAVEL

When planning to take your kids on a tour, look for companies that specialize in family travel.

➤ FAMILY-FRIENDLY TOUR OPERATORS: **Families Welcome!** (⊠ 92 N. Main St., Ashland, OR 97520, ☎ 541/482–6121 or 800/326–0724, FAX 541/482–0660). **Grandtravel** (⊠ 6900 Wisconsin Ave., Suite 706, Chevy Chase, MD 20815, ☎ 301/986–0790 or 800/247–7651) for people traveling with grandchildren ages 7–17.

HOTELS

Most hotels in Rome allow children under a certain age to stay in their parents' room at no extra charge, but others charge them as extra adults; be sure to **ask about the cutoff age for children's discounts.**

CONSUMER PROTECTION

Whenever possible, **pay with a major credit card** so you can cancel payment or be reimbursed if there's a problem, as long as you can provide documentation. This is the best way to pay, whether you're buying travel arrangements before your trip or shopping at your destination.

If you're doing business with a particular company for the first time, **contact your local Better Business Bureau and the attorney general's offices** in your state and the company's home state, as well. Have any complaints been filed?

Finally, if you're buying a package or tour, always **consider travel insurance** that includes default coverage (☞ Insurance, *below*).

➤ LOCAL BBBs: **Council of Better Business Bureaus** (⊠ 4200 Wilson Blvd., Suite 800, Arlington, VA 22203, ☎ 703/276–0100, FAX 703/525–8277).

CUSTOMS & DUTIES

When shopping, **keep receipts** for all of your purchases. Upon reentering the country, **be ready to show customs officials what you've bought.** If you feel a duty is incorrect, appeal the assessment. If you object to the way your clearance was handled, get the inspector's badge number. In either case, first ask to see a supervisor, then write to the appropriate authorities, beginning with the port director at your point of entry. Check to **find out whether your state imposes import duties** in addition to those assessed by the federal government; if you fail to pay on returning to the country, you may be assessed fines as well as the state duty.

IN ITALY

Of goods obtained anywhere outside the EU or goods purchased in a duty-free shop within an EU country, the allowances are: (1) 200 cigarettes or 100 cigarillos or 50 cigars or 250 grams of tobacco; (2) 2 liters of still table wine or 1 liter of spirits over 22% volume or 2 liters of spirits under 22% volume or 2 liters of fortified and sparkling wines; and (3) 50 milliliters of perfume and 250 milliliters of toilet water.

Of goods obtained (duty and tax paid) within another EU country, the allowances are: (1) 800 cigarettes or 400 cigarillos or 400 cigars or 1 kilogram of tobacco; (2) 90 liters of still table wine plus (3) 10 liters of spirits over 22% volume plus 20 liters of spirits under 22% volume plus 60 liters of sparkling wines plus 110 liters of beer.

IN AUSTRALIA

Australia residents who are 18 or older may bring back $A400 worth of souvenirs and gifts (including jewelry), 250 cigarettes or 250 grams of tobacco, and 1,125 ml of alcohol (including wine, beer, and spirits). Residents under 18 may bring back $A200 worth of goods.

➤ INFORMATION: **Australian Customs Service** (Regional Director, ⊠ Box 8, Sydney, NSW 2001, ☎ 02/921–32000, FAX 02/921–34000).

IN CANADA

Canadian residents who have been out of Canada for at least seven days may bring in C$500 worth of goods duty-free. If you've been away less than seven days but more than 48 hours, the duty-free allowance drops to C$200; if your trip lasts 24–48 hours, the allowance is C$50. You may not pool allowances with family

SMART TRAVEL TIPS / THE GOLD GUIDE

members. Goods claimed under the C$500 exemption may follow you by mail; those claimed under the lesser exemptions must accompany you. Alcohol and tobacco products may be included in the seven-day and 48-hour exemptions but not in the 24-hour exemption. If you meet the age requirements of the province or territory through which you reenter Canada, you may bring in, duty-free, 1.14 liters (40 imperial ounces) of wine or liquor *or* 24 12-ounce cans or bottles of beer or ale. If you are 16 or older you may bring in, duty-free, 200 cigarettes and 50 cigars.

You may send an unlimited number of gifts worth up to C$60 each duty-free to Canada. Label the package UNSOLICITED GIFT—VALUE UNDER $60. Alcohol and tobacco are excluded.

➤ INFORMATION: **Revenue Canada** (⊠ 2265 St. Laurent Blvd. S, Ottawa, Ontario K1G 4K3, ☎ 613/993–0534, 800/461–9999 in Canada).

IN NEW ZEALAND

Although greeted with a "Haere Mai" ("Welcome to New Zealand"), homeward-bound residents with goods to declare must present themselves for inspection. If you're 17 or older, you may bring back $700 worth of souvenirs and gifts. Your duty-free allowance also includes 4.5 liters of wine or beer; one 1,125-ml bottle of spirits; and either 200 cigarettes, 250 grams of tobacco, 50 cigars, or a combo of all three up to 250 grams.

➤ INFORMATION: **New Zealand Customs** (⊠ Custom House, ⊠ 50 Anzac Ave., Box 29, Auckland, New Zealand, ☎ 09/359–6655, ☎ 09/309–2978).

IN THE U.K.

If you are a U.K. resident and your journey was wholly within the European Union (EU), you won't have to pass through customs when you return to the United Kingdom. If you plan to bring back large quantities of alcohol or tobacco, check EU limits beforehand.

➤ INFORMATION: **HM Customs and Excise** (⊠ Dorset House, ⊠ Stamford St., London SE1 9NG, ☎ 0171/202–4227).

IN THE U.S.

Non-U.S. residents ages 21 and older may import into the United States 200 cigarettes or 50 cigars or 2 kilograms of tobacco, 1 liter of alcohol, and gifts worth $100. Prohibited items include meat products, seeds, plants, and fruits.

➤ INFORMATION: **U.S. Customs Service** (Inquiries, ⊠ Box 7407, Washington, DC 20044, ☎ 202/927–6724; complaints, Office of Regulations and Rulings, ⊠ 1301 Constitution Ave. NW, Washington, DC 20229; registration of equipment, Resource Management, ⊠ 1301 Constitution Ave. NW, Washington, DC 20229, ☎ 202/927–0540).

DISABILITIES & ACCESSIBILITY

ACCESS IN ROME

Italy has only recently begun to provide facilities such as ramps, telephones, and rest rooms for people with disabilities; such things are still the exception, not the rule. Travelers' wheelchairs must be transported free of charge, according to Italian law, but the logistics of getting a wheelchair on and off trains and buses can make this requirement irrelevant. High, narrow steps for boarding trains create problems. Seats are reserved for people with disabilities on public transportation, but few buses have lifts for wheelchairs. Rome's newer gray and red city buses are equipped for easy boarding and securing of wheelchairs. In many monuments and museums, even in some hotels and restaurants, architectural barriers make it difficult, if not impossible, for people with disabilities to gain access. In Rome, however, St. Peter's, the Sistine Chapel, and the Vatican Museums are all accessible by wheelchair. The terminals of Fiumicino Airport–Rome Ostiense rail connection have elevators for wheelchairs.

Throughout Rome parking spaces near major monuments and public buildings are reserved for cars transporting people with disabilities. In the narrow streets of the city's center, parked cars hugging the buildings, the lack of sidewalks, and bumpy, uneven, cobblestone pavements make for hard going.

Bringing a Seeing Eye dog into Italy requires an import license, a current certificate detailing the dog's inoculations, and a letter from your veterinarian certifying the dog's health. Contact the nearest Italian consulate for particulars.

➤ LOCAL RESOURCES: The **Italian Government Travel Office** (ENIT; ☞ Visitor Information, *below*) can provide a list of accessible hotels and the addresses of Italian associations for travelers with disabilities.

MAKING RESERVATIONS

When discussing accessibility with an operator or reservations agent, **ask hard questions.** Are there any stairs, inside *or* out? Are there grab bars next to the toilet *and* in the shower/tub? How wide is the doorway to the room? To the bathroom? For the most extensive facilities meeting the latest legal specifications, **opt for newer accommodations,** which are more likely to have been designed with access in mind. Older buildings may have more limited facilities. Be sure to **discuss your needs before booking.**

TRANSPORTATION

➤ COMPLAINTS: **Aviation Consumer Protection Division** (☞ Air Travel, *above*) for airline-related problems. **Disability Rights Section** (✉ U.S. Department of Justice, Civil Rights Division, ✉ Box 66738, Washington, DC 20035–6738, ☎ 202/514–0301 or 800/514–0301, TTY 202/514–0383 or 800/514–0383, FAX 202/307–1198) for general complaints.

TRAVEL AGENCIES & TOUR OPERATORS

As a whole, the travel industry has become more aware of the needs of travelers with disabilities. In the U.S., the Americans with Disabilities Act requires that travel firms serve the needs of all travelers. Note, though, that some agencies and operators specialize in making travel arrangements for individuals and groups with disabilities.

➤ TRAVELERS WITH MOBILITY PROBLEMS: **Access Adventures** (✉ 206 Chestnut Ridge Rd., Rochester, NY 14624, ☎ 716/889–9096), run by a former physical-rehabilitation coun-

selor. **Accessible Journeys** (✉ 35 W. Sellers Ave., Ridley Park, PA 19078, ☎ 610/521–0339 or 800/846–4537, FAX 610/521–6959), for escorted tours exclusively for travelers with mobility impairments. **Flying Wheels Travel** (✉ 143 W. Bridge St., Box 382, Owatonna, MN 55060, ☎ 507/451–5005 or 800/535–6790, FAX 507/451–1685), a travel agency specializing in customized tours and itineraries worldwide. **Hinsdale Travel Service** (✉ 201 E. Ogden Ave., Suite 100, Hinsdale, IL 60521, ☎ 630/325–1335), a travel agency that benefits from the advice of wheelchair traveler Janice Perkins.

DISCOUNTS & DEALS

Be a smart shopper and **compare all your options** before making any choice. A plane ticket bought with a promotional coupon may not be cheaper than the least expensive fare from a discount ticket agency. For high-price travel purchases, such as packages or tours, keep in mind that what you get is just as important as what you save.

CLUBS & COUPONS

Many companies sell discounts in the form of travel clubs and coupon books, but these cost money. You must use participating advertisers to get a deal, and only after you recoup the initial membership cost or book price do you begin to save. If you plan to use the club or coupons frequently, you may save considerably. Before signing up, find out what discounts are free.

➤ DISCOUNT CLUBS: **Entertainment Travel Editions** (✉ 2125 Butterfield Rd., Troy, MI 48084, ☎ 800/445–4137; $20–$51, depending on destination). **Great American Traveler** (✉ Box 27965, Salt Lake City, UT 84127, ☎ 801/974–3033 or 800/548–2812; $49.95 per year). **Moment's Notice Discount Travel Club** (✉ 7301 New Utrecht Ave., Brooklyn, NY 11204, ☎ 718/234–6295; $25 per year, single or family). **Privilege Card International** (✉ 237 E. Front St., Youngstown, OH 44503, ☎ 330/746–5211 or 800/236–9732; $74.95 per year). **Sears's Mature Outlook** (✉ Box 9390, Des Moines, IA 50306, ☎ 800/336–6330; $19.95

per year). **Travelers Advantage** (✉ CUC Travel Service, ✉ 3033 S. Parker Rd., Suite 1000, Aurora, CO 80014, ☎ 800/548–1116 or 800/648–4037; $59.95 per year, single or family). **Worldwide Discount Travel Club** (✉ 1674 Meridian Ave., Miami Beach, FL 33139, ☎ 305/534–2082; $50 per year family, $40 single).

CREDIT-CARD OR AUTO-CLUB BENEFITS

When you use your credit card to make travel purchases you may get free travel-accident insurance, collision-damage insurance, and medical or legal assistance, depending on the card and the bank that issued it. American Express, MasterCard, and Visa provide one or more of these services, so **get a copy of your credit card's travel-benefits policy.** If you are a member of an auto club, always **ask hotel and car-rental reservations agents about auto-club discounts.** Some clubs offer additional discounts on tours, cruises, and admission to attractions.

DISCOUNT RESERVATIONS

To save money, **look into discount-reservations services** with toll-free numbers, which use their buying power to get a better price on hotels, airline tickets, even car rentals. When booking a room, always **call the hotel's local toll-free number** (if one is available) rather than the central reservations number—you'll often get a better price. Always ask about special packages or corporate rates.

When shopping for the best deal on hotels and car rentals, **look for guaranteed exchange rates,** which protect you against currency fluctuations.

➤ AIRLINE TICKETS: **☎ 800/359–4537.**

➤ HOTEL ROOMS: **Hotels Plus** (☎ 800/235–0909). **International Marketing & Travel Concepts** (☎ 800/790–4682). **Steigenberger Reservation Service** (☎ 800/223–5652). **Travel Interlink** (☎ 800/888–5898).

PACKAGE DEALS

Packages and guided tours can save you money, but don't confuse the two. When you buy a package, your travel remains independent, just as though you had planned and booked the trip yourself. Fly/drive packages, which combine airfare and car rental, are often a good deal. In cities, ask the local visitor's bureau about hotel packages. These often include tickets to major museum exhibits and other special events.

ELECTRICITY

To use your U.S.-purchased electric-powered equipment, **bring a converter and adapter.** The electrical current in Italy is 220 volts, 50 cycles alternating current (AC); wall outlets take Continental-type plugs, with two round prongs.

If your appliances are dual-voltage, you'll need only an adapter. Don't use 110-volt outlets, marked FOR SHAVERS ONLY, for high-wattage appliances such as blow-dryers. Most laptops operate equally well on 110 and 220 volts and so require only an adapter.

EMERGENCIES

➤ CONSULATES: **U.S. Consulate** (✉ Via Veneto 121, ☎ 06/46741). **Canadian Consulate** (✉ Via Zara 30, ☎ 06/445–981). **U.K. Consulate** (✉ Via Venti Settembre 80A, ☎ 06/482–5441).

➤ EMERGENCIES: Dial 113 for police, 115 for fire, 118 for medical emergency and ambulance. Also, 112 for Carabinieri (militarized police) and 116 for the Italian Automobile Club.

➤ PHARMACIES: You will find American and British products, or their equivalents, and English-speaking staff at: **Farmacia Cola di Rienzo** (✉ Via Cola di Rienzo 213, ☎ 06/324–3130). **Farmacia Internazionale Barberini** (✉ Piazza Barberini 49, ☎ 06/482–5456). **Farmacia Internazionale Capranica** (✉ Piazza Capranica 96, ☎ 056/679–4680). Most are open 8:30–1 and 4–8; some are open all night. Sunday opening is by rotation.

ETIQUETTE & BEHAVIOR

In churches, any kind of revealing dress is taboo; shorts, tank tops, and miniskirts are banned; shoulders must be covered.

GAY & LESBIAN TRAVEL

Local gays and lesbians generally maintain low visibility in Rome;

favorite clubs and bars are usually mixed rather than exclusively homosexual.

➤ GAY AWARENESS ORGANIZATIONS: **Arcigay Arcilesbica Pegaso** (✉ Via Acciaresi 7, ☎ 06/4173–0752). **Circolo Mario Mieli** (✉ Via Ostiense 202, ☎ 06/541–3985).

➤ GAY- AND LESBIAN-FRIENDLY TRAVEL AGENCIES: **Corniche Travel** (☎ 8721 Sunset Blvd., Suite 200, West Hollywood, CA 90069, ☎ 310/854–6000 or 800/429–8747, FAX 310/659–7441). **Islanders Kennedy Travel** (✉ 183 W. 10th St., New York, NY 10014, ☎ 212/242–3222 or 800/988–1181, FAX 212/929–8530). **Now Voyager** (✉ 4406 18th St., San Francisco, CA 94114, ☎ 415/626–1169 or 800/255–6951, FAX 415/626–8626). **Yellowbrick Road** (✉ 1500 W. Balmoral Ave., Chicago, IL 60640, ☎ 773/561–1800 or 800/642–2488, FAX 773/561–4497). **Skylink Travel and Tour** (✉ 3577 Moorland Ave., Santa Rosa, CA 95407, ☎ 707/585–8355 or 800/225–5759, FAX 707/584–5637), serves lesbian travelers.

HEALTH

FOOD & DRINK

The Centers for Disease Control and Prevention (CDC) in Atlanta caution that most of Southern Europe is in the "intermediate" range for risk of contacting traveler's diarrhea. Part of this risk may be attributed to an increased consumption of olive oil and wine, which can have a laxative effect on stomachs used to a different diet. The CDC also advises all international travelers to swim only in chlorinated swimming pools, unless they are absolutely certain the local beaches and freshwater lakes are not contaminated.

MEDICAL PLANS

No one plans to get sick while traveling, but it happens, so **consider signing up with a medical-assistance company.** Members receive doctor referrals, emergency evacuation or repatriation, 24-hour telephone hot lines for medical consultation, cash for emergencies, and other personal and legal assistance. Coverage varies by plan, so **review the benefits of each carefully.**

➤ MEDICAL-ASSISTANCE COMPANIES: **International SOS Assistance** (✉ 8 Neshaminy Interplex, Suite 207, Trevose, PA 19053, ☎ 215/245–4707 or 800/523–6586, FAX 215/244–9617; ✉ 12 Chemin Riantbosson, 1217 Meyrin 1, Geneva, Switzerland, ☎ 4122/785–6464, FAX 4122/785–6424; ✉ 10 Anson Rd., 14-07/08 International Plaza, Singapore, 079903, ☎ 65/226–3936, FAX 65/226–3937).

HOLIDAYS

January 1 (New Year's Day); January 6 (Epiphany); Easter Sunday and Monday; April 25 (Liberation Day); May 1 (Labor Day or May Day); June 29 (St. Peter, Rome's patron saint); August 15 (Assumption of Mary, also known as Ferragosto); November 1 (All Saints' Day); December 8 (Immaculate Conception); December 25, 26 (Christmas Day and Boxing Day).

INSURANCE

Travel insurance is the best way to **protect yourself against financial loss.** The most useful plan is a comprehensive policy that includes coverage for trip cancellation and interruption, default, trip delay, and medical expenses (with a waiver for preexisting conditions).

Without insurance, you will lose all or most of your money if you cancel your trip, regardless of the reason. Default insurance covers you if your tour operator, airline, or cruise line goes out of business. Trip-delay covers unforeseen expenses that you may incur due to bad weather or mechanical delays. **Compare the fine print regarding trip-delay coverage** when reviewing policies.

For overseas travel, one of the most important components of travel insurance is its medical coverage. Supplemental health insurance will pick up the cost of your medical bills should you become sick or be injured while traveling. U.S. residents should note that Medicare generally does not cover health-care costs outside the United States, nor do many privately issued policies. Residents of the United Kingdom can buy an annual travel-insurance policy valid for most

THE GOLD GUIDE / SMART TRAVEL TIPS

vacations taken during the year in which the coverage is purchased. If you are pregnant or have a pre-existing condition, make sure you're covered. British citizens should buy extra medical coverage when traveling overseas, according to the Association of British Insurers. Australian travelers should buy travel insurance, including extra medical coverage, whenever they go abroad, according to the Insurance Council of Australia.

Always **buy travel insurance directly from the insurance company**; if you buy it from a cruise line, airline, or tour operator that goes out of business you probably will not be covered for the agency or operator's default, a major risk. Before you make any purchase, **review your existing health and home-owner's policies** to find out whether they cover expenses incurred while traveling.

➤ TRAVEL INSURERS: In the U.S., **Access America** (✉ 6600 W. Broad St., Richmond, VA 23230, ☎ 804/285–3300 or 800/284–8300). **Travel Guard International** (✉ 1145 Clark St., Stevens Point, WI 54481, ☎ 715/345–0505 or 800/826–1300). In Canada, **Mutual of Omaha** (✉ Travel Division, ✉ 500 University Ave., Toronto, Ontario M5G 1V8, ☎ 416/598–4083, 800/268–8825 in Canada).

➤ INSURANCE INFORMATION: In the U.K., **Association of British Insurers** (✉ 51 Gresham St., London EC2V 7HQ, ☎ 0171/600–3333). In Australia, the **Insurance Council of Australia** (☎ 613/961–41077, FAX 613/961–47924).

LANGUAGE

In Rome, language is no problem. You can always find someone who speaks at least a little English, albeit with a heavy accent; remember that the Italian language is pronounced exactly as it is written (many Italians try to speak English as it is written, with disconcerting results). You may run into a language barrier in the countryside, but a phrase book and close attention to the Italians' astonishing use of pantomime and expressive gestures will go a long way.

Try to **master a few phrases for daily use,** and familiarize yourself with the terms you'll need to decipher signs and museum labels. To get the most out of museums, you'll need English-language guidebooks to exhibits; look for them in bookstores and on newsstands, as those sold at the museums are not necessarily the best.

LANGUAGES FOR TRAVELERS

A phrase book and language tape set can help get you started.

➤ PHRASE BOOKS AND LANGUAGE-TAPE SETS: *Fodor's Italian for Travelers* (☎ 800/733–3000, 800/668–4247 in Canada, FAX 212/5722–6045 international orders; audio set $16.95 [$23.50 in Canada]).

LANGUAGE-STUDY PROGRAMS

Private language schools and U.S.- and U.K.-affiliated educational institutions offer a host of Italian language study programs in Rome.

➤ LANGUAGE SCHOOLS: **American U. of Rome** (✉ Via Pietro Rosselli 4, ☎ 06/5833–0919). **Loyola U.** (✉ Via dei Massimi 114, ☎ 06/355881). **Rome International U.** (✉ Via Bissolati 20, ☎ 06/4200–1422). **Temple U.** (✉ Lungotevere Arnaldo da Brescia 15, ☎ 06/3600–1544).

LODGING

APARTMENT & VILLA RENTALS

If you want a home base that's roomy enough for a family and comes with cooking facilities, **consider a furnished rental.** These can save you money, especially if you're traveling with a large group of people. Home-exchange directories list rentals (often second homes owned by prospective house swappers), and some services search for a house or apartment for you (even a castle if that's your fancy) and handle the paperwork. Some send an illustrated catalog; others send photographs only of specific properties, sometimes at a charge. Up-front registration fees may apply.

➤ RENTAL AGENTS: **Drawbridge to Europe** (✉ 5456 Adams Rd., Talent, OR 97540, ☎ 541/512–8927 or 888/268–1148, FAX 541/512–0978). **Europa-Let/Tropical Inn-Let** (✉ 92 N. Main St., Ashland, OR 97520, ☎ 541/482–5806 or 800/462–4486,

FAX 541/482–0660). **Hometours International** (✉ Box 11503, Knoxville, TN 37939, ☎ 423/690–8484 or 800/367–4668). **Interhome** (✉ 124 Little Falls Rd., Fairfield, NJ 07004, ☎ 973/882–6864 or 800/882–6864, FAX 973/808–1742). **Property Rentals International** (✉ 1008 Mansfield Crossing Rd., Richmond, VA 23236, ☎ 804/378–6054 or 800/220–3332, FAX 804/379–2073). **Rent-a-Home International** (✉ 7200 34th Ave. NW, Seattle, WA 98117, ☎ 206/789–9377 or 800/488–7368, FAX 206/789–9379). **Vacation Home Rentals Worldwide** (✉ 235 Kensington Ave., Norwood, NJ 07648, ☎ 201/767–9393 or 800/633–3284, FAX 201/767–5510). **Villas International** (✉ 605 Market St., San Francisco, CA 94105, ☎ 415/281–0910 or 800/221–2260, FAX 415/281–0919). **Hideaways International** (✉ 767 Islington St., Portsmouth, NH 03801, ☎ 603/430–4433 or 800/843–4433, FAX 603/430–4444; membership $99) is a club for travelers who arrange rentals among themselves.

➤ ITALY-ONLY AGENCIES: **Cuendet USA** (✉ 165 Chestnut St., Allendale, NJ 07041, ☎ 201/327–2333; ✉ Suzanne T. Pidduck, c/o Rentals in Italy, 1742 Calle Corva, Camarillo, CA 93010, ☎ 800/726–6702). **Vacanze in Italia** (✉ 22 Railroad St., Great Barrington, MA 01230, ☎ 413/528–6610 or 800/533–5405).

➤ IN THE U.K.: **CV Travel** (✉ 43 Cadogan St., London SW3 2PR, England, ☎ 0171/581–0851). **Magic of Italy** (✉ 227 Shepherds Bush Rd., London W6 7AS, England, ☎ 0181/748–7575).

HOME EXCHANGES

If you would like to exchange your home for someone else's, **join a home-exchange organization,** which will send you its updated listings of available exchanges for a year and will include your own listing in at least one of them. It's up to you to make specific arrangements.

➤ EXCHANGE CLUBS: **HomeLink International** (✉ Box 650, Key West, FL 33041, ☎ 305/294–7766 or 800/638–3841, FAX 305/294–1148; $83 per year).

HOSTELS

No matter what your age, you can **save on lodging costs by staying at hostels.** In some 5,000 locations in more than 70 countries around the world, Hostelling International (HI), the umbrella group for a number of national youth hostel associations, offers single-sex, dorm-style beds and, at many hostels, "couples" rooms and family accommodations. Membership in any HI national hostel association, open to travelers of all ages, allows you to stay in HI-affiliated hostels at member rates (one-year membership is about $25 for adults; hostels run about $10–$25 per night). Members also have priority if the hostel is full; they're eligible for discounts around the world, even on rail and bus travel in some countries.

➤ HOSTEL ORGANIZATIONS: **Hostelling International—American Youth Hostels** (✉ 733 15th St. NW, Suite 840, Washington, DC 20005, ☎ 202/783–6161, FAX 202/783–6171). **Hostelling International—Canada** (✉ 400-205 Catherine St., Ottawa, Ontario K2P 1C3, ☎ 613/237–7884, FAX 613/237–7868). **Youth Hostel Association of England and Wales** (✉ Trevelyan House, ✉ 8 St. Stephen's Hill, St. Albans, Hertfordshire AL1 2DY, ☎ 01727/855–215 or 01727/845–047, FAX 01727/844–126); membership in the U.S. $25, in Canada C$26.75, in the U.K. £9.30).

➤ IN ROME: The **IYHF Ostello della Gioventù Foro Italico** (✉ Viale Olimpiadi 61, Foro Italico sports complex, near Tiber north of downtown Rome, ☎ 06/323–6279, FAX 06/324–2613) can be reached from Termini station by taking Metro A to Ottaviano/S. Pietro station (Via Barletta exit), then bus 32.

HOTELS

Italian hotels are classified from five-star (deluxe) to one-star (very basic hotels and small inns). Stars are assigned according to standards set by regional boards, but rates are set by each hotel. During slack periods, or when a hotel is not full, it is often possible to negotiate a discounted rate. Room rates are on a par with other European capitals: Rates in $$$$ hotels can be downright extravagant. In those categories, ask for one of the better rooms, as less desirable rooms—and there usually are some—don't give you what you're paying for. Except in $$$$ and some $$$ hotels, rooms may be very small compared to U.S. standards.

In all hotels there is a rate card inside the door of your room, or inside the closet door; it tells you exactly what you will pay for that particular room (rates in the same hotel may vary according to the location and type of room). On this card, breakfast and any other optionals must be listed separately. Any discrepancy between the basic room rate and that charged on your bill is cause for complaint to the manager and to the local tourist office.

Except for most $$$$ establishments, hotels quote room rates including breakfast. Many of the hotels we recommend offer generous buffet breakfasts instead of simple, even skimpy "continental breakfasts." Remember, if the latter is the case, you can eat for less at the nearest coffee bar.

Hotels that we list as $$ and $—moderate to inexpensively priced accommodations—may charge extra for optional air-conditioning. In older hotels the quality of the rooms may be very uneven; if you don't like the room you're given, request another. This applies to noise, too. Front rooms may be larger and have a view, but they also may have significant street noise. If you're a light sleeper, request a quiet room when making reservations. Specify whether you care about having either a bath or shower, since not all rooms have both.

Rome has no official off-season as far as hotel rates go, though some hotels will reduce rates during the slack seasons (January–March and July–August) upon request. Always inquire about special rates.

➤ MAJOR CHAINS: Atahotels (✉ Via Lampedusa 11/A, 20141 Milano, ☎ 02/895–261 or toll-free in Italy 1678/23013, FAX 02/846–5568; some bookable through E&M Associates, ☎ 212/599–8280 or 800/223–9832). ITT-Sheraton/The Luxury Collection (✉ 745 5th Ave., New York, NY

10151, ☎ 800/221–2340 or toll-free in Italy 1678–835035, FAX 212/421–5929). Jolly (☎ 800/247–1277 in New York state, 800/221–2626 elsewhere, 800/237–0319 in Canada, toll-free in Italy 1670–7703). Starhotels (✉ Via Belfiore 27, 50144 Florence, ☎ 055/36921 or toll-free in Italy 1678–60200 or book through 800/448–8355, FAX 055/36924).

➤ ASSOCIATIONS OF INDEPENDENTLY HELD HOTELS: Best Western (☎ 800/528–1234). Italhotels (☎ toll-free in Italy 1678/01004). Space Hotels (☎ toll-free in Italy 1678/13013; or book through Supranational, 416/927–1133 or 800/843–3311).

MAIL

POSTAL RATES

Airmail letters (lightweight stationery) to the United States and Canada cost 1,300 lire for the first 19 grams and an additional 500 lire for every additional unit of 20 grams. Airmail postcards cost 1,200 lire if the message is limited to a few words and a signature; otherwise, you pay the letter rate. Airmail letters and postcards to the United Kingdom cost 900 lire. You can buy stamps at tobacconists'.

Outgoing mail will arrive much faster if mailed from the Vatican, with Vatican stamps. You can buy them in the post offices on either side of Piazza San Pietro, one next to the information office and the other under the colonnade opposite. During peak tourist seasons a Vatican Post Office mobile unit is set up in St. Peter's Square.

RECEIVING MAIL

Mail service is generally slow; allow up to 10 days for mail from Britain, 15 days from North America. Correspondence can be addressed to you care of the Italian post office. Letters should be addressed to your name, "c/o Ufficio Postale Centrale," followed by "Fermo Posta" on the next line, and the name of the city (preceded by its postal code—Rome's central post office's is 00187) on the next. You can collect it at Rome's central post office at Piazza San Silvestro by showing your passport or photo-bearing ID and paying a small fee. American Express also has a general-delivery service. There's no charge for cardholders, holders of American Express Traveler's checks, or anyone who booked a vacation with American Express.

MONEY

COSTS

Rome's prices are comparable to those in other major capitals, such as Paris and London. The days when Italy's high-quality attractions came with a comparatively low Mediterranean price tag are long gone. With the cost of labor and social benefits rising and an economy weighed down by the public debt, Italy is therefore not a bargain, but there is an effort to hold the line on hotel and restaurant prices, which had become inordinately high by U.S. standards. Depending on season and occupancy, you may be able to obtain unadvertised lower rates in hotels; always inquire. If you want the luxury of $$$$ and $$$ hotels, be prepared to pay top rates.

Admission to the Vatican Museums is 15,000 lire. The cheapest seat at Rome's Opera House runs 30,000 lire; a movie ticket is 12,000 lire. A daily English-language newspaper is 2,400 lire.

A Rome taxi ride (1 mile) costs 10,000 lire. An inexpensive hotel room for two, including breakfast, is about 190,000 lire; an inexpensive dinner is 40,000 lire, and a ½-liter carafe of house wine, 6,000 lire. A simple pasta item on the menu runs about 13,000 lire, a cup of coffee 1,200–1,400 lire, and a Rosticceria lunch, about 15,000 lire. A McDonald's Big Mac is 4,800 lire, a Coke (standing) at a café is 2,200 lire, and a pint of beer in a pub is 7,000 lire.

CREDIT & DEBIT CARDS

Should you use a credit card or a debit card when traveling? Both have benefits. A credit card allows you to delay payment and gives you certain rights as a consumer (☞ Consumer Protection, *above*). A debit card, also known as a check card, deducts funds directly from your checking account and helps you stay within your budget. When you want to rent a car, though, you may still need an old-fashioned credit card. Although you can always *pay* for your car with a debit card, some agencies will not allow you to *reserve* a car with a debit card.

Otherwise, the two types of plastic are virtually the same. Both will get you cash advances at ATMs worldwide if your card is properly programmed with your personal identification number (PIN). (For use in Rome, your PIN must be five digits long.) Both offer excellent, wholesale exchange rates. And both protect you against unauthorized use if the card is lost or stolen. Your liability is limited to $50, as long as you report the card missing.

➤ ATM LOCATIONS: **Cirrus** (☎ 800/424–7787). **Plus** (☎ 800/843–7587) for locations in the U.S. and Canada, or visit your local bank.

➤ REPORTING LOST CARDS: To report lost or stolen credit cards, call the following toll-free numbers: **American Express** (☎ 800/327–2177); **Master Card** (☎ 800/307–7309); and **Visa** (☎ 800/847–2911).

CURRENCY

The unit of currency in Italy is the lira. There are bills of 500,000 (practically impossible to change, except in a bank), 100,000, 50,000, 10,000, 5,000, 2,000, and 1,000 lire. Coins are 1,000, 500, 200, 100, and 50 lire. At press time, the exchange rate was about 1,640 lire to the U.S. dollar, 1,060 lire to the Canadian dollar, and 2,740 lire to the pound sterling. The Euro, the new single European currency, will not yet be circulating in Italy in 1999, though it will begin to appear in high-level financial quotations.

EXCHANGING MONEY

For the most favorable rates, **change money through banks.** Although fees charged for ATM transactions may be higher abroad than at home, Cirrus and Plus exchange rates are excellent, because they are based on wholesale rates offered only by major banks. You won't do as well at exchange booths in airports or rail and bus stations, in hotels, in restaurants, or in stores, although you may find their

THE GOLD GUIDE / SMART TRAVEL TIPS

hours more convenient. To avoid lines at airport exchange booths, **get a bit of local currency before you leave home.**

➤ EXCHANGE SERVICES: **Chase** *Currency To Go* (☎ 800/935−9935; 935−9935 in NY, NJ, and CT). **International Currency Express** (☎ 888/842−0880 on the East Coast, 888/278−6628 on the West Coast). **Thomas Cook Currency Services** (☎ 800/287−7362 for telephone orders and retail locations).

TRAVELER'S CHECKS

Do you need traveler's checks? It depends on where you're headed. If you're taking side trips to rural areas and small towns, go with cash; traveler's checks are best used in the city. Lost or stolen checks can usually be replaced within 24 hours. To ensure a speedy refund, buy your own traveler's checks—don't let someone else pay for them: irregularities like this can cause delays. The person who bought the checks should make the call to request a refund.

PACKING

LUGGAGE

How many carry-on bags you can bring with you is up to the airline. Most allow two, but the limit is often reduced to one on certain flights. Gate agents will take excess baggage—including bags they deem oversize—from you as you board and add it to checked luggage. To avoid this situation, make sure that everything you carry aboard will fit under a seat. Also, get to the gate early and request a seat at the back of the plane; you'll probably board first while the overhead bins are still empty. As big, bulky baggage attracts the attention of gate agents and flight attendants on a busy flight, make sure your carry-on is really a carry-on. Finally, a carry-on that's long and narrow is more likely to remain unnoticed than one that's wide and squarish.

If you are flying internationally, note that baggage allowances may be determined not by piece but by weight—generally 88 pounds (40 kilograms) in first class, 66 pounds (30 kilograms) in business class, and 44 pounds (20 kilograms) in economy.

Airline liability for baggage is limited to $1,250 per person on flights within the United States. On international flights it amounts to $9.07 per pound or $20 per kilogram for checked baggage (roughly $640 per 70-pound bag) and $400 per passenger for unchecked baggage. You can buy additional coverage at check-in for about $10 per $1,000 of coverage, but it excludes a rather extensive list of items, shown on your airline ticket.

Before departure, **itemize your bags' contents** and their worth, and label the bags with your name, address, and phone number. (If you use your home address, cover it so that potential thieves can't see it readily.) Inside each bag, **pack a copy of your itinerary.** At check-in, **make sure that each bag is correctly tagged** with the destination airport's three-letter code. If your bags arrive damaged or fail to arrive at all, file a written report with the airline before leaving the airport.

PACKING LIST

Rome generally has mild winters and hot, sticky summers. Take a medium-weight coat for winter; a lightweight all-weather coat for spring and fall, and a lightweight jacket or sweater for summer evenings, which may be cool. Brief summer thunderstorms are common, so take a folding umbrella. As interiors can be cold and sometimes damp in the cooler months, take woolens or flannels. Plan your wardrobe in layers, no matter what the season. Casual clothes are the general rule, especially during the summer. In all seasons, Italians dress exceptionally well; to them, casual means easy but elegant, even in jeans. Though men aren't required to wear jackets or ties anywhere, except in the grander hotel dining-rooms and some deluxe restaurants, they are expected to look reasonably sharp. Formal wear is the exception rather than the rule at the opera, though people in expensive seats usually do get dressed up. Wear sturdy walking shoes or sandals, preferably with thick soles, to get around in comfort on Rome's many cobblestone streets and the gravel paths that surround some of the historic buildings.

The dress codes are strict for visits to St. Peter's and the Vatican Museums: For both men and women, shorts, tank tops halter tops are taboo. Shoulders must be covered. Women should carry a scarf or shawl to cover bare arms if the custodians insist. Those who do not comply with the dress code are refused admittance. Although there are no specific dress rules for the huge outdoor papal audiences, you will be turned away if you're in shorts or a revealing outfit. The Vatican Information Office in St. Peter's Square will tell you the dress requirements for smaller audiences. Dress codes for churches are similar, though less strictly applied.

To protect yourself against purse snatchers and pickpockets, carry a money pouch or belt. Don't keep your passport and large sums of money in your handbag or hip pocket. Any kind of bag, shoulder bag, or camera case is a target. If you must carry one, choose one with long straps that you can sling across your body, bandolier style. Avoid carrying a bag if you can, or carry one that is obviously just a tote for your guide book and sundries.

In your carry-on luggage **bring an extra pair of eyeglasses or contact lenses** and **enough of any medication you take** to last the entire trip. You may also want your doctor to write a spare prescription using the drug's generic name; brand names may vary from country to country. **Never put prescription drugs or valuables in luggage to be checked.** To avoid customs delays, carry medications in their original packaging. And don't forget to copy down and carry addresses of offices that handle refunds of lost traveler's checks.

PASSPORTS & VISAS

When traveling internationally, **carry a passport even if you don't need one** (it's always the best form of I.D.), and make **two photocopies of the data page** (one for someone at home and another for you, carried separately from your passport). If you lose your passport, promptly call the nearest embassy or consulate and the local police.

ENTERING ITALY

All U.S., Canadian, U.K., Australian, and New Zealand citizens, even infants, need only a valid passport to enter Italy for stays of up to 90 days.

PASSPORT OFFICES

The best time to apply for a passport or to renew is during the fall and winter. Before any trip, be sure to check your passport's expiration date and, if necessary, renew it as soon as possible. (Some countries won't allow you to enter on a passport that's due to expire in six months or less.)

➤ AUSTRALIAN CITIZENS: **Australian Passport Office** (☎ 13/1232).

➤ CANADIAN CITIZENS: **Passport Office** (☎ 819/994–3500 or 800/ 567–6868).

➤ NEW ZEALAND CITIZENS: **New Zealand Passport Office** (☎ 04/494– 0700 for information on how to apply, 0800/727–776 for information on applications already submitted).

➤ U.K. CITIZENS: **London Passport Office** (☎ 0990/21010), for fees and documentation requirements and to request an emergency passport.

➤ U.S. CITIZENS: **National Passport Information Center** (☎ 900/225– 5674; calls are charged at 35¢ per minute for automated service, $1.05 per minute for operator service).

SAFETY

The best way to protect yourself against purse snatchers and pickpockets is to wear a money belt. (See ☞ Packing, *above*.) Wear a bag or camera slung across your body bandolier-style, and don't rest your bag or camera on a table or chair at a sidewalk café or restaurant. In Rome, beware of pickpockets on buses, especially Line 64 (Termini-St. Peter's) and subways and when making your way through the corridors of crowded trains. Pickpockets may be active wherever tourists gather, including the Roman Forum, Piazza Navona, and St. Peter's Square. Purse snatchers work in teams on a single motor scooter or motorcycle: one drives and the other grabs.

"Gypsy" children and young women, often with babes in arms, present around sights popular with tourists throughout Europe, are rife in Rome and are adept pickpockets. One modus operandi is to approach a tourist and proffer a piece of card-board with writing on it. While the unsuspecting victim attempts to read the message on it the children's hands are busy under it, trying to make off with wallets and valuables. If you see such a group (usually recognizable by their unkempt appearance), do not even allow them near you—they are quick and know more tricks than you do. The phrases "Vai via" (Go away!) and "Chiamo la polizia" (I'll call the police) usually keep them at bay.

SCOOTERS

➤ RENTAL AGENCIES: **Scoot-a-Long** (✉ Via Cavour 302, ☎ 06/678–0206). **St. Peter Moto** (✉ Via di Porta Castello 43, ☎ 06/687–5714). Riders are required by law to wear helmets.

SENIOR-CITIZEN TRAVEL

Senior-citizen discounts are not widely offered in Italy unless they are part of a tour package (see below). EU citizens over 60 are entitled to free admission to state museums as well as to many other museums—always ask at the ticket office. Older travelers may be eligible for special fares on Alitalia and other airlines. When renting a car, **ask about promotional car-rental discounts,** which can be cheaper than senior-citizen rates.

Senior travelers should be aware that few public buildings, including muse-ums, restaurants, and shops, in Rome are air-conditioned. Public toilets are few and far between, other than those in restaurants and hotels, and in department stores. Toilets in coffee bars may be locked to keep out unde-sirables; ask for the key at the cashier. There are public toilets in St. Peter's Square, Piazza di Spagna, at the Roman Forum, and in a few other strategic locations.

➤ EDUCATIONAL PROGRAMS: **Elder-hostel** (✉ 75 Federal St., 3rd floor, Boston, MA 02110, ☎ 617/426–8056). **Folkways Institute** (✉ 14600 Southeast Aldridge Rd., Portland, OR 97236-6518, ☎ 503/658–6600 or 800/225–4666, FAX 503/658–8672).

Interhostel (✉ University of New Hampshire, ✉ 6 Garrison Ave., Dur-ham, NH 03824, ☎ 603/862–1147 or 800/733–9753, FAX 603/862–1113).

SHOPPING

The notice PREZZI FISSI (fixed prices) means just that; in shops displaying this sign it's a waste of time to bar-gain unless you're buying a sizable quantity of goods or a particularly costly object. Always bargain, how-ever, at outdoor markets (except food markets) and when buying from street vendors. For a comprehensive intro-duction to the joys of shopping, Italian-style, ☞ Pleasures & Pastimes *in* Chapter 1.

SIGHTSEEING TOURS

ORIENTATION TOURS

American Express, Appian Line, Car-rani, CIT, and other operators offer three-hour tours in air-conditioned 60-passenger buses with English-speaking guides. There are four itine-raries: "Ancient Rome" (including the Roman Forum and Colosseum); "Classic Rome" (including St. Peter's Basilica, Trevi Fountain, and the Janiculum Hill); "Christian Rome" (including some major churches and the catacombs); and "The Vatican Museums and Sistine Chapel." Most cost about 53,000 lire, but the Vatican Museums tour costs about 60,000 lire. American Express tours depart from Piazza di Spagna and CIT from Piazza della Repub-blica, both with some hotel pickups; Carrani and Appian Line pick you up at centrally located hotels.

American Express and other opera-tors can provide a luxury car for up to three people, a limousine for up to seven, a minibus for up to nine, all with English-speaking driver, but guide service is extra. Almost all operators offer "Rome by Night" tours, with or without dinner and entertainment. You can book tours through travel agents.

Though operators and names change, a sightseeing bus following a continu-ous circle route through the center of town is usually operating. It makes scheduled stops at important sites, where you can get on and off at will. Check with the Rome tourist information kiosks or inquire at your hotel for the name of the current operator and schedules.

The least expensive organized sightseeing tour of Rome is that run by ATAC, the municipal bus company. Bus 110 tours leave from Piazza dei Cinquecento, in front of Termini Station, last about three hours, and cost about 15,000 lire. The driver provides a commentary, and you're given an illustrated guide with which to identify the sights. Buy tickets at the ATAC information booth in front of Termini Station. There is at least one tour daily, departing at 2:30 PM (3:30 in summer).

The least expensive sightseeing "tours" of Rome are the routes followed by certain buses and trams that pass major sights. With a single 1,500-lire ticket you can get in 75 minutes of sightseeing (or an entire day, with a 6,000 giornaliero ticket). Time your ride to avoid rush hours. The little electric Bus 116 scoots through the heart of Old Rome, with stops near the Pantheon, the Spanish Steps, and Piazza del Popolo, among others. The route of Bus 117 takes in San Giovanni in Laterano, the Colosseum, and the Spanish Steps.

➤ BUS LINE: **ATAC** (☎ 167–431784).

➤ TOUR OPERATORS: **American Express** (☎ 06/67641), **Appian Line** (☎ 06/488–4151), **Carrani** (☎ 06/489–03564), **CIT** (☎ 06/47941).

SPECIAL-INTEREST TOURS

You can make your own arrangements (at no cost) to attend a public papal audience at the Vatican or at the pope's summer residence at Castelgandolfo (☞ The Vatican in Chapter 2). You can also book through a travel agency for a package that includes coach transportation to the Vatican for the audience and some sightseeing along the way, returning you to your hotel, for about 40,000 lire. The excursion outside Rome to Castel Gandolfo on summer Sundays for the pope's blessing costs about 45,000 lire. Agencies that arrange these tours include Appian Line, Carrani, and CIT.

Tourvisa Italia organizes boat trips on the Tiber, leaving from Ripa Grande, at Ponte Sublicio. Depending on the season, they may include excursions to Ostia Antica, with a guided visit of the excavations and return by bus. A scheduled river bus service operates from spring to fall, depending on the conditions of the river.

➤ TOUR OPERATORS: **Appian Line** (☎ 06/488–4151). **Carrani** (☎ 06/488–0510). **CIT** (☎ 06/47941). **Tourvisa Italia** (✉ Via Marghera 32, ☎ 06/445–3224).

WALKING TOURS

Scala Reale organizes day and evening walking tours, theme walks, and excursions for very small groups, together with personalized consulting on what to see and do. Genti e Paesi is an Italian cultural association that offers walking tours and museum visits in English. Book at least one day in advance. If you have a reasonable knowledge of Italian, you can take advantage of the free guided visits and walking tours organized by Rome's cultural associations and the city council for museums and monuments. These usually take place on weekends. Programs are announced in the daily papers and in *Roma C'è*.

➤ TOUR OPERATORS: **Genti e Paesi** (✉ Via Adda 11, ☎ 06/853–01755). **Scala Reale** (✉ Via Varese 52, ☎ 888/467–1986, ℻ 617/249–0186 in U.S., ☎ ℻ 06/447–00898 in Italy).

EXCURSIONS

Most operators offer half-day excursions to Tivoli to see the fountains and gardens of Villa D'Este. Appian Line's morning tour to Tivoli also includes a visit to Hadrian's Villa, with its impressive ancient ruins. Again, most operators have full-day excursions to Assisi, to Pompeii and/or Capri, and to Florence.

➤ TOUR OPERATOR: **Appian Line** (☎ 06/488–4151).

PERSONAL GUIDES

You can arrange for a personal guide through American Express, CIT, or the main EPT Tourist Information Office.

SMART TRAVEL TIPS

THE GOLD GUIDE / SMART TRAVEL TIPS

➤ TOUR OPERATORS: **American Express** (☎ 06/67641). **CIT** (☎ 06/47941). **EPT Tourist Information Office** (☎ 06/488–3748).

STUDENT TRAVEL

LOCAL RESOURCES

The **Centro Turistico Studentesco** (CTS) is a student and youth travel agency with offices in major Italian cities; CTS helps its clients find low-cost accommodations and bargain fares for travel in Italy and elsewhere and also serves as a meeting place for young people of all nations. CTS is also the Rome representative for EuroTrain International.

➤ AGENCY: **Centro Turistico Studentesco** (✉ Via Genova 16, near railroad station, ☎ 06/467–9271).

TRAVEL AGENCIES

To save money, **look into deals available through student-oriented travel agencies.** To qualify you'll need a bona fide student I.D. card. Members of international student groups are also eligible.

➤ STUDENT I.D.S & SERVICES: **Council on International Educational Exchange** (✉ CIEE, ✉ 205 E. 42nd St., 14th floor, New York, NY 10017, ☎ 212/822–2600 or 888/268–6245, FAX 212/822–2699), for mail orders only, in the United States. **Travel Cuts** (✉ 187 College St., Toronto, Ontario M5T 1P7, ☎ 416/979–2406 or 800/667–2887) in Canada.

➤ STUDENT TOURS: **AESU Travel** (✉ 2 Hamill Rd., Suite 248, Baltimore, MD 21210-1807, ☎ 410/323–4416 or 800/638–7640, FAX 410/323–4498). **Contiki Holidays** (✉ 300 Plaza Alicante, Suite 900, Garden Grove, CA 92840, ☎ 714/740–0808 or 800/266–8454, FAX 714/740–2034).

SUBWAY TRAVEL

The Metro is the easiest and fastest way to get around Rome. There are stops near most of the main tourist attractions. The Metro has two lines—A and B—which intersect at Termini Station. Line A runs from the eastern part of the city, with stops, among others, at San Giovanni in Laterano, Piazza Barberini, Piazza di Spagna, Piazzale Flaminio (Piazza del Popolo), and Ottaviano/San Pietro, near St. Peter's and the Vatican Museums. Line B has stops near the Colosseum, the Circus Maximus, the Pyramid (Ostiense Station and trains for Ostia Antica), and the basilica of San Paul's Outside the Walls. The metro opens at 5:30 AM, and the last trains leave the last station at either end at 11:30 PM (on Saturday night the last train leaves at 12:30 AM). The fare is 1,500 lire. (☞ Metrebus *in* Bus & Tram Travel, *above*.)

TAXES

HOTELS

The service charge and IVA, or Value-Added Tax, are included in the rate except in five-star deluxe hotels, where the IVA (15% on luxury hotels) may be a separate item added to the bill at departure.

RESTAURANTS

Many, but not all, Rome restaurants have eliminated extra charges for service and for pane e coperto (a cover charge that includes bread, whether you eat it or not). If it is an extra, the service charge may be 12–15%. Only part, if any, of this amount goes to the waiter, so an additional tip is appreciated (see Tipping).

VALUE-ADDED TAX (V.A.T.)

Value-added tax (IVA), is 20% on luxury goods. On most consumer goods, it is already included in the amount shown on the price tag; on services, such as car rentals, it is an extra item.

To get an IVA refund, when you are leaving Italy take the goods and the invoice to the customs office at the airport or other point of departure and have the invoice stamped. (If you return to the United States or Canada directly from Italy, go through the procedure at Italian customs; if your return is, say, via Britain, take the Italian goods and invoice to British customs.) Under Italy's IVA-refund system, a non-EU resident can obtain a refund of tax paid after spending a total of 300,000 lire in one store (before tax—and note that price tags and prices quoted, unless otherwise stated, include IVA). Shop with your passport and ask the store for an invoice itemizing the article(s), price(s), and the amount of tax. Once back home—and within 90 days of the date of purchase—mail the stamped invoice to the store, which will forward the IVA rebate to you. A growing number of stores in Italy (and Europe) are members of the Tax-Free Shopping System, which expedites things by providing an invoice that is actually a Tax-Free Cheque in the amount of the refund. Once stamped, it can be cashed at the Tax-Free Cash refund window at major airports and border crossings. You can also have the refund credited to your credit card or bank account, or sent directly home. To save a step at the airport or border, you can send the Cheque to a Tax-Free Shopping address.

TAXIS

Taxis in Rome do not cruise, but if free they will stop if you flag them down. They wait at stands but can also be called by phone, in which case you're charged a supplement. The meter starts at 4,500 lire; there are supplements for night service (5,000 lire extra from 10 PM–7 AM) and on Sundays and holidays, as well as for each piece of baggage. Unfortunately, these charges do not appear on the meter, causing countless misunderstandings. If you take a taxi at night and/or on a Sunday, or if you have baggage or have had the cab called by phone, the fare will legitimately be more than the figure shown on the meter. Use only licensed, metered white or yellow cabs, identified by a numbered shield on the side, an illuminated taxi sign on the roof, and a plaque next to the license plate reading SERVIZIO PUBBLICO. Avoid unmarked, unauthorized, unmetered gypsy cabs (numerous at Rome airports and train stations), whose drivers actively solicit your trade and may demand astronomical fares.

➤ CALLING A CAB: To call a cab, dial 3875, 3570, 4994, or 8433. **Radio Taxi** (☎ 06/3875) accepts American Express and Diner's Club. Specify when calling that payment will be made by credit card.

TELEPHONES

COUNTRY CODES

The country code for Italy is 39. The area code for Rome is 06. When dialing an Italian number from abroad, do not drop the initial 0 from the local area code.

DIRECTORY & OPERATOR INFORMATION

For general information in English, dial 176. To place international telephone calls via operator-assisted service (or for information), dial 170 or long-distance access numbers (see below).

INTERNATIONAL CALLS

Hotels tend to overcharge, sometimes exorbitantly, for long-distance and international calls. Use your **AT&T, MCI** (see below), or **Sprint** cards. Or buy an international phone card, which you can use from designated pay phones. Or make your calls from Telefoni offices, designated TELECOM), where operators will assign you a booth, sell you an international telephone card, and help you place your call. You can make collect calls from any phone by dialing 172–1011, which will get you an English-speaking operator. (When calling from pay telephones, insert a 200-lire coin, which will be returned upon the completion of your call). You automatically reach an operator in the country of destination. Rates to the United States are lowest round the clock on Sunday and 10 PM–8 AM, Italian time, on weekdays.

AT&T, MCI, and Sprint international access codes make calling the United States relatively convenient, but you may find the local access number blocked in many hotel rooms. First ask the hotel operator to connect you. If the hotel operator balks, ask for an international operator, or dial the international operator yourself. One way to improve your odds of being connected to your long-distance carrier is to travel with more than one company's calling card (a hotel may block Sprint, for example, but not MCI). If all else fails, call from a pay phone in the hotel lobby.

THE GOLD GUIDE / SMART TRAVEL TIPS

➤ ACCESS CODES: **AT&T Direct** (☎ 172–1011; ☎ 800/435–0812 for other areas). **MCI WorldPhone** (☎ 172–1022; ☎ 800/444–4141 for other areas).

PUBLIC PHONES

Pay phones take either a 200-lire coin, two 100-lire coins, a 500-lire coin, or a *scheda telefonica* (prepaid calling card). Many phones accept only a *scheda telefonica.* You buy the card (values vary—5,000 lire, 10,000 lire, and so on) at Telefoni offices, post offices, newsstands, and tobacconists. Tear off the corner of the card and insert it in the slot. When you dial, its value appears in the window. After you hang up, the card is returned so you can use it until its value runs out. The *scheda telefonica internazionale* (values vary from 12,000 to 100,000 lire) is an international calling card that can be used at designated public phones to call many foreign countries, including Canada and the U.S.

TIPPING

Many Rome restaurants have done away with the service charge of about 12%–15% that used to appear as a separate item on your check. It's customary to leave an additional 5%–10% tip for the waiter, depending on the quality of service. Tip checkroom attendants 500–1,000 lire per person, rest room attendants 500 lire; in both cases tip more in expensive hotels and restaurants. Tip 100 lire for whatever you drink standing up at a coffee bar, 500 lire or more for table service in a café. At a hotel bar tip 2,000 lire and up for a round or two of cocktails, more in the grander hotels.

Tip taxi drivers 5%–10% of the meter amount. Railway and airport porters charge a fixed rate per bag. Tip an additional 1,000 lire, more if the porter is very helpful. Not all theater ushers expect a tip; if they do, tip 500 lire per person, more for very expensive seats. Give a barber 2,000–3,000 lire and a hairdresser's assistant 3,000–8,000 lire for a shampoo or cut, depending on the type of establishment and the final bill; 5%–10% is a fair guideline.

On sightseeing tours, tip guides about 2,000 lire per person for a half-day group tour, more if they are very good. In museums and other places of interest where admission is free, a contribution is expected; give anything from 500 to 1,000 lire for one or two persons, more if the guardian has been especially helpful. Service station attendants are tipped only for special services.

In hotels, give the portiere (concierge) about 15% of his bill for services, or 5,000–10,000 lire if he has been generally helpful. For two people in a double room, leave the chambermaid about 2,000 lire per day, or about 5,000–10,000 a week, in a moderately priced hotel; tip a minimum of 1,000 lire for valet or room service. Increase these amounts by one-half in an expensive hotel, and double them in a very expensive hotel. In very expensive hotels, tip doormen 1,000 lire for calling a cab and 2,000 lire for carrying bags to the check-in desk, bellhops 3,000–5,000 lire for carrying your bags to the room and 3,000–5,000 lire for room service.

TOUR OPERATORS

Buying a prepackaged tour or independent vacation can make your trip to Rome less expensive and more hassle-free. Because everything is prearranged, you'll spend less time planning.

Operators that handle several hundred thousand travelers per year can use their purchasing power to give you a good price. Their high volume may also indicate financial stability. But some small companies provide more personalized service; because they tend to specialize, they may also be more knowledgeable about a given area.

BOOKING WITH AN AGENT

Travel agents are excellent resources. In fact, large operators accept bookings made only through travel agents. But it's a good idea to **collect brochures from several agencies,** because some agents' suggestions may be influenced by relationships with tour and package firms that reward them for volume sales. If you have a special interest, **find an agent with** expertise in that area; ASTA (☞ Travel Agencies, *below*) has a database of specialists worldwide.

Make sure your travel agent knows the accommodations and other services. Ask about the hotel's location, room size, beds, and whether it has a pool, room service, or programs for children, if you care about these. Has your agent been there in person or sent others you can contact?

Do some homework on your own, too: Local tourism boards can provide information about lesser-known and small-niche operators, some of which may sell only direct.

BUYER BEWARE

Each year consumers are stranded or lose their money when tour operators—even very large ones with excellent reputations—go out of business. So **check out the operator.** Find out how long the company has been in business, and ask several travel agents about its reputation. If the package or tour you are considering is priced lower than in your wildest dreams, **be skeptical.** Try to **book with a company that has a consumer-protection program.** If the operator has such a program, you'll find information about it in the company's brochure. If the operator you are considering does not offer some kind of consumer protection, then ask for references from satisfied customers.

In the U.S., members of the National Tour Association and United States Tour Operators Association are required to set aside funds to cover your payments and travel arrangements in case the company defaults. It's also a good idea to choose a company that participates in the American Society of Travel Agents' Tour Operator Program (TOP). This gives you a forum if there are any disputes between you and your tour operator; ASTA will act as mediator.

➤ Tour-Operator Recommendations: **American Society of Travel Agents** (☞ Travel Agencies, *below*). **National Tour Association** (✉ NTA, ✉ 546 E. Main St., Lexington, KY 40508, ☎ 606/226–4444 or 800/ 755–8687). **United States Tour Operators Association** (✉ USTOA, ✉ 342 Madison Ave., Suite 1522, New York, NY 10173, ☎ 212/599– 6599 or 800/468–7862, 𝙵𝙰𝚇 212/ 599–6744).

COSTS

The more your package or tour includes, the better you can predict the ultimate cost of your vacation. Make sure you know exactly what is covered, and **beware of hidden costs.** Are taxes, tips, and service charges included? Transfers and baggage handling? Entertainment and excursions? These can add up.

Prices for packages and tours are usually quoted per person, based on two sharing a room. If traveling solo, you may be required to pay the full double-occupancy rate. Some operators eliminate this surcharge if you agree to be matched with a roommate of the same sex, even if one is not found by departure time.

GROUP TOURS

Among companies that sell tours to Rome, the following are nationally known, have a proven reputation, and offer plenty of options. The classifications used below represent different price categories, and you'll probably encounter these terms when talking to a travel agent or tour operator. The key difference is usually in accommodations, which run from budget to better, and better-yet to best.

➤ Super-Deluxe: **Abercrombie & Kent** (✉ 1520 Kensington Rd., Oak Brook, IL 60521-2141, ☎ 630/954– 2944 or 800/323–7308, 𝙵𝙰𝚇 630/ 954–3324). **Travcoa** (✉ Box 2630, 2350 S.E. Bristol St., Newport Beach, CA 92660, ☎ 714/476–2800 or 800/ 992–2003, 𝙵𝙰𝚇 714/476–2538).

➤ Deluxe: **Central Holidays** (✉ 206 Central Ave., Jersey City, NJ 07307, ☎ 201/798–5777 or 800/935– 5000). **Donna Franca Tours** (✉ 470 Commonwealth Ave., Boston, MA 02215, ☎ 617/375–9400 or 800/ 225–6290). **Globus** (✉ 5301 S. Federal Circle, Littleton, CO 80123- 2980, ☎ 303/797–2800 or 800/221– 0090, 𝙵𝙰𝚇 303/347–2080). **Maupintour** (✉ 1515 St. Andrews Dr., Lawrence, KS 66047, ☎ 785/

843–1211 or 800/255–4266, FAX 785/843–8351). **Perillo Tours** (✉ 577 Chestnut Ridge Rd., Woodcliff Lake, NJ 07675, ☎ 201/307–1234 or 800/431–1515). **Tauck Tours** (✉ Box 5027, 276 Post Rd. W, Westport, CT 06881-5027, ☎ 203/226–6911 or 800/468–2825, FAX 203/221–6866).

➤ FIRST-CLASS: **Brendan Tours** (✉ 15137 Califa St., Van Nuys, CA 91411, ☎ 818/785–9696 or 800/421–8446, FAX 818/902–9876). **Caravan Tours** (✉ 401 N. Michigan Ave., Chicago, IL 60611, ☎ 312/321–9800 or 800/227–2826, FAX 312/321–9845). **Insight International Tours** (✉ 745 Atlantic Ave., #720, Boston, MA 02111, ☎ 617/482–2000 or 800/582–8380, FAX 617/482–2884 or 800/622–5015). **Trafalgar Tours** (✉ 11 E. 26th St., New York, NY 10010, ☎ 212/689–8977 or 800/854–0103, FAX 800/457–6644).

➤ BUDGET: **Cosmos** (☞ Globus, *above*). **Trafalgar** (☞ *above*).

PACKAGES

Like group tours, independent vacation packages are available from major tour operators and airlines. The companies listed below offer vacation packages in a broad price range.

➤ AIR/HOTEL: **Continental Vacations** (☎ 800/634–5555). **Delta Vacations** (☎ 800/872–7786). **DER Tours** (✉ 9501 W. Devon St., Rosemont, IL 60018, ☎ 800/937–1235, FAX 847/692–4141 or 800/282–7474, 800/860–9944 for brochures). **4th Dimension Tours** (✉ 7101 S.W. 99th Ave., #105, Miami, FL 33173, ☎ 305/279–0014 or 800/644–0438, FAX 305/273–9777). **TWA Getaway Vacations** (☎ 800/438–2929). **US Airways Vacations** (☎ 800/455–0123).

➤ FROM THE U.K.: **British Airways Holidays** (✉ Astral Towers, Betts Way, London Rd., Crawley, West Sussex RH10 2XA, ☎ 01293/722–727, FAX 01293/722–624). **Carefree Italy** (✉ Allied Dunbar House, East Park, Crawley, West Sussex RH10 6AJ, ☎ 01293/552–277). **Italian Escapades** (✉ 227 Shepherds Bush

Rd., London W6 7AS, ☎ 0181/748–2661). **Page and Moy Holidays** (✉ 136–140 London Rd., Leicester, LE2 1EN, ☎ 0116/250–7676).

SPECIAL-INTEREST TOURS

You can make your own arrangements (at no cost) to attend a public papal audience at the Vatican or at the pope's summer residence at Castelgandolfo (☞ The Vatican, *below*). You can also book through a travel agency for a package that includes coach transportation to the Vatican for the audience and some sightseeing along the way, returning you to your hotel, for about 40,000 lire. The excursion outside Rome to Castel Gandolfo on summer Sundays for the pope's blessing costs about 45,000 lire. Agencies that arrange these tours include Appian Line, Carrani, and CIT.

Tourvisa Italia organizes boat trips on the Tiber, leaving from Ripa Grande, at Ponte Sublicio. Depending on the season, they may include excursions to Ostia Antica, with a guided visit of the excavations and return by bus. A scheduled river bus service operates from spring to fall, depending on the conditions of the river.

Gemini Tours, which offers private car tours of Rome and the surrounding sites, specializes in researching family histories and locating hometowns and historical records for travelers of Italian descent.

➤ TOUR OPERATORS: **Appian Line** (☎ 06/488–4151). **Carrani** (☎ 06/488–0510). **CIT** (☎ 06/47941). **Gemini Tours** (☎ 06/303–11002). **Tourvisa Italia** (✉ Via Marghera 32, ☎ 06/445–3224).

THEME TRIPS

➤ ART: **IST Cultural Tours** (✉ 225 W. 34th St., New York, NY 10122-0913, ☎ 212/563–1202 or 800/833–2111, FAX 212/594–6953).

➤ FOOD & WINE: **Annemarie Victory Organization** (✉ 136 E. 64th St., New York, NY 10021, ☎ 212/486–0353, FAX 212/751–3149). **Cuisine International** (✉ Box 25228, Dallas, TX 75225, ☎ 214/373–1161 or FAX 214/373–1162). **Donna Franca Tours** (☞ Group Tours, *above*).

➤ LEARNING: **Smithsonian Study Tours and Seminars** (⌗ 1100 Jefferson Dr. SW, Room 3045, MRC 702, Washington, DC 20560, ☎ 202/357–4700, FAX 202/633–9250).

➤ SPAS: **Great Spas of the World** (⌗ 55 John St., New York, NY 10038, ☎ 212/267–5500 or 800/772–8463, FAX 212/571–0510). **Spa-Finders** (⌗ 91 5th Ave., #301, New York, NY 10003-3039, ☎ 212/924–6800 or 800/255–7727). **Spa Trek Travel** (⌗ 475 Park Ave. S., New York, NY 10016, ☎ 212/779–3480 or 800/272–3480, FAX 212/779–3471).

➤ TENNIS: **Championship Tennis Tours** (⌗ 8040 E. Morgan Trail #12, Scottsdale, AZ 85258, ☎ 602/443–9499 or 800/468–3664, FAX 602/443–8982). **Steve Furgal's International Tennis Tours** (⌗ 11828 Rancho Bernardo Rd., #123–305, San Diego, CA 92128, ☎ 619/675–3555 or 800/258–3664).

TRAIN TRAVEL

State-owned FS trains are part of the Metrebus system (☞ Bus & Tram Travel, *above*) and also serve some destinations on side trips outside Rome. The main FS stations in Rome are Termini, Tiburtina, Ostiense, and Trastevere. Suburban trains use all of these stations. The Ferrovie COTRAL line, departing from a terminal in Piazzale Flaminio, connects Rome with Viterbo; shut down for improvement in 1998, the line should be operating by 1999.

FS trains have first and second classes. On local trains the higher, first-class fare gets you a clean doily on the headrest of your seat, a little more legroom, and a little less crowding. On long-distance trains (to Florence and Venice, for instance), first-class travel is worth the difference, and **it is essential to make seat reservations in either class, easy to do in advance at travel agencies.** For destinations within 100 km (62 mi) of Rome, you can buy a kilometrico ticket. Like bus tickets, they can be purchased at some newsstands and in ticketing machines, as well as at FS ticket windows. Buy them in advance so you won't waste time in line at station ticket booths. Like all train tickets, they must be date-stamped in

the little yellow or red machines near the track before you board. Within a range of 100 km they are valid for six hours from the time they are stamped, and you can get on and off at will at stops in between for the duration of the ticket's validity.

TRAVEL AGENCIES

A good travel agent puts your needs first. Look for an agency that has been in business at least five years, emphasizes customer service, and has someone on staff who specializes in your destination. In addition, **make sure the agency belongs to a professional trade organization,** such as ASTA in the United States. If your travel agency is also acting as your tour operator, *see* Buyer Beware in Tour Operators, *above*).

➤ LOCAL AGENT REFERRALS: **American Society of Travel Agents** (ASTA, ☎ 800/965–2782 24-hr hot line, FAX 703/684–8319). **Association of British Travel Agents** (⌗ 55–57 Newman St., London W1P 4AH, 0171/637–2444, FAX 0171/637–0713). **Association of Canadian Travel Agents** (⌗ Suite 201, 1729 Bank St., Ottawa, Ontario K1V 7Z5, ☎ 613/521–0474, FAX 613/521–0805). **Australian Federation of Travel Agents** (☎ 02/926–43299). **Travel Agents' Association of New Zealand** (☎ 04/499–0104).

TRAVEL GEAR

Travel catalogs specialize in useful items, such as compact alarm clocks and travel irons, that can **save space when packing.** They also offer dual-voltage appliances, currency converters, and foreign-language phrase books.

➤ CATALOGS: **Magellan's** (☎ 800/962–4943, FAX 805/568–5406). **Orvis Travel** (☎ 800/541–3541, FAX 540/343–7053). **TravelSmith** (☎ 800/950–1600, FAX 800/950–1656).

U.S. GOVERNMENT

Government agencies can be an excellent source of inexpensive travel information. When planning your trip, **find out what government materials are available.**

➤ ADVISORIES: **U.S. Department of State** (⌗ Overseas Citizens Services

THE GOLD GUIDE / SMART TRAVEL TIPS

THE GOLD GUIDE / SMART TRAVEL TIPS

Office, ⊠ Room 4811 N.S., Washington, DC 20520; ☏ 202/647–5225 or ℻ 202/647–3000 for interactive hot line; ☏ 301/946–4400 for computer bulletin board); enclose a self-addressed, stamped, business-size envelope.

➤ PAMPHLETS: **Consumer Information Center** (⊠ Consumer Information Catalogue, Pueblo, CO 81009, ☏ 719/948–3334 or 888/878–3256) for a free catalog that includes travel titles.

VISITOR INFORMATION

TOURIST INFORMATION

➤ AT HOME: **Italian Government Tourist Board** (ENIT; ⊠ 630 5th Ave., New York, NY 10111, ☏ 212/245–4822, ℻ 212/586–9249; ⊠ 401 N. Michigan Ave., Chicago, IL 60611, ☏ 312/644–0990, ℻ 312/644–3019; ⊠ 12400 Wilshire Blvd., Suite 550, Los Angeles, CA 90025, ☏ 310/820–0098, ℻ 310/820–6357; ⊠ 1 Pl. Ville Marie, Suite 1914, Montréal, Québec H3B 3M9, ☏ 514/866–7667, ℻ 514/392–1429; ⊠ 1 Princes St., London W1R 8AY, ☏ 0171/408–1254, ℻ 0171/493–6695).

➤ IN ROME: EPT (⊠ Via Parigi 5, ☏ 06/488–3748). ◷ Mon.–Sat. 9–7. There are also EPT and city tourist information booths at Termini Station and Leonardo da Vinci Airport. For information on places other than Rome there is a booth at the **ENIT** (National Tourist Board; ⊠ Via Marghera 2, ☏ 06/497–1222).

WEB SITES

Do check out the World Wide Web when you're planning. You'll find everything from up-to-date weather forecasts to virtual tours of famous cities. Fodor's Web site, www.fodors.com, is a great place to start your on-line travels.

➤ SUGGESTED WEB SITES: For more information specifically on Italy, visit: http://www.initaly.com and http://www.wel.it.

WHEN TO GO

The main tourist season in Rome starts shortly before Easter (when the greatest number of visitors flock to the city) and runs through October. Spring and fall are the best seasons in Rome, as far as the weather goes, though tourist attractions are still crowded. It's neither too hot nor too cold, there's usually plenty of sun, and the famous Roman sunsets are at their best. In July and August, come if you like, but learn to do as the Romans do—get up and out early, seek shady refuge from early afternoon heat, take a nap if you can, resume activities in the late afternoon, and stay up late to enjoy the evening breeze. During August many shops and restaurants close, and on the August 15 holiday Rome is a ghost town. Roman winters are relatively mild, with some persistent rainy spells. During the winter months, especially January–March, you have a better chance of getting into the major tourist attractions without having to wait in line.

CLIMATE

The following are average daily maximum and minimum temperatures for Rome.

➤ FORECASTS: **Weather Channel Connection** (☏ 900/932–8437), 95¢ per minute from a Touch-Tone phone.

ROME

Jan.	52F	11C	May	74F	23C	Sept.	79F	26C
	40	5		56	13		62	17
Feb.	55F	13C	June	82F	28C	Oct.	71F	22C
	42	6		63	17		55	13
Mar.	59F	15C	July	87F	30C	Nov.	61F	16C
	45	7		67	20		49	10
Apr.	66F	19C	Aug.	86F	30C	Dec.	55F	13C
	50	10		67	20		44	6

1 Destination: Rome

THE LAYERS OF ROME

Rome is like a big layer cake that can be pried open to get a feel for each of the layers. You'll find pieces of Ancient Rome casually strewn about, topped by Medieval and Renaissance Rome, topped by Fascist Rome, and finally today's Rome, where decades of political apathy are giving way to a revitalized city.

The Colosseum is the most intact reminder of Ancient Rome. Climb up into it and you can almost picture it full of screaming toga-clad citizens enjoying a spectacle of gladiators and wild beasts in mortal combat. Pick your way among the ruins in the Forum, trying to reconstruct what it might have been like to stroll here a few centuries before Christ. View the mathematical perfection of the round Pantheon, erected in 27 BC, rebuilt around AD 120, and modified in AD 608 when it became a church. Walk up to the top of the Capitoline hill, one of the seven Rome was built on, and look out across the Forum toward the Palatine hill, where the Colosseum looms in the background, to see a spectacular view of the whole city spread out before you.

Medieval and Renaissance Papal Rome are brought to life by the works of the architects, sculptors, and artists of those periods, still very much in evidence around the city. In the immense Vatican Museums you walk through the Raphael rooms radiant with frescoes by the artist, including *The School of Athens,* and finally reach the Sistine Chapel where, up on the ceiling, Michelangelo's hand of God reaches to give life to Adam, and on the wall at the far end writhing bodies ascend and descend in the artist's *Last Judgment.*

For a taste of the grim side of the Renaissance, you can visit the sumptuous Borgia apartments in the Vatican, frescoed by Pinturicchio, where Cesare Borgia is supposed to have murdered his sister Lucrezia's husband, Alphonse of Aragon.

In the Baroque layer, you come to the Rome of Bernini. From the piazza in front of St. Peter's to the Four Rivers Fountain in Piazza Navona, Bernini and others of his time transformed the face of Rome. Visit the spectacular Galleria Borghese, reopened in 1997 after more than a decade of restoration, to see a stunning collection of Bernini sculpture, including the 6-foot-tall marble *David.*

In the next layer, you'll find Nicola Salvi's dramatic, Rococo Trevi fountain, completed in 1762. This was the setting for the scene in Fellini's *La Dolce Vita* in which Marcello Mastroianni wades into the fountain after Anita Ekberg. *La Dolce Vita* highlighted Roman contradictions still evident today. In the film, Romans celebrate life in a never-ending party filled with drinking and sex, while at the same time citizens turn out in hordes for a child's primitive vision of the Madonna. Today, try purchasing Italy's equivalent of *Time* or *Newsweek* at a newsstand a few feet from the Pope's residence, and chances are it will feature a topless woman on the cover. Romans are sexually uninhibited—as you'll find on a walk through any park—yet devout Catholics who also find it tough to shed ancient superstitions.

On the flamboyant side of Rome—and we hit another layer—is the 19th-century Vittorio Emanuele monument facing Piazza Venezia. This excessive landmark, known as the wedding cake or the typewriter, with its white staircases spilling into the street, doesn't seem to reflect any particular style or historic message, except Rome's greed for grandeur.

Rome's next layer records the period of Fascism. Anyone who knows how unruly Italians are by nature would be astonished to see old film footage showing Mussolini addressing masses of Italians filling piazzas in perfect order and responding in unison, as their troops parade impeccably. Somehow, Mussolini managed to put Italians in marching order, appealing to their age-old desire for greatness. Il Duce was promising to bring back the Roman Empire, or nearly. So Romans happily allowed him to raise monolithic white stone buildings to house ministries and state-owned industry, elevating the bureaucrat and making the state's presence felt everywhere. Many major industrial and financial offices are still located in EUR, a neighborhood in the suburbs of Rome that's a museum of fascist architecture.

Today in the city, a fresh layer is beginning to show. Corruption scandals have overthrown a whole generation of politicians. A new law under which mayors are elected directly by the citizens has made local governments more accountable. Rome's mayor, environmentalist Francesco Rutelli, reelected to a second four-year term in 1998, has made the city cleaner and more livable. Rome is a little less chaotic than it once was, and traffic a little less perilous. It still takes time to get used to some Roman habits, like the scooters that zigzag in and out of traffic nearly tipping their adolescent, bare-headed riders, or having to look out for daredevil drivers when crossing the street on a pedestrian crosswalk. But as the mayor of nearby Naples, Antonio Bassolino, puts it, there's a transformation underway within Italians, from a "cynic sense" to a "civic sense."

In modern, bustling Rome, life and work take place outdoors. People lunch outside, sitting at tables that overflow from restaurants and bars onto sidewalks and into piazzas. That means people mix with each other: At lunch under a bright blue sky and hot sun in Piazza San Lorenzo in Lucina, not far from Parliament, you might see a crazy beggar woman chatting with important politicians and journalists. Italian teenagers know how to pick up girls on the Spanish Steps in every language. To witness Italian politicians in their daily task of horse-trading—exchanging support of one bill for this or that favor—try the bar in Via Uffici del Vicario. Or just watch them pacing in front of Parliament barking into their mobile phones.

In the new Italy, such enterprises as reviving the Galleria Borghese and opening the Palazzo Altemps—a Roman sculpture museum—have become possible where once bureaucracy was too much for good intentions. Palazzo Altemps has the extra appeal of plunging you into many of Rome's layers simultaneously. Once the residence of Cardinal Marco Sittico Altemps, the palazzo was redone in the Renaissance, but some 4th-century tombs in the foundations and part of a Medieval wall have been exposed. Ancient Roman statues are displayed in the rooms, but they aren't all totally authentic: Renaissance collectors sometimes commissioned contemporary sculptors to add arms and legs; in the museum collection is a Roman

statue of a seated Ares with a foot added later by Bernini.

Rome's layers are manifest everywhere. But some aspects of the city cut right through all the layers. Rome is romantic and unforgettable, just as it was for Audrey Hepburn in *Roman Holiday*. It's a perfect city for honeymooners. Just take an evening stroll through Piazza Navona, and you'll feel the inexplicable, indescribable thrill that has beguiled many visitors to Rome over the centuries into staying forever.

— Lucy Villeneuve

NEW AND NOTEWORTHY

During 1999 the rush to finish public works and infrastructure planned for the Jubilee Year of 2000 reaches a paroxysm of activity, to the detriment of traffic in certain parts of the city, especially around the Vatican itself. Many churches and public buildings are still shrouded as restorations continue up to the 2000 deadline. The cleaning of the facade of **St. Peter's** should be completed well before the end of 1999. On the fringes of the Vatican, within a bastion of the Vatican walls, construction work continues on a giant underground garage for tour buses. The new **Musei Vaticani** (Vatican Museums) station of Metro A opens at the beginning of 1999. Meanwhile, the Vatican Museums are receiving an entirely new entrance near the former entrance on Viale Vaticano; as visitors are to be channeled on a one-way route, itineraries within the museums may be altered. The new order of the itineraries will be posted at the entrance and may not correspond exactly to that described in this book.

The opening hours of a number of Rome's museums, along with others throughout Italy, have been extended; most are now open from 9 AM to 10 PM on weekdays, except for one weekly closing day. Most are open late on Sunday. In Rome the list includes the newly refurbished and highly popular **Galleria Borghese** as well as the recently opened archaeological museums of **Palazzo Altemps** and **Palazzo Massimo alle Terme,** and the **Galleria dell'Arte Antica** in Palazzo Barberini. **Castel Sant'Angelo** is open until 10, and the views of Rome by night from the terraces are spectacular. Also open late, the **Gallera d'Arte Moderna** in Villa Borghese has been endowed with a terrace café-restaurant that has become a chic rendezvous.

Following the discovery of a rare fresco of a cityscape and other images by 1st-century-AD artists in the Cryptoporticus (a tunnel-like gallery) on the site of Nero's **Domus Aurea** (Golden House), the Domus Aurea is scheduled to be partially reopened to visitors by spring 1999, after having been closed for 17 years.

Rome loses one obelisk and gains another. The obelisk of Axum, a victory trophy brought from Ethiopia by Mussolini and placed near the Circus Maximus, has been returned to that country as a gesture of reconciliation. And U.S. architect Richard Meier is putting up a new obelisk as part of his redesign of **Piazza dell'Augusteo** and of the building containing the Ara Pacis. Many of Rome's piazzas, large and small, central and not, have been done over as part of a beautification project focused on the Jubilee Year 2000.

Throughout Italy the **telephone** dialing system has changed. Now, even for local calls you must dial the area code. For example, for calls within Rome you must dial 06, which is the area code, before you dial the number of the person you are calling. To call Rome from outside Italy you must dial 39-06- plus the number you want. No area code is required for emergency numbers such as 112 (Carabinieri) or 118 (ambulance, health emergency).

Although the **euro,** the new European currency, will not yet be circulating in 1999, you may start to see prices quoted in euros. The euro will wholly supplant the lira by mid-2002.

The Holy Year: Jubilee 2000

The Holy Year, or Jubilee, in 2000 will bring an estimated 35 million pilgrims to Rome to visit the major basilicas, see the Pope, and pay homage to the tomb of St. Peter. The city of Rome and the Vatican are working together to see that these record crowds can be welcomed, housed, fed, and moved about more or less efficiently. Romans themselves shudder at the thought of their city's being invaded by hordes of pilgrims, making it impossible for them

carry on as usual. While the Vatican has been quietly going ahead with its plans, cleaning up the front of St. Peter's Basilica, installing a new entrance-exit system for the Vatican Museums, and organizing the practical aspects of the Holy Year program, Rome's administrators have had to cope with some glitches in their plans. A projected underpass that would have sped traffic past a perennial bottleneck at Castel Sant'Angelo and a new Metro line in the city center are among the public works that have been scrapped for technical reasons (archaeological risk and bureaucratic delays). On the bright side, part of the funds for those projects will instead be spent on improving tourist services such as hotels and information.

The city has pledged to do what it calls a restyling of the areas around the basilicas, enlarging sidewalks and Metro stations to handle the anticipated crowds of passengers. Even before 1998, Rome had started sprucing up for the Jubilee, restoring buildings and revamping museums. Special concerts and exhibitions are planned throughout the year.

The Vatican, of course, emphasizes the religious aspect of the Jubilee year. Though it is on the eastern outskirts of Rome at Tor Tre Teste, where few non-pilgrims will get to see it, an important new church is being built as a symbol of the Jubilee. Designed by Richard Meier, it was started behind schedule, so heavenly intervention may be required to get it finished on time.

Highlights of the Jubilee calendar are the opening and closing ceremonies in St. Peter's. The event officially begins before midnight on December 24, 1999, when the pope strikes with a silver hammer at the Holy Door in St. Peter's, symbolically opening it. The door is to remain open for 54 weeks. Special prayer vigils are being held in St. Peter's on December 31, 1999, and December 31, 2000; on both occasions, at midnight the bells of the world's Roman Catholic churches will be rung. The Holy Doors in San Giovanni in Laterano and Santa Maria Maggiore will be opened at ceremonies on December 25. That at San Paolo fuori le Mura will be opened January 18. St. Peter's feast day on June 29 is sure to be a major celebration, with up to 250,000 people packed into Piazza San Pietro for a papal mass outdoors. August 19–20, culmination of the week-long Youth Jubilee, may be a date not to be in Rome (unless you're participating), as some 2 million young people are expected for a mega-prayer meeting at a site on the city's outskirts. The Pope should be in Rome most of the year, with the exception of his much-heralded visit to the Holy Land. Every evening when he is in Rome throughout the Holy Year, the Pope will appear at a window of the Vatican Palace to pray with and to bless pilgrims in the square.

Magnets for Jubilee pilgrims during the year will be the four patriarchal basilicas in Rome: St. Peter's, Santa Maria Maggiore, San Giovanni in Laterano, and San Paolo fuori le Mura. Churches in general and such religious sites as the catacombs will be crowded throughout Holy Year, which ends with the closing of the Holy Door by the Pope on January 6, 2001, in St. Peter's. Closing ceremonies at the three other major basilicas in Rome will be held the preceding day, January 5.

WHAT'S WHERE

Rome's population of about 3 million lives in a sprawling urban district that is Italy's largest, extending southwest to the sea at Ostia. But practically all of the capital's myriad sights are crammed into the centro storico, or historic center, a relatively small part of that area. Historic Rome is defined by the impressive Aurelian Wall that encompasses the city's core. In AD 7, the emperor Augustus organized ancient Rome into 14 *regiones,* administrative divisions that were the origin of the historic *rioni,* many of which still have Latin-sounding names, like Subura, Esquilino, and Monti. The outline of most of the seven original hills has been dulled by landfill and development, but the Palatino and Aventino are still prominent heights. Modern Rome's neighborhoods may be known by ancient names, or by the names of key streets or piazzas.

Ancient Rome

The geographic center of the city is at Piazza Venezia, site of a late-19th-century monument that incongruously marks the heart of ancient Rome. The most evocative ruins of the ancient city extend from the Campidoglio across the Foro Romano to the Colosseo and the Terme di Caracalla and include the Palatino and Circo Massimo. This is one of the world's most striking and significant concentrations of historic remains, and it is destined to become an archaeological park of enormous dimensions. Except on the fringes, this area has no residents except lazy lizards and complacent cats. Scattered throughout the city are many more ruins, reminders of just how vast ancient Rome really was.

The Vatican

Seat of Roman Catholicism and residence of the popes, Vatican City has religious resonance and artistic splendors. Mostly enclosed within high walls that recall the papacy's stormy history, the Vatican opens the arms of the Bernini colonnade to embrace the world at Piazza San Pietro, an immense meeting place for the faithful and scene of the pope's public appearances. The Basilica di San Pietro, or St. Peter's, astounds for its size and glorious interior, and the Vatican Museums for their endless art collections. The Sistine Chapel is Michelangelo's magnificent artistic legacy. Between the Vatican and the once-moated bulk of Castel Sant'Angelo, the pope's covered passageway flanks an enclave of workers and crafts people, the old Borgo neighborhood, whose workaday charm is beginning to succumb to gentrification.

Old Rome

Packed with churches and patrician palaces, the land between the Roman Forum and the banks of the Tiber across from the Vatican and Castel Sant'Angelo is layered with history. The magnificent Pantheon, one of the world's greatest buildings, and the 3rd-century BC temples at Largo Argentina evoke ancient Rome. Piazza Navona is Bernini's most lighthearted tribute to the Baroque style; Borromini's more cerebral architectural responses are close by. Prelates' palaces, especially Palazzo della Cancelleria and Palazzo Farnese, make strong statements about the riches and power of the papal court. Churches like Il Gesù tell even more about an era of religious triumph and turmoil. In between are narrow streets and intriguing little shops, interspersed with eating places and cafés that are a focus of Rome's easygoing, itinerant nightlife.

The Spanish Steps and Trevi Fountain

A shopper's paradise, this district has its more polished side in the triangle that extends north of Via del Tritone to Piazza del Popolo. The density of high-fashion boutiques and trendy little shops leaves little room for residents, and the neighborhoods on either side of Via del Tritone are sparsely populated. The Spanish Steps are a magnet all day and well into the night for teenage Romans and camera-toting tourists. Especially on weekends, the Piazza di Spagna–Via del Corso zone is sometimes jammed with swarms of Rome's young and very young, in from the city's outlying districts for a ritual stroll that resembles a chaotic migration of lemmings in blue jeans. The scene around the Fontana di Trevi is equally crowded, forcing the wishful to toss their coins into the fountain from center field.

From Trajan's Market to San Giovanni in Laterano: Monti and the Esquilino

Monti is the old Subura, where the plebs of ancient Rome lived in dark tenements, with a high wall between their mean streets and the glories of the Imperial Fora. The neighborhood has a workaday, picturesque part along Via Panisperna and Via dei Serpenti, streets that follow the declivity of the Esquilino (Hill) and are lined with offbeat shops and little restaurants. Artistic treasures appear in out-of-the-way corners, like Michelangelo's *Moses* in the church of San Pietro in Vincoli. The great basilicas of Santa Maria Maggiore and San Giovanni in Laterano loom at the end of the broad avenues laid out centuries ago by the popes to make the pilgrims' way through Rome a little easier. Via Nazionale, instead, is a 19th-century thoroughfare that intersects the area, providing a direct link between Piazza Venezia and Termini Station. One of the Romans' favorite shopping streets, Via Nazionale is the unofficial showcase on Carnival weekends for tots parading in costume. The Termini Station neighborhood is a patchwork of dignified and seamy blocks; the patterns shift from time to time, but the area in general seems to be putting its better face forward in the wake of urban renewal projects. The Piazza Vittorio area is an ethnic kaleidoscope, full of African, Asian, and Middle Eastern shops and restaurants.

From the Quirinale to Piazza della Repubblica

The massive Palazzo Quirinale marks the more sober limit of a district laid out in the late 19th century, after the unification of Italy under the Savoy kings and the pope's retreat to the Vatican, which left the city free to become the capital of the new kingdom. A bit of Old Rome can still be seen around Piazza Barberini, where Bernini's Fontana del Tritone and Palazzo Barberini are reminders of the Baroque age. Pompous ministry buildings and a plethora of offices and banks mark this area as central Rome's principal business district. An oasis of ease appears on Via Veneto, heart of the Ludovisi neighborhood, where a former Savoy palace is now the American Embassy and where grand hotels and elegant cafés bask in the afterglow of La Dolce Vita. Piazza della Repubblica is another example of how Rome's history is revealed in layers: the vast ruins of the Terme di Diocleziano were transformed into a Renaissance monastery and the church of Santa Maria degli Angeli, designed by Michelangelo; the Baroque church of Santa Maria della Vittoria harbors a Bernini masterpiece; and the piazza itself, a paragon of late-19th-century urban planning, echoes the outline of the ancient baths.

Villa Borghese to the Ara Pacis

Much of this district accommodates Rome's most central park, dotted with pines and fountains and neoclassical "ruins." The lush park of Villa Borghese is a happy conjunction of the pleasure gardens and palaces of Renaissance prelates on the site of ancient Roman villas. The expanse of greenery is studded with the world-class museums of the Galleria Borghese and Villa Giulia, both with histories of their own, and the emphatically neoclassic gallery that somewhat incongruously houses collections of modern and contemporary art, the Galleria Nazionale d'Arte Moderna. The Pincio, the ancient Pincian Hill, is a belvedere over the city and a vantage point over elegantly planned Piazza del Popolo, below. The piazza's cafés are, in turn, vantage points from which to enjoy the variegated passersby. Crossing the piazza are dedicated shoppers heading for Via del Corso's emporia, art students on mopeds veering toward Via Ripetta and the Academy of Fine Arts, and more subdued types on their way to the art and antiques galleries on Via del Babuino or Via Margutta. In the opposite direction, mothers push babies in strollers through Porta del Popolo toward the business and residential Flaminio neighborhood to the north.

Trastevere and the Ghetto

The Tiberina Island, with bridges on either side, links two of the city's most picturesque neighborhoods: the Jewish Ghetto on the Tiber's left bank and Trastevere across the river. Both were bustling neighborhoods even in the earliest Roman times. What was to become the Ghetto in the 1500s was at the edge of ancient Rome's river port and wholesale marketplace; Trastevere was the place where immigrants from the empire's eastern colonies lived, among them ancient Rome's large Jewish community, which moved across the Tiber during the Middle Ages. Despite creeping gentrification, the Ghetto still preserves the flavor of Old Rome and a sense of community revolving around Via Portico d'Ottavia and the nearby Synagogue. Somewhat schizophrenic, Trastevere is trying to find its equilibrium on a fine line between its historic, authentic Roman character and *faux* folksy. It is afflicted with too many cute little restaurants and pizzerias, clubby tea rooms and esoterically trendy shops, and noisy late-night activity. But it has one of Rome's most beautiful, comfortably homey piazzas, Santa Maria in Trastevere, and many sections, totally off the beaten track, that have faithfully preserved the aura of past centuries.

The Aventino to St. Paul's

The Aventino, one of Rome's seven hills, is now an upscale residential neighborhood lush with private gardens, several early Christian churches, a famous keyhole with a view of St. Peter's, and Parco Savelli, known for orange trees and a great view up the Tiber toward Old Rome. The view of the Palatino from the northern approaches to the Aventino gives an insight into the scale of Imperial Rome's palaces. Beyond, Testaccio is a working-class neighborhood that is enjoying new popularity as a trendy place to eat and stay up late, perhaps disco dancing at the foot of Mount Testaccio, a manmade hill that started life as a dump for shards of the amphorae that the ancient Romans used to transport foodstuffs. Other than the Piramide, a monumental Roman tomb, there is not much to see between here and the basilica of San Paolo fuori le Mura, which is in the drab Ostiense residential neighborhood.

Celio and Caracalla

Almost entirely given over to parks and churches and ruins, the district encompassing the Celio (the Celian Hill) and the ancient Terme di Caracalla includes islands of quiet that seem far removed from the streams of traffic swirling around it. Several early Christian churches and the towering brick structures of the baths provide historical interest.

The Via Appia

The ancient Via Appia starts at Porta San Sebastiano, in a bucolic enclave that reaches right into the heart of the city and will be the core of the proposed archaeological park encompassing many of ancient Rome's most majestic sites. To the east lies the Via Appia Nuova, which starts in front of the basilica of San Giovanni in Laterano and cuts through miles of highly developed residential neighborhood to reach the Capannelle racetrack, Ciampino Airport, and points southeast. The Via Appia Antica, so called to distinguish it from the modern thoroughfare, leads past walled gardens to the catacombs and the Mausoleo di Cecilia Metella, where the lush countryside is dotted with evocative ruins and the arches of ancient aqueducts. This exclusive area is home to such personalities as Gina Lollobrigida and Franco Zeffirelli.

PLEASURES AND PASTIMES

Dining

Rome is a city distinguished more by its good attitude toward eating out than by a multitude of outstanding restaurants.

Don't look for star chefs here, or the latest trends—with a few notable exceptions, the city's food scene is a bit like its historic sites, well-worn but still standing. Nonetheless, Romans have been known since ancient times for great feasts and banquets, and though the days of the triclinium and the saturnalia are long past, dining out is still all the nightlife most Romans need. In fact, a lingering meal al fresco is one of Rome's great pleasures.

There was a time when you could predict the clientele and prices of a Roman eating establishment by whether it was called a *ristorante* (restaurant), a trattoria, or an *osteria* (tavern). These names have since become interchangeable. A rustic-looking spot that calls itself an osteria may turn out to be chic and anything but cheap. Generally speaking, however, a trattoria is a family-run place, simpler in decor, cuisine, and service—and slightly less expensive—than a ristorante. At no establishment should you feel compelled to eat a "full" meal (antipasto, first course, second course, side dish, and dessert), but ordering just a green salad will likely be frowned upon (Italians can't really seem to understand why someone would go out to a restaurant and then not eat). Lunch is served from noon to 3, dinner from 8 until about 10:30 or 11, but some restaurants stay open later, especially in summer, when patrons linger at sidewalk tables to enjoy the *ponentino* (evening breeze).

The Passeggiata (Strolling)

A favorite pastime of Romans (and most Italians) is the *passeggiata,* literally, the promenade. In the late afternoon, especially on weekends, couples, family groups, and packs of teenagers stroll in the main streets and piazzas. The passeggiata usually includes some café-sitting and window-shopping as well. Your own version of the passeggiata, different from all that purposeful walking you have to do to see the sights, could take you on an aimless stroll into Rome's byways. As you amble down the narrow streets, take time to peek into courtyards and look up at open windows as dusk falls to see lights go on, illuminating carved or frescoed ceilings on upper floors. The perfect accompaniment to a passeggiata is a gelato, or ice cream, either cone or cup, to be enjoyed as you ramble through Rome.

Shopping

The city's most famous shopping district is conveniently compact, fanning out at the foot of the Spanish Steps in a galaxy of boutiques offering gorgeous wares with glamorous labels. Here you can ricochet from Gucci to Prada to Valentino and Versace with less effort than it takes to pull out your platinum credit card. Even if your budget is designed for lower altitudes, you can find great clothes and accessories at prices you can afford. But buying is not necessarily the point. The greatest pleasure is in browsing, admiring window displays that are works of art, imagining you or yours in a little red dress by Valentino or a lean Armani suit, and dreaming that all this could be yours—if your name were Bill Gates.

Sidewalk Cafés

Café-sitting is the most popular leisure-time activity in Rome, practiced by all and involving nothing more strenuous than gesturing to catch the waiter's eye. Cafés are meant for relaxing, chatting with a companion, and/or eyeing the passing parade, possibly within view of one of the city's spectacular fountains or churches, in a square that would seem naked without a fringe of bright café umbrellas or awnings. For tourists and shoppers, part of this particular pleasure is resting tired feet. You will never be rushed, no matter how long you sit, and not even when café tables are crowded at aperitif time, just before lunch and, especially, supper. It's said that you can tell people by the café they sit at—from the toney types at Teichner in Piazza San Lorenzo in Lucina to the intellectuals and celebrities at the Antico Caffè della Pace, to all of the above—plus the rest of the world—at Tre Scalini in Piazza Navona.

GREAT ITINERARIES

Rome presents a particular challenge for visitors: just as you begin to fall in love with the city, you realize you don't have the time—let alone the energy—to see more than a fraction of its treasures. It's wise to take this into account from the start, and follow a focused yet flexible itinerary.

A ramble through a picturesque quarter of Old Rome can be just as enlightening as a chapel redolent of incense or a trek through marbled miles of museum corridors.

Though large, Rome invites walking; the bus and Metro systems are also feasible options for weary legs, once you get the hang of them. Carry an up-to-date transport route map. The Metro is easy to use, especially if you buy your tickets at a tobacconist or newsstand so you don't have to cope with ticket vending machines. Plan your day to take into account the varying opening hours you will encounter. You will probably be mixing classical and Baroque, museums and parks, the center and environs, and the variety lends spice to your visit. Most churches are usually open from 7 or 8 until noon or 12:30, and from 3 or 4 to about 7. You are expected to refrain from sightseeing in churches if a service is under way. Major basilicas are open all day.

If You Have 4 days

➤ DAY 1: Begin your first day at the **Campidoglio** and survey Rome from atop the Colle Capitolino (Capitoline Hill). Next, explore the **Foro Romano** (Roman Forum) and see the **Colle Palatino** (Palatine Hill) and the **Colosseo** (Colosseum). In the afternoon, combine sightseeing with shopping and make your way through the neighborhood around the **Scalinata di Spagna** (Spanish Steps).

➤ DAY 2: The following morning visit the **Musei Vaticani** (Vatican Museums) and the **Cappella Sistina** (Sistine Chapel), then the **Basilica di San Pietro** (St. Peter's Basilica). From October to mid-March the Vatican Museums are open only until 12:45, so you have no choice but to see them before you go to St. Peter's Basilica, which is open all day. At other times the museum is open until 3:45, allowing you more flexibility. Relax in the afternoon, perhaps exploring the neighborhood around your hotel.

➤ DAY 3: In the morning explore Old Rome and make your way to **Trevi Fountain**. In the afternoon you can visit a museum of interest (such as Castel Sant'Angelo) or watch the passing parade from a sidewalk café in one of the city's beautiful piazzas. You could walk from the **Mercati Traianei** (Trajan's Market) to the great basilicas of **Santa Maria Maggiore** and **San Giovanni in Laterano**.

➤ DAY 4: Get in some more shopping and/or a museum—**Galleria Borghese** (Borghese Gallery), perhaps—and spend your final afternoon and evening exploring the picturesque **Ghetto** and **Trastevere** neighborhoods.

If You Have 6 Days

Spend your first four days as above.

➤ DAY 5: In the morning wander through **Villa Borghese** and, if you haven't done so already, see the Canova and Bernini sculptures in the **Galleria Borghese**. Explore the **Piazza del Popolo** area and make your way to the **Ara Pacis**. In the afternoon see **Piazza del Quirinale** and make your way to **Piazza della Repubblica**.

➤ DAY 6: Make an excursion either to the **Appian Way** or to the ancient city of **Ostia Antica**. In the afternoon, stroll on the **Aventine** or **Celian** hills.

If You Have 10 Days

This will allow you to see Rome with more leisure.

➤ DAY 1: Start at the **Capitoline Hill,** see the **Forum** and **Palatine** and then the **Colosseum**. In the afternoon visit one of the archaeological museums (**Palazzo Altemps** or **Palazzo Massimo**).

➤ DAY 2: In the morning see the **Vatican Museums** and **St. Peter's,** and in the afternoon see part of **Old Rome**.

➤ DAY 3: Set off in the morning through **Villa Borghese** to the **Galleria Borghese** and then continue westward to the Tiber and the **Ara Pacis**. In the afternoon explore the shopping streets around **Piazza di Spagna** and toss a coin into **Trevi Fountain**.

➤ DAY 4: Start from **Trajan's Market** and make your way to the basilicas of **Santa Maria Maggiore** and **San Giovanni in Laterano**. In the afternoon explore the area between the **Quirinal Hill** and **Piazza della Repubblica**.

➤ DAY 5: Make an excursion to **Ostia Antica**.

➤ DAY 6: Devote the morning to a museum or neighborhood of your choice, and spend the afternoon exploring the **Celian Hill** and the **Baths of Caracalla**.

➤ DAY 7: Walk from the **Ghetto** through **Trastevere** and continue up to the **Gianicolo** (Janiculum Hill).

➤ DAY 8: Explore the **Aventine** and make your way to **San Paolo fuori le Mura** (St. Paul's outside the Walls).

➤ DAY 9: Make an excursion to the **Appian Way** and spend the afternoon shopping or relaxing.

➤ DAY 10: Take in a museum or neighborhood that interests you, and ramble through **Old Rome.**

FODOR'S CHOICE

Churches

★ **San Clemente.** Delve deep into the excavations below this church for an idea of how Rome, and its religions, grew.

★ **Santa Maria Maggiore.** The ceiling gleams with gold from the New World, but the mosaics in this magnificent place of worship were put here centuries before anyone had ever thought of setting sail across the Atlantic.

★ **Sant'Andrea al Quirinale.** Bernini designed it, and when it was finished he used to come here just to sit and enjoy his own handiwork.

★ **Santi Quattro Coronati.** An enclave of peace where nuns chant their prayers, this is one of the city's most intriguing churches, for it is part fortress, too.

Classical Sites

★ **The Baths of Caracalla.** The grandest of Rome's public baths is still a wonderful place to stroll and dream of what this social club-cum-spa must have been like in its heyday.

★ **Hadrian's Villa.** In what is now an archaeological park, Hadrian had replicas of the classical world's most famous buildings erected for his pleasure.

★ **Ostia Antica.** Perhaps even more than Pompeii, the excavated port city of ancient Rome conveys a picture of everyday life in a busy commercial center.

Hotels

★ **Cavalieri Hilton.** The short time it takes to commute from downtown by taxi or courtesy bus is amply rewarded by superior facilities, attention to creature comforts, and breathtaking views of Rome. $$$$

★ **Eden.** Stylish without being self-conscious, this hotel has exceptional atmosphere and a restaurant/roof terrace boasting superlative cuisine and views. $$$$

★ **Britannia.** An impeccably run boutique hotel where guests are quite literally pampered by an attentive staff. It is small, elegant, and excellent. $$$

★ **Farnese.** An old mansion has been converted into a hotel in art deco style with up-to-the-minute comfort and a friendly staff. $$$

★ **Locarno.** The location, near Piazza del Popolo, is convenient, the atmosphere is welcoming, and the rooms have Old World charm. $$

★ **Margutta.** This small hotel is the happy sum of an absolutely central location, friendly management, and quite adequate rooms at reasonable rates. $

Monuments

★ **The Colosseum.** The shouts of gladiators, the cries of the crowd, and echoes of pitiless persecutions (though the Christians were probably martyred elsewhere) come faintly from these ancient stones.

★ **Monumento a Vittorio Emanuele II.** For sheer size and conspicuousness, this is Rome's most visible and bombastic landmark.

★ **The Pantheon.** Take time to absorb the harmonious proportions of this pagan temple that was later consecrated as a church, and stand under the oculus (opening in the roof) to look up at the eye of heaven.

★ **The Pyramid of Gaius Cestius.** One of Rome's oddest monuments, this white marble pyramid testifies to the boundless self-esteem of a Roman official.

Museums

★ **Galleria Borghese.** Resplendent with frescoes and stuccoes, this museum harbors Canova's *Pauline Borghese* and several Bernini works that define the essence of Baroque sculpture.

★ **Etruscan Museum of Villa Giulia.** A beautiful papal summer palace holds the art and artifacts of the highly civilized people who ruled central Italy even before the Romans.

★ **Palazzo Massimo alle Terme.** If only for the frescoes from the Casa di Livia (House of Livia) and from the Farnesina, this museum would deserve a place of honor, but it has all manner of other classical finds, too.

Off the Beaten Track

★ **The excavations under St. Peter's.** This is where archaeologists found a cemetery niche that they identified as the actual tomb of St. Peter. The visit also gives you insight into how the great basilica above came into being.

★ **The private apartments of the Doria Pamphili Palace** (Palazzo Doria Pamphili). After eyeing the family's fabulous art collection, take a look at some of the private salons that this aristocratic clan calls home.

★ **Isola Tiberina.** If the Tiber's waters permit, stroll on the embankments of the island that the ancient Romans clad with marble to heighten its resemblance to a ship.

Quintessential Rome

★ **Foro Romano** (Roman Forum). The place where the Caesars walked stirs an awareness of the grandeur that was Rome, and if that's not enough, the Colosseum is just down the street.

★ **Piazza Navona.** The exuberant spirit of the Baroque Age is embodied in Bernini's fantastic Fontana dei Quattro Fiumi (Fountain of the Four Rivers), set off by the curves and steeples of Borromini's church of Sant'Agnese, and admired by colorful crowds devouring *gelati*.

★ **Piazza di San Pietro** (St. Peter's Square). No other place in the world is quite like it. Stand near the obelisk and take in the size and significance of the physical core of Christianity, an almost aggressively defined urban space with an intrinsic harmony.

★ **Piazza Santa Maria in Trastevere.** In a neighborhood that blends authentic Roman flavor with a shot of bohemian spirit and a dash of just plain seediness, sit at the café facing Santa Maria in Trastevere at dusk as hidden spotlights suddenly illuminate the golden mosaics high on the front of the church.

★ **The Appian Way.** Ancient paving stones are bared along this thoroughfare, where tall cypresses guard melancholy tombs, ruins of emperors' villas rise in green fields, and processions of 2,000-year-old arches carry aqueducts toward the city's fountains.

Restaurants

★ **La Pergola.** Warmly elegant with trompe l'oeil ceilings, handsome wood paneling, and large windows, the dining room has amply spaced tables and low lighting that create an intimate atmosphere. Dishes are balanced and light, and presentation is striking. (Vatican) $$$$

★ **La Rosetta.** At this elegant, wood-paneled restaurant, first-rate fish is the specialty. Try such treats as *vongole veraci* (large, tasty sautéed clams) or sea bass with black truffle. (Old Rome) $$$$

★ **Myosotis.** Central location, an extensive menu that rides the delicate line between tradition and innovation, and great value make Myosotis a place to return to. (Old Rome) $$

★ **Antico Arco.** Run by three friends with a passion for wine and fine food, the restaurant serves such delights as *petto d'anatra con salsa di lamponi* (duck breast with raspberry sauce). (Trastevere/Testaccio) $–$$

★ **Dal Toscana.** This great family-run Tuscan trattoria has an open wood-fired grill and classic dishes such as *ribollita* (thick bread and vegetable soup) and *pici* (fresh thick pasta served with wild hare sauce). (Vatican) $

Walks

★ **Anywhere in Old Rome early on a Sunday.** This is the perfect time to see the piazzas and palaces free of the bustle of everyday business and to get an uncluttered view of Rome's architecture. But come back again on a weekday to get the feel of life in the city.

★ **Via Condotti and vicinity.** The essence of Italian style is yours for the looking as you window-shop your way through some of Rome's most elegant shopping streets near the Piazza di Spagna.

★ **Villa Borghese and the Pincio.** In fair weather this walk affords a more bucolic perspective on Rome's beauties, with the added bonus of three major museums within the park's confines.

Works of Art

★ **The ceiling of the Sistine Chapel.** No matter how many pictures have prepared you for the sight of Michelangelo's masterpiece, it never ceases to amaze.

★ **The head of Constantine in the courtyard of the Capitoline Museums.** Now in the courtyard of the Conservators' Palace, this is a fragment of the 40-foot-high statue of the emperor enthroned that stood in the Basilica of Maxentius (Basilica di Massenzio).

⭐ **The Ludovisi sarcophagus in Palazzo Altemps.** The intricacy of this massive work steals the show from other stellar sculptures in the Museo Nazionale Romano's collections.

⭐ **Canova's sculpture of Pauline Borghese in the Galleria Borghese.** Napoléon's sister couldn't have cared less about the gossip this statue caused, and that little smile on her lips hints that she probably enjoyed all the attention.

⭐ **Raphael's Stanze in the Vatican.** These rooms, filled with Raphael's marvelous compositions, stunning colors and forms, and secret portraits of some of the artist's most famous contemporaries, are a highlight of the Vatican Museums.

FESTIVALS AND SEASONAL EVENTS

Contact the Italian State Tourist Office (☞ Visitor Information, *above*) for exact dates and further information on all the festivals held in Rome.

WINTER

➤ JAN. 5–6: On the eve of **Epiphany,** Piazza Navona's toy fair explodes in joyful conclusion, with much noise and rowdiness to encourage Befana, an old woman who brings toys to good children and pieces of coal (represented by similar-looking candy) to the naughty.

➤ FEB.: **Carnival** celebrations reach a peak of masquerading fun on the Sunday and Tuesday before Lent begins. On the evening of Martedí Grasso (Mardi Gras) many restaurants hold special carnival parties—you'll need to make reservations well in advance.

SPRING

➤ APR.: **Easter** is the big event of the month, preceded by the solemn rites of Holy Week, in which the pope takes an active part. The Good Friday procession, staged near the Colosseum, is both moving and spectacular. The Monday after Easter, known as Pasquetta, is a holiday and traditionally a day for an outing into the country.

➤ LATE APR.: The Piazza di Spagna bursts into bloom, with the Spanish Steps covered with azaleas. Nearby, Via Margutta holds an **outdoor art show.**

➤ LATE APR.–EARLY MAY: T he **International Horse Show** (Federazione Italiana Sport Equestri, ✉ Viale Tiziano 74, ☎ O6/3685–8528) brings sleepy Piazza di Siena, an amphitheater in Villa Borghese, to life with stirring competition and a chic crowd of spectators.

➤ EARLY MAY: The **Rose Show** (Roseto Comunale, ✉ Via della Murcia, ☎ 06/574– 6810) opens at Valle Murcia on the slopes of the Aventine Hill overlooking the Circus Maximus and continues into June.

➤ MID-MAY: An **antiques fair** is held in the beautiful old Via dei Coronari in Old Rome, when shops stay open late and the street is lit by torches. It is repeated in October.

➤ LATE MAY: The **Italian International Tennis Tournament** (Federazione Italiana Tennis, ✉ Viale Tiziano 74,☎ 06/3685–8510) is held at Foro Italico.

SUMMER

➤ MID-JUNE–MID-JULY: The **Festival of Baroque Music** is held in Viterbo.

The **Pontine Music Festival** is held in the Caetani castle in Sermoneta and in the abbeys of Fossanova and Valvisciolo, all within reach of Rome.

➤ JUNE 23: On the eve of the **Feast of St. John the Baptist,** June 24, the neighborhood of San Giovanni bursts with festive activities, mainly gastronomic.

➤ JUNE 29: The **Feast of St. Peter,** patron saint of Rome, is marked by solemn celebrations in St. Peter's basilica, when the interior of the church is ablaze with light, and by showy fireworks over the Aventine Hill.

➤ MID-JUNE–LATE JULY: The **French Academy** at Villa Medici holds a **festival of performing arts** featuring leading French artists. The **Romaeuropa Festival** showcases leading European talents in the performing arts in indoor and outdoor venues throughout the city.

➤ MID-JULY: The **Festa di Noantri** in Trastevere combines religious processions with concerts of traditional Roman music and a sidewalk fair.

➤ AUG. 5: The **Feast of the Madonna of the Snow** is marked in the Basilica of Santa Maria Maggiore by a high mass, during which rose petals are thrown to represent the miraculous August snowfall that indicated where the church should be built.

➤ AUG. 15: **Ferragosto** marks the height of the summer vacation period. Most shops, restaurants, and museums are closed, public transport is at a minimum, and the city is the quietest it will ever be. There are special celebrations in the church of Santa Maria in Trastevere.

AUTUMN

➤ LATE SEPT.–EARLY OCT.: A **Handicrafts Fair** brings torchlight, street stalls, and animation to Via dell'Orso.

➤ EARLY OCT.: In the Alban Hills southeast of

Rome, the **Grape Harvest Festival** in Marino features parades and fountains spouting wine.

➤ DEC. 1–8: **Museum Week** highlights special exhibitions and free admission.

➤ DEC. 8: This is the day of the **Feast of the Immaculate Conception,** when Rome's fire department replaces the garland atop the statue of the Virgin Mary in Piazza di Spagna, and the pope comes over from the Vatican to pay his respects.

➤ MID-DEC.: Rome's **Opera** season begins.

➤ LATE DEC.: **Presepi** (Christmas crèches) go on display in many churches; some of them are antique and quite elaborate.

➤ DEC. 24 AND 25: **Christmas** is very much a family holiday in Rome. There are no public celebrations other than solemn religious rites, beginning on Christmas Eve; these are especially beautiful in the city's older churches and in St. Peter's, where the pope officiates both at midnight mass and at the late-morning mass on Christmas Day before imparting his blessing to the faithful in the square.

2 Exploring Rome

Rome is a heady blend of artistic and architectural masterpieces, classical ruins, and extravagant Baroque churches and piazzas. The places evoke the people—Roman emperors concerned with outdoing their predecessors in grandeur, powerful prelates enmeshed in intricate scandals, geniuses summoned by the popes to add to the Vatican's treasures, a dictator who left his mark on the city before his imperial dreams were shattered, and the Romans themselves, full of the earthy energy that makes this a city of unique vitality.

FROM ANCIENT TIMES, Romans have been piling the present on top of the past, blithely building, layering, and overlapping their more than 2,500 years of history to create the colorful, interwoven fabric of an excitingly beautiful city. Rome is exuberant and occasionally exasperating. The city's core is visually stunning, with its heady mix of antiquity, art, style, and good living. Not even the noise, the lines at the museums, the crowded buses can take the edge off the city's nonchalant grandeur. Here you can stroll casually past some of Western civilization's greatest monuments, have gelato in a square designed by Bernini, and sleep in a Renaissance palace. Rome's extraordinary settings and glowing colors give everything you do here a tinge of romance, a hint of adventure, a taste of beauty.

Don't be self-conscious in your wanderings about the city. Poke and pry under the surface of things. Walk boldly through gates that are just ajar to peek into the hidden world of Roman courtyards. But do it with a smile, the surest way to break down a stern custodian's reserve. Generally warm and straightforward, the Romans are pleased to give you a glimpse of the nooks and crannies of their hometown, of which they are inordinately proud. They are also just as happy to leave to you the joy of discovering them for yourself. The emotion of walking in the Roman Forum, the fun of people-watching in Piazza Navona, the glorious sight of ocher-colored palaces under the blue sky in the sublime light of late afternoon are very personal and very Roman experiences.

During your stay, you are also likely to share with the Romans some of the problems that afflict them—of which the biggest is traffic, with its corollaries of noise and air pollution. But things are improving. Sizable areas of the city center have been designated for pedestrians only, so you can sightsee without feeling as if you are a combatant in World War III targeted by the buzz bombs known here as *motorini* (mopeds).

Keep your sightseeing flexible. This city is so richly stocked with attractions that you won't be able to cover all the sights anyway. Be selective, concentrating on what interests you most. You'll probably be walking most of the time, mixing classical sites with Baroque, museums with parks, churches with shops, the center with the environs. However you do it, be sure to take plenty of time out for simply sitting and observing this kaleidoscopic city and the passing pageant.

ANCIENT ROME

Rome, as everyone knows, was built on seven hills—Colle Capitolino (the Camipdoglio, as it is known commonly), Monte Palatino, Monte Esquilino, Monte Viminale, Monte Cello, Monte Quirinale, and Monte Aventino. Two of these historic hills—the Campidoglio and the Palatine—formed the hub of ancient Rome, the center of the civilized world. The Campidoglio has always been the seat of Rome's government; its Latin name is echoed in the designation of national and state capitol buildings. On the Palatine the earliest recorded inhabitants of Rome lived in modest mud huts; later, its position made it Rome's most exclusive residential zone, site of the emperors' vast and luxurious palaces. Between the hills, in the Forum, the Romans worshipped, discussed politics, and carried on commerce. Between the Palatine and the Tiber were the markets where livestock and produce arrived by boat. Though it remained the heart of monumental and religious Rome, the Forum was later dwarfed by the Imperial Fora, built by a succession of emperors to augment the original, overcrowded Forum and to make sure that the people would have tangible evidence of their generosity.

More than any other, this part of Rome is a perfect example of that layering of historic eras, the overlapping of ages, of religions, of a past that is very much a part of the present. Christian churches rise on the foundations of ancient pagan temples. An immense marble monument to an 18th-century king of a newly united Italy shares a square with a medieval palace built by a pope. But it is the history and memory of ancient Rome that dominate the area. After a more than 27-centuries-long parade of pageantry, it is not surprising that Shelley and Gibbon reflected on the sense of *sic transit gloria mundi* they felt here. The ruins and monuments, the Colosseum and the triumphal arches have stood through the centuries as emphatic reminders of the genius and power that made Rome the center of the Western world.

Numbers in the text and margin correspond to points of interest on the Ancient Rome map.

The Campidoglio

The Campidoglio has been the seat of civic government since Rome itself began. Though most of the buildings here date from the Renaissance, this hill was once the epicenter of the Roman Empire. Originally, the Capitoline Hill consisted of two peaks: the Capitolium and the Arx. The hollow between them was known as the Asylum; it was here, in the days before the republic was founded in 510 BC, that prospective settlers came to acknowledge the protection of Romulus, legendary first king of Rome, and to be granted "asylum." Later, during the republic, the austere, public-spirited period in which the Roman Empire was established, Roman temples occupied both peaks, and, later still, in 78 BC, the Tabularium, or Record Office, was built to house the city archives. It was incorporated into the foundations of Palazzo Senatorio, rebuilt in the 1500s, which is still Rome's city hall. Throughout the Middle Ages an earlier incarnation of Palazzo Senatorio was just about the only building on the Campidoglio, then an unkempt hill strewn with the classical rubble of temples and used mainly as a goat pasture. Nonetheless the fame of the Campidoglio lingered on—Petrarch, the 14th-century Italian poet, was just one of many to extol its original splendor though its sumptuous marble palaces and temples had long since crumbled.

The Romans of the Renaissance achieved a fairly sophisticated understanding of ancient Rome and were conscious of the glory of the ancient city and of the decline it had endured for so long. Nevertheless, their attempts at restoration mostly took the form of carrying away what remained of the original buildings to use as materials for their own construction projects or buying newly unearthed statues and other works of art to display in their new sculpture galleries and their palaces.

In 1537 Pope Paul III called in Michelangelo and charged him with restoring the Campidoglio. The aim was not just to re-create its former glory but to provide a fitting setting for the imminent visit of Charles V, the Holy Roman emperor, ruler of Spain and much of central Europe. The purpose of his visit was to receive the praise of a grateful pope for a notable victory over the Moors in North Africa. It was decided—very much in emulation of ancient Roman triumphal processions—that Charles V should proceed through the city to the Campidoglio, following what was believed to have been the route used by the ancient emperors after their triumphs. Much of Michelan-

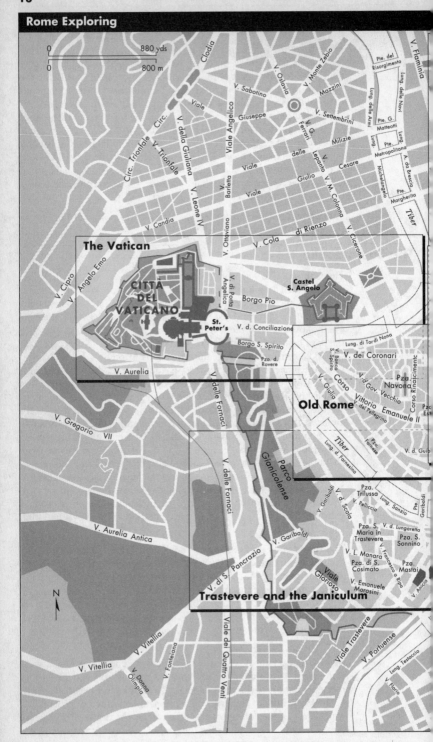

The Vatican

CITTÀ DEL VATICANO

Castel S. Angelo

St. Peter's

Old Rome

Trastevere and the Janiculum

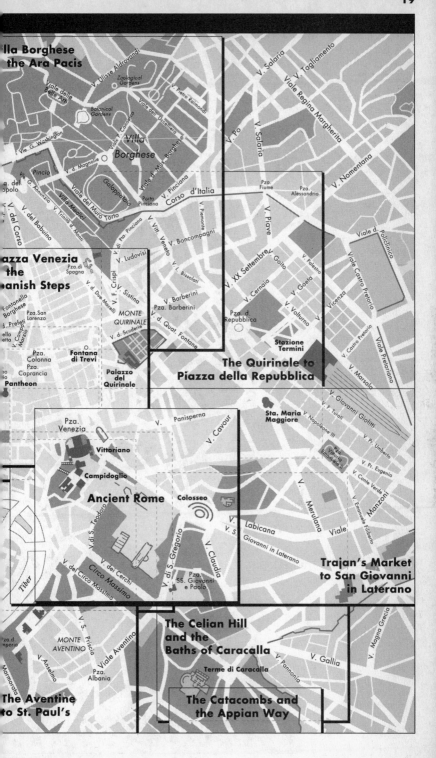

**lla Borghese
the Ara Pacis**

**azza Venezia
the
anish Steps**

**The Quirinale to
Piazza della Repubblica**

Ancient Rome

**Trajan's Market
to San Giovanni
in Laterano**

**The Celian Hill
and the
Baths of Caracalla**

**The Aventine
to St. Paul's**

**The Catacombs and
the Appian Way**

20

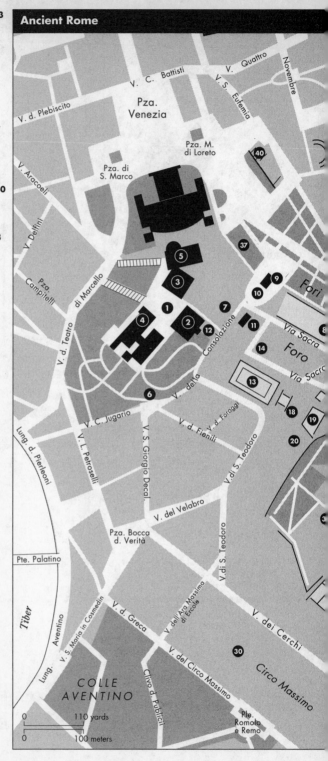

Ancient Rome

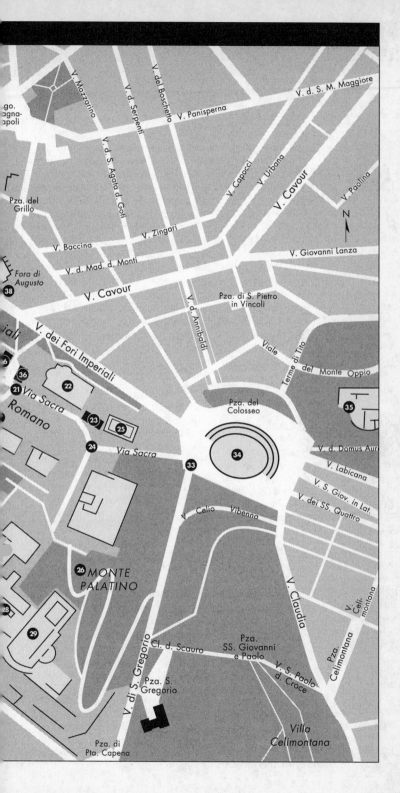

ROME'S GOVERNMENTS

ALTHOUGH IT'S BEEN THE capital of the Republic of Italy only since 1946, Rome has been the capital of *something* for more than 2,500 years, and it shows. The magnificent ruins of the Palatino, the massive complex of the Forum, the balanced lines of the Campidoglio, the imperial majesty of the Colonna di MarcoAurelio, not to mention St. Peter's, capital of Catholic Christianity, are all part of Rome's longest-lasting identity—that of seat of government, one of the world's most enduring. The Roman Republic, founded in the 6th century BC, was the philosophical base of modern republics; the Roman Senate the inspiration for modern senates (complete with dynastic rule and seat-buying). Even the language of modern government comes from Rome: the English words "capitol" and "palace" come from the names of the Capitoline (Campidoglio) and Palatine (Palatino) Hills, the ancient sites of, respectively, the government halls and imperial residences.

This is not to say that it's been an easy 2½ millennia: The birth of modern government seems to have brought with it the birth of modern politics, and with very few exceptions, Roman rulers throughout the ages have found their position to be anything but secure. While senators of the Roman Republic contented themselves with buying influence, would-be emperors of later centuries found much more permanent ways of getting their opponents out of office. The end of the Roman Republic and the beginning of the Roman Empire was marked by the ambush and murder of Julius Caesar, while Nero ascended to the throne with the help of his mother, who cleared the way by poisoning Claudius with death's-head mushrooms. Popes elected to rule in medieval times were frequently challenged by anti-Popes, rival pontiffs chosen in opposition elections; many anti-popes "ruled" concurrently with official popes, starting with Hippolytus in 217 and continuing until Felix V in 1439. Hundreds of years later, with the advent of the democratic Italian Republic, political methods have become tamer, and, perhaps for this reason, the turnover rate has increased: Prime Minister Romano Prodi's Olive Coalition holds the postwar record for continuing rule—a whopping two years, in September of 1998.

Rome's major sights constitute a tour through the governments of the ages. The Imperial Fora, monuments to the power and wealth of the emperors, nestle up against the monument to Victor Emanuel II, the first king of a united Italy; next door is the Campidoglio, home of the municipal records building in Republican times, now the site of modern Rome's City Hall. Across the street on Piazza Venezia is the Palazzo Venezia, from whose balcony Fascist dictator Benito Mussolini gave his most famous addresses, and up the Quirinale Hill is the Palazzo Quirinale, once home to popes, then kings, and now to the Italian President. Modern Italian politics are played right in the center of it all: at Palazzo Madama (the Italian Senate), next to Piazza Navona; Palazzo Chigi (the Prime Minister's office), on Piazza Colonna; and the Chamber of Deputies, next door at Piazza Montecitorio. After all, if Italy's government bureaucracy is legendary, it only stands to reason that its most legendary city should be its home.

gelo's plan was not finished for almost a century, but nearly everything here today follows his original designs.

A Good Walk

Begin your walk on the **Campidoglio** ①, or Capitoline Hill, site of Michelangelo's spectacular Piazza del Campidoglio and Rome's ceremonial city hall, **Palazzo Senatorio** ②. Take in the view from the piazza, putting your back to the replica of the ancient bronze statue of Marcus Aurelius. In front of you, to the north, stretch the rooftops of central Rome, punctuated by tapered domes and steeples, with the heights of Monte Mario in the distance. Flanking the Palazzo Senatorio are both elegant late-Renaissance halves of Rome's most noteworthy museum complex, the **Musei Capitolini,** made up of the **Museo Capitolino** ③ and the **Palazzo dei Conservatori** ④, which contain works of art gathered by Pope Sixtus V. Off to the southeast flank of the Museo Capitolino, at the head of the hill's formidable flight of steep steps, stands the ancient redbrick church of **Santa Maria in Aracoeli** ⑤. From vantage points in the Campidoglio gardens and belvederes on the left of Palazzo Senatorio you can look out onto the Imperial Fora and the Roman Forum itself.

From the southwest flank of Palazzo Senatorio, take Via del Campidoglio and then Via del Tempio di Giove for a look at the Roman Forum from the **Belvedere Tarpeo** ⑥; imagine what the area looked like when most of these magnificent ruins were covered over by marshy pastureland, and cows grazed beside half-buried columns and trod 2,000-year-old marble paving slabs. From the belvedere on the northeast side of Palazzo Senatorio, descend Via San Pietro in Carcere, actually a flight of stairs, to the gloomy **Carcere Mamertino** ⑦.

TIMING

This walk can be done in about two hours, depending on how long you linger in the Musei Capitolini. Take the walk and those exploring the Foro Romano and Palatino on one of your first days in Rome in order to get a sense of where and how the city began and how it expanded. Fair weather helps, but it is not essential, as the Musei Capitolini and the church of Santa Maria dell'Ara Coeli are indoor sights. Late evening is an option for this walk; though the church is closed, the museums are open late, and the views of the city lights and the illuminated Monumento a Vittorio Emanuele and Foro Romano are striking.

Sights to See

❻ Belvedere Tarpeo (Tarpeian Belvedere). A vantage point with a view of the Palatine Hill that held a particular fascination for the city's 18th- and 19th-century grand tourists, who had come to contemplate the glory of the ancient city, this was the infamous Tarpeian Rock from which traitors were dashed to the ground below. Here, in the 7th century BC, Tarpeia betrayed the Roman citadel to the besieging Sabines, sworn enemies of the early Romans, asking, in return, for what they wore on their left arms, thinking of their heavy gold bracelets. The scornful Sabines did indeed shower her with their gold as they passed, but added the crushing weight of their heavy shields, also carried on their left arms. ⊠ *Via del Tempio di Giove.*

❼ Carcere Mamertino (Mamertine Prison). A minor attraction amid the glories of ancient Rome, the prison consists of two gloomy subterranean cells where Rome's vanquished enemies, most famously the Goth Jugurtha and the indomitable Gaul Vercingetorix, were imprisoned and died of starvation or strangulation. In the lower cell, St. Peter himself is believed to have been held prisoner and to have miraculously brought forth a spring of water in order to baptize his jailers. That explains why a church, San Giuseppe dei Falegnami, was built over the prison. ⊠ *Via di San Pietro in Carcere.* 🖼 *Donations requested.* ☉ *Daily 9– 12:30 and 2–7:30.*

★ **Musei Capitolini** (Capitoline Museums). Today, the buildings on the east and west sides of Piazza del Campidoglio, both with facades designed by Michelangelo, are museums. Palazzo Senatorio, the central building, also is destined to become part of the museum complex. The museums' collections are based on those assembled in the 15th century by Pope Sixtus IV, one of the earliest of the great papal art lovers and collectors of antiquities. To your right, as you face Palazzo Senatorio, is Palazzo dei Conservatori; to your left is Palazzo Nuovo, which houses the Museo Capitolino. Your ticket is good for both.

The collections include some of the finest and most celebrated sculptures of the ancient world. Up to now, seeing them in serried ranks in the Capitoline's dark galleries was hardly an ideal introduction to works that inspired generations of artists from the 15th century onward. It's also worth remembering that many of these statues have been restored by overconscientious 18th- and 19th-century collectors, who added limbs and heads with considerable abandon, and that originally almost all these works would have been brilliantly colored and gilded. Remember, too, that many of the works here are Roman copies of Greek originals. For hundreds of years, family businesses in ancient Rome prospered by copying Greek statues—they used a process called "pointing," by which exact copies could be made—but, though faithful, their copies are often strangely lifeless. Portraiture was one area in which the Romans outstripped the Greeks. The hundreds of Roman portrait busts in the collections are probably the highlight of a visit here.

Note: During restoration of the Capitoline Museums, most of the collections, especially the most famous pieces, have been moved to another venue. Until they are returned to the Campidoglio on an indefinite date toward the end of 1999, they can be seen at the **Centrale Montemartini** (⊠ Viale Ostiense 106, ☏ 06/699–1191; 🖼 12,000 lire; ☉ Tues.–Fri. 10–6, weekends 10–7). Here, classical archaeology is juxtaposed with industrial archaeology in the former Montemartini power plant. ⊠ *Piazza del Campidoglio,* ☏ *06/671–03069.* 🖼 *10,000 lire; free last Sun. of month; ticket office in Palazzo dei Conservatori.* ☉ *Tues.–Sun. 9–9.*

❸ **Museo Capitolino** (Capitoline Museum). As you enter the courtyard you'll find the reclining figure of Marforio, to which anonymous political protests and satirical poems were affixed in ancient times. The original gilded bronze equestrian statue of Marcus Aurelius is behind glass here. The collection begins with a few Egyptian sculptures, but most of the interesting pieces are upstairs, where the first room contains the poignant sculpture *Dying Gaul* and the delicate *Marble Faun* that inspired 19th-century novelist Nathaniel Hawthorne's novel of the same name. The Sala del Fauno next door displays the delightful red-marble *Drunken Faun* and the *Child with a Goose,* both Roman copies of Greek bronzes. In the large room there's a basalt statue of an obese *Hercules as a Boy,* as well as two much finer pieces: an old and a young centaur in gray marble. The *Wounded Amazon,* in the same room, is a famous Roman copy of a 5th-century BC Greek original.

Next, the fascinating **Sala dei Filosofi** and **Sala degli Imperatori** present you with row upon row of portrait busts, a kind of ancient *Who's Who.* In the Sala degli Imperatori, look for the handsomely austere Augustus; for cruel Caracalla and vicious Nero; for the haughty Marcus Aurelius; and for the dissolute, eerily modern Heliogabalus. And don't miss the extraordinary bust of an unidentified Roman matron with an incredibly elaborate hairdo. (☞ Musei Capitolini, *above*.)

❹ **Palazzo dei Conservatori** (Conservators' Palace). Here the Conservators, the city's elected magistrates, met in the Middle Ages. In the courtyard stand a huge head and hand, fragments of a colossal statue of the emperor Constantine, which tourists like to use as props for souvenir photographs. You ascend a monumental staircase to the resplendent **Salon of the Orazi and Curiazi,** occasionally used by city authorities for official ceremonies, with a magnificent gilt ceiling and carved wooden doors providing the setting for some glorious 16th-century frescoes by Cavalier d'Arpino. At either end of the salon reign statues of the Baroque period's most important popes: Bernini's marble sculpture of his patron, Urban VIII, and Algardi's portrait in bronze of Innocent X.

In the rooms that follow you'll find more frescoes depicting scenes of ancient Roman history; a colorful geometric mosaic unearthed during the construction of the Via Nazionale in the 19th century; and the *Capitoline Wolf,* an Etruscan bronze of the 6th century BC (the figures of the twins Romulus and Remus were added in 1509). Romulus and Remus were, legend claims, the founders of Rome. They were found, as infants, on the banks of the Tiber by a she-wolf, who suckled them (hence this statue). They had been dispossessed by a wicked uncle, but were really the sons of the god Mars and a Latin princess. A shepherd adopted the twins, and they grew to become strong and ambitious young men. The gods favored them and encouraged them to build a city. The spot they chose in 753 BC was near the place where they had been found by the she-wolf, close by the Palatine. During the building of the city the brothers quarreled and, in a fit of anger, Romulus killed Remus—which is how the city became Roma, not Rema. In the corner room, the lovely *Boy with a Thorn* attracts the most attention. Here also is the impressive bust in bronze of an austere and intense *Brutus,* a portrait of Junius Brutus, founder of the Roman Republic and ancestor of the last of the great Republicans, the Brutus who stabbed Julius Caesar, the warrior-turned-statesman-turned-emperor who ushered in the Imperial age of ancient Rome.

When restorations have been completed, the **Galleria degli Orti Lamiani** will again contain sculptures found on the Esquiline Hill (today the site of the church of Santa Maria Maggiore), including the *Esquiline Venus.* At the end of the corridor is the **Passaggio del Muro Romano,** formed by great gray stone blocks that made up the base of the Temple of Jupiter, most sacred spot in ancient Rome and center of Roman religious life. These blocks, dating from 509 BC, are believed to be among the oldest fragments of any building in the city. In its heyday, the temple was lavishly decorated with gold, precious jewels, and numerous tablets, banners, and medallions. It was here that Roman military triumphs were celebrated. The conquering general, dressed in a purple toga and painted a brilliant red like the statue of Jupiter in the temple, would offer up his sacrifice. Simultaneously, his vanquished enemies would be done to death in the Mamertine prison below the Capitol. (Much later, Julius Caesar and Augustus were granted the right to wear these sumptuous robes whenever they chose.) The riches of the temple were plundered by successive waves of invading Goths and Vandals when the empire fell. Gradually, what remained of the building was carried away for use in other structures around the city, until all that was left were these bare stone slabs.

Upstairs, the **Pinacoteca Capitolina** has some splendid paintings: a Tintoretto *Magdalene,* Rubens's *Romulus and Remus,* a portrait of Bernini by Velázquez, Caravaggio's *Young St. John,* and, in another room, one of his versions of *The Fortune Teller.* (☞ Musei Capitolini, *above.*)

❷ Palazzo Senatorio. Rome's city hall thrusts its foundations deep into the Tabularium, the ancient city's hall of records. During the Middle Ages it looked like the medieval town halls you see in Tuscan hill towns, part fortress and part assembly hall. The building was entirely rebuilt in the 1500s as part of Michelangelo's revamping of the Campidoglio for Pope Paul III. What you see is an adaptation of the master's design by later architects, who wisely left the Michelangelo-designed front staircase as the focus of the facade. The ancient statue of Minerva in the niche at the center was opportunely renamed the Goddess Rome, and the river gods (the Tiber, right, and the Nile, left) were hauled over from the Terme di Costantino on the Quirinal Hill. Used up to now as ceremonial seat of the city government, Palazzo Senatorio will soon be opened to the public as part of the Capitoline Museum complex. ⊠ *Piazza del Campidoglio.*

Piazza del Campidoglio. On the summit of the Camipdoglio, this is one of Rome's most beautiful sites, thanks mainly to Michelangelo's vision of spatial harmony. You approach the Campidoglio up a gently sloping ramp, the *cordonata.* As you climb it, the buildings and spatial effects of the site gradually reveal themselves. The equestrian **statue of the emperor Marcus Aurelius** that stands in the center of the piazza is a copy of the original bronze statue placed here by Michelangelo as a visual reference to the link between the rank of Charles V and that of the ancient emperor. The original statue, now in the Musei Capitolini (☞ *above*), is one of the finest ancient Roman works to have survived, though it's likely that it owes its survival principally to the fact that it was mistakenly believed to have been a likeness of the Christian Emperor Constantine rather than of the pagan Marcus Aurelius. It's claimed that Michelangelo was so struck by the statue's vivid naturalism that, having placed it in the piazza, he commanded it to walk. Another legend claims that if the statue's original gold patina returns (only traces of it are left) the end of the world will be imminent. ⊠ *Via del Teatro Marcello.*

❺ Santa Maria in Aracoeli. On the north slope of the Capitoline Hill, a steep flight of steps parallels the gentler cordonata leading to the Campidoglio. Atop the 122 steps looms the stark, redbrick church. This slope of the hill has served as a religious site since the dawn of Rome. The ancient Romans came up here to worship at the Temple of Juno Moneta, which also housed the Roman mint (hence the origin of the word money). Legend recounts that here the Sybil predicted to Augustus the coming of a Redeemer. The emperor responded by erecting an altar, the Ara Coeli—the Altar of Heaven—on the spot. The site subsequently saw the building of one of the first Christian churches in Rome. The church passed to the Benedictines in the 10th century and in 1250 to the Franciscans, who restored and enlarged it in Romanesque-Gothic style. In the Middle Ages, before the present Campidoglio was built, the city elders used to meet here to discuss affairs of state, just as the ancient Romans had met in the Temple of Jupiter.

Inside the church you'll find evidence of the successive eras of Rome's past. There are classical columns and large marble fragments from pagan buildings and a 13th-century Cosmatesque pavement—so called because, like so many other brilliantly colored mosaics of the period, this was the work of the prolific Cosmati family, who used bits of the precious marbles of ancient Rome in their compositions. The rich Renaissance gilded ceiling commemorates the naval victory of Lepanto in 1571 over the Turks. Among these artistic treasures, the first chapel on the right is noteworthy for Pinturicchio's calm 16th-century frescoes of *San Bernardino of Siena.* There's a Byzantine madonna over the altar, where the emperor Augustus and the Sybil are depicted in the apse amid saints and angels, a most unusual position for a pagan emperor, to put it mildly. In the third chapel on the left you can admire Gozzoli's 15th-century fresco *St. Anthony of Padua;* on the right of the main portal there's a handsome polychrome monument to Cardinal D'Albret by Bregno, and next to it a tombstone by Donatello, worn by the passage of time and the faithful, now finally moved to an upright position. ⊠ *Via del Teatro di Marcello.*

Foro Romano

The original Roman Forum is only one part of the labyrinthine archaeological complex that goes by that name. Don't confuse it, either, with the later Imperial Forums (or, more properly, Fora), built by Julius Caesar and the emperors as the city's needs grew. The Roman Forum lies in what was once a marshy valley between the Capitoline and Palatine hills, a valley crossed by a mud track and used as a cemetery by the Iron Age settlers on the Palatine. Over the years, a marketplace and some huts were established here, and after the land was drained in the 6th century BC the site eventually became the Forum. The Forum became a symbol of the values that had inspired Republican Rome's conquest of an empire—the stern moral authority of the republic. It was the historic and monumental heart of ancient Rome that had existed long before the emperors and the pleasure-loving, ever-more-corrupt imperial Rome of the 1st to the 4th centuries AD.

Centuries of plunder and the unstoppable urge of later Romans to carry off what was left of the better building materials reduced the Forum to its current desolate state. It is almost impossible to imagine this enormous area as the pulsating heart of a Rome that ruled over a vast empire, filled with stately and extravagant buildings—temples, palaces, and shops—and crowded with people from all corners of that empire. Adding to the confusion is the fact that the Forum developed over many hundreds of years; what you see today are not the ruins from just one period but from almost 900 years, from about 500 BC to AD 400. As the original buildings became too small or were thought too old-fashioned for a Rome that grew ever more powerful, they were pulled down and replaced by larger, more lavish structures. But as often as not, the foundations of the older buildings remained, and many have survived to the present, pitted and scarred with age, alongside their later cousins.

A Good Walk

Head for Via dei Fori Imperiali and the entrance to the **Foro Romano.** Here you can find what remains of the various buildings in the Forum: The **Basilica Emilia** ⑧, not a church but a civic hall; the **Curia** ⑨, where the Senate met; the **Comitium** ⑩, where Mark Antony eulogized Caesar. The **Arco di Settimio Severo** ⑪, the remaining columns of the **Tempio di Vespasiano** ⑫, and the **Colonna di Foca** ⑭ rise above the ruins, while the **Basilica Giulia** ⑬ is little more than a large raised platform. The **Tempio di Cesare** ⑮, on the spot where Caesar was cremated, is hardly distinguishable. The **Tempio di Antonino e Faustina** ⑯ met with better luck; incoporated into a church, its columned front has been well preserved. You can't miss the small, round **Tempio di Vesta** ⑰, with a few columns still standing. The **Tempio di Castore e Polluce** ⑱ and the **Fonte di Giuturna** ⑲ have to be imagined, as little is left of them. Off to one side, you can see but not visit the church of **Santa Maria Antiqua** ⑳, built into what was originally a vestibule of the imperial palace on the Palatino.

Stroll east along the **Via Sacra** ㉑, and turn left into the **Basilica di Massenzio** ㉒. The 10th-century church of **Santa Francesca Romana** ㉓ stands atop a rise next to the Basilica di Massenzio. The Via Sacra ends at the **Arco di Tito** ㉔, where a carved menorah recalls Rome's recapture of Jerusalem after the great Jewish revolt. The **Tempio di Venere e Roma** ㉕, one of architecturally savvy emperor Hadrian's projects, was begun on the site of the vast vestibule of Nero's grandiose Domus Aurea in AD 121.

TIMING

It takes about one hour to explore the Forum, more if you want to try to identify the principal ruins. There is a municipal information kiosk at Piazza del Tempio della Pace, on Via dei Fori Imperiale near the entrance to the Foro Romano. With the exception of mobile refreshment stands along Via dei Fori Imperiali, there are few places within easy reach where you can take a break for lunch or a snack. Consider bringing along some sustenance to keep you going. As this walk is practically entirely outdoors, good weather is a must; the beaten-earth paths of the Foro Romano are muddy and slippery in the rain. The route is a magical one for a late-evening stroll, when the archaeological area and monuments are stunningly illuminated. During the summer the sights may be open until quite late; check locally.

Sights to See

⓫ **Arco di Settimio Severo** (Arch of Septimius Severus). The most richly decorated arch ever seen by the ancient Romans, it was built in AD 203 to celebrate the emperor Severus's victory over the Parthians. It was topped by a bronze statuary group of a chariot drawn by four or perhaps as many as six life-size horses. The sculptured stone reliefs on the arch were probably based on huge painted panels depicting the event, a kind of visual report that the emperor sent home to Rome to make sure his subjects were duly impressed by his foreign campaigns. ⊠ *West end of Foro Romano.*

㉔ **Arco di Tito** (Arch of Titus). This triumphal arch stands at a slightly elevated position at the northern approach to the Palatine Hill. It was erected in AD 81 to celebrate the recapture of Jerusalem 10 years earlier, after the great Jewish revolt. It's famous for a relief representing the seven-branched candlestick—a menorah—that was part of the spoils of war. ⊠ *East end of Via Sacra.*

㉒ **Basilica di Massenzio** (Basilica of Maxentius). The great arched vaults of the structure dominate the north side of the Via Sacra. Begun under the Emperor Maxentius about AD 306, the edifice was a center of judicial and commercial activity, the last of its kind to be built in Rome. What remains is only one third of the original. Like so many other Roman monuments, it served as a quarry for building materials and was stripped of its lavish marble and stucco decorations. Its coffered vaults, like the coffering inside the Pantheon's dome, were later copied by many Renaissance artists and architects. ⊠ *Via Sacra.*

⓼ **Basilica Emilia** (Aemilian Basilica). Once a great colonnaded hall, this was a meeting place for merchants and a kind of community center of the 2nd century BC, later rebuilt in the 1st century AD by Augustus. The term *basilica* refers not to a church as such, but to a particular architectural form developed by the Romans. A rectangular hall flanked by colonnades, it served as a court of law or a center for business and commerce. Some Roman basilicas were later converted into churches, and the early models proved remarkably enduring in the design of later Roman churches; there are 13th-century churches in the city that are fundamentally no different from many built in the 5th and 6th centuries AD. ⊠ *On right as you descend into Roman Forum from Via dei Fori Imperiali entrance.*

⑬ Basilica Giulia (Julius Caesar Basilica). The Basilica Giulia owes its name to Julius Caesar, who had it built. One of several such basilicas in the center of Rome, this one was where the Centumviri, the hundred-or-so judges forming the civil court, met to hear cases. The open space between the Basilica Emilia and this basilica was the heart of the Forum proper, prototype of Italy's famous piazzas, and center of civic and social activity in ancient Rome. ⊠ *Via Sacra.*

⑭ Colonna di Foca (Column of Phocas). The last monument to be added to the Forum was erected in AD 608 in honor of a Byzantine emperor who had donated the Pantheon to Pope Boniface IV. ⊠ *West end of Foro Romano.*

⑩ Comitium. The open space in front of the Curia (☞ *below*) was the political center of ancient Rome. Julius Caesar had rearranged the Comitium, moving the Curia to its present site and transferring the Imperial **Rostra,** the podium from which orators spoke to the people (decorated originally with the prows of captured ships, or *rostra,* hence the term *rostrum*), to a spot just south of the Arch of Septimius Severus. It was from this platform that Mark Antony delivered his funeral address in Caesar's honor. Also here, under protective roofing, is the black pavement that supposedly marks the **burial place of Romulus,** first king of Rome, in the primitive settlement's burial ground near the mud track that gave rise to the Forum. Legend is supported by the fact that the tombstones underlying the black pavement bear the earliest-known Latin inscription in characters somewhat resembling Greek. On the left of the Rostra rises the **Tempio di Saturno** (Temple of Saturn), where ancient Rome's state treasury was kept. ⊠ *West end of Foro Romano.*

⑨ Curia (Senate Hall). The large and well-preserved brick building in the northwest part of the Forum was built in the era of Diocletian in the late 3rd century AD. By that time the Senate, which met in the Curia, had lost practically all of the power and prestige that it had possessed during the Republican era, becoming a mere echo chamber for decisions taken in other centers of power. ⊠ *Via Sacra, northwest corner of Foro Romano.*

⑲ Fonte di Giuturna (Spring of Juturna). Legend says that as Castor and Pollux carried the news of a great victory to Rome they paused to water their horses at the rectangular, marble-lined pool near what became their temple (☞ Tempio di Castore e Polluce, *below*). ⊠ *Via Sacra.*

★ Foro Romano (Roman Forum). Today, as massive archaeological investigations continue, the Forum seems little more than a baffling series of ruins, with roofless buildings, isolated columns, occasional paving stones, and grass everywhere, growing up, around, and between what's left. Making sense of these gaunt and craggy ruins is no easy business. This is why it's worth investing in a little booklet that shows in transparency what the place looked like in its heyday over a photo of the site as it is today. ⊠ *Entrances on Via dei Fori Imperiali, Via San Teodoro (Via Teatro di Marcello), and Piazza Santa Maria Nova (Colosseum),* ☎ *06/699–0110.* ⊞ *Free.* ☉ *Mon.–Sat. 9–5 (no entry after 4), Sun. 9–2 (no entry after 1). Audioguide available at Via dei Fori Imperiali entrance.*

㉓ Santa Francesca Romana. The church, a 10th-century edifice with a Renaissance facade, is dedicated to the patron saint of motorists; on her feast day, March 9, cars and taxis crowd the roadway below the church for a special blessing. Its incomparable setting also makes it a favorite for society weddings. ⊠ *Piazza di Santa Francesca Romana.*

⑳ **Santa Maria Antiqua.** An imperial construction, it was converted into a Christian church some time in the 5th or 6th centuries. Within are some exceptional but faded frescoes of Eastern saints, similar to those in the rock churches of Cappadocia in Turkey. It is rarely open. ⊠ *South of temple of Castor and Pollux, at foot of Palatine Hill.*

⑯ **Tempio di Antonino e Faustina** (Temple of Antoninus and Faustina). The temple was erected by the Senate in honor of Faustina, deified wife of emperor Antoninus Pius (138–161), Hadrian's successor, and dedicated to the emperor himself upon his death. Because it was transformed into a church, it is one of the best-preserved ancient structures in the Forum. ⊠ *North of Via Sacra.*

⑱ **Tempio di Castore e Polluce** (Temple of Castor and Pollux). This temple was dedicated in 484 BC to the twin brothers of Helen of Troy. Legend relates that they were the divine messengers who carried to Rome the news of the victory of Lake Regillus, southeast of Rome, and the definitive defeat of the deposed Tarquin dynasty, a battle won thanks to their heavenly intervention. The brothers literally flew on their fabulous white steeds over the 20-km (12-mi) distance between the lake and the city to bring the news to the people before mortal messengers could arrive. ⊠ *West of House of the Vestals.*

⑮ **Tempio di Cesare** (Temple of Caesar). Built by Augustus, Caesar's successor, the temple stands over the spot where Julius Caesar's body was cremated on a pyre improvised by distraught and grief-crazed citizens who fed the flames with their own possessions. ⊠ *Between two forks of Via Sacra.*

㉕ **Tempio di Venere e Roma** (Temple of Venus and Rome). The truncated columns of this temple, begun by Hadrian in AD 121, frame a view of the Colosseum. ⊠ *East of Arco di Tito.*

⑫ **Tempio di Vespasiano** (Temple of Vespasian). All that remains are three graceful Corinthian columns. They marked the site of the Forum through the centuries when the rest was hidden beneath overgrown rubble. Nearby is the ruined platform that was the **Tempio di Concordia** (Temple of Concord). ⊠ *West end of Foro Romano.*

⑰ **Tempio di Vesta** (Temple of Vesta). The small, circular temple is where the haughty and highly privileged vestal virgins kept the sacred flame alive. Next to the temple, the ruins of the **Casa delle Vestali** (House of the Vestals) give no hint of the splendor in which the women lived out their 30-year vows of chastity. Inside was the garden courtyard of their palace, surrounded by airy colonnades, behind which lay at least 50 rooms. Chosen when they were between six and ten years old, the six vestal virgins dedicated their lives for 30 years to keeping the sacred fire, a tradition that dated back to the very earliest days of Rome, when guarding the community's precious fire was essential to its well-being. Their standing in Rome was considerable, indeed they were second in rank only to the empress. Their intercession could save a condemned man, and they did, in fact, rescue Julius Caesar from the lethal vengeance of his enemy Sulla. The virgins were handsomely maintained by the state, but if they allowed the sacred fire to go out they were scourged by the high priest, and if they broke their vows they were buried alive. The vestal virgins were one of the last of ancient Rome's institutions to die out, enduring to as late as the end of the 4th century AD, even after Rome's emperors had become Christian. They were finally suppressed by Theodosius. ⊠ *South side of Via Sacra.*

㉑ **Via Sacra.** The basalt-paved road that loops through the Roman Forum, lined with temples and shrines, was also the route of religious and triumphal processions. It is now little more than a dirt track, with occasional patches of the paving stones trod by Caesars and plebs, rutted with the ironclad wheels of Roman wagons. Yet it is one of the most evocative walks in Rome. ⊠ *Foro Romano*.

Monte Palatino

There are few more atmospheric places to wander in Rome than the Palatino, discovering hidden corners and restful, shady lanes, glimpsing sudden views of the modern city past centuries-old ruins, and allowing yourself to enjoy a sense of the far-off majesty that was Rome. Though picnicking is frowned on, you might well bring along a circumspect snack and enjoy it in this unique setting.

A Good Walk

The ticket office and entrance to **Monte Palatino** ㉖ are at the base of the hill near the Arco di Tito. Follow the path known as the Clivus Palatinus, whose worn, original paving stones were trodden by both slaves and emperors, up to the flat hilltop where the ruins of the emperors' palaces stand. The palace complex built by Domitian includes the **Domus Flavia** ㉗ on the west, the **Domus Augustana** ㉘ at the center, and the **Stadio Palatino** ㉙ on the east. Below and south of the Palatino lies the **Circo Massimo** ㉚, and beyond that is the Colle Aventino (Aventine Hill). The **Casa di Livia** ㉛ and the **Orti Farnesiani** ㉜, which are adjacent, on the northwest crest of the Palatino, represent two of the Palatino's golden ages: the first when it was prime real estate covered with ancient Roman patrician residences, and the second when it became the private property of one of Renaissance Rome's most powerful families.

TIMING

A leisurely stroll on the Palatino, with stops for the views and a visit to the Museo Palatino, takes about an hour. Fair weather is a must, as are good walking shoes for dusty slopes that are slippery when damp. Paths lead to an alternative exit on the east slope of the Palatino, on Via di San Gregorio, but the exit is not always open.

Sights to See

★ **Casa di Livia** (House of Livia). Atop the Palatine are the excavations of one of the few remaining examples of a well-to-do Republican family's dwelling, rarely open to the public. Its delicate, delightful frescoes reflect the sophisticated taste of wealthy Romans, whose love of beauty and theatrical conception of nature was inherited, much later, by their descendants during the Renaissance. ⊠ *Northwest crest of Palatino*.

㉚ **Circo Massimo** (Circus Maximus). Ancient Rome's oldest and largest racecourse lies in a natural hollow between two hills. From the imperial box in their palace on the Palatine Hill, the emperors could look out over the elongated oval course. Stretching about 650 yards from end to end, the Circus Maximus could hold more than 300,000 spectators. On certain occasions there were as many as 24 races a day, and meetings could last for 15 days. The noise, the color, and the excitement of the crowd must have been astounding. Later, when Rome was ruled by the popes, another kind of spectacle drew crowds to the site to witness the execution of criminals and transgressors of papal laws. ⊠ *Mursia valley between Palatine and Aventine hills*.

㉘ **Domus Augustana.** In the Palazzi Imperiali complex (☞ *below*), this building consisted of private apartments for Domitian and his family. ⊠ *Southern crest of Palatino*.

㉗ **Domus Flavia** (Palace of the Flavians). In the Palazzi Imperiali complex (☞ *below*), this palazzo served Domitian for official functions and ceremonies. Also called Palazzo dei Flavi, it included a basilica where the emperor could hold judiciary hearings. There was also a large audience hall, a peristyle (a columned courtyard), and the imperial triclinium (dining room). ⊠ *Southern crest of Palatino.*

㉖ **Monte Palatino** (Palatine Hill). This hill, rising above and to the south of the Forum, is the oldest inhabited site in Rome. Archaeologists have uncovered remains of an Iron Age settlement here dating as far back as the 9th century BC. In fact, the ancient Romans always believed that Romulus, founder of Rome, lived on the Palatine. During the Republican era it was an exclusive residential area for wealthy families such as the Flacci and the Crassi, and in the Imperial age, the emperors took it over as a suitable site for their huge and splendid palaces. Until parts of his imperial residence were excavated recently, it was believed that Augustus, the first emperor to live on the Palatine, had tactfully chosen to keep the modest house he had lived in as a private citizen. Now it seems that he, like his successors, opted for suitably regal quarters. Tiberius was one of the first to build a full-fledged palace here; others followed. From the **Belvedere**, you have panoramic views of the Circus Maximus, the green slopes of the Aventine and Celian hills, the bell tower of Santa Maria in Cosmedin, and the immense white marble block of the United Nations Food and Agriculture Organization headquarters. ⊠ *East end of Via Sacra; ticket office and entrance at base of hill near Arco di Tito.* 🎫 *12,000 lire.* ☉ *Daily, Nov.–Mar. 9–3, Apr. –Oct. 9–4.*

㉜ **Orti Farnesiani** (Farnese Gardens). Alessandro Farnese, a nephew of Pope Paul III, commissioned the 16th-century architect Vignola to lay out the archetypal Italian garden over the ruins of the Palace of Tiberius, up just a few steps from the House of Livia. This pleasure garden was originally much larger than it is now, and the existing aviary had a twin. The adjacent **Museo Palatino** holds finds from the excavations (visitors are admitted in groups of up to 30, twice an hour); also adjacent is the newly restored **Loggia Mattei**, with early 16th-century frescoes. ⊠ *Monte Palatino.*

Palazzi Imperiali (Imperial Palaces). Late in the 1st century AD the Emperor Domitian outdid them all. He ordered his architects to put up two separate palaces and a stadium or garden (☞ Domus Augustana, Domus Flavia, *above,* and Stadio Palatino, *below*). His architects undertook the task of adapting the Palatine to the emperor's wishes. Older dwellings were razed, hollows were filled in, and terraces were extended out toward the Circus Maximus to increase the surface area.

㉙ **Stadio Palatino** (Palatine Stadium). Next to his palace, Domitian created a vast open space. It may have been his private hippodrome, or it may simply have been an immense sunken garden; alternatively, perhaps it was used to stage games and other amusements for the benefit of the emperor. ⊠ *Southeast crest of Palatino.*

Arco di Costantino and Colosseo

A Good Walk

The exit of the Palatino leads again to the Arco di Tito, where you turn east toward the Colosseo. To the right is the **Arco di Costantino** ㉝. Next, you can explore the **Colosseo** ㉞, one of antiquity's largest and most famous monuments. Cross Piazza del Colosseo and stroll through the park on the **Colle Oppio** ㉟, where most of Nero's fabulous palace, the **Domus Aurea**, is hidden under the remains of the monumental baths that were built over it. The park has some good views over the Colosseo (one of the best vantage points is the terrace at the top of the escalator just inside the Colosseum Metro station). Though the park has been sorely neglected, new archaeological finds among the ruins of Nero's palace have sparked cleanup efforts.

TIMING

A look at the Arco di Costantino won't take up more than 15 minutes of your time, but the Colosseo deserves more. You can give it a cursory look in 30 minutes, but if you want to climb to the upper tiers, allow an hour or more.

Sights to See

㉝ **Arco di Costantino** (Arch of Constantine). The majestic arch, studded with rich marble decorations, stands near the Colosseum. It is one of Rome's most imposing monuments, erected in AD 315 to commemorate Constantine's victory over Maxentius at the Milvian Bridge. It was just before this battle, in AD 312, that Constantine—the emperor who converted Rome to Christianity—had a vision of a cross in the heavens and heard the words "In this sign thou shalt conquer." The economy-minded Senate ordered that many of the decorations for the arch be taken from earlier monuments; perhaps this was a tacit recognition of the greater artistic value of these earlier sculptures in comparison with the slipshod reliefs commissioned for the arch. It is easy to picture ranks of Roman legionnaires marching under the arch's great barrel vault. ⊠ *Piazza del Colosseo.*

㉟ **Colle Oppio** (Oppian Hill). This ridge of the Esquiline Hill was the site of Nero's fabulous **Domus Aurea.** To build this extravagant palace, the capricious emperor confiscated a vast tract of land right in the center of Rome, earning the animosity of most of his subjects. The palace was huge and sumptuous, with a facade of pure gold, seawater piped into the baths, decorations of mother-of-pearl and other precious materials, and vast gardens. Not much has survived of all this; a good portion of the buildings and grounds were buried under the public works with which subsequent emperors sought to make reparation to the Roman people for Nero's phenomenal greed.

The largest of the buildings put up by later emperors over the Domus Aurea was the great complex of baths built by Trajan. As a result, the site of the Domus Aurea itself remained unknown for many centuries; indeed, when a few of Nero's original halls were discovered underground at the end of the 15th century, no one realized that they actually were part of the palace. Raphael was one of the artists who had themselves lowered into the rubble-filled rooms, which resembled grottoes. The artists copied the original painted Roman decorations, barely visible by torchlight, and, like modern, ill-mannered tourists, scratched their names on the ceilings. Raphael later used these models—known as *grotesques* because they were found in the so-called grottoes—in his decorative motifs for the Vatican Loggia. Today the pleasant park laid out around the ruins of Trajan's Baths is a meeting place for Rome's growing colony of immigrants from Africa. ⊠ *Piazza del Colosseo and Via Labicana.*

★ **Colosseo** (Colosseum). The most stupendous extant monument of ancient Rome was begun by the Flavian emperor Vespasian in AD 72 and was inaugurated by Titus eight years later with a program of games and shows lasting 100 days. On the opening day alone, 5,000 wild beasts perished in the arena. Its construction was a remarkable feat of engineering, for it stands on marshy terrain reclaimed by draining an artificial lake on the grounds of Nero's Domus Aurea; Vespasian thus intended to make amends to the Roman people for Nero's confiscation of the land. Originally known as the Flavian amphitheater, it came to be called the Colosseum by later Romans who identified it with the site of the Colossus of Nero, a 115-foot-tall gilded bronze statue of the emperor in the guise of sun god that stood at the entrance to what is now Via dei Fori Imperiali. Twelve pairs of elephants were needed to transport the statue here from its original site at the entrance to the Domus Aurea; it was pulled down and destroyed by order of Pope Gregory the Great at the end of the 6th century.

The Colosseum was designed to hold more than 50,000 spectators for gory entertainments such as combats between wild beasts and gladiators. It has a circumference of 573 yards and was faced with stone from Tivoli. A *velarium,* an ingenious system of sail-like awnings—rigged on ropes maneuvered by sailors culled from the imperial fleet—could be unfurled to protect the arena's occupants from sun or rain.

In one of the arches on the metro station side, look for the traces of ancient Roman stucco decoration that once adorned most of the arena. Explore the upper levels, where behind glass you can see a scale model of the Colosseum as it was, sheathed with marble and studded with statues. From the upper tiers you can get a good view of the labyrinthine passageways on the subterranean level of the arena.

Legend has it that as long as the Colosseum stands, Rome will stand; and when Rome falls, so will the world. This prophecy didn't deter Renaissance princes from using the Colosseum as a quarry for building materials for such noble dwellings as Palazzo Barberini and Palazzo Farnese. Earlier, the Colosseum had been seriously damaged by earthquakes and, during the Middle Ages, had been transformed into a fortress. Some experts maintain that it was in Rome's circuses, and not here, that thousands of early Christians were martyred. Still, tradition has reserved a special place for the Colosseum in the story of Christianity, and it was Pope Benedict XIV who stopped the use of the building as a quarry when, in 1749, he declared it sanctified by the blood of the martyrs. A tiny chapel built in the 6th century under one of the Colosseum's arches was restored and reconsecrated for the 1983 Holy Year. ⊠ *Piazza del Colosseo,* ☎ *06/700–4261.* 🎫 *10,000 lire.* ☉ *Mon.–Sat. 9–5 (no entry after 4), Sun. 9–2 (no entry after 1).*

NEED A BREAK?   About half a block east of the Colosseum is **Pasqualino** (⊠ Via dei Santi Quattro 66), a neighborhood trattoria with sidewalk tables providing a view of the arena's marble arches. For delicious gelato try **Ristoro della Salute** (⊠ Piazza del Colosseo 2a), on the east side of the piazza, one of Rome's best *gelaterie* (ice-cream parlors).

Fori Imperiali

A complex of five grandly conceived squares flanked with colonnades and temples, the Imperial Fora formed the magnificent monumental core of ancient Rome, together with the original Roman Forum. When the broad Via dei Fori Imperiali was laid out over the ruins of the Imperial Fora to provide a suitable setting for what Mussolini expected would be his own imperial victories, a statue of every emperor who had built a forum was set up in front of his particular structure.

A Good Walk

From Piazza del Colosseo, head northwest on Via dei Fori Imperiali toward Piazza Venezia. On the walls on your left, plaques in marble and bronze put up by Mussolini show the extension of the ancient Roman Empire in various ages. The dictator's own dreams of empire led him to construct this avenue, cutting brutally through the Imperial Fora area, so that he would have a suitable venue for parades celebrating his own military triumphs. Beyond the ancient brick walls behind the Imperial

Fora lay the *suburra,* the mean streets of ancient Rome, where the plebs lived in crowded and unsanitary tenements. **Santi Cosma e Damiano** ㊱, a little gem, started life as a library in the Forum of Vespasian, and it holds a marvelous early Christian mosaic. Among the Fori Imperiali along the avenue you can see **Foro di Cesare** ㊲ and the **Foro di Augusto** ㊳. The grandest of all the Imperial Fora was the **Foro Traiano** ㊴, with its huge semicircular **Mercati Traianei** and the **Colonna di Traiano** ㊵.

TIMING

The walk along Via dei Fori Imperiali, with a stop at the church of Santi Cosma e Damiano and a look at the Fori Imperiali from sidewalk level, takes only about 30 minutes. To explore the emperors' fora more closely, allow another 30 minutes or so. The fora are lit up at night and may be open for evening visits, when guided tours in English may also be offered (guided tours take about one hour).

Sights to See

㊵ **Colonna di Traiano** (Trajan's Column). The remarkable series of reliefs spiraling up this column celebrate the emperor's victories over the Dacians in what today is Serbia. The scenes on the column represent just about the best primary source material on the Roman army and its tactics, and they are so important that the state of preservation of the column is monitored continuously. It has stood in this spot since AD 113. An inscription on the base declares that the column was erected in Trajan's honor and that its height corresponds to the height of the hill that was razed to create a level area for the grandiose project of Trajan's Forum (☞ *below*). The emperor's ashes, no longer here, were kept in a golden urn in a chamber at the column's base, and his statue stood atop the column until 1587, when the pope had it replaced with a statue of St. Peter. ⊠ *Via del Foro di Traiano.*

㊳ **Foro di Augusto** (Forum of Augustus). Its ruins, along with those of the **Foro di Nerva** (Forum of Nerva), on the northeast side of Via dei Fori Imperiali give only a hint of what must have been impressive edifices. ⊠ *Via dei Fori Imperiali.*

㊲ **Foro di Cesare** (Caesar's Forum). The first to be built, Caesar's appeared in the middle of the 1st century BC. Without fail, on the Ides of March, an unknown hand lays a bouquet at the foot of Caesar's statue. ⊠ *Via dei Fori Imperiali.*

㊴ **Foro Traiano** (Trajan's Forum). The largest and most imposing of all the Fori Imperiali, it was a magnificently planned complex, designed by architect Apollodorus of Damascus. A vast basilica, two libraries, and a temple were laid out around the square. To make room for it, Trajan razed a hill that connected the Capitoline and Quirinal hills (☞ Colonna di Traiano, *above*). North of the forum was the huge, semicircular **Mercati Traianei** (Trajan's Market; ☞ Trajan's Market to San Giovanni in Laterano, *below*). ⊠ *Via dei Fori Imperiali.*

㊱ **Santi Cosma e Damiano.** This church was adapted in the 6th century from two ancient buildings: the library in Vespasian's Forum of Peace and a hall of the Temple of Romulus (dedicated to the son of Maxentius). It was restored in the 17th century by the Barberini Pope Urban VIII, who added a few bees from his family's coat of arms to the lower left-hand side of the mosaic in the apse. There's a Neapolitan *presepio,* or Christmas crèche, on permanent display in a side chapel. ⊠ *Off Via Sacra, opposite Tempio di Antonino e Faustina.*

THE VATICAN

St. Peter's and the Vatican are the heart and headquarters of the Roman Catholic Church. The massive walls surrounding Vatican City strongly underscore the fact that this is an independent, sovereign state, established by the Lateran Treaty of 1929, which was signed by the Holy See—the pope—and the Italian government. Vatican City covers 108 acres on a hill west of the Tiber and is separated from the city on all sides by high walls, except at Piazza di San Pietro. Inside the walls, about 1,000 people live as residents. The Vatican newspaper, *L'Osservatore Romano,* is consulted throughout the world. The Vatican issues its own stamps, strikes commemorative coins, and has its own postal system. Within its territory are administrative and foreign offices, a pharmacy, banks, an astronomical observatory, a print shop, a mosaic school and art restoration institute, a tiny train station, a supermarket, a small department store, and several gas stations. Radio Vaticano, a powerful transmitting station, broadcasts in 35 languages to six different continents.

The sovereign of this little state is Pope John Paul II who, until his election on October 16, 1978, was Cardinal Karol Wojtyla, archbishop of Cracow. He is the 264th pope of the Roman Catholic Church, the first non-Italian for 456 years, and the first-ever Pole to hold the office. He has full legislative, judicial, and executive powers, with complete freedom under the Lateran Treaty to organize armed forces within his state (the Swiss Guards and the Vatican police) and to live in or move through Italian territory whenever he so desires. The pope reigns over 700 million Roman Catholics throughout the world and is assisted in his task by the College of Cardinals and, increasingly in recent years, by Synods of Bishops. The intricate rules of etiquette that were once characteristic of the Vatican have been greatly relaxed by recent popes, and much of the Apostolic Palace has been redecorated in severely simple style. But the colorful dress uniforms of the Swiss Guards are a reminder of past ostentation and worldly power.

The Basilica of St. Peter, one of the world's largest and most splendid Christian churches, is the expression of an age when the popes wielded considerable temporal power together with enormous religious authority. The tangible sign of the greatness of the Roman Catholic Church is St. Peter's, where worldly grandeur is somehow infused with spiritual significance. One of the most magnificent structures ever built, with a dome that is a vision of heavenly glory, St. Peter's, to many, does not seem like a church at all. But no one could consider a visit to Rome complete without seeing it—and without visiting the Vatican Museums' collections, of staggering richness and diversity, and the Sistine Chapel, Michelangelo's masterpiece.

Numbers in the text and margin correspond to numbers on the Vatican map.

A Good Walk

To enter the Vatican Museums, the Sistine Chapel, and St. Peter's you must comply with the Vatican's dress code, or you will be turned away by the implacable custodians at the doors. For both men and women, shorts and tank tops are taboo, as are miniskirts and otherwise revealing clothing. Wear a jacket or shawl over sleeveless tops. Start at the **Musei Vaticani** ①. The new entrance on Viale Vaticano (there is a separate exit on the same street) can be reached by the bus 49 from Piazza Cavour, which stops right in front; or on foot from the bus 81 or tram 19, which stop at Piazza Risorgimento; or from the Ottaviano–S. Pietro Metro Line A stop. The collections of the Museums are immense, covering

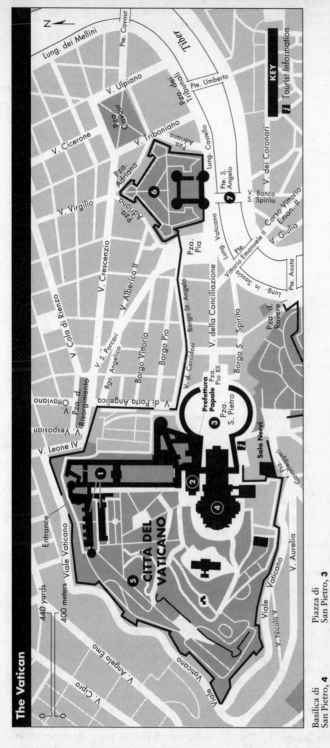

The Vatican

KEY

i Tourist Information

Basilica di
San Pietro, **4**
Capella Sistina, **2**
Castel Sant'Angelo, **6**
Giardini Vaticani, **5**
Musei Vaticani, **1**

Piazza di
San Pietro, **3**
Ponte Sant'Angelo, **7**

about 7 km (4½ mi) of displays. Special posters at the entrance and throughout the museum plot out a choice of four color-coded itineraries. You can rent a taped commentary in English explaining the Sistine Chapel and the Raphael Rooms. You're free to photograph what you like, barring use of flash, tripod, or other special equipment, for which permission must be obtained. To economize on time and effort, once you've seen the frescoes in the Borgia rooms, you can skip the collections of modern religious art in good conscience and get on with your tour. Lines at the entrance to the **Capella Sistina** ② move fairly quickly, as lingering inside is discouraged.

The Vatican runs a bus service between the Museums and a stop near the Information Office in Piazza di San Pietro. The bus takes a route through the Vatican gardens and saves you the long walk around the Vatican walls. The fare is 2,000 lire. It runs Monday–Tuesday, Thursday–Saturday 8:45–12:45, on the half hour.

Piazza di San Pietro ③ is at the west end of Via della Conciliazione. Explore the **Basilica di San Pietro** ④, visiting the Museo Storico-Artistico and the Grotte Vaticane. Take the elevator to the roof of the basilica, a strange fairytale landscape of little cupolas and towers. Climb the short staircase to the gallery inside the base of the huge dome for a dove's-eye view of the papal altar below. If you can't handle a steep, claustrophobic, one-way-only climb, don't attempt the ascent to the lantern at the top of the dome. Next, you can join a tour of the elegant **Giardini Vaticani** ⑤.

You can continue your walk to **Castel Sant'Angelo** ⑥, on Borgo Pio, where there are a number of trattorias and cafés. The huge medieval fortress, built over the tomb of emperor Hadrian himself, saved at least one pope's life, when Clemente VII took refuge here during the Sack of Rome in 1527. From Castel Sant'Angelo's terraces you get a bird's-eye view of **Ponte Sant'Angelo** ⑦, the graceful bridge adorned with statues designed by Bernini that spans the Tiber here.

TIMING

If possible, break up this itinerary into two half-days. You could do St. Peter's and Castel Sant'Angelo one day and devote another day to the Vatican Museums. To do all three on the same day takes stamina and dedication, even if you choose the shortest museum itinerary. Besides, you run the risk of suffering cultural indigestion. As the Vatican is close to the Via Cola di Rienzo and Via Ottaviano shopping areas, you might want to combine sightseeing with shopping. Another option would be to add Castel Sant'Angelo to the end of the Old Rome tour (☞ A Good Walk *in* Old Rome, *below*).

Start at the Museums, which close earlier, so you can take your time in St. Peter's and Castel Sant'Angelo (which is open late some evenings). Alternatively, time your visit to the Museums so you will finish at closing hour, as they are less likely to be crowded as the day wears on. With every visitor to Rome, including countless school groups, anxious to see the Museums and especially the Sistine Chapel, the crowds can be like those at a popular ball game: Get there either very early, before the pressure builds up, or late, as the crowds thin out. The recommended tours of the Vatican Museums take from 90 minutes (but you can cheat and do it in an hour if you don't have to wait in line at the Sistine Chapel) to five hours (this, too can be done in less). Allow an hour for St. Peter's and an hour for Castel Sant'Angelo. To do all three sights, including walking from one to another, would take from five to six hours, not counting breaks.

THE WORLD'S SMALLEST COUNTRY

IN ADDITION TO THE COLOSSEUM, the Forum, and the other sights that make the city unique, another institution makes Rome different from any other city in the world: it is the only Catholic diocese with an elected bishop. He's not just any bishop, of course; the Bishop of Rome is none other than the Pope, elected for life by the 120 members of the College of Cardinals in an election that arguably affects more of the world's people than any other. Although his primary role is as the leader of the Catholic Church, this job title brings with it sovereignty over Vatican City and ecclesiastical responsibility for the city of Rome from Rome's cathedral, San Giovanni in Laterano (St. John in Lateran).

The complicated relationship between Rome and the Vatican was laid down in 1929 in the terms of the Lateran Concordat and Treaty, signed by Fascist strongman Benito Mussolini and Pope Pius XI. Under Italian unification in 1870, the land area controlled by the Church, the Papal States, had been annexed by the Kingdom of Italy, giving rise to complaints that dependence on a political body compromised the Pope's ability to the direct the Church. Nearly 60 years later, a compromise was reached, establishing the Vatican's autonomy but requiring its sworn political neutrality and establishing Catholicism as the Italian state religion. This is the agreement that exists today, and it's responsible for the delicate, sometimes awkward, and frequently bizarre relationship between Italy and the world's smallest country, tucked away in the center of Rome.

Vatican City is completely surrounded by the city of Rome, and although it's possible to pass through without ever knowing you've left the sovereignty of the Italian state, closer inspection reveals a number of differences more striking than the low brick walls that mark the city limits. There are no border controls or passport stamps, but the Vatican is an autonomous political body, with independent leadership and diplomatic relationships like any other country. The country is ruled by the Pope and the various papally appointed Pontifical Councils that advise him; although technically the Pope is an elected official, the electorate is not the population of Vatican City but the College of Cardinals, who have chosen a leader from among their number in every election since 1378. Although its population is just over 1,000 (including his Holiness John Paul II, who lives in the Apostolic Palace), the Vatican has its own postal system, reputedly much more reliable than the Posta Italiana (look for blue boxes marked Posta Vaticana). To use the Vatican Post, you'll have to buy special stamps at the Posta Vaticana, just off to the right before St. Peter's Cathedral, for which you can pay in either Italian or Vatican lire—the Vatican has its own currency, linked to the lira, that is legal tender all over Italy.

The relationship between Italy and Vatican City grows complicated when it comes to matters that affect both countries. A prime and thorny example is the Jubilee Year in 2000, a Church-declared Holy Year expected to bring millions of extra pilgrims to the already visitor-swamped Vatican. In preparation, the city of Rome has embarked on large-scale civic improvements to accommodate the visitors. Although Rome cannot help but benefit from the influx of tourist money, the Vatican, as the seat of the church, is the main attraction. In this instance, at least, it's clear that in practical matters, the separation of Vatican Church and Italian state is far from complete.

Sights to See

★ **Basilica di San Pietro** (St. Peter's Basilica). The largest church in the world, built over the tomb of St. Peter, it is also the most imposing and breathtaking architectural achievement of the Renaissance. Its story goes back to AD 319, when the emperor Constantine built a basilica over the site of the tomb of St. Peter. The original church stood for more than 1,000 years, undergoing a number of restorations and alterations, until it threatened to collapse toward the middle of the 15th century. In 1452 a reconstruction job was begun; it was quickly abandoned for lack of cash. In 1506 Pope Julius II instructed the architect Bramante to raze all the existing buildings and to build a new basilica, one that would surpass even Constantine's for grandeur. But it wasn't until 1626 that the basilica was completed and dedicated. Five of Italy's greatest Renaissance artists died during the time of their work on the new and greater St. Peter's—Bramante, Raphael, Peruzzi, Antonio Sangallo the Younger, and Michelangelo.

Though Bramante made only little progress in rebuilding St. Peter's, he succeeded nonetheless in outlining a basic plan for the church, and, crucially, he built the piers of the crossings—the massive pillars supporting the dome. After Bramante's death in 1514, Raphael, the Sangallos, and Peruzzi all proposed variations on the original plan at one time or another. Again, however, lack of finance, rivalries between the architects, and, above all, the turmoil caused by the Sack of Rome in 1527 and the mounting crisis of the Reformation conspired to ensure that little serious progress was made. In 1546, however, Pope Paul III turned to Michelangelo and more or less forced the aging artist to complete the building. Michelangelo, in turn, insisted on having carte blanche to do as he thought best. He returned to Bramante's first idea of having a centralized Greek-cross plan—that is, with the "arms" of the church all the same length—and completed most of the exterior architecture except for the dome and the facade. His design for the dome, however, was modified after his death by Giacomo della Porta. The nave, too, was altered after Michelangelo's death. Pope Paul V wanted a Latin-cross church (a church with one "arm" longer than the rest), so Carlo Maderno lengthened one of the arms to create a nave. He was also responsible for the facade. This was much criticized at the time because it hides the dome from observers below. It is also wider than it is high.

As you climb the shallow steps up to the great church, flanked by the statues of saints Peter and Paul, you'll see the **Loggia delle Benedizioni** (Benediction Loggia) over the central portal. This is the balcony where newly elected popes are proclaimed and where they stand to give their apostolic blessing on solemn feast days. The vault above you is encrusted with rich stucco work, and the mosaic above the central entrance to the portico is a much-restored work by the 14th-century painter Giotto that was in the original basilica. The bronze doors of the main entrance also were salvaged from the old basilica. The sculptor Filarete worked on them for 12 years; they show scenes from the Council of Florence and the Life of Pope Eugene IV (1431–47), his patron. The large central figures are saints Peter and Paul. In the basilica, look at the inside of these doors for the amusing "signature" at the bottom in which Filarete shows himself and his assistant dancing with joy, tools in hand, at having completed their task. To the left are two modern bronze doors, the so-called *Doors of Death,* in both of which you'll see Pope John XXIII. On the right of the main entrance are the *Door of the Sacraments* and the *Holy Door,* opened only during Holy Years.

Pause a moment to judge the size of the great building. The people near the main altar seem dwarfed by the incredible dimensions of this im-

St. Peter's

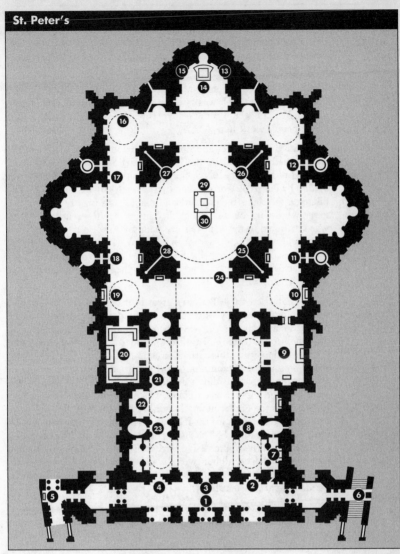

Alexander VII monument, **17**

Bronze Baldacchino, **29**

Central Door, **3**

Chapel of the Choir, **20**

Chapel of the Column; Altar and tomb of St. Leo the Great, **16**

Chapel of the Holy Sacrament, **9**

Chapel of the Pietà; Pietà (Michelangelo), **7**

Chapel of the Presentation; John XXIII monument, **22**

Charlemagne, **5**

Christina of Sweden monument, **8**

Clement XIII monument, **12**

Clementina Sobieski; Monument, opp. Pillar of the last Stuarts; Exit from Cupola, **23**

Clementine Chapel; (under altar: St. Gregory the Great tomb), **19**

Confession, **30**

Emperor Constantine, **6**

Entrance to Cupola, **11**

Gloria, with St. Peter's Chair, **14**

Gregorian Chapel, **10**

Holy Door, **2**

Innocent VIII monument, **21**

Manzù Door, **4**

Paul III monument, **15**

Pius V monument (below: entrance to Sacristy), **18**

St. Andrew, **28**

St. Helen, **26**

St. Longinus; entrance to crypt, **25**

St. Peter, **24**

Urban VIII monument, **13**

The Veronica, **27**

Vestibule: The Ship, Giotto mosaics, **1**

mense temple. The statues, the pillars, and the holy-water stoups borne by colossal cherubs are all imposing. Brass inscriptions in the marble pavement down the center of the nave indicate the approximate length of the world's principal Christian churches, all of which fall far short of the apse of St. Peter's.

Immediately to your right is Michelangelo's *Pietà,* one of the world's most famous statues. It was safely screened behind shatterproof glass after being damaged by a maniac in 1972 and masterfully restored in the Vatican's workshops.

Exquisite bronze grilles and doors by Borromini open into the third chapel in the right aisle, the **Cappella del Santissimo Sacramento** (Chapel of the Most Holy Sacrament), with a Baroque fresco of the *Trinity* by Pietro da Cortona and carved angels by Bernini. At the last pillar on the right (the pier of St. Longinus) is a bronze statue of *St. Peter,* whose big toe is kissed by the faithful. Until recently the statue was attributed to the 13th-century sculptor Arnolfo da Cambio, but experts now say that it is a much earlier work. In the right transept, over the door to the **Cappella di San Michele** (Chapel of St. Michael), usually closed, Canova created a brooding neoclassical monument to Pope Clement XIII.

In the central crossing, Bernini's great bronze *baldacchino*—a huge, spiral-columned canopy—rises high over the **altare papale** (papal altar). Bernini's Barberini patron, Pope Urban VIII, had no qualms about stripping the bronze from the Pantheon in order to provide Bernini with the material to create this curious structure. The Romans reacted with the famous quip, *"Quod non fecerunt barbari, fecerunt Barberini."* ("What the barbarians didn't do, the Barberini did.") A curious legend connected with the baldacchino, which swarms with Barberini bees (the bee was the Barberini family symbol), relates that the pope commissioned it in thanks for the recovery of a favorite niece who had almost died in childbirth. The story is borne out by the marble reliefs on the bases of the columns: The Barberini coat of arms is surmounted by a series of heads, all but two of which seem to represent a woman in what might be the pain of labor, while a smiling baby's face appears on the base at the right front.

The antique casket in the niche by the papal altar contains the *pallia,* bands of white wool that are conferred by the pope on archbishops as a sign of authority. These pallia are made by nuns from the wool of two lambs blessed every year in the Church of St. Agnes on her feast day, January 21. When completed, they are blessed by the pope during the rites of the feast of St. Peter on June 29 and are stored in the casket that you see. Beautiful bronze vigil lights flicker around the **confessio** under the papal altar. This is the ceremonial entrance to the crypt, and its location more or less corresponds with the spot where St. Peter was buried, in a cemetery, or catacomb, over which the foundations of the basilica were built.

The splendid gilt-bronze **Cattedra di San Pietro** (throne of St. Peter) in the apse above the main altar was designed by Bernini to contain a wooden and ivory chair that St. Peter himself is said to have used, though in fact it doesn't date back further than medieval times. (You can see a copy of the chair in the treasury.) Above it, Bernini placed a window of thin alabaster sheets that diffuses a golden light around the dove, symbol of the Holy Spirit, in the center.

Two of the major papal funeral monuments in St. Peter's are located on either side of the apse and unfortunately are usually dimly lit. To the right is the **tomb of Pope Urban VIII;** to the left is the **tomb of Pope**

Paul III. Paul's tomb is the earlier, designed between 1551 and 1575 by della Porta, the architect who completed the dome of St. Peter's after Michelangelo's death. The nude figure of Justice was widely believed to be a portrait of the pope's beautiful sister, Giulia. The charms of this alluring figure were such that in the 19th century, it was thought that she should no longer be allowed to distract worshipers from their prayers and she was swathed in marble drapery. It was very much in emulation of this splendid late-Renaissance tomb that Urban VIII ordered Bernini to design his tomb. Notice the skeleton figure of Death writing the pope's name on a marble slab. The **tomb of Pope Alexander VII,** also designed by Bernini, stands to the left of the altar as you look up the nave, behind the farthest pier of the crossing.

Under the Pope Pius V monument, the entrance to the sacristy leads also to the **Museo Storico-Artistico e Tesoro** (Historical-Artistic Museum and Treasury; ⊠ 3,000 lire; ⊙ daily, Apr.–Sept. 9–6:30, Oct.–Mar. 9–5:30), a small collection of Vatican treasures. They range from the massive and beautifully sculptured 15th-century tomb of Pope Sixtus IV by Pollaiuolo, which you can view from above, to a jeweled cross dating from the 6th century and a marble tabernacle by the Florentine mid-15th-century sculptor Donatello. Among the other priceless objects are a platinum chalice presented to Pope Pius VI by Charles III of Spain in the middle of the 18th century and an array of sacred vessels in gold, silver, and precious stones.

Continue on down the left nave past Algardi's monument to Pope Leo XI. The handsome bronze grilles in the **Capella del Coro** (Chapel of the Choir) here were designed by Borromini to complement those opposite in the **Cappella del Santissimo Sacramento.** The next pillar holds a rearrangement of the Pollaiuolo brothers' austere monument to Pope Innocent VIII, the only major tomb to have been transferred from the old basilica. The next chapel contains the handsome bronze monument to Pope John XXIII by contemporary sculptor Emilio Greco. On the last pier in this nave stands a monument by the late-18th-century Venetian sculptor Canova marking the spot in the crypt below where the last of the ill-fated Stuarts—the 18th-century Roman Catholic claimants to the British throne, who were long exiled in Rome—were buried.

Between the Gregorian Chapel and the right crossing, take the elevator or climb the long flight of shallow stairs to the **roof** (⊠ 5,000 lire including elevator to roof, 4,000 lire via spiral ramp or stairs; ⊙ daily, Apr.–Aug. 8–6, Sept.–Mar. 8–5) of the church, a surreal landscape of vast sloping terraces punctuated by cupolas that serve as skylights over the various chapels. The roof affords unusual perspectives on the dome above and the piazza below. The terrace is equipped with the inevitable souvenir shop and with toilets. A short flight of stairs leads to the entrance of the drum—the base of the dome—where, appropriately enough, there's a bust of Michelangelo, principal designer of the dome. Within the drum, another short ramp and staircase give access to the **gallery** encircling the base of the dome. From here you have a dove's-eye view of the interior of the church. It's well worth the slight effort to make your way up here, though not if you suffer from vertigo.

Only if you're stout of heart and sound of wind should you then make the taxing climb from the drum of the dome up to the **tamburo** (lantern) at the very apex of the dome. A narrow, seemingly interminable staircase follows the curve of the dome between inner and outer shells, finally releasing you into the cramped space of the lantern balcony for an absolutely gorgeous panorama of Rome and the countryside on a clear day. There's also a nearly complete view of the palaces, courtyards, and gardens of the Vatican. Be aware, however, that it's a tiring, slightly claustrophobic, and a one-way-only climb: you can't turn back if you change your mind!

The entrance to **Le Sacre Grotte Vaticane** (Tombs of the Popes; ⊠ free; ☉ daily, Apr.–Sept. 7–6, Oct.–Mar. 7–5) is at the base of the pier dedicated to St. Longinus. As the only exit from the crypt leads outside St. Peter's, it is best to leave this visit for last. The crypt is lined with marble-faced chapels and simple tombs occupying the area of Constantine's basilica and standing over the cemetery in which recent excavations have brought to light what is believed to be the tomb of St. Peter himself.

With advance notice you can tour the **Necropoli precostantiniana, or scavi** (excavations) under the basilica, which give a fascinating glimpse of early Christian Rome. Guides are available, or you can use a taped guide. Apply by fax (FAX 06/698–85518) two or three months in advance. You can also apply in person to the Ufficio Scavi (Excavations Office; ☎ 06/698–85318; ☉ Mon.–Sat. 9–5), on the right beyond the Arco delle Campane entrance to the Vatican, left of the basilica. Tell the Swiss guard you want the Ufficio Scavi and he will let you enter the confines of Vatican City. Tickets (⊠ 10,000 lire), however, may not be available on short notice. ⊠ *Piazza di San Pietro.* ⊠ *Free.* ☉ *Daily, Apr.–Sept. 7–7, Oct.–Mar. 7–6. Free one-hour guided tours Mon.–Sat. 10:15 and 3 PM (no tour Wed. AM), Sun. 2:30; inquire at desk inside portico of St. Peter's (daily 10–12 and 3–5, except Wed. AM).*

NEED A BREAK?   **Insalata Ricca** (Piazza Risorgimento 6), about halfway between the Vatican Museums and St. Peter's, offers light meals, chiefly pasta, salads, and pizza.

★ **Cappella Sistina** (Sistine Chapel). The chapel where important papal ceremonies are held is Michelangelo's masterpiece, a milestone in the history of Western art. In 1508, the redoubtable Pope Julius II commissioned Michelangelo to fresco the more than 10,000 square feet of the Sistine Chapel's ceiling. The task took four years, and it's said that for many years afterward Michelangelo couldn't read anything without holding it up over his head! The result, however, was the masterpiece that you see. A pair of binoculars, incidentally, helps greatly.

Before the chapel was consecrated in 1483, its lower walls had been decorated by a group of artists including Botticelli, Ghirlandaio, Perugino, and Signorelli, all working under the direction of Pinturicchio. They had painted scenes from the life of Moses on one wall and episodes from the life of Christ on the other. Later, Julius II, dissatisfied with the simple vault decoration—it consisted of no more than stars painted on the ceiling—decided to call in Michelangelo. At the time, Michelangelo was carving Julius II's gargantuan tomb—a project that never came near completion—and, considering himself a sculptor first and a painter second, had no desire to give the project up in order to paint a ceiling (painting was in any case a task he considered to be unworthy of him). Julius was not, however, a man to be trifled with, and Michelangelo reluctantly began work. The project proceeded fitfully until Michelangelo decided that he would paint the ceiling himself, and he dismissed his assistants (by contrast, substantial sections of Raphael's *Stanze* [☞ Musei Vaticani, *below*] were the work of assistants; probably only the principal figures are actually by Raphael himself).

Michelangelo's subject was the story of humanity before the coming of Christ. It is told principally by means of the scenes depicted in nine main panels. These show, working from the altar: the *Separation of*

Light from Darkness, the *Creation of the Heavenly Bodies,* the *Separation of Land and Sea,* the *Creation of Adam,* the *Creation of Eve,* the *Fall of Man and the Expulsion from Paradise,* the *Sacrifice of Noah,* the *Flood,* and the *Drunkenness of Noah.* These focal scenes appear in an architectural framework, further embellished with Old Testament figures, prophets, sybils, and 20 *ignudi,* or nude youths. In the lunettes below, the spaces between the windows, Michelangelo painted the ancestors of Christ.

The ceiling, cleaned and restored in the early 1990s, is vibrantly colored, a startling contrast to the dark and veiled tones known for so many years. The cleaning, not without controversy, has led art historians to reevaluate Michelangelo's influence on the Mannerist style, which favored similarly vivid colors. What remains unchanged, however, is the remarkable power and imagination of the ceiling. Notice the way that the later scenes—the *Creation of Adam* is a good example—are larger and more simply painted than the relatively more detailed early scenes. As the work advanced, so Michelangelo became progressively bolder in his treatment, using larger forms and simpler colors.

More than 20 years later, Michelangelo was called on again, this time by the Farnese Pope Paul III, to add to the chapel's decoration by painting the *Last Judgment* on the wall over the altar. The subject was well suited to the aging and embittered artist, who had been deeply moved by the horrendous Sack of Rome in 1527 and the confusions and disturbances of the Reformation. The painting stirred up controversy even before it was unveiled in 1541, shocking many Vatican officials, especially one Biagio di Cesena, who criticized its "indecent" nudes. Michelangelo retaliated by painting Biagio's face on the figure with donkey's ears in Hades, in the lower right-hand corner of the work. Biagio pleaded with Pope Paul to have Michelangelo erase his portrait, but the pontiff replied that he could intercede for those in purgatory but had no power over hell. Michelangelo painted his own face on the wrinkled human skin in the hand of St. Bartholomew. ⊠ *Vatican Palace; entry only through Vatican Museums (☞ below).*

NEED A BREAK?

You will get glimpses of the Passetto, a passageway along Via dei Corridori and Borgo Sant'Angelo that served the popes as an emergency exit leading to the safety of Castel Sant'Angelo. The street-level **park** surrounding the castle is a pleasant place to rest on a fair day before you tackle the castle itself. The entrance to Castel Sant'Angelo is on the lower level of the park, in what was once a moat into which the Tiber's waters flowed, skirting the edifice.

⑥ Castel Sant'Angelo (Holy Angel Castle). A great circular building with one of the most distinctive silhouettes of any structure in Rome, it stands between the Tiber and the Vatican. Castel Sant'Angelo's loggias and terraces have wonderful views. The structure was in fact built as a mausoleum for the emperor Hadrian. Work began in AD 135 and was completed by the emperor's son, Antoninus Pius, about five years later. When first finished, it consisted of a great square base topped by a marble-clad cylinder on which was planted a ring of cypress trees. Above them towered a gigantic statue of Hadrian. From about the middle of the 6th century AD the building became a fortress, the military key to Rome for almost 1,000 years and the place of refuge for numerous popes during wars and sieges. Its name dates from 590, when Pope Gregory the Great, returning to the Vatican during a terrible plague, saw an angel standing on the summit of the castle in the act of sheathing its sword. Taking this as a heavenly sign that the plague was at an end, the pope built a chapel on the spot where he had seen the angel. Next to it he had a statue of the angel placed. Henceforth, it became known as Castel Sant'Angelo.

Enter the building from the former moat, and through the original Roman door of Hadrian's tomb. From here you pass through a courtyard that was enclosed in the base of the classical monument. You enter a vaulted brick corridor that hints at grim punishments in dank cells. On the right, a spiral ramp leads up to the chamber in which Hadrian's ashes were kept. Where the ramp ends, the Borgian Pope Alexander VI's staircase begins. Part of it consisted of a wooden drawbridge, which could isolate the upper part of the castle completely. The staircase ends at the Cortile dell'Angelo, a courtyard that has become the resting place of the marble angel that stood above the castle. (It was replaced by a bronze sculpture in 1753.) The stone cannonballs piled in the courtyard look like oversize marble snowballs. In the rooms on the right of the Cortile dell'Angelo there's a small collection of arms and armor; on the left, some frescoed halls, which are used for temporary exhibitions, and the **Cappella di Papa Leone X** with a facade by Michelangelo.

In the courtyard named for Pope Alexander VI, a wellhead bears the Borgia coat of arms. The courtyard is surrounded by gloomy cells and huge storerooms that could hold great quantities of oil and grain in case of siege. Benvenuto Cellini, the rowdy 16th-century Florentine goldsmith, sculptor, and boastful autobiographer, spent some time in Castel Sant'Angelo's foul prisons; so did Giordano Bruno, a heretical monk who was later burned at the stake in Campo dei Fiori, and Beatrice Cenci, accused of patricide and incest and executed just across Ponte Sant'Angelo. Her story forms the lurid plot of Shelley's verse drama *The Cenci*.

Take the stairs at the far end of the courtyard to the open terrace. From here, you have some wonderful views of the city's rooftops and of the lower portions of the castle. You can also see the Passetto, the fortified corridor connecting Castel Sant'Angelo with the Vatican. Pope Clement VII used it to make his way safely to the castle during the Sack of Rome in 1527. Opening off the terrace are more rooms containing arms and military uniforms. There's also a bar where you can pause for refreshments.

Continue your walk along the perimeter of the tower and climb the few stairs to the **appartamento papale** (papal apartments). Though used by the popes mainly in times of crisis, these splendid rooms are far from spartan. The sumptuous Sala Paolina (Pauline Room), the first you enter, was decorated in the 16th century by Pierino del Vaga and his assistants with lavish frescoes of scenes from the Old Testament and the lives of St. Paul and Alexander the Great. Look for the trompe l'oeil door with a figure climbing the stairs. From another false door, a black-clad figure peers into the room. This is believed to be a portrait of an illegitimate son of the powerful Orsini family. The Camera del Perseo (Perseus Room), next door, is named for a frieze in which del Vaga represents Perseus with damsels and unicorns. The classical theme is continued in the next room, the Camera del Amore e Psiche (Amor and Psyche Room), used by the popes as a bedroom. From the Pauline Room a curving corridor covered with grotesques (based on ancient Roman wall paintings seen by the artists of the time in the grottolike ruins of Nero's palace) leads to the library, some smaller rooms, and the treasury. Here the immense wealth of the Vatican was brought for safekeeping during times of strife; it was stored in the large 16th-century strongboxes you see today. You can continue on to the upper terrace at the feet of the bronze angel for a magnificent view. ⊠ *Lun-*

gotevere Castello 50, ☎ 06/687–5036. ☎ 8,000 lire. ☉ Open Mon.–Sat. 9–7; Thurs.–Sat. also 8:30 PM–11:30 PM; closed 2nd and 4th Tues. of month.

A tiny pastry shop, **Dolceborgo** (✉ Borgo Pio 162), is one of the area's best.

❺ Giardini Vaticani (Vatican Gardens). Extending over the hill behind St. Peter's is Vatican City's enclave of neatly trimmed lawns and flower beds dotted with some interesting constructions and other, duller ones that serve as office buildings. The Vatican Gardens occupy almost 40 acres of land on the Vatican hill, behind St. Peter's. Tours begin in front of the Information Office on Piazza San Pietro, where you board a bus that takes you through the Porta delle Campane (Gate of the Bells) on the south side of the square, into the precincts of Vatican city. You visit the little-used Vatican railroad station, which now houses a museum of coins and stamps made in the Vatican, and the Torre di San Giovanni (Tower of St. John), restored by Pope John XXIII as a place where he could retreat to work in peace and now used as a residence for distinguished guests. The tower is at the top of the hill, which you explore on foot. The plantings include a formal Italian garden, a flowered French garden, a romantic English landscape, and a small forest. Regulations prohibit photographing the gardens, but souvenir snapshots are allowed. The visit includes considerable walking and climbing stairs and slopes. Wear suitable shoes, and observe the Vatican dress code. Book the tour as far in advance as possible at the Vatican Information office. Tickets must be picked up at least 24 hours ahead. Reservations can be made by fax but can be confirmed only in person at the Vatican Information Office. ✉ *South side of Piazza San Pietro,* ☎ *06/698–84466,* FAX *06/698–85100.* ☎ *18,000 lire.* ☉ *Mar.–Oct., Mon., Tues., Thurs.–Sat. 10; Nov.–Feb., Sat. 10. Vatican dress code applies.*

★ Musei Vaticani (Vatican Museums). This vast museum complex is part of the **Vatican Palace**, residence of the popes since 1377. The palace consists of a number of individual buildings containing an estimated 1,400 rooms, chapels, and galleries. The pope and his household occupy only a small part of the palace, most of the rest of which is given over to the Vatican Library and Museums.

Among the extraordinary riches contained in the small area of Vatican City, probably the single most important is the Sistine Chapel. All museum itineraries include the Sistine Chapel (☞ Cappella Sistina, *above*), but the routes are subject to change because of the opening of the new museum entrance and the anticipated heavy flow of visitors for Holy Year in 2000.

The longer itineraries usually start at the **Egyptian Museum** (in which Room II reproduces an underground chamber tomb of the Valley of Kings). The **Chiaramonti Museum** was organized by the neoclassical sculptor Canova and contains almost 1,000 copies of classical sculpture. The gems of the Vatican's sculpture collection are in the **Pio-Clementino Museum,** however. Just off the hall in Room X, you'll find the *Apoxyomenos* (The Scraper), a beautiful 1st-century AD copy of a bronze statue of an athlete. There are other even more famous pieces in the **Octagonal Courtyard,** where Pope Julius II had them moved in 1503 from his private collection. In the left-hand corner stands the celebrated *Apollo Belvedere.* In the far corner, on the same side of the courtyard, is the *Laocoön* group, found on Rome's Esquiline Hill in 1506, held to be possibly the single most important antique sculpture group in terms of its influence on Renaissance artists.

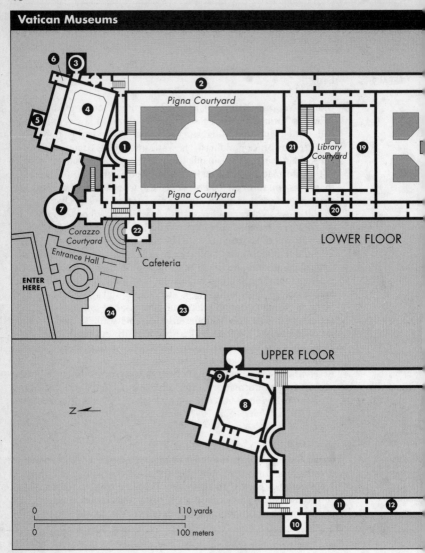

## 48

Vatican Museums

Antiquarium, **9**
Borgia Rooms, **18**
Candelabra Gallery, **11**
Chiaramonti Museum, **2**
Egyptian Museum, **1**
Etruscan Museum, **8**
Gallery of Busts, **5**

Hall of the Immaculate Conception, **16**
Map Gallery, **13**
Mask Room, **6**
New Wing, **21**
Octagonal Courtyard, **4**

Pagan, Christian Antiquities, and Ethnological Museums, **24**
Pinacoteca Gallery, **23**
Pio-Clementino Museum, **3**
Pius V Rooms, **14**
Quattro Cancelli, **22**

Raphael Rooms, **17**
Room of the Rotunda, **7**
Sala della Biga, **10**
Sobieski Room, **15**
Tapestry Gallery, **12**
Vatican Library, **19, 20**

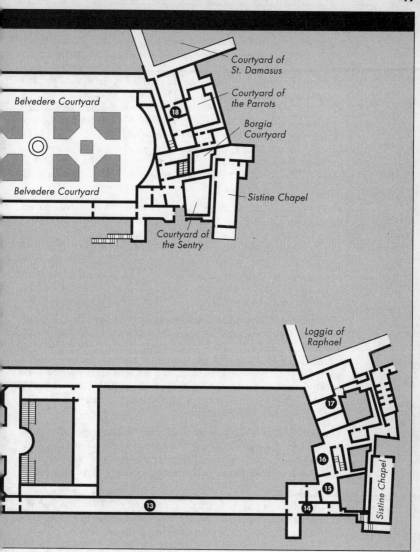

Courtyard of
St. Damasus

Courtyard of
the Parrots

Borgia
Courtyard

Belvedere Courtyard

18

Belvedere Courtyard

Sistine Chapel

Courtyard of
the Sentry

Loggia of
Raphael

17

16

15

13

14

Sistine Chapel

An adjacent hall dedicated to animals is filled with sculpture and mosaics done in colored marble, some of them very charming. There is a gallery of classical statues and a room of busts; the smallish Mask Room displays a lively mosaic pavement from the emperor Hadrian's Villa at Tivoli just outside Rome, and a copy of the 4th-century BC Greek sculptor Praxiteles' *Cnidian Venus*. In the **Hall of the Muses**, the *Belvedere Torso* occupies center stage: This is a fragment of a 1st-century BC statue, probably of Hercules, all rippling muscles and classical dignity much admired by Michelangelo. The lovely neoclassical room of the Rotonda has an ancient mosaic pavement and a huge porphyry basin from Nero's palace, as well as several colossal statues. The room on the Greek-cross plan contains two fine porphyry sarcophagi (great marble burial caskets), one of Costantia and one of St. Helena, mother of the Emperor Constantine.

The **Etruscan Museum** holds extraordinarily rich objects from the Regolini-Galassi find near Cerveteri, and a wealth of other material as well. Adjacent are three sections of limited interest: the Antiquarium, with Roman originals; three small rooms of Greek originals (followed by a broad staircase lined with Assyrian reliefs); and a vase collection. The domed Sala della Biga comes next. The *biga* (chariot) group at the center was extensively reconstructed in 1780. The chariot itself is original and was used in the Church of San Marco as an episcopal throne.

All itineraries merge in the **Candelabra Gallery,** where the tall candelabra—immense candlesticks—under the arches are, like the sarcophagi and vases, of ancient origin. In the **Tapestry Gallery**, the walls facing the windows are hung with magnificent tapestries executed in Brussels in the 16th century from designs by Raphael. On the window walls are tapestries illustrating the life of Pope Urban VIII. They were done in a workshop that the Barberini family set up in Rome in the 17th century expressly for this purpose.

The long **Gallery of Maps** is frescoed with 40 topographical maps of Italy and the papal territories, commissioned by Pope Gregory XIII in 1580. On each map is a detailed plan of the region's principal city. The ceiling is decorated with episodes from the history of the regions.

In the **Apartment of Pius V** is a small hall hung with tapestries. Facing the windows are the precious 15th-century *Passion* and *Baptism of Christ* from Tournai, in Belgium. The Sobieski Room gets its name from a huge painting by the Polish artist Lalejko. It shows the *Victory of Vienna*, a decisive defeat of the invading Ottoman forces in the late 17th century. A massive display case in the Hall of the Immaculate Conception shows some preciously bound volumes containing the text of the papal bull promulgating that particular dogma.

Rivaling the Sistine Chapel for artistic interest are the **Stanze** (Raphael Rooms), which are directly over the Borgia apartments (☞ *below*). Pope Julius II moved into this suite of rooms in 1507, four years after his election, reluctant to continue living in the Borgia apartments with their memories of his ill-famed predecessor, Alexander VI. He called in Raphael and his assistants to decorate the rooms. The Incendio Room was the last to be painted in Raphael's lifetime, and was executed mainly by Giulio Romano, who worked from Raphael's drawings for the new pope, Leo X. It served as the pope's dining room. The frescoes depict stories of previous popes called Leo, the best of them showing the great fire in the Borgo (the neighborhood between the Vatican and Castel Sant'Angelo), which threatened to destroy the original St. Peter's in the year AD 847. Miraculously, Pope Leo IV extinguished it with the sign of the cross. The other frescoes show the coronation of Charlemagne by Leo III in St. Peter's, the *Oath of Leo III,* and a naval battle with the Saracens at Ostia in AD 849, after which Pope Leo IV showed clemency to the defeated.

The Segnatura Room, the first to be frescoed, was painted almost entirely by Raphael himself. The theme of the room—which may broadly be said to be "learning"—reflects the fact that this was Julius's private library. Theology triumphs in the fresco known as the *Disputa,* or *Debate on the Holy Sacrament,* on the wall behind you as you enter. Opposite, the *School of Athens* glorifies philosophy in its greatest exponents. Plato is on the right (perhaps a portrait of Leonardo da Vinci) debating a point with Aristotle. The pensive figure on the stairs is sometimes thought to be Raphael's rival, Michelangelo, who was painting the Sistine Chapel at the same time that Raphael was working here. In the foreground on the right is Euclid, a portrait of the architect Bramante, and, on the far right, the handsome youth just behind the white-clad older man is Raphael himself. Over the window on the left are Parnassus, who represents poetry, and Apollo, the Muses, and famous poets, many of whom are likenesses of Raphael's contemporaries. In the lunette over the window opposite, Raphael painted figures representing and alluding to the Cardinal and Theological Virtues, and subjects showing the establishment of written codes of law. Beautiful personifications of the four subject areas, Theology, Poetry, Philosophy, and Jurisprudence, are painted in circular pictures on the ceiling above.

Third in the series of rooms is the Eliodoro Room, a private antechamber. Working on the theme of Divine Providence's miraculous intervention in defense of endangered faith, Raphael depicted Leo the Great's encounter with Attila; it's on the wall as you enter. The *Expulsion of Heliodorus from the Temple of Jerusalem,* opposite the entrance, refers to Pope Julius II's insistence on the Church's right to temporal possessions. He appears on the left, watching the scene. On the left window wall, the *Liberation of St. Peter* is one of Raphael's best-known and most effective works.

Adjacent to the Raphael Rooms, the **Hall of Constantine** was decorated by Giulio Romano and other assistants of Raphael after the latter's untimely death in 1520. The frescoes represent various scenes from the life of the Emperor Constantine. A door in the corner leads to the **Loggia,** or terrace, designed and frescoed by Raphael with Old Testament subjects and with the grotesques, the small decorative patterns he had copied from the walls of Nero's Domus Aurea (☞ Colle Oppio *in* Arco di Costantino and Colosseo *in* Ancient Rome, *above*) after the discovery of its ruins in the early 16th century. The richly decorated Chiaroscuri Room contains Michelangelo's model for the dome of St. Peter's. The tiny **chapel of Nicholas V,** aglow with Fra Angelico frescoes of episodes from the life of St. Stephen (above) and St. Lawrence (below), is a gem of Renaissance art. If it were not under the same roof (or roofs) as Raphael's and Michelangelo's works, it would undoubtedly draw the attention it deserves.

In the **Borgia apartments,** some intriguing historic figures are depicted in the elaborately painted ceilings, designed but only partially executed by Pinturicchio at the end of the 15th century and greatly retouched in later centuries. In the Room of the Sybil, it's generally believed that Cesare Borgia murdered his sister Lucrezia's husband, Alphonse of Aragon. In the Room of the Saints, Pinturicchio painted his self-portrait in the figure to the left of the possible portrait of the architect Antonio da Sangallo (his profession is made clear by the fact that he holds a T square). The lovely picture of St. Catherine of Alexandria is said to be a representation of Lucrezia Borgia herself. The Resurrection scene in the next room, the Room of the Mysteries, offers excellent portraits of the kneeling Borgia pope, of Cesare Borgia (the soldier with a lance at the center), and of the young Francesco Borgia (the Roman at the soldier's side), who also was probably assassinated by Cesare. These and the other rooms of the Borgia apartments have been given over to exhibits of the Vatican's collection of modern religious art, which continues interminably on lower levels of the building.

In the frescoed exhibition halls that are part of the Museums, the Vatican Library displays precious illuminated manuscripts and documents from its vast collections. The **Room of the Aldobrandini Marriage** contains beautiful ancient frescoes of a Roman nuptial rite, named for their subsequent owner, Cardinal Aldobrandini.

The **Braccio Nuovo** (New Wing) holds an additional collection of ancient Greek and Roman statues, the most famous of which is the *Augustus of Prima Porta,* in the fourth niche from the end on the left. It's considered a faithful likeness of the emperor Augustus, 40 years old at the time. Note the workmanship in the reliefs on his armor. The two gilt bronze peacocks in the gallery were in the courtyard of the original basilica of St. Peter's. Before that it's likely that they stood in the emperor Hadrian's mausoleum, today Castel Sant'Angelo (☞ *above*). To the ancient Romans the peacock was a symbol of immortality.

The paintings in the **Pinacoteca** (Picture Gallery) are almost exclusively of religious subjects and are arranged in chronological order, beginning with what in the 19th century were called the "primitives" of the 11th and 12th century. Room II has a marvelous Giotto triptych, painted on both sides, which stood on the high altar in the old St. Peter's. In Room III you'll see Madonnas by the Florentine 15th-century painters Fra Angelico and Filippo Lippi. The Raphael Room contains the exceptional *Transfiguration,* the *Coronation of the Virgin,* and the *Foligno Madonna* as well as the tapestries that Raphael designed to hang in the Sistine Chapel. The next room contains Leonardo's *St. Jerome* and a Bellini *Pietà.* In the courtyard outside the Pinacoteca you can admire the reliefs from the base of the Colonna di Marco Aurelio, the column in Piazza Colonna.

The **Museo Gregoriano Profano** (Museum of Pagan Antiquities) contains classical statues and other objects found in the territory of the Papal States (much of antiquity-rich central Italy) over the centuries. Up-to-date display techniques here heighten interest in this extensive collection of Roman and Greek sculptures.

In the **Museo Pio Cristiano** (Museum of Christian Antiquities), the most famous piece is the 3rd-century AD statue, the *Good Shepherd,* much reproduced as a devotional image. The **Museo Missionario-Etnologico** (Ethnological-Missionary Museum), usually open only Wednedsay and Saturday, has artifacts from exotic places all over the world. There are some precious Oriental statuettes and vases, scale models of temples, and full-scale Melanesian spirit huts. The **Museo Storico** (Historical Museum) displays a collection of state carriages—including an early version of the Popemobile, an ordinary car adapted to take an armchair in the back—uniforms, arms, and banners. ⊠ *Vatican Museums:* ⊠ *Viale Vaticano,* ☏ *06/698–83041.* 🎟 *15,000 lire; free last Sun. of month.* ☉ *Easter Week and mid-Mar.–Oct., Mon.–Fri. 8:45–3:45 (no admission after 2:45), Sat. and last Sun. of month 8:45–12:45 (no admission after 11:45); Oct.–mid-Mar. (except Easter Week), Mon.–Sat. and last Sun. of month 8:45–12:45 (no admission after 11:45). Closed religious holidays: Jan. 1, Jan. 6, Feb. 11, Mar. 19, Easter Sun. and Mon., May 1, Ascension Thurs., Corpus Christi, June 29, Aug. 15–16, Nov. 1, Dec. 8, Dec. 25–26.*

NEED A
BREAK?

About five minutes from the Vatican Museums exit are two good neighborhood trattorias that are far less touristy than those opposite the Museums. At **Dino e Toni** (✉ Via Leone IV 60) you can dine on typical Roman fare, fresh from the nearby outdoor market on Via Andrea Doria, and pizza. **La Caravella** (✉ Via degli Scipioni 32 at Via Vespasiano, off Piazza Risorgimento) serves classic Roman food and pizza.

★ **Piazza di San Pietro** (St. Peter's Square). The piazza is at the west end of Via della Conciliazione, a broad, rather soulless avenue begun by Mussolini in 1936 to celebrate the "conciliation" between the Vatican and the Italian government, a conciliation brought about by the Lateran Pact of 1929, which thereafter regulated the relationship between church and state. The road links the Vatican with the center of Rome, across the Tiber. It was, when built, a physical sign of the newfound accord between the secular and the spiritual powers. To make way for it, two old streets and a row of houses were razed. The approach to St. Peter's along Via della Conciliazione gives you time to become accustomed to the enormous dimensions of the square and the huge church beyond it.

The vast piazza was designed by Bernini as a grandiose prelude to St. Peter's basilica, a suitable setting for the pomp and panoply of processions and for great gatherings of pilgrims. The work began in 1656 and was completed just 11 years later. Though it is called a square, it isn't actually square at all; in fact, though it appears to be circular, it's an ellipse, the sides of which are formed by two immense colonnades, each consisting of four rows of giant columns. If you stand on either of the two stone discs set into the ground in front of each of the two colonnades (they're about midway between the obelisk in the dead center of the square and the two fountains to either side of it), the colonnades seem to consist of a single row of columns.

The 85-foot-high Egyptian **obelisk** was brought to Rome by Caligula in AD 38 and was probably placed in his circus, believed to have been near here. It was moved to its present site in 1586 by Pope Sixtus V. The monumental task of raising it almost ended in disaster when the ropes started to give way. In the absolute silence—the spectators had been threatened with death if they made a sound—a voice called "Water on the ropes!" Thus a Genoese sailor saved the day and was rewarded with the papal promise that thereafter the palms used in St. Peter's on Palm Sunday should come from Bordighera, the sailor's hometown.

The emblem at the top of the obelisk is the Chigi star, placed here in honor of Alexander VII, the Chigi pope under whom the piazza was built. Alexander had been categorical in dictating to Bernini his requirements for the design of the piazza. It had to make the pope visible to as many people as possible from the Benediction Loggia and from his Vatican apartments; it had to provide a covered passageway for papal processions; and it had to skirt the various existing buildings of the Vatican, while incorporating the obelisk and the fountain already there. (This fountain was moved to its present position, and a twin fountain was installed to balance it.)

Piazza San Pietro is the scene of mass papal audiences as well as special commemorations, masses, and beatification ceremonies. When he is in Rome, the pope makes an appearance every Sunday at noon, at the window of the Vatican Palace. He addresses the crowd and blesses all present. The pope holds mass audiences on Wednesday mornings at about 11, and at 10 in the hottest months. Whether or not they are held in the square depends on the weather and sometimes on the pope's health. There is an indoor audience hall adjacent to the basilica. While the pope is vacationing at Castel Gandolfo in the Castelli Romani, he gives a talk and blessing from a balcony of the papal palace there. For admission to an audience, apply for tickets, which are free, in advance (in writing by mail or by fax, FAX 06/6988–5863), indicating the date you prefer, the language you speak, and the hotel in which you will stay. Or apply for tickets on the Monday or Tuesday before the Wednesday audience at the Prefettura della Casa Pontificia (Papal Prefecture; ☎ 06/698–8301, Mon. and Tues. 9–1), which you reach through the **Portone di Bronzo** (Bronze Door) in the right-hand colonnade. For a fee that includes transportation from your hotel and some sketchy sightseeing along the way, some travel agencies will arrange tickets for an audience.

On the south side of the square are the **Vatican Information Office** (☎ 06/698–4466, Mon.–Sat. 8:30–7), where you can book tours of the Vatican Gardens, and the **Vatican Bookshop** (weekdays 8:30–7, Saturday 8:30–2). There are Vatican post offices (known for fast handling of outgoing mail) on either side of St. Peter's Square, and in peak tourist season, a blue-and-white post office van is parked in the square. You can buy Vatican stamps and coins at the shop annexed to the information office. Public toilets are near the Information Office, under the colonnade opposite, and outside the exit of the crypt. Religious objects and souvenirs are sold at strategically located, Vatican-run shops. ⊠ *West end of Via della Conciliazione.*

❼ **Ponte Sant'Angelo** (Sant'Angelo Bridge). One of the most beautiful of central Rome's 20 or so bridges is lined with Baroque angels designed by Bernini, Baroque Rome's most prolific architect and sculptor. Bernini himself carved only two of the angels, both of which were moved to the Church of Sant'Andrea delle Fratte shortly afterward for safekeeping. Though copies, the angels on the bridge today convey forcefully the grace and characteristic sense of movement—a key element of Baroque sculpture—of Bernini's best work. ⊠ *Between Lungotevere Castello and Lungotevere Altoviti.*

OLD ROME

A district of narrow streets with curious names, airy Baroque piazzas, and picturesque courtyards, Old Rome (Vecchia Roma) occupies the horn of land that pushes the Tiber westward toward the Vatican. During the Renaissance, when the popes ruled both from the Vatican and from the Lateran, this area in between became the commercial hub of the city. Artisans and shopkeepers toiled in the shadow of the huge palaces built to consolidate the power and prestige of the leading personages of the papal court. Writers and artists, such as the satirist Aretino and the goldsmith-sculptor Cellini, made sarcastic comments on the alternate fortunes of the courtiers and courtesans who populated the area. Artisans and artists still live in Old Rome, but their numbers are diminishing as the district becomes gentrified. Two of the liveliest piazzas in Rome, Piazza Navona and Piazza del Pantheon, are the lodestars in a constellation of cafés, trendy shops, eating places, clubs, and wineshops.

Old Rome is an area to be seen on foot, both on weekdays, when the little shops are open and it hums with activity, and on Sundays, when there's much less traffic and noise to distract you and you can take a leisurely look at the old palaces and churches to appreciate their scale and harmonious forms. This walk is a long one and could well be divided into two or even three sections, to include other sights on the fringes, such as Castel Sant'Angelo, the Gallery Doria Pamphili or the

Ghetto. It is a walk on which you can give free rein to your curiosity, poking into corners, peeking into courtyards, stepping into esoteric little shops, and finding picturesque vistas at every turn.

Numbers in the text and margin correspond to points of interest on the Old Rome map.

A Good Walk

Near **Piazza Venezia** ①, start at **Il Gesù** ②, the grandmother of all Rome's Baroque churches, with its spiraling ceiling frescoes. Cross Corso Vittorio and take Via del Gesù, a typical byway, turning left onto Via Pié di Marmo (literally, Street of the Marble Foot, named for the broken-off foot of what must have been a very large classical statue that was found here; the foot is at the corner of Via Santo Stefano del Cacco). Via Pié di Marmo leads into Piazza Santa Caterina di Siena and into Piazza della Minerva. On the right is the church of **Santa Maria sopra Minerva** ③, the only major church in Rome in Gothic style.

Straight ahead is the curving, brickbound mass of the **Pantheon** ④. What you see is the side and rear of the building, where you can observe how the Romans built a series of weight-carrying arches into the walls of the building to support the huge dome, a technique later taken up by Renaissance architects. Follow Via della Minerva to Piazza della Rotonda and go to the north end of the square to get an overall view of the temple's columned portico. The piazza is the focus of a busy café and *gelati* scene that starts in the morning and continues until late at night. Streets throughout this area are lined with gelaterie, pubs, pizzerias, restaurants, clubs, and discos.

Take Via Orfani north to Piazza Capranica and follow Via della Guglia into Piazza Montecitorio. Off the west side of the piazza, head into Via Uffizi del Vicario. Continue west on Via della Stelletta. Ahead of you, across Via della Scrofa, is Via dei Portoghesi and the **Torre della Scimmia** ⑤. More a piazza than a street, Via dei Portoghesi leads almost immediately into Via dell'Orso, lined with the shops of artisans, cabinet makers, and antiques-restorers. It ends at Via dei Soldati; climb the short flight of street stairs in front of the Hostaria dell'Orso, which has been serving guests since the 15th century, to see the **Museo Napoleonico** ⑥. Highly conspicuous across the Tiber is the huge Palazzo di Giustizia (Court Building), a bombastic late-19th-century travertine marble monster. Instead of heading south on heavily trafficked Via Zanardelli, go back down the street stairs and follow Via dei Soldati to **Palazzo Altemps** ⑦, which houses a fine collection of classical antiquities. Piazza Navona is just across Piazza Sant' Apollonia, but you can save it for later. Instead, head east, under the arch, to the church of **Sant'Agostino** ⑧, which harbors a Caravaggio masterpiece. To see more Caravaggios, turn right on Via della Scrofa to reach Via della Dogana Vecchia and the church of **San Luigi dei Francesi** ⑨. Continue south on Via della Dogana Vecchia to Piazza Sant'Eustachio, which offers a couple of oddities. One is a bronze stag's head perched atop the little church of Sant'Eustachio, in reference to the legend of the saint's conversion. Another is the bizarre pinnacle crowning the dome of Sant'Ivo, which you can see from the piazza (the church's rear entrance is on the west side of Piazza Sant'Eustachio). Via del Salvatore skirts the flank of **Palazzo Madama** ⑩, Italy's Senate building, and leads to Corso Rinascimento. Go left on Corso Rinascimento to number 40, where you can get a frontal view of the church of **Sant'Ivo alla Sapienza** ⑪. The huge church looming at the end of Corso Rinascimento is **Sant'Andrea della Valle** ⑫, setting of the first act of *Tosca*. The slightly curved, columned facade on the north side of Corso Vittorio Emanuele is that of **Palazzo Massimo alle Colonne** ⑬, one of Rome's oldest patrician homes and still residence of the Colonna family. On the south side of this major traffic artery is the **Museo Baracco** ⑭. Opposite, Palazzo Braschi, on the north side of the avenue, is a museum of the city of Rome that has been undergoing renovations for years and is closed for an indefinite period; it opens only sporadically to house temporary exhibitions.

From Piazza San Pantaleo, Via della Cuccagna (Street of the Greased Pole, a favorite game in Piazza Navona) gives access to **Piazza Navona** ⑮, a celebrated 17th-century example of Baroque exuberance, with Bernini's **Fontana dei Quattro Fiumi** ⑯ as a centerpiece. Flanking the Piazza are the **Palazzo Pamphili** ⑰ and the church of **Sant'Agnese in Agone** ⑱.

From the west side of Piazza Navona, enter Via di Tor Millina and turn right at pretty Piazza della Pace. Narrow alleys curve around either side of the church of **Santa Maria della Pace** ⑲. They lead to Via dei Coronari (street of the crown makers, where craftsmen fashioned crowns and wreaths for sacred images, a flourishing business in papal Rome). This attractive street is lined with art galleries and antiques shops. About halfway along Via dei Coronari is large Piazza San Salvatore in Lauro and on it the church of **San Salvatore in Lauro** ⑳. Continue west along Via dei Coronari to Via Panico. Turn right and follow Via Panico to Ponte Sant'Angelo. The little piazza at this end of Ponte Sant'Angelo was the scene in 1599 of the execution of Beatrice Cenci and others of her family involved in the tragic affair that later inspired Shelley's play, *The Cenci*.

Next, turn left, away from the river, into Via del Banco di Santo Spirito. On the right-hand side of this byway is an arched passageway, the Arco dei Banchi, entrance to Renaissance financier Agostino Chigi's counting rooms. A marble inscription on the left pillar of the arch states that the street was often flooded by the Tiber, a problem finally solved in the 1800s when embankments were put up along the course of the river. In the pretty little edifice on the corner of Via dei Banchi Nuovi, Rome's oldest bank, the Banco di Santo Spirito (Bank of the Holy Spirit, now Banca di Roma), has operated since the early 1600s.

Cross Largo Tassoni to the west side of Corso Vittorio, where both Via del Consolato and Via dei Cimatori lead to the graceful church of **San Giovanni dei Fiorentini** ㉑, on Piazza dell'Oro (Square of Gold), heart of Renaissance Rome's gold district. One of Old Rome's most stately and historic streets, **Via Giulia** ㉒, begins at the south end of Piazza dell'Oro.

From Via Giulia, take Via Farnese, flanking the great palace, to Piazza Farnese. On July 14, Rome helps the French Embassy in **Palazzo Farnese** ㉓ celebrate Bastille Day with music and dancing in the piazza. On the south side of Piazza Farnese, Via della Quercia leads to Piazza Capo di Ferro and **Palazzo Spada** ㉔. From Piazza della Quercia take Via dei Balestrari or Vicolo delle Grotte east to **Campo dei Fiori** ㉕, one of the most picturesque of Rome's piazzas. Northeast of Campo dei Fiori is the immense **Palazzo della Cancelleria** ㉖. Head northwest on Via del Pellegrino (the route pilgrims took to reach St. Peter's). Turn right into Via Larga to reach busy Corso Vittorio Emanuele, dominated here by the huge **Santa Maria in Valicella (Chiesa Nuova)** ㉗ and the **Oratorio dei Filippini** ㉘. To return to Piazza Navona, go east on Via del Governo Vecchio. The street takes its name from the 15th-century Palazzo Nardini, at number 39, once seat of Rome's papal governors and later a law court.

Not a walk for a rainy day, this tour can, however, be broken up and resumed again to suit your program and energy. To do the entire walk, spending about 40 minutes in Palazzo Altemps, would take about five hours, not counting breaks. But taking breaks is what this walk is all about: The route takes you past a plethora of piazzas to linger in and cafés where you can sit and take in the sights over coffee or a gelato.

Sights to See

㉕ Campo dei Fiori (Field of Flowers). A bustling marketplace in the morning and bohemian haunt the rest of the day (and night), this piazza has plenty of earthy charm. Except for the pizzerie and gelaterie, it looks much as it did in the early 1800s. Brooding over the piazza is a hooded statue of the philosopher Giordano Bruno, who was burned at the stake here in 1600 for heresy. His was the first of the executions that drew Roman crowds to Campo dei Fiori in the 17th century. The Campo dei Fiori area is full of shops selling crafts goods and second-hand furniture, and it is known for interesting eating places in all price ranges. ⊠ *Junction of Via dei Baullari, Via Giubbonari, Via del Pellegrino, Piazza della Cancelleria.*

⑯ Fontana dei Quattro Fiumi (Fountain of the Four Rivers). Piazza Navona's most famous work of art, planted right in the center, was created for Pope Innocent X by Bernini in 1651. The obelisk rising out of the fountain, a Roman copy, had stood in the Circus of Maxentius on Via Appia Antica. Bernini's powerful figures of the four rivers represent the four corners of the world: the Nile, with its face covered in allusion to its unknown source; the Ganges; the Danube; and the Plata, with its hand raised. ⊠ *Piazza Navona.*

❷ Il Gesù. The mother church of the Jesuits in Rome is the grandmother of all Baroque churches. Its architecture (the overall design was by Vignola, the facade by Della Porta) influenced ecclesiastical building in Rome for more than a century and was exported by the Jesuits throughout Europe. Though consecrated in 1584, the church wasn't decorated inside for 100 years or more. It had been intended originally that the interior be left plain to the point of austerity—but, when it was finally embellished, no expense was spared. For sheer, unadulterated grandeur, no church in Rome, save perhaps St. Peter's, compares with this one. The most striking element is the ceiling, covered with frescoes swirling down from on high and merging with the painted stucco figures at their base, the illusion of space in the two-dimensional painting becoming the reality of three dimensions in the sculpted figures. Baciccia, their painter, achieved extraordinary effects in these frescoes, especially in *The Triumph of the Holy Name of Jesus,* over the nave. Here, the heretics cast out of heaven seem to be hurtling down onto the observer. Further grandeur is represented in the altar in the Chapel of St. Ignatius in the left-hand transept. This is surely the most sumptuous Baroque altar in Rome; as is typical, the enormous globe of lapis lazuli that crowns it is really only a shell of lapis over a stucco base—after all, Baroque decoration prizes effects and illusions. The heavy bronze altar rail by architect Carlo Fontana is in keeping with the tone of magnificence.

The architectural significance of Il Gesù extends far beyond the splendid interior. The first of the great Counter-Reformation churches, it was put up after the Council of Trent (1545–63) had signaled the determination of the Roman Catholic Church to fight back against the Reformed Protestant heretics of northern Europe. Il Gesù spawned imitations throughout Italy and the other Catholic countries of Europe. ⊠ *Piazza del Gesù, off Via del Plebiscito.*

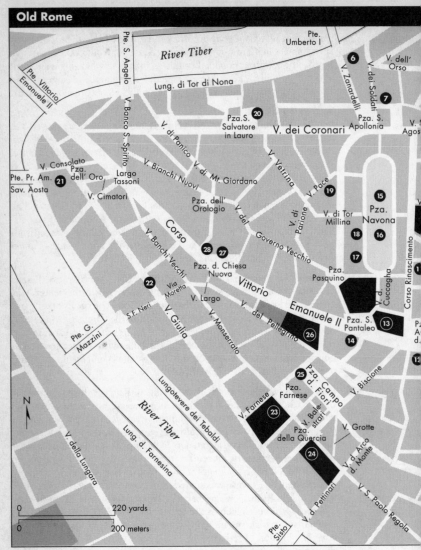

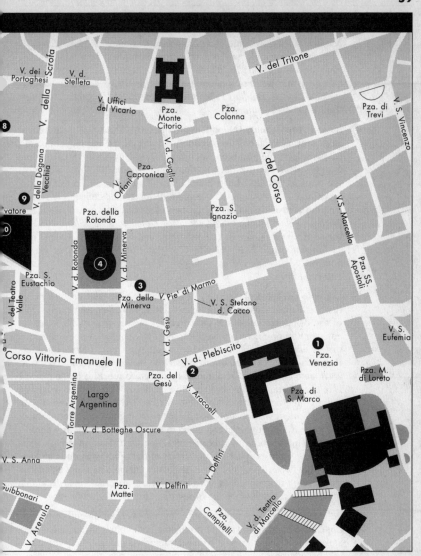

⓮ **Museo Baracco** (Baracco Museum). This small but select museum offers a compact overview of sculpture in the ancient civilizations of the Mediterranean area, incuding Egyptian, Assyrian, and Greek works. The chronologically ordered collection is housed in a Renaissance building commissioned by a French prelate, a member of the papal court. Lilies—symbols of France—are prominent in the frieze circling the exterior. ✉ *Via dei Baullari 1*, ☎ *06/688–06848.* ◪ *10,000 lire.* ☉ *Open Tues.–Sat. 9–7, Sun. 9–1.*

⑥ **Museo Napoleonico** (Napoléonic Museum). This small museum in 16th-century Palazzo Primoli contains a specialized and rich collection of Napoléon memorabilia, including a bust by Canova of Pauline Borghese. On the top floor of the same building (separate entrance) the unusual **Museo Mario Praz** (Mario Praz Museum) preserves the apartment in which a noted Italian art historian and collector lived and accumulated an astounding collection of neoclassical art and antiques. ✉ *Museo Napoleonico: Piazza di Ponte Umberto I,* ☎ *06/688–06286.* ◪ *3,750 lire.* ☉ *Open Tues.–Sat. 9–7, Sun. 9–1. Museo Mario Praz:* ✉ *Via Zanardelli 1,* ☎ *06/686–1089.* ◪ *4,000 lire.* ☉ *Open Tues.– Sun. 9–1, 2:30–6:30; Mon. 2:30–6:30. Hourly guided visits only; reservations advised.*

㉘ **Oratorio dei Filippini** (Oratory of the Philippines). This religious residence is named for Rome's favorite saint, Philip Neri, founder in 1551 of the Congregation of the Oratorians. Like the Jesuits, the Oratorians—or Philippini, as they were known—were one of the new religious orders established in the mid-16th century as part of the Counter-Reformation. The Oratorians, under the benign leadership of Philip Neri, acted under a code of humility and good works. Neri, a man of rare charm and wit, insisted that the members of the order—most of them young noblemen whom he had recruited personally—not only renounce their worldly goods and declare their good intentions by acts such as parading the streets dressed in rags, but also work as common laborers in the building of Neri's great church of Santa Maria in Valicella. The Oratory itself, headquarters of the order, was built by Borromini between 1637 and 1662. Its gently curving facade is typical of Borromini's near obsession with introducing movement into his buildings. ✉ *Piazza della Chiesa Nuova (Corso Vittorio Emanuele).*

⑦ **Palazzo Altemps.** The palace's sober exterior belies a magnificence that appears as soon as you walk into the majestic courtyard, studded with statues and covered in part by a rectractable awning. The awning is a reconstruction of a nicety used in many a patrician abode, a throwback to the type of awning that shaded the ancient Romans in the Colosseum. The restored interior hints at the splendid Roman lifestyle of the 16th through 18th centuries and serves as a stunning showcase for the most illustrious pieces from the Museo Nazionale Romano's collection of ancient Roman sculpture, which includes famous pieces from the Ludovisi family collection. In the frescoed salons you can see the *Galata,* a poignant work portraying a barbarian warrior who chooses death for himself and his wife rather than humiliation by the enemy. Another highlight is the so-called Ludovisi sarcophagus, large and magnificently carved of marble. In a place of honor is the Ludovisi throne, which at least one authoritative art historian considers a colossally over-rated fake. Look for the framed explanations of the exhibits that detail (in English) how and exactly where Renaissance sculptors, Bernini among them, added missing pieces to the classical works. In the lavishly frescoed Loggia stand busts of the Caesars. ✉ *Piazza Sant'Apollinare 46,* ☎ *06/683–3759.* ◪ *10,000 lire.* ☉ *Open Tues.–Sun. 9*AM*–10*PM*.*

26 Palazzo della Cancelleria (Chancery Palace). Occupying a massive site in a neighborhood of splendid palaces, this is the largest and one of the most beautiful of the city's Renaissance palaces. It was built for a nephew of the Riario Pope Sixtus IV toward the end of the 15th century and reputedly paid for by the winnings of a single night's gambling by another nephew. The Riario family symbol of the rose appears on the windows of the main floor and in the pillars and pavement of the courtyard. The palace houses the offices of the Papal Chancery and is part of the Vatican's extraterritorial possessions. You can step inside to see the courtyard; some salons are occasionally open to the public as concert venues.

Inconspicuously tucked into a corner of the palace, the church of **San Lorenzo in Damaso** was probably added by Bramante during the construction of the Cancelleria at the beginning of the 16th century. The original church of that name, on another part of the site, was one of the oldest churches of Rome, founded in the 4th century. When Napoléon occupied Rome, the 16th-century church was used as a law court and later had to be reconsecrated. ⊠ *Piazza della Cancelleria, off Corso Vittorio Emanuele II.*

23 Palazzo Farnese. It is the most beautiful of all of Rome's Renaissance palaces, the result of the combined talents of architects Sangallo the Younger, Michelangelo, and Giacomo della Porta, in that order. The imposing building was commissioned by Alessandro Farnese, later Pope Paul III, while he was still cardinal. In the piazza, twin fountains fall into massive Egyptian granite basins found in the ruins of the Baths of Caracalla. The palace is now the French Embassy. You can, if you apply a month or so in advance, visit the Galleria, the palace's most celebrated interior. (Fax a request to the Office of Culture, French Embassy, Rome, FAX 06/686–01331.) The reason for seeing the room is the magnificent ceiling fresco, painted between 1597 and 1604 by Annibale Caracci. ⊠ *Piazza Farnese.*

10 Palazzo Madama. The handsome 17th-century palace is a onetime Medici residence, now seat of the Italian Senate. It is occasionally open for guided visits. ⊠ *Corso Rinascimento,* ☎ *06/488–991, Rome EPT (Tourist Information Office).*

13 Palazzo Massimo alle Colonne. A curving, columned portico identifies this otherwise inconspicuous palace on a traffic-swept bend of busy Corso Vittorio Emanuele. In the 1530s architect Baldassare Peruzzi adapted the structure of an earlier palace belonging to the Massimo family, transforming it to suit the clan's high rank in the papal aristocracy and its status as the oldest of Rome's noble families, older than even the Colonna and Orsini clans. If you're here on March 16, you'll be able to go upstairs in the palace, seeing the antique livery on the servants and at the courtyard and loggias on your way to the family chapel. On this day the public is invited inside to take part in commemorations of a prodigious miracle performed here in 1583 by Philip Neri, who is said to have recalled a young member of the family, one Paolo Massimo, from the dead. ⊠ *Corso Vittorio Emanuele II 141.*

17 Palazzo Pamphili. Sometimes in the evening you can get a tantalizing glimpse of Pietro da Cortona's magnificent frescoes through the great illuminated windows of this palace. It is now the Brazilian Embassy. ⊠ *Piazza Navona 14.*

24 Palazzo Spada. In this neighborhood of huge, austere palaces, Palazzo Spada strikes an almost frivolous note, with its upper stories covered with stuccos and statues and its pretty ornament-encrusted courtyard. The little garden gallery is a delightful example of the sort of architectural games rich Romans of the 17th century found irresistible. From the end of the gallery, an imposing colonnaded loggia appears to stretch to a distant statue. In fact, the loggia is all of about 30 feet long and the statue is tiny, no more than about two feet high. What's happening, of course, is that the gallery grows progressively narrower and the columns progressively smaller as they near the statue, hence the illusion of depth. Step into the far end and you practically have to bend double. It was long thought that Borromini was responsible for this ruse; in fact it's now known that it was designed by an Augustinian priest, Giovanni Maria da Bitonto. The picture gallery in the palace has some outstanding works. Among them are Breughel's *Landscape with Windmills,* Titian's *Musician,* and Andrea del Sarto's *Visitation.* ⊠ *Piazza Capo di Ferro 3 (entrance on Vicolo del Polverone),* ☎ 06/ 686–1158. 🎫 *10,000 lire.* ☉ *Mon.–Sat. 9–7, Sun. 9–1.*

❹ Pantheon. This onetime pagan temple, a marvel of architectural harmony and proportion, is the best-preserved monument of Imperial Rome. It was entirely rebuilt by the emperor Hadrian around AD 120 on the site of an earlier pantheon (temple of all the gods) erected in 27 BC by Augustus's general Agrippa. The majestic circular building was actually designed *by* Hadrian, as were many of the temples, palaces, and lakes of his enormous villa outside the city at Tivoli. Curiously, however, Hadrian retained the inscription over the entrance from the original building that named Agrippa as the builder, in the process causing enormous confusion among historians until, in 1892, archaeologists discovered that all the bricks used in the Pantheon were stamped AD 120.

The most striking thing about the Pantheon is not its size, immense though it is (until 1960 the dome was the largest ever built), nor even the phenomenal technical difficulties posed by so vast a construction; rather, it is the remarkable unity of the building, "the calm and majestic sense of the classical world," as one writer put it, that it exudes. You don't have to look far to find the reason for this harmony: The diameter of the dome is exactly equal to the height of the walls. It is the use of such simple mathematical balance that gives classical architecture its characteristic sense of proportion and its nobility and timeless appeal.

Why, alone among the major monuments of Imperial Rome, did the Pantheon survive intact? The answer is that it became a church, in AD 608. No building, church or not, escaped some degree of plundering through the turbulent centuries of Rome's history after the fall of the empire. In 655, for example, the gilded bronze covering the dome was stripped. Similarly, in the early 17th century, Pope Urban VIII removed the bronze that covered the wooden beams of the portico, using the metal to produce the *baldacchino* (canopy) that covers the high altar at St. Peter's. Nonetheless, the exterior of the Pantheon is substantially the same as it was when built. Inside, the coffered vault was once faced with ornamental stuccos, now lost, but the pavement has been restored in the style of the original. The Pantheon holds the tombs of several more or less illustrious figures. The most famous is Raphael's (between the second and third chapels on the left as you enter). The inscription reads "Here lies Raphael; while he lived, mother Nature feared to be outdone; and when he died, she feared to die with him." Two of Italy's 19th-century kings are buried here, too: Vittorio Emanuele II and Umberto I. The tomb of the former was partly made from bronze taken from the Pantheon by Urban VIII, cast as cannons by him, and then symbolically remelted and returned here. The great opening at the apex of the dome, the oculus, is nearly 30 feet in diameter and was the temple's only source of light. It was intended as a symbol of the "all-seeing eye of heaven." ☒ *Piazza della Rotonda.* ☎ *Free.* ☉ *Mon.–Sat. 9–6:30, Sun. 9–1.*

NEED A
BREAK?

On Via degli Orfani, on the east side of Piazza del Pantheon, the **Tazza d'Oro** coffee bar (no tables, no frills) is the place for serious coffee drinkers, who indulge in *granita di caffè con panna* (coffee ice with whipped cream). This area is ice-cream heaven, with some of Rome's best *gelaterie* within a few steps of each other. Romans consider **Giolitti** (☒ Via Uffizi del Vicario 40) superlative; the scene at the counter often looks like the storming of the Bastille. Remember to pay the cashier first, and hand the stub to the counterperson when you order your cone. Giolitti has a good snack counter, also.

⑮ Piazza Navona. Here everything that makes Rome unique is compressed into one beautiful Baroque piazza. It has antiquity, Bernini sculptures, a gorgeous fountain (☞ Fontana dei Quattro Fiumi, *above*), a graceful church (☞ Sant'Agnese in Agone, *below*) and, above all, the excitement of people out to enjoy themselves—strolling, café-sitting, seeing, and being seen. An ancient Roman circus (which accounts for its oval shape), Piazza Navona has been an entertainment venue for Romans down through the centuries. It stands over the ruins of Domitian's circus; you can see a section of the ancient arena's walls just around the corner on Piazza Tor Sanguigna. Piazza Navona still has the carefree air of the days when it was the scene of Roman circus games, medieval jousts, and 17th-century carnivals. Even now it's the site of a lively Epiphany fair in January and the place where revelers gather for many other entertainment events throughout the year.

Glamorous televized fashion events are occasionally staged in this fabulous setting, but most of the time the square is simply Rome's most popular place to meet, have ice cream and coffee, take the children and dogs for a walk, and watch the passing parade. The piazza still looks much as it did during the 17th and 18th centuries, after the Pamphili Pope Innocent X decided to make it a monument to the Pamphili family (☞ Palazzo Pamphili, *above*) that would rival the Barberinis' palace at the Quattro Fontane. Some of the low houses have enviable terrace gardens.

The piazza dozes in the morning, when small groups of pensioners sun themselves on stone benches and children pedal tricycles around the big fountain. In the late afternoon, the sidewalk cafés fill up for the aperitif hour. In the evening, especially in good weather, Piazza Navona comes to life with a colorful throng of vendors, street artists, tourists, and Romans out for their evening *passeggiata* (promenade). ☒ *Junction of Via della Cuccagna, Corsia Agonale, Via di Sant'Agnese, Via Agonale.*

NEED A
BREAK?

The sidewalk tables of the **Tre Scalini** (☒ Piazza Navona 30) café offer a grandstand view of the piazza and the action. This is the place that invented the *tartufo,* a luscious chocolate ice-cream specialty. The restaurant-pizzeria annex (the menu features Pizza Navona) has the same view.

❶ Piazza Venezia. The geographic heart of Rome, this is the spot from which all distances from Rome are calculated and it is the principal crossroads of city traffic. Piazza Venezia stands at what was the beginning of Via Flaminia, the ancient Roman road that leads east across Italy to Fano on the Adriatic Sea. Via Flaminia was, and still is, a vital artery. The initial tract of Via Flaminia, from Piazza Venezia to Piazza del Popolo, is now known as the Corso (Via del Corso, one of the busiest shopping streets in the city), after the horse races (*corse*) hat were run here during the wild Roman carnivals of the 17th and 18th centuries. The podium near the beginning of the Corso is still the domain of Rome's most practiced traffic policemen, whose imperious gestures and imperative whistles are a spectacle not to be missed. The massive female bust, a fragment of antiquity, near the church San Marco in the corner of the piazza is known to the Romans as Madama Lucrezia; it was one of the "talking statues" on which anonymous poets hung verses pungent with political satire, a practice that has not entirely disappeared. From the enclosed wooden veranda of the palace on the corner of Via del Plebiscito and the Corso, Napoléon's mother had a fine view of the goings-on below during the many years that she lived in Rome. ⊠ *Junction of Via del Corso, Via Plebiscito, Via Cesare Battisti.*

㉑ **San Giovanni dei Fiorentini.** This graceful church dedicated to Florence's patron Saint, John the Baptist, stands in what was the heart of the Florentine colony in Old Rome. Many of these Florentines were goldsmiths who contributed to the building of the church. Talented goldsmith and sculptor Benvenuto Cellini of Florence, known for his vindictive nature as much as for his genius, lived nearby. Inside the church, Borromini executed a splendid altar for the Falconieri family chapel in the choir. The animal-loving pastor allows well-behaved pets to keep their owners company at services. ⊠ *Piazza dell'Oro.*

❾ **San Luigi dei Francesi.** The church is famous for its three magnificent Caravaggios, painted at the beginning of the 17th century. It is also the official church of Rome's French colony (San Luigi is St. Louis, patron of France). The Caravaggios are in the Chapel of St. Matthew (at the altar end of the left nave). Put some coins in the machine to light up these canvases, and Caravaggio's mastery of light effects takes it from there. The works are, from the left, *The Calling of St. Matthew, Matthew and the Angel,* and *Matthew's Martyrdom.* When painted, they caused considerable consternation to the clergy of San Luigi, who thought the artist's dramatically realistic approach was scandalously disrespectful. A first version of the altarpiece was rejected; the priests were not particularly happy with the other two either. Time has fully vindicated Caravaggio's patron, Cardinal Francesco del Monte, who commissioned these works and stoutly defended them. They're recognized to be among the artist's greatest paintings. ⊠ *Piazza San Luigi dei Francesi.* ☉ *Open Fri.–Wed. 7:30–12:30 and 3:30–7, Thurs. 7:30–12:30.*

⓴ **San Salvatore in Lauro.** Outside and in, this church looks more Venetian than Roman. It was designed along the lines of models by the Venetian architect Palladio. If the church is not open, ring the bell at number 15 for admission to the interior and to the charming little 15th-century cloister that is used by a civic association. ⊠ *Piazza San Salvatore in Lauro.*

⓲ **Sant'Agnese in Agone** (St. Agnes in Navona). The church's name comes from *agona,* the source of the word *Navona* and a corruption of the Latin *agonalis,* describing the type of games held there in Roman times. The graceful Baroque facade is by Borromini. ⊠ *Piazza Navona*

❽ **Sant'Agostino.** Caravaggio's celebrated *Madonna of the Pilgrims*—which scandalized all Rome because a kneeling pilgrim is pictured, all too realistically for the taste of the time, with dirt on the soles of his feet— is in the first chapel on the left. In a niche just inside the door of the church is Sansovino's sculptured *Madonna and Child,* known to the Romans as the Madonna del Parto (of Childbirth) and piled high with ex-votos. ⊠ *Piazza Sant'Agostino.*

19 **Santa Maria della Pace.** A semicircular portico stands in front of the 15th-century church. It was an architectural solution devised by Pietro da Cortona, who was commissioned in 1656 to restore the church and design its facade. He demolished a few buildings here and there to create the relatively spacious approach to the church. Then he added arches to give architectural unity to the piazza, which has become the core of a trendy café scene. The church is usually closed, but if it happens to be open when you pass by, stop in to see Raphael's fresco of the Sybils above the first altar on your right, and the fine decorations of the Cesi Chapel, second on the right, designed in the mid-16th century by Sangallo. ⊠ *Piazza Santa Maria della Pace.*

27 **Santa Maria in Vallicella,** or **Chiesa Nuova** (the New Church). Like Il Gesù, the New Church was built toward the end of the 16th century, in the fervor of the Counter Reformation at the urging of St. Philip Neri. It has a sturdy Baroque interior, all white and gold, with ceiling frescoes by Pietro da Cortona and three magnificent altarpieces by Rubens. An enormous statue of the saint is in the sacristy. ⊠ *Piazza della Chiesa Nuova, Corso Vittorio Emanuele II.*

3 **Santa Maria sopra Minerva.** The name of the church reveals that it was built over *(sopra)* the ruins of a temple of Minerva, goddess of wisdom. Erected in 1280 by the Dominicans on severe Italian Gothic lines, it has undergone a number of more or less happy restorations to the interior. Certainly, as the city's only Gothic church, it provides a refreshing contrast to Baroque flamboyance. Have some coins handy to illuminate the **Carafa Chapel** in the right transept, where Filippino Lippi's glowing 15th-century frescoes are well worth the small investment. Under the main altar is the tomb of Italy's patron saint, Catherine of Siena. Left of the altar you'll find Michelangelo's *Risen Christ* and the tomb of the gentle artist Fra Angelico, behind a modern sculptured bronze screen. Bernini's unusual and little-known monument to the Blessed Maria Raggi is on the fifth pier from the door on the left as you leave the church. In front of the church, the little obelisk-bearing elephant carved by Bernini is perhaps the city's most charming sculpture. An inscription on the base reads something to the effect that it takes a strong mind to sustain solid wisdom, a subtle reference to the church's site. ⊠ *Piazza della Minerva.*

12 **Sant'Andrea della Valle.** This huge 17th-century church has the highest dome (by Maderno) in Rome after St. Peter's. Imposing though its dimensions are, the church is remarkably balanced in design. Inside, where Puccini set the first act of *Tosca,* note the early 17th-century frescoes in the choir vault by Domenichino and those by Lanfranco in the dome, one of the earliest ceilings in full Baroque style. Richly marbled and decorated chapels flank the nave. ⊠ *Corso Vittorio Emanuele II.*

11 **Sant'Ivo alla Sapienza.** The main facade of this eccentric Baroque church, probably Borromini's best, is on the stately courtyard of an austere building that once housed Rome's university. Sant'Ivo has what must surely be one of the most delightful domes in all Rome—a golden spiral said to have been inspired by a bee's stinger. The bee symbol is a reminder that Borromini built the church on commission from the Barberini Pope Urban VIII. The geometrically conceived interior is worth a look, especially if you share a taste for Borromini's complex mathematical architectural idiosyncrasies. ⊠ *Corso Rinascimento 40 (another entrance off Piazza Sant'Eustachio).* ☉ *Daily 9–noon.*

5 **Torre della Scimmia** (Monkey Tower). A medieval tower atop the building that stands at the junction of Via dei Portoghesi with Via dei Pianellari, it figures in a chapter in the lore of Old Rome. In the building, so the story goes, a pet monkey ran amok one day, seizing a baby and carrying it to the top of the tower. Here the crazed animal seemed about to dash the child to the street below. A crowd of neighbors and bystanders invoked the Madonna's intercession, and the monkey carefully descended with the baby, carrying it to safety. In gratitude, the father placed a statue of the Madonna on the tower, along with a vigil light, both of them still neighborhood landmarks. (One version of the story relates that the monkey was sold to pay for the statue.) ⊠ *Via dei Portoghesi.*

㉒ **Via Giulia.** The street was named for Pope Julius II, who commissioned it in the early 1500s as part of a scheme to open up a grandiose approach to St. Peter's. Though the pope's plans to change the face of the city were only partially completed, this street became an important thoroughfare in Renaissance Rome. Via Giulia was the first street in Rome since ancient times to be laid out in a straight line, and it was flanked with elegant churches and palaces. It has again become one of Rome's most exclusive addresses, with antiques shops at street level and fabulous rooftop penthouses overlooking the Tiber. Among the buildings that should attract your attention are **Palazzo Sacchetti** (⊠ Via Giulia 66), with an imposing stone portal, and the forbidding brick building that housed the **Carceri Nuove**(⊠ Via Giulia 52), Rome's prison for more than two centuries. Now it contains judiciary offices and a small criminology museum. Near the bridge that arches over the southern end of Via Giulia is the Church of **Santa Maria dell'Orazione e Morte** (Holy Mary of Prayer and Death), with stone skulls on its door. These are a symbol of a confraternity that was charged with burying the bodies of the unidentified dead found in the city streets. There are several other curious old churches along this route, but most of them are closed except on special occasions. The **Palazzo Falconieri** (⊠ Via Giulia 1), adjacent to Santa Maria dell'Orazione e Morte, was designed by Bramante. The arch over the street served as a link in the Farnese enclave, which included Palazzo Farnese, on the east side of Via Giulia, and Villa Farnesina, directly across the river, in Trastevere. ⊠ *Between Piazza dell'Oro and Piazza San Vincenzo Pallotti.*

TOWARD THE SPANISH STEPS AND THE TREVI FOUNTAIN

The Corso and Piazza di Spagna area is not only a shopper's paradise. Major attractions include a series of imposing Renaissance and Baroque palaces—among them Palazzo Borghese, the luxurious home of one of Rome's most talked-about families—and a number of striking churches. Sumptuously theatrical Roman ecclesiastical architecture, in particular heroic illusionistic ceiling painting, is in ample supply here. The highlights of this area are the Spanish Steps, 18th-century Rome's most famous example of city planning, and the Trevi Fountain, the most ornate and thrilling of the city's great fountains.

Numbers in the text and margin correspond to points of interest on the Piazza Venezia to the Scalinata di Spagna map.

A Good Walk

Begin at Piazza Venezia (☞ Old Rome, *above*), the square in front of the elaborate marble mountain that is the **Monumento a Vittorio Emanuele II** ①. On the west side of the piazza looms **Palazzo Venezia** ②, built in the 15th century for the Venetian Cardinal Pietro Barbo, who became Pope Paul II and who totally renovated the adjacent church of **San Marco** ③, on Piazza San Marco on the south side of the palace. From Piazza Venezia, head north on Via del Corso, but walk on the

THREE COINS AND A TRITON

ANY VISITOR WHO'S EVER thrown a coin backward over his or her shoulder into the Fontana di Trevi to ensure a return to Rome appreciates the particular magic of the city's fountains. From the magnificence of the Fontana dei Quattro Fiumi at Piazza Navona to the graceful caprice of the Fontana delle Tartarughe in the Ghetto, the ever-flowing sculptures seem as essential to the *piazze* they inhabit as the cobblestones and ocher buildings that surround them. In fact, much of central Rome was established well before most of its fountains were put in place, and it was more than a hundred years after this that the creations came to be regarded as anything more than public services.

In the late 16th century, after the running-water heyday of the Roman Empire and before the 20th century's municipal pipelines, the primary purpose of the Roman fountain was simply to provide water. To mark the completion of the Virgin Aqueduct, architect Giacomo della Porta designed 18 unassuming, functional fountains, all consisting of a large basin with two or three levels of smaller basins in the center, which were built and placed throughout the city at points along the water line. (Or, as in the case of the Fontana delle Tartarughe in Piazza Mattei, at points where the locals wanted the water line to be; the residents of this part of the Ghetto managed to convince the city to install the fountain despite the lack of water and then engineered a deviation from the aqueduct line to supply it). Although nearly all of Della Porta's fountains remain, their spare Renaissance style is

virtually unrecognizable, as most were elaborately redecorated after his death with dolphins, obelisks, and sea monsters, in keeping with the flamboyant styles of the Baroque.

Of this next generation of Baroque fountaineers, the most famous is Gian Lorenzo Bernini (who is thought, incidentally, to be responsible for the addition of the delicate turtles in della Porta's fountain at Piazza Mattei). Bernini's writhing, muscular creatures of myth adorn most of Rome's most visible fountains, including the Fontana di Trevi (so named for the three streets—*tre vie*—that converge at its piazza), the Fontana di Nettuno, with its tritons, at Piazza Barberini, and, in the center of Piazza Navona, the Fontana dei Quattro Fiumi, whose hulking figures represent the four great rivers of the known world: the Nile, the Ganges, the Danube and the Rio de la Plata.

Surprisingly, the most common type of fountain in Rome is also the kind least noted by visitors: the small, inconspicuous drinking fountains that burble away from sidestreet walls, old stone niches, and even fire-hydrantlike installations on street corners. You can drink this water—many of these *fontanelle* even have pipes fitted with a little hole up from which water shoots when you hold your hand under the main spout. If you want to combine the glorious Roman fountain with a cool drink of water, head to Piazza di Spagna, where the Barcaccia fountain (designed by Pietro Bernini, fountainmaster Gian Lorenzo's father) is outfitted with spouts, spurts—and platforms from which thirsty admirers can wet their whistles.

right-hand side of the street so that you can get a good view of the attractive facade of **Palazzo Doria-Pamphili** ④, one of Rome's grandest. The entrance to the palace's sumptuous art gallery and state apartments is on Piazza del Collegio Romano, where Rome's most famous and enormously influential Jesuit school was conducted for three centuries until 1870. After glimpsing how an aristocratic family lives, take Via di Sant' Ignazio to the enchanting 18th-century Rococo Piazza di Sant'Ignazio, designed by architect Raguzzini as if it were a stage set. But then, of course, theatricality was a key element of almost all the best Baroque and Rococo art. And nowhere is this more evident than in the church of **Sant'Ignazio** ⑤, where the ceiling frescoes hold a surprise or two.

Behind the "stage set," Via del Burro leads to Piazza di Pietra, where the Rome Stock Exchange is set inside the columns of an ancient temple. From here it's just a few steps along Via dei Bergamaschi to Piazza Colonna, named for the celebrated **Colonna di Marco Aurelio** ⑥ at its center. North of the column, Palazzo Chigi, a 16th- and 17th-century building, is where the Italian government has its cabinet offices. Next door is the Chamber of Deputies in **Palazzo Montecitorio** ⑦.

Just off Via del Tritone is little **Santa Maria in Via** ⑧, where you can have a sip of some very special water. Across Via del Tritone, a busy thoroughfare that climbs to Piazza Barberini and Via Veneto, Piazza San Silvestro is a hub of public transportation and location of the main post office. It is also on the edge of a shopping district that has few equals elsewhere in the world. From Via del Tritone on the south to Piazza del Popolo on the north, from the Tiber on the west to Villa Borghese on the east, this is a fabulous trove of specialty shops and boutiques offering all types of fashions, jewelry, household goods, and anything else you might want—including the well-maintained restroom facilities in the Rinascente department store, which occupies the block at the corner of Via del Corso and Largo Chigi. You can detour in and out of the area's narrow byways as your fancy takes you, attracted by stunning window displays. At some point, head north on Via del Corso again to Piazza San Lorenzo in Lucina to see the Bernini works in **San Lorenzo in Lucina** ⑨ and perhaps linger in the café, a fashionable haunt, on this pretty square. At the west end of the square, take Via del Leone to Largo Fontanella Borghese to see the portal of **Palazzo Borghese** ⑩ and browse at the stalls selling old books and prints around the corner in airy Piazza della Fontanella Borghese, where you can get an even better idea of the palace's size. Follow Via della Fontanella Borghese, lined with smart shops, to Largo Goldoni, site of an information kiosk.

From Largo Goldoni you enter Via Condotti and get a head-on view of the **Scalinata di Spagna** ⑪ and the church of **Trinità dei Monti** ⑫. On Via Condotti you can carom from Bulgari to Gucci to Valentino to Ferragamo with no effort at all, except perhaps that of pushing through the crowds. On weekend and holiday afternoons the square, along with Via del Corso and neighboring streets, is packed with teenagers out for a mass stroll. They perch on the steps and around the low-lying **Fontana della Barcaccia** ⑬ in the middle of the piazza. To the right of the Spanish Steps, the **Keats and Shelley Memorial House** ⑭ gives you an idea of how England's Romantic poets lived in what was then Rome's bohemian quarter. On the left at the foot of the steps is Babington's Tea Room, which has catered to the refined cravings of Anglo-Saxon travelers since its establishment by two genteel English ladies in 1896. Now it's an overpriced enclave favored by wealthy Italian Anglophiles. The ancient column in adjacent Piazza Mignanelli, where the American Express office is located, supports a statue of the Immaculate Conception. Each December 8, a crack unit of the Rome Fire Department sends one of its best men up a ladder to replace the garland crowning the Madonna, and the pope usually stops by in the afternoon to pay his respects. At the far end of this part of the piazza stands **Palazzo di Propaganda Fide** ⑮, brain center of the far-flung missionary activities of the Jesuits.

Follow Via di Propaganda to the church of **Sant'Andrea delle Fratte** ⑯, where you can pause under the orange trees in the cloister. From Via Sant'Andrea delle Fratte, turn left onto Via del Nazareno and cross busy Via del Tritone to Via della Stamperia. On the right-hand side of Via della Stamperia is Palazzo Poli, which houses the **Calcografia dello Stato** ⑰. A few paces beyond, as you continue south, is the old building in which the **Accademia di San Luca** ⑱, with a gallery of old masters, is located. As you near the end of Via della Stamperia you can probably hear the sound of **Fontana di Trevi** ⑲, a Baroque extravaganza of sculpture and cascading waters. From Trevi Fountain, Via Lucchesi leads you to Piazza della Pilotta and Via della Pilotta, where picturesque bridges overhead connect **Palazzo Colonna** ⑳ with the Colonna family's gardens on the slope of the Quirinal Hill. The west side of the palace is flanked by the church of **Santi Apostoli** ㉑. On the ceiling, the early 18th-century artist Baciccia painted one of his swooping, swirling illusionist frescoes. Opposite the church is another of Rome's splendid patrician palaces, 17th-century Palazzo Odescalchi, used as a model for aristocratic palaces throughout Europe.

TIMING

Not counting shopping, this walk could take from 3½ to 5 hours, allowing for visits to the galleries and for a few coffee or ice cream breaks. It certainly should be done on days when the shops are open, even if you're only window shopping. When they are closed, even for the lunch break, most shops hide their windows behind heavy metal shutters, depriving you of spotlighted previews of Roman style. Though the Galleria Doria Pamphili is open most days of the week, the Galleria in Palazzo Colonna is open only on Saturday morning.

Sights to See

⑱ **Accademia di San Luca.** A private academy of the arts founded by a group of painters in the 1400s, it is housed in 16th-century Palazzo Carpegna. Its gallery is open to the public and contains some fine Renaissance paintings, including a charming putto by Raphael and his *Madonna of St. Luke.* ⊠ *Piazza dell'Accademia di San Luca 77,* ☎ *06/679–8850.* 🎟 *Free.* ۞ *Open Mon., Wed., Fri., and last Sun. of month, 10–1.*

⑰ **Calcografia dello Stato** (National Graphics Institute). Together with similar institutes in Paris and Madrid, it preserves the world's most important collections of copper engraving plates by artists from the 1500s up to the present. There is an exhibition space on the ground floor, where samples of its historic treasures and contemporary work may be on display. The historic collection includes invaluable antique presses and engraving plates by 18th-century Roman artist Piranesi. ⊠ *Via della Stamperia 6,* ☎ *06/688–06565.* 🎟 *Free.* ۞ *Open Mon. Sat. 9–1.*

⑥ **Colonna di Marco Aurelio** (Column of Marcus Aurelius).The 2nd-century AD column, for a time mistakenly believed to celebrate Antoninus Pius and still called the Colonna Antonina by many, is composed of 28 blocks of marble covered with a series of reliefs that spiral up to a statue of St. Paul, which dispossessed the effigy of Marcus Aurelius in the 16th century. The column is the centerpiece of Piazza Colonna. ⊠ *Piazza Colonna.*

70

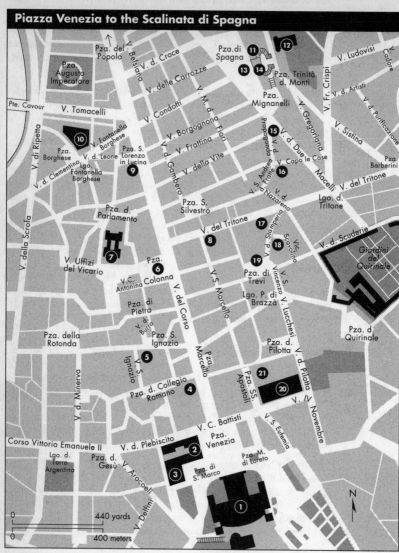

Piazza Venezia to the Scalinata di Spagna

⑬ Fontana della Barcaccia (Barcaccia Fountain). At the center of the Piazza di Spagna, this curious fountain represents a half-sunken boat. The water spills out of the sunken fountain rather than cascading dramatically as in most other Roman fountains; it may have been designed that way to make the most of the area's low water pressure. It was thanks to the Barberini Pope Urban VIII, who commissioned the fountain, that there was any water at all in this area, which was becoming increasingly built-up during the 17th century. He restored one of the ancient Roman aqueducts that once channeled water here. The bees and suns on the boat constitute the Barberini trademark. Some insist that the Berninis (Pietro and his more famous son Gian Lorenzo) intended the fountain to be a reminder that this part of town was often flooded by the Tiber; others that it represents the Ship of the Church; and still others that it marks the presumed site of the emperor Domitian's water stadium in which sea battles were re-enacted in the glory days of the Roman Empire. On August dog days, when there's no one around, tourists use it as a refreshing footbath. ⊠ *Piazza di Spagna.*

⑲ Fontana di Trevi (Trevi Fountain). This aquatic marvel, all the more effective for its cramped setting in the tiny piazza, is one of the city's most exciting sights. Backing up a wall of Palazzo Poli, it is alive with rushing waters and marble sea creatures commanded by an imperious Oceanus. The work of Nicola Salvi—though it's thought that Bernini may have been responsible for parts of the design—it was completed in 1762 and is a perfect example of the Rococo taste for dramatic theatrical effects. The water comes from the Acqua Vergine aqueduct, built by the ancient Romans, and is so called because of the legend that it was a young girl, a *vergine*, who showed its source to thirsty Roman soldiers. The story is pictured in the relief on the right of the figure of Oceanus. Usually thickly fringed with tourists tossing coins into the basin to ensure their return to Rome (the fountain grosses about 230 million lire a year, most of it donated to charity), the fountain was the backdrop for a memorable Mastroianni-Ekberg scene in *La Dolce Vita*. (Unfortunately, the water is turned off during the wee hours and occasionally at other times for cleaning; if that is the case when you arrive, make a point of returning another day to see it in full gush.) ⊠ *Piazza di Trevi.*

NEED A BREAK?	**Gelateria San Crispino** (⊠ Via della Panetteria 42), closed Tuesday, is a relatively recent contender for top honors for the city's best ice cream. The northern Italian family that runs it takes almost fanatic pride in using only genuine ingredients, and they won't serve their gelato in a cone—they say it alters the flavor. At **Gelateria Trevi** (⊠ Via del Lavatore 84), closed Thursday, also known as Cecere, the atmosphere is more easygoing.

⑭ Keats and Shelley Memorial House. The English Romantic poet Keats lived here, in what was the colorful bohemian quarter of 18th- and 19th-century Rome, especially favored by the English. You can visit his rooms, which have been preserved as they were when he died here in 1821. They contain a rather quaint collection of memorabilia of English literary figures of the period—Byron, Shelley, Joseph Severn, and Leigh Hunt as well as Keats—and an exhaustive library of works on the Romantics. ⊠ *Piazza di Spagna 26,* ☎ *06/678–4235.* 🎟 *5,000 lire.* ⊙ *Weekdays, May–Sept. 9–1 and 3–6, Oct.–Apr. 9–1 and 2:30–5:30.*

❶ Monumento a Vittorio Emanuele II, or Altare della Patria (Victor Emmanuel Monument, or Altar of the Nation). Romans say you can avoid seeing it only if you're standing on it. The huge white mass of the Victor Emmanuel Monument is an inescapable and handy Roman landmark. Some have likened it to a huge wedding cake; others, to an immense Victorian typewriter in white marble. However modern eyes may look at it, it was the splendid focus of civic pride to turn-of-the-century Romans. In order to create this elaborate marble monster and the vast piazza in which it stands, its architects blithely destroyed many ancient and medieval buildings and altered the slope of the Capitoline Hill, which abuts it. Built to honor the unification of Italy and the nation's first king, Victor Emmanuel II, it also shelters the eternal flame at the tomb of Italy's Unknown Soldier, guarded day and night by sentinels, and the Institute of the History of the Risorgimento—relics of the struggle for the unification of Italy in the 19th century. After having been closed to the public for many years, it is occasionally open to visitors (check with the tourist office). The views from the top of its gleaming white staircases and those from the loggia and terraces are among Rome's best, so if it is open make an effort to see them. ✉ *Piazza Venezia.*

⑩ Palazzo Borghese. One of the princely palaces of Rome's aristocratic families, this is a huge, rambling, Renaissance building that goes on for blocks and has several portals. The palace was begun in 1590 for a Spanish cardinal by architect Martino Longhi, who designed the sturdy facade facing Largo Fontanella Borghese. In 1605 Cardinal Borghese celebrated his election as Pope Paul V by purchasing the palace; it later passed to his nephew, Cardinal Scipione Borghese, who assembled his magnificent art collection here. Still used by the Borghese family, though part of it is rented out, the palace is closed to the public. You can get as far as the gate inside the main portal on Largo Fontanella Borghese to take a peek at the double courtyard. ✉ *Largo Fontanella Borghese.*

⑳ Palazzo Colonna. An immense palace, it faces Piazza Santi Apostoli on one side and the Quirinal Hill on the other. A little bridge over Via della Pilotta links the palace with the gardens on the hill. Palazzo Colonna is home to one of Rome's oldest and most patrician families, whose picture gallery is open to the public one day a week. The gallery itself is a setting of aristocratic grandeur; centerpiece of one of the salons is the ancient red marble column (*colonna* in Italian) that is the family's emblem. Adding redundant lustre to the opulently stuccoed and frescoed salons are works by Poussin, Tintoretto, and Veronese, and a number of portraits of illustrious members of the family such as Vittoria Colonna—Michelangelo's muse and long-time friend—and Marcantonio Colonna, who had a hand in the great naval victory at Lepanto in 1577. ✉ *Via della Pilotta 17,* ☎ *06/679–4362* ✉ *10,000 lire.* ☉ *Sept.–July, Sat. 9–1.*

⑮ Palazzo di Propaganda Fide (Palace of the Propagation of the Faith). Jesuit missionary activity is headquartered here. Bernini created the simpler facade on the piazza in 1644, while his archrival Borromini designed the more elaborate one on Via di Propaganda not long before his death in 1667. ✉ *Piazza di Spagna 48.*

④ Palazzo Doria-Pamphili. The beauty of the graceful 18th-century facade of this patrician palace may escape you unless you take time to step to the opposite side of the street for a good view. The foundations of the immense complex of buildings probably date back to classical times. The present building dates from the 15th century, with the exception of the facade. It passed through several hands before it became the property of the famous seafaring Doria family of Genoa, who had married into the Roman Pamphili clan. As in most of Rome's older patrician residences, the family still lives in part of the palace but rents out some of its 1,000 rooms, five courtyards, and four monumental staircases to various public and private enterprises to help pay the taxes. The incredibly rich family art collection is open to the public, along with part of the private apartments. Set like the family jewels that they are in an alcove off the gallery are the famous Velázquez portrait and the Bernini bust of the Pamphili Pope Innocent X. Of the three Caravaggios in the collection, the *Rest on the Flight to Egypt* is the finest. You'll also find a Titian and some splendid 17th-century landscapes by Claude Lorrain and Gaspar Dughet. The guided tour of the private apartments includes a Baroque chapel, a ballroom, and three authentically furnished 18th-century salons. In the private apartments are an *Annunciation* by Filippo Lippi, a family portrait by Lotto, and a stately portrait of Andrea Doria by Sebastiano del Piombo. It's the glimpse of an aristocratic lifestyle that makes this tour special. ⊠ *Piazza del Collegio Romano 2,* ☎ *06/679–7323.* ☒ *Picture gallery, 12,000 lire; private apartments, 5,000 lire.* ☉ *Fri.–Wed. 10–5. Guided visits to the private apartments offered at regular intervals 10:30–12:30.*

❼ Palazzo Montecitorio. The Chamber of Deputies meets here. The huge palace occupies two city blocks and has two facades, one facing Piazza del Parlamento. The facade on Piazza Montecitorio was designed by Bernini and is adorned with a 6th-century BC Egyptian obelisk. The obelisk once served as the pointer of an immense sundial traced in the pavement of the Campo Marzio, a vast open area set aside under the emperor Augustus in the 1st century AD. Embellished with gardens and promenades, it extended as far as the Tiber and included the Augusteo (the emperor's family mausoleum) and the Ara Pacis. Almost entirely hidden by subsequent constructions, parts of the area's original pavement, with symbols of the planets, lie under the buildings on Piazza San Lorenzo in Lucina. ⊠ *Piazza Montecitorio.*

❷ Palazzo Venezia. Built for Venetian Cardinal Pietro Balbo, who became Pope Paul II, Palazzo Venezia was the backdrop used by Mussolini to harangue crowds massed in the vast piazza below, proclaiming his ill-fated dreams of empire from the balcony over the main portal. The palace shows a mixture of Renaissance grace and heavy medieval lines, and it houses an eclectic collection of decorative objects, paintings, sculptures, and ceramics in handsome salons, some of which Mussolini used as his offices. (A light burned permanently in one window during Mussolini's reign, a typically bombastic attempt by the Italian dictator to prove he never slept.) The café on the loggia is a pleasant place for a pause with a view over the garden courtyard. ⊠ *Via del Plebiscito 118,* ☎ *06/699–94221.* ☒ *8,000 lire.* ☉ *Tues.–Sat. 9–2:30, Sun. 9–1.*

❸ San Marco. The ancient church was used for official ceremonies by Venetian Pope Paul II, who resided in the palace he built next door. Tradition relates that St. Mark wrote his gospel in Rome, and the church is dedicated to the evangelist, as well as to the 4th-century Pope Mark, whose relics are under the main altar. One of many Roman churches built as a basilica, the original edifice was destroyed by fire and replaced in the 6th century. The third church, the one you see today, was built in the 9th century by Pope Gregory IV, as the dedication in the Byzantine apse mosaics testifies. The church is a perfect example of Rome's layering of history, of periods and styles built up one upon another, from the early Christian architectural motifs to the Romanesque bell tower; from the Byzantine mosaics to the windows in the nave, there are obvious transitions from convoluted Gothic to spacious early Renaissance. Then there's the full flowering of Renaissance style in the magnificent gilt ceiling and the ample portico that Pope Paul II built to provide shelter for himself and his retinue during outdoor rites in bad weather. On the right wall of the portico is the tomb of Vannozza Cattanei. The mistress of the Borgia Pope Alexander VI, she bore him three children, including Lucrezia and Cesare. Originally located in the Church of Santa Maria del Popolo, the tomb was moved here under mysterious circumstances. No one has ever been able to discover why, when, or by whom. ⊠ *Piazza San Marco, off Piazza Venezia.*

⑤ Sant'Ignazio. This 17th-century church harbors some of the magnificent illusions typical of the Baroque style. To get the full effect of the marvelous illusionistic ceiling by priest-artist Andrea del Pozzo, stand on the small disk set into the floor of the nave. The heavenly vision above you, seemingly extending upward almost indefinitely, represents the *Glory of St. Ignatius Loyola* and is part of Del Pozzo's cycle of works in this church exalting the early history of the Jesuit Order, whose founder was the mystic Ignatius of Loyola. The artist repeated this illusionist technique, so popular in the late 17th century, in the false dome, which is actually a flat canvas. The overall effect of the frescoes is dazzling (be sure to have coins handy for the machine that switches on the lights) and was fully intended to rival that produced by Baciccia in the nearby church of Il Gesù. ⊠ *Piazza Sant'Ignazio.*

⑨ San Lorenzo in Lucina. The church was probably founded on the site of an early Christian meeting place under the aegis of a Roman matron named Lucina, whose name was added to that of St. Lawrence to distinguish it from other churches dedicated to him. Behind its 12th-century portico and campanile (bell tower), the interior is not especially interesting. There's one exception, however: the **Cappella Fonseca** (Fonseca Chapel), the fourth on the right, designed by Bernini. His bust of Fonseca, Innocent X's physician, represents the donor in moving contemplation. On the chapel's right wall, a 17th-century painting shows Elisha pouring salt into the waters of Jericho in order to purify them; it's a clear reference to Fonseca's concern with purifying the malarial waters of Rome and its *campagna,* the area surrounding the city. The 17th-century *Crucifixion* over the main altar is by Guido Reni. The church guards relics of the grill on which the early Christian martyr St. Lawrence was roasted alive. ⊠ *Piazza San Lorenzo in Lucina.*

⑯ Sant'Andrea delle Fratte. On either side of the choir are the two original angels that Bernini himself carved for the Ponte Sant'Angelo, where copies now stand. The door in the right aisle leads into one of Rome's hidden gardens, where orange trees bloom in the cloister. Borromini's contributions—the dome and a curious bell tower—are best seen from Via Capo le Case, across Via Due Macelli. ⊠ *Via Sant'Andrea delle Fratte (Via della Mercede).*

⑧ Santa Maria in Via. This small 16th-century church is something of a collector's item: It is the only church in Rome with a tiny spa inside it. In a little chapel, on the right as you enter, an attendant dispenses curative water that comes from a spring that bubbles up on the site; the spring once brought up, it's claimed, the icon of the Madonna that's now over the altar. ⊠ *Via di Santa Maria in Via (Via del Tritone).*

㉑ Santi Apostoli (Holy Apostles). The Basilica of Santi Apostoli is a mixture of architectural styles, the result of successive restorations of an ancient church. The grandiose ceiling fresco by Baciccia, who did an even grander one for the Jesuits at Il Gesù, celebrates the founding of the Franciscan Order. One of the church's best features is the lovely double portico on the facade, dating from the 15th century. The church is often the scene of the weddings and funerals of Rome's aristocracy, and the piazza frequently serves as a gathering place for heated political rallies and demonstrations. ⊠ *Piazza Santi Apostoli.*

NEED A
BREAK? The **Birreria Tempera** (✉ Via San Marcello 19, closed Sun.), off Piazza Santi Apostoli, is open all day (and until late). You can have a good light lunch or supper here in congenial surroundings.

⑪ **Scalinata di Spagna** (Spanish Steps). This spectacular staircase takes its name from the Spanish Embassy to the Holy See—the Vatican—which has occupied the historic palace facing what is now the American Express office since the 17th century. However, the idea for a monumental staircase connecting the piazza with the French Church of Trinità dei Monti at the top of the hill originated with the French minister Mazarin. Its construction in 1723 was partially financed by French funds. Perfect for sitting and lounging on and for photographing from all angles, the steps have always attracted a picturesque crowd, from 19th-century artists' models in folk costumes to present-day tourists from the four corners of the earth. Romans don't linger here; they leave the steps and square to the tourists. But they don't fail to stop by in mid-April and early May, when the Spanish Steps are gloriously blanketed with huge azaleas in bloom. ✉ *Piazza di Spagna, junction of Via Condotti, Via del Babuino, Via Due Macelli.*

NEED A
BREAK? You may prefer to limit your shopping here to the window variety, but there's one thing on Via Condotti that everybody can afford, and that's a stand-up coffee at the bar at the **Antico Caffè Greco** (✉ Via Condotti 86, closed Sun.), a 200-year-old institution, the haunt of artists and literati. With its tiny, marble-topped tables and velour settees, it's a nostalgic old place. Goethe, Byron, and Liszt were habitués; Buffalo Bill stopped in when his road show hit Rome. It's still a haven for writers and artists, and for ladies carrying Gucci shopping bags. Remember, table service is costly here.

⑫ **Trinità dei Monti.** Standing high above the Spanish Steps, this church is beautiful not so much in itself but for its dramatic location and magnificent views. It is occasionally used as a concert venue. ✉ *Piazza Trinità dei Monti.*

TRAJAN'S MARKET TO SAN GIOVANNI IN LATERANO

In ancient times, the Subura (the present-day Suburra) was one of Rome's most populous neighborhoods. It lay east of the Imperial Fora and the huge market built by Trajan, where staples and delicacies from the four corners of the Empire could be found. A high stone wall separated the Suburra's mean streets from the Imperial Fora and acted as a barrier during the great fire of 64 BC, keeping the flames from spreading to Rome's most august monuments. The Suburra was a dark warren of many-storied dwellings, the cramped home of a substantial portion of ancient Rome's citizens, who numbered more than one million by the 1st century AD.

This neighborhood is clearly different from that of Old Rome, near the Vatican to the west. Here, instead, you find the stamp of a much more remote past—the heritage of ancient Rome. You can see the Colosseum's marble-clad walls looming at the end of narrow, shadowy streets with Latin-sounding names: Panisperna, Baccina, Fagutale. Other walls, built for the Caesars, shore up medieval tower-houses; streets dip and climb, hugging the curves of two of the seven hills on which Romulus founded his city. Emerging from antiquity, the great churches of the Christian era stand out like islands connected by broad avenues. The new streets laid out by the popes or, later, by the planners of the capital of the new Italy slice through the meandering byways, providing a shorter, surer route for pilgrims and commerce. Majestic Santa Maria Maggiore, its interior gleaming with gold from the New World, and San Giovanni in Laterano, coolly grand and echoing with vastness, are among the oldest of the city's churches, though restored and remodeled down through the centuries. They are also major pilgrimage churches, the focus of Holy Year rites for Roman Catholics, and a magnet for anyone interested in art and architecture. Another lodestone is the smaller, hard-to-find church of San Pietro in Vincoli, which hoards its hidden treasure—Michelangelo's statue of Moses.

Numbers in the text and in the margin correspond to numbers on the Trajan's Market to San Giovanni in Laterano map.

A Good Walk

Using Piazza Venezia (☞ Old Rome, *above*) as a landmark, start on Via Quattro Novembre, which curves uphill from the piazza, and explore the **Mercati Traianei** ①, ancient Rome's multistoried shopping mall. At the top of Via Quattro Novembre, off Largo Magnanapoli, turn into Via Panisperna, a double-dip street that links the Quirinal Hill, on which you are standing, with the Viminal and Esquiline hills (Santa Maria Maggiore is on the Esquiline). To see one of Rome's quaintest little piazzas, turn right, going downhill on Salita del Grillo. The attractions here are the medieval Torre del Grillo, 18th-century Palazzo del Grillo, a portion of the ancient wall put up to separate the Forum of Augustus from the Suburra, and the 15th-century house of the Knights of Malta. Follow the Roman walls along Via Tor de' Conti and turn left onto either Via Baccina or Via Madonna dei Monti. The latter leads directly into Via Leonina. On the right-hand side of Via Leonina, climb the street staircase up to Via Cavour, cross this busy thoroughfare, and climb the street staircase opposite, named Via San Francesco da Paola but otherwise known as the Salita dei Borgia. The dark staircase passes under what was once Palazzo Borgia, hotbed of Renaissance intrigue. On the piazza is the church of **San Pietro in Vincoli** ②, to which Michelangelo's *Moses* attracts throngs of tourists.

Returning to Via Cavour, turn right and head northeast on Via Cavour or on quieter, parallel Via Urbana. Make a brief detour to the left, or west, to see the mosaics in the church of **Santa Pudenziana** ③. Both Via Urbana and Via Cavour lead straight to Piazza dell'Esquilino and the sweeping staircase at the rear of **Santa Maria Maggiore** ④. You can enter the church here to save steps, but be sure when you exit from the front doors to turn back and take a good look at the facade on Piazza Santa Maria Maggiore, preferably from the far side of the piazza, to get the full effect of facade, loggia, and bell tower. On narrow Via di Santa Prassede, which is at the southwest corner of Piazza Santa Maria Maggiore, is the little church of **Santa Prassede** ⑤, with a tiny porch marking the portal and 9th-century mosaics inside. Returning to parallel Via Merulana, you reach Largo Brancaccio. On your right is the large **Museo Nazionale d'Arte Orientale** ⑥, Italy's chief collection of art and artifacts from the East and Middle East. The area between Via Merulana and Stazione Termini, to the east, with Piazza Vittorio as its fulcrum, is as multi-ethnic as Rome gets. Asian, Indian, and African grocery stores and restaurants abound.

Via Merulana was laid out as a pilgrim's route in the 1500s and runs straight as an arrow between the basilicas of Santa Maria Maggiore and **San Giovanni in Laterano** ⑦, with its medieval cloister. Attached to the north flank of the church is the **Palazzo Lateranense** ⑧. The **Scala Santa** ⑨ is in the churchlike edifice diagonally across from the Lateran

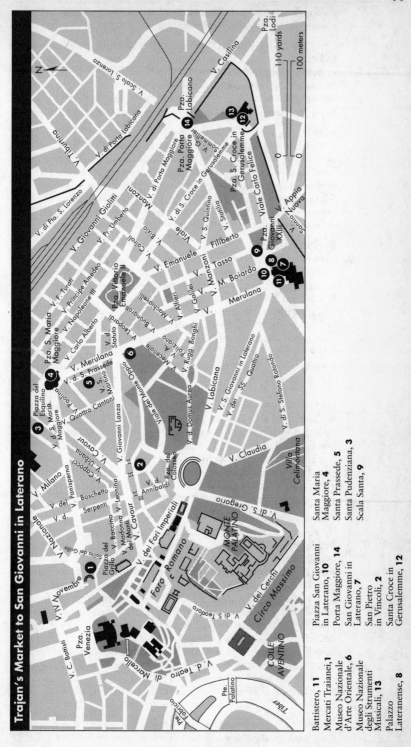

Trajan's Market to San Giovanni in Laterano

100 meters
110 yards

Battistero, **11**
Mercati Traianei, **1**
Museo Nazionale
d'Arte Orientale, **6**
Museo Nazionale
degli Strumenti
Musicali, **13**
Palazzo
Lateranense, **8**

Piazza San Giovanni
in Laterano, **10**
Porta Maggiore, **14**
San Giovanni in
Laterano, **7**
San Pietro
in Vincoli, **2**
Santa Croce in
Gerusalemme, **12**

Santa Maria
Maggiore, **4**
Santa Prassede, **5**
Santa Pudenziana, **3**
Scala Santa, **9**

Palace. Turn south into **Piazza San Giovanni in Laterano** ⑩. On the square is the octagonal **Battistero** ⑪.

From Piazza di Porta San Giovanni and the ancient city walls, pierced to let traffic through, go east on Viale Carlo Felice to reach the church of **Santa Croce in Gerusalemme** ⑫. Behind the church is the **Museo Nazionale degli Strumenti Musicali** ⑬. Then you can head back to San Giovanni's Metro stop and bus lines, or continue northeast to see **Porta Maggiore** ⑭, a part of the Acqua Claudia aqueduct.

TIMING

The walk takes about 3½ hours, including visits to the Mercati Traianei and the basilicas. The market and basilicas are open through lunch hour, but if you want to see Michelangelo's Moses in San Pietro in Vincoli, you have to get there before 12:30 or after 3:30. Santa Pudenziana and Santa Prassede also close from about noon to 3 or 4. Allow an additional 30 minutes for a visit to the Museo d'Arte Orientale and 20 to 30 minutes for a cursory look at the Museo di Strumenti Musicali.

Sights to See

⑪ **Battistero** (Baptistry). Though much altered through the centuries, The Baptistry of San Giovanni is the forerunner of all such buildings where baptisms take place, a ritual of key importance in the Christian faith. It was built by Constantine in the 4th century and enlarged by Pope Sixtus III about 100 years later. It stands on the site of the baths attached to the home of Constantine's second wife, Fausta, who, emperor's wife or not, was suffocated in the hot room of the baths after having falsely accused Constantine's son by his first wife of having tried to rape her. This exceedingly unpleasant death is an example of one of the accepted Roman methods of dealing with members of the ruling classes who were implicated in scandals of this type. Of the four chapels ranged around the walls of the baptistry, the most interesting is the first on the right (as you enter). It has a set of ancient bronze doors whose hinges send out a musical sound when the doors are opened and closed. They probably came from the Baths of Caracalla. But notice also the splendid porphyry columns that support the entire structure, typical of the Romans' love of luxurious and exotic materials. ✉ *Piazza San Giovanni in Laterano.* ☉ *Daily 8:30–12:30 and 3–6.*

① **Mercati Traianei** (Trajan's Market). A huge, multistoried brick complex of shops, covered and open walkways, and terraces overlooking the ruins of the Imperial and Roman fora, the market that Trajan had built as part of his own forum is the forerunner of a modern shopping mall, and not very different from it. Though much better preserved than most of the buildings that stood in the neighboring Forum and the Imperial Fora, the market gives only a hint of its original splendor. When built in the early 2nd century AD, at the order of the emperor Trajan—whose military exploits are celebrated on the reliefs spiraling up Trajan's Column in the Forum below—the market was immediately considered one of the wonders of the classical world. The designer of both Forum and market was Apollodorus of Damascus, by far the most successful architect of the day. In addition to the market buildings, discussed below, the Forum contained temples and libraries, statues and fountains, all decked out in the most luxurious materials that could be found.

The market stands on the site of what was originally a low hill running between the Quirinale Hill to the northeast and the Capitoline Hill to the west. It speaks volumes for the confidence of Apollodorus and his patron—not to mention the almost unlimited slave labor at their disposal—that they could so blithely remove this great quantity of earth just to build a market, even one as splendid as this. In fact the architectural centerpiece of the market is the enormous curved wall—technically known as an exedra, a form of apse—that shores up the side of the Quirinale Hill that had been exposed by Apollodorus's gangs of laborers. Here the Romans would come to meet and to gossip, sitting on the seats Apollodorus thoughtfully provided, which extended the length of the exedra.

Enter the large, vaulted hall in front of you. Two stories of shops rise up on either side. It's thought that they were probably a bazaar or a similar sort of specialty market. Head for the flight of steps at the far end that leads down to Via Biberatica, Pepper Street (in fact *biberatica* is a medieval corruption of the Latin *piper,* meaning *pepper*). Here the superrich came to buy this much sought-after luxury and other spices. Head back to the three tiers of shops that line the upper levels of the great exedra and look out over the remains of the Forum. Though empty and bare today, the cubicles were once ancient Rome's busiest market stalls. Wine, oils, flowers, perfumes, shoes, clothing, and household goods were all sold in this thriving market—everything a burgeoning and sophisticated population desired. Though it seems to be part of the market, the **Torre delle Milizie** (Tower of the Militia), the tall brick tower that is a prominent feature of Rome's skyscape, was built in the early 1200s. In those times wealthy families vied with one another to build the strongest, highest defensive towers. Pope Boniface VIII bought this one from the Conti family so that he could use it as a stronghold to defend his Roman territory against his arch-enemies, the Colonnas. ✉ *Via Quattro Novembre 94,* ☎ *06/671–03613.* ☎ *3,000 lire.* ☉ *Apr.– Sept., Tues.–Sat. 9–1:30, Sun. 9–1, Tues. and Thurs. also open 4–7; Oct.–Mar., Tues.–Sat. 9–1:30, Sun. 9–1.*

⑥ Museo Nazionale d'Arte Orientale (National Museum of Oriental Art). The museum's extensive collection of Middle Eastern and East Asian art is being continually enriched by the finds of Italian archaeological expeditions. Italian archaeologists have also been in on some of the most important finds of recent decades, such as Ebla in Syria. ✉ *Via Merulana 248,* ☎ *06/487–4415.* ☎ *8,000 lire.* ☉ *Mon., Wed., Fri., Sat. 9–2, Tues. and Thurs. 9–7, Sun. 9–1. Closed 1st and 3rd Sun. of month.*

NEED A
BREAK?

Across from the museum, on the opposite side of Via Merulana, **Pannella** (✉ Largo Leopardi 2) is a large, highly specialized bread store with a tempting array of products to sample on the spot. It has a small coffee bar and also offers take-out dishes and ice cream.

⑬ Museo Nazionale degli Strumenti Musicali (National Museum of Musical Instruments). Just behind Santa Croce is this museum housing a sizable collection of instruments from prehistory to the present, arranged by type, including folk instruments, mechanical instruments, a 16th-century clavichord, and the richly carved 17th-century Barberini Harp. ✉ *Piazza Santa Croce in Gerusalemme 9/a,* ☎ *06/701–4796.* ☎ *4,000 lire.* ☉ *Tues.–Sat. 9–2, Sun. 9–1.*

⑧ Palazzo Lateranense (Lateran Palace). The building flanking the basilica of San Giovanni was the popes' official residence until their exile to Avignon in the south of France in the 14th century. The present palace was built by Domenico Fontana in 1586. Still technically part of the Vatican, it now houses the offices of the Rome Diocese and the Vatican Historical Museum, which includes the historic Papal Apartment, with antique furnishings, medieval sculptures, and Renaissance tapestries; and the Sala della Conciliazione, with a magnificent carved and painted wood ceiling dated 1589. ✉ *Entrance in atrium of church.* ☎ *8,000* *lire.* ☯ *Sat. and first Sun. of each month; guided tours in Italian at 9, 10, 11, 12.*

⑩ Piazza San Giovanni in Laterano. At the center of the plaza stands Rome's oldest and tallest obelisk. This originally stood in front of the Temple of Ammon in Thebes, Egypt, in the 15th century BC. It was brought to Rome by Constantine in AD 357 to stand in the Circus Maximus, and finally was set up here in 1588. On one side of the square is the big, rambling city hospital of San Giovanni, which was founded in the Middle Ages as a kind of infirmary of the Lateran Palace. ⊠ *Junction of Via Merulana, Via Amba Aradam.*

⑭ Porta Maggiore. The massive 1st-century AD monument is not really a city gate (porta) but was part of the Acqua Claudia aqueduct. It gives you an idea of the scale of Roman public works, and also of the level of the ancient city—you have to look down from present sidewalk level to that of the gate. On the Piazzale Labicano side of the portal, to the east, is the curious **Baker's Tomb,** erected in the 1st century BC by the grieving wife of a prosperous baker. She saw to it that the tomb was decorated with stone ovens and charming friezes illustrating her deceased husband's trade. ⊠ *Junction of Via Eleniana, Via di Porta Maggiore, Via Casilina.*

⑦ San Giovanni in Laterano (St. John in Lateran). This is one of Rome's four patriarchal basilicas, as well as one of the city's most imposing churches. Historically speaking, it is the most important church in the city, more so even than St. Peter's. As the official seat of the bishop of Rome—otherwise known as the pope—it is the place where he officiates in all ceremonies concerned specifically with Rome as opposed to those concerned with the papacy in general. The towering facade dates from 1736 and was modeled on that of St. Peter's. On it are 15 colossal statues: Christ, John the Baptist, John the Evangelist, and 12 apostles of the church look out on the sea of dreary suburbs that have spread out from Porta San Giovanni to the lower slopes of the Alban Hills.

San Giovanni was founded in the 4th century on land donated by the emperor Constantine, who had obtained it from the wealthy patrician family of the Laterani. And that's why its name refers to its location—in Laterano. Vandals, earthquakes, and fire damaged the original and successive constructions. Finally, in 1646, Pope Innocent X commissioned Borromini to rebuild the church, and it's Borromini's rather cool, tense Baroque interior that you see today.

Under the portico on the left stands an ancient statue of Constantine. Another link with Rome's past are the central portal's ancient bronze doors, brought here from the Curia building in the Forum. Inside, little is left of the early decorations. Supposedly by the 14th-century Florentine painter Giotto, a famous fragment of a fresco on the first pillar in the double aisle on the right depicts Pope Boniface VIII proclaiming the first Holy Year in 1300. The mosaic in the apse was reconstructed from a 12th-century original by Torriti, the same Franciscan friar who executed the apse mosaic in Santa Maria Maggiore. The papal altar at the center of the church contains a wooden table believed to have been used by St. Peter to celebrate the Eucharist. The altar's rich Gothic tabernacle dates from 1367 and, somewhat gruesomely, contains what are believed to be the heads of saints Peter and Paul.

You shouldn't miss the **cloisters,** with their little twin columns and frieze encrusted with 13th-century Cosmatesque mosaics by the Vassallettos, a father-and-son team. Enter the cloister from the last chapel at the end of the left aisle. ⊠ *Piazza di Porta San Giovanni.*

San Giovanni in Laterano

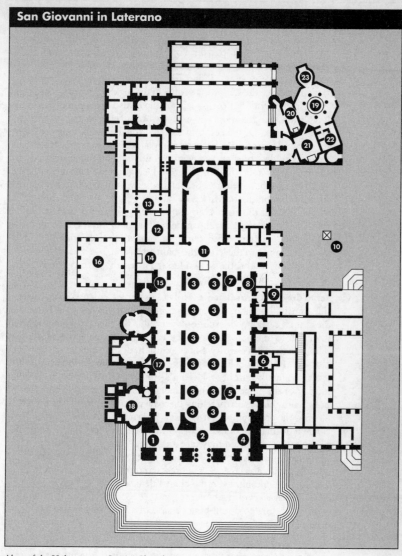

Altar of the Holy
Sacrament (four
Roman columns), 14

Ancient statue of
Constantine, 1

Caracciolo
monument, 17

Chapel of SS. Seconda
and Rufina, 20

Cloisters, 16

Colonna Chapel, 12

Constantine
Baptistry, 19

Corsini Chapel, 18

Entrance to the
Cloisters, 15

Farnese tomb, 7

Giotto fresco, 5

Henry IV of France, 9

Holy Door, 4

Martinez de Chiaves
tomb, 8

Massimo Chapel, 6

Obelisk, 10

Papal Altar, 11

Roman bronze
doors, 2

Sacristy, 13

St. John the Baptist
Chapel (ancient
doors), 23

St. John the
Evangelist Chapel, 22

St. Venanzio
Chapel, 21

The 12 Apostles, 3

② **San Pietro in Vincoli** (St. Peter Enchained). What has put this otherwise anonymous church on the map is the monumental statue of Moses carved by Michelangelo in the early 16th century for the never-completed tomb of his patron, Pope Julius II. The fierce power of this remarkable sculpture dominates its setting, a reduced version of Michelangelo's original design for the enormous tomb. People say that you can see the sculptor's profile in the lock of Moses's beard right under his lip, and that the pope's profile is also there somewhere. But don't let the search distract you from the overall effect of this marvelously energetic work. Of the rest of the design for the tomb, only the flanking statues *Leah* and *Rachel* were completed. In high season it's a madhouse of guided tours and souvenir vendors; if you're lucky you'll find it fairly empty and you'll be able to take a good look at the sculpture. As for the rest of the church, St. Peter, after whom the church is named, takes second billing to Moses. What are reputed to be the chains that bound St. Peter during his imprisonment by the Romans in Jerusalem are in a bronze and crystal urn under the main altar. Other treasures in the church include a 7th-century mosaic of St. Sebastian in front of the second altar on the left of the main altar, and, by the door, the tomb of the Pollaiuolo brothers, two lesser Florentine 15th-century artists. ⌧ *Piazza San Pietro in Vincoli.*

⑫ **Santa Croce in Gerusalemme** (Holy Cross of Jerusalem). From the outside, much like Santa Maria Maggiore and San Giovanni in Laterano, the church certainly doesn't look very old. There's a Romanesque bell tower off to one side, put up in the 12th century, while the facade was rebuilt in the 18th century. But the church, despite extensive 17th- and 18th-century remodeling of the interior, dates from the 4th century AD. It was originally part of St. Helena's 4th-century AD palace. St. Helena, mother of the emperor Constantine, was an indefatigable collector of holy relics. Her most precious discovery was fragments of the Holy Cross—the cross on which Christ was crucified—which she had unearthed during one of many forays through the Holy Land. The relics of the cross—if indeed these are authentic—are in the modern chapel at the end of the left aisle. There are otherwise few indications of the church's venerable age. To all intents and purposes you seem to be in a Baroque building. Even the chapel dedicated to St. Helena, located in the lower level of the building, was redecorated in the 15th century with a dazzling gold-and-blue version of an earlier mosaic. ⌧ *Piazza Santa Croce in Gerusalemme.*

❹ **Santa Maria Maggiore** (St. Mary Major). The exterior of the church, from the broad sweep of steps on Via Cavour to the more elaborate facade on Piazza Santa Maria Maggiore, is that of a gracefully curving 18th-century building, the very model of Baroque architecture of that period. But, in fact, Santa Maria Maggiore is one of the oldest churches in Rome, built around 440 by Pope Sixtus III. Not only is it one of the seven great pilgrimage churches of Rome, it is also by far the most complete example of an early Christian basilica in the city—one of the immense, hall-like buildings derived from ancient Roman civic buildings and divided into thirds by two great rows of columns marching up the nave. The other six basilicas—San Giovanni in Laterano and St. Peter's are the most famous—have been entirely transformed, or even rebuilt. Paradoxically, the major reason why this church is such a striking example of early Christian design is that the same man who built the incongruous exteriors about 1740—Ferdinando Fuga—also conscientiously restored the interior, throwing out later additions and, crucially, replacing a number of the great columns.

It was long believed that the basilica came to be built when the Virgin Mary appeared in a dream to Pope Sixtus III and ordered him to build

Santa Maria Maggiore

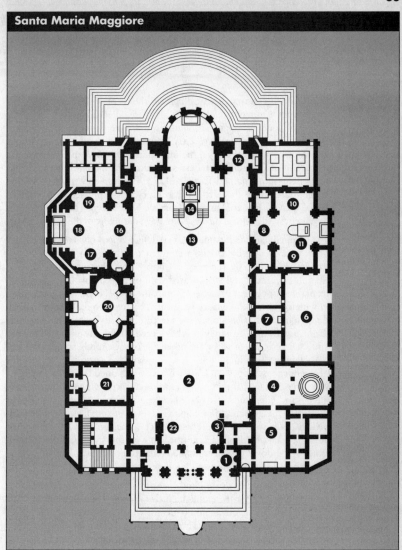

a church in her honor. It was to stand on the spot where snow would fall on the night of August 5, an event about as likely in a Roman August as snow in the Sahara. True or false, the legend is commemorated every August 5, the feast of the Madonna of the Snows, with a special mass in the Sistine Chapel at which a shower of white rose petals falls from the ceiling.

Precious 5th-century mosaics high on the nave walls and on the triumphal arch in front of the main altar are splendid testimony to the basilica's venerable age. Those along the nave show 36 scenes from the Old Testament (unfortunately, they are hard to see clearly without binoculars), while those on the arch illustrate the Annunciation and the Youth of Christ. The majestic mosaic in the apse was created by a Franciscan monk named Torriti in 1275. The resplendent carved wood ceiling dates from the early 16th century; it's supposed to have been gilded with the first gold brought from the New World. The Cosmatesque pavement in the central nave is even older, dating from the 12th century.

The **Cappella Sistina** (Sistine Chapel), which opens onto the right-hand nave, was created by architect Domenico Fontana for Pope Sixtus V in 1585. (*Sistine,* by the way, is simply the adjective from *Sixtus.*) Elaborately and heavily decorated with precious marbles "liberated" from the monuments of ancient Rome, the chapel includes a lower level in which some 13th-century sculptures by Arnolfo da Cambio are all that's left of what was once the incredibly richly endowed chapel of the *presepio,* the Christmas crèche, looted during the Sack of Rome in 1527. Directly opposite, on the other side of the church, stands the **Cappella Paolina** (Pauline Chapel), a rich Baroque setting for the tombs of the Borghese popes Paul V—who commissioned the chapel in 1611 with the declared intention of outdoing Sixtus's chapel across the nave—and Clement VIII. The *Madonna* above its altar is a precious Byzantine image painted perhaps as early as the 8th century. The **Cappella Sforza** (Sforza Chapel) next door was designed by Michelangelo and completed by Della Porta (the same partnership that was responsible for the dome of St. Peter's). ⊠ *Piazza Santa Maria Maggiore; rear entrance on Piazza Esquilino.*

⑤ Santa Prassede. This small and inconspicuous 9th-century church is known above all for the exquisite little **Chapel of San Zenone.** It's just to the left of the entrance, and it gleams with vivid mosaics that reflect their Byzantine inspiration. Though much less classical and naturalistic than the earlier mosaics of Santa Pudenziana, they are no less splendid. Note the square halo over the head of Theodora, mother of St. Pasquale I, the pope who built this church. It indicates that she was still alive when she was depicted by the artist. The chapel also contains one curious relic: a miniature pillar, supposedly part of the column at which Christ was flogged during the Passion. It was brought to Rome in the 13th century. Next to the entrance to the chapel is an early work of Bernini, a bust of Bishop Santoni, executed when the sculptor was in his mid-teens. Over the main altar, the magnificent mosaics on the arch and apse are also in rigid Byzantine style; in them Pope Pasquale I wears the square halo of the living and holds a model of his church. ⊠ *Via di Santa Prassede.*

③ Santa Pudenziana. This much-restored early Christian church is well worth a visit for its strikingly colored 5th-century apse mosaic representing Christ and the Apostles, in which Sts. Praxides and Pudenziana hold wreaths over the heads of Sts. Peter and Paul. ⊠ *Via Urbana.*

⑨ Scala Santa (Holy Steps). A 16th-century building encloses the Holy Steps, which tradition holds to be the staircase from Pilate's palace in Jerusalem, brought to Rome by St. Helena, mother of the Emperor Constantine. Wood protects the 28 marble steps worn smooth by the knees of pilgrims through the centuries. There are two other staircases that you can ascend to see the **Sancta Sanctorum,** the private chapel of the popes in the old Lateran Palace. Visible only through a window grate, it's a masterpiece of Cosmatesque mosaics. ⊠ *Piazza San Giovanni in Laterano.* ⊙ *Daily, Oct.–Mar. 6:15–noon and 3–6:15, Apr.–Sept. 6:15–noon and 3:30–6:45.*

THE QUIRINALE TO PIAZZA DELLA REPUBBLICA

The area east of Old Rome and northeast of the Roman Forum owes its broad streets and dignified palazzi, rather seedy in some stretches, to the city's transformation after 1870, when it became the capital of a newly united Italy. The influx of ministries and new businesses set off a frenzied building boom and a rush to modernize the city's infrastructure. Vast tracts of gardens and vineyards, once part of the parks of patrician villas, were divided and developed, as in the Via Veneto and Quirinale areas. Distinguished turn-of-the-century architecture became the neighborhood's hallmark. Broad avenues were laid out and given the patriotic names of Via Nazionale and Via Venti Settembre (September 20 was the date when Italian troops breached Porta Pia to claim Rome as the kingdom's new capital). A new railroad station was built at Termini, where Pope Pius IX had established a terminal for the various rail lines entering Rome. Piazza della Repubblica was laid out to serve as a monumental foyer between the station and the rest of the city. After World War II the old Termini station was replaced with a then-daring modern construction, and the huge Piazza dei Cinquecento in front of it was laid out. After its 1950s and early '60s heyday as the focus of Dolce Vita excitement, Via Veneto declined into dullness. Though the area immediately adjacent to Termini station slid more dramatically downhill, current urban renewal projects and increased policing are pulling it up again. Basically unchanging, the Quirinal and Via Veneto neighborhoods have preserved their solid, bourgeois palaces and enormous ministries. And Via Veneto keeps trying to woo back the mainstream of Roman sidewalk café society from the lively scenes at Piazza del Pantheon and Piazza Navona—as yet to no avail.

Numbers in the text and margin correspond to points of interest on the Quirinale to Piazza della Repubblica map.

A Good Walk

The Quirinal hill boasts some of the key Baroque buildings of Rome, notably the two churches of Sant'Andrea al Quirinale and San Carlo alle Quattro Fontane. On the hill's lower slopes is the imposing Palazzo Barberini. Begin your walk at **Piazza del Quirinale** ①. The square marks the summit of the Quirinal Hill, highest of the seven hills of Rome. The front of the largest palace on the plaza, **Palazzo del Quirinale** ② (easily identified by the sentinels at the portal), is quite plain, though it houses the president of Italy. Make a brief detour onto Via XXIV Maggio, which links Piazza del Quirinale with Via Nazionale. On the right, a double ramp of stairs and an ornate stone portal mark the entrance to the gardens of Villa Colonna, domain of the Colonna family, whose palazzo is at the foot of the hill, on Piazza Santi Apostoli (☞ Palazzo Colonna *in* Toward the Spanish Steps and the Trevi Fountain, *above*). Opposite, on the east side of Via XXIV Maggio, **Palazzo Pallavicini Rospigliosi** ③ belongs to another of Rome's aristocratic clans.

Take Via del Quirinale, on the right of the presidential palace. The featureless, 1,188-ft-long wing of the palace on the left side of the street hides the Quirinale gardens. On the right is Bernini's favorite architectural creation, the church of **Sant'Andrea al Quirinale** ④. Borromini's perfectly proportioned church of **San Carlo alle Quattro Fontane** ⑤ stands at the end of Via del Quirinale, at the **Quattro Fontane** ⑥ intersection.

Turn northwest, or left, into Via Quattro Fontane, where the **Galleria Nazionale d'Arte Antica** ⑦, housed in the Palazzo Barberini, stands about halfway down the hill. The grandest of 17th-century Rome's stately palaces, it was decorated with illusionist frescoes by Pietro da Cortona. Downhill from the palace (turn right when you leave) you'll come upon **Piazza Barberini** ⑧, a handy starting point for exploring the 19th-century Ludovisi district and Via Veneto. On the east corner of Via Vittorio Veneto, the tree-lined, uphill avenue at the north end of the piazza, is the **Fontana delle Api** ⑨, attributed in part to Bernini. Walk uphill into the sedate lower reaches of Via Veneto. At the church of **Santa Maria della Concezione** ⑩, thousands of bones of monks are artistically but grimly arranged in the crypt. The broad avenue curves up the hill past travel agencies and hotels, with a sidewalk café or two where the only clients seem to be tired tourists and bank employees. At the intersection with Via Bissolati, the pace picks up. The big white palace on the right is **Palazzo Margherita** ⑪, built in 1890 as the residence of Italy's Queen Margherita. It's now the U.S. Embassy; security is inconspicuous but tight, and you couldn't get inside if you wanted to.

Turn right and follow Via Bissolati to the end and cross Largo Santa Susanna to the intersection with Via Venti Settembre. On Piazza San Bernardo, the Baroque church of **Santa Susanna** ⑫ is Rome's American Catholic church. On the northeast corner of Via Venti Settembre, the **Fontanone dell' Acqua Felice** ⑬ features smugly spouting lions. On the northwest corner, the church of **Santa Maria della Vittoria** ⑭ harbors Bernini's surprisingly earthy interpretation of a mystical vision. At this point you can elect to make a detour by bus or taxi to the early Christian churches of Sant'Agnese and Santa Costanza, 3.2 km (2 mi) northeast of here, beyond the old city walls. You can either walk—head straight up Via Venti Settembre, past **Porta Pia** ⑮—or take the bus: Bus 60 stops on the southwest side of Largo Santa Susanna. As you walk or ride northeast along Via Nomentana, you pass through some of Rome's older residential suburbs and **Villa Torlonia** ⑯, a public park, on the right; inside the park, in the Casa delle Civette, is art nouveau stained glass. Bus 60 stops on Via Nomentana near the church of **Sant'Agnese** ⑰; the church's entrance is on Via di Sant'Agnese, and you walk uphill on the grounds to the church of **Santa Costanza** ⑱.

Return to Piazza della Rebubblica (Bus 60 stops near the church of Santa Maria della Vittoria) by way of Via Vittorio Emanuele Orlando, passing the historic Grand Hotel and the **Aula Ottagonale** ⑲, on the corner of Via Parigi. In **Piazza della Repubblica** ⑳, two neoclassical exedrae (hemicycles) stand more or less over similar, ancient exedrae that were part of the Baths of Diocletian. A simple cross high on stark brick walls identifies the church of **Santa Maria degli Angeli** ㉑, once the great hall of the Roman baths. You can see how parts of the ancient bath complex were adapted to serve as a monastery as you visit the halls and cloister of the **Terme di Diocleziano** ㉒, a section of the Museo Nazionale Romano. Off the southeast end of Piazza della Repubblica, Via delle Terme di Diocleziano leads to **Palazzo Massimo alle Terme** ㉓, where you can see more of the antiquities that make up the Museo Nazionale Romano's collections.

TIMING

This is a long walk, involving some major museums and a lengthy detour to the church of Sant'Agnese. If the length of your stay in Rome permits, break it up into two shorter walks, and make the detour to Sant'Agnese a separate walk, also. The walk from Piazza del Quirinale to Piazza della Repubblica, not counting the detour to Sant'Agnese, takes about 90 minutes, plus 10 to 15 minutes for every church visited, and at least 90 minutes each for visits to the Galleria Nazionale d'Arte Antica in Palazzo Barberini and the section of the Museo Nazionale Romano in Palazzo Massimo alle Terme. The detour to Sant'Agnese by bus takes about two hours.

Sights to See

⑲ Aula Ottagonale (Octagonal Hall). Once part of the Baths of Diocletian, this octagonal hall had a twin on what is now the middle of Viale Einaudi, the street leading toward Termini station. The hall, part of the Museo Nazionale Romano, harbors some very large and beautiful ancient Roman bronze sculptures. ⊠ *Via Romita (Piazza della Repubblica),* ☎ *06/487–0690.* ⊒ *Free.* ☉ *Daily 9–7.*

⑨ Fontana delle Api (Fountain of the Bees). The upper shell and the inscription are from a fountain that Bernini designed for Urban VIII; the rest was lost when the fountain had to be moved to make way for a new street. This inscription was the cause of a considerable scandal when the fountain was first put up in 1644. It stated that the fountain had been erected in the 22nd year of the pontiff's reign, while in fact the 21st anniversary of Urban's election to the papacy was still some weeks away. The last numeral was hurriedly erased, but to no avail— Urban died eight days before the beginning of his 22nd year as pope. The superstitious Romans, who had immediately recognized the inscription as an almost foolhardy tempting of fate, were vindicated. ⊠ *Via Vittorio Veneto at Piazza Barberini.*

NEED A BREAK?

Along Via degli Avignonesi and Via Rasella (both narrow streets off Via delle Quattro Fontane, opposite Palazzo Barberini) there are some good, moderately priced trattorias. One of the most popular with Romans is **Gioia Mia** (⊠ Via degli Avignonesi 34, closed Wed.).

---

⑬ Fontanone dell'Acqua Felice (Fountain of Acqua Felice). Though its name could be translated as "The Big Fountain of the Happy Water," like something from *Hiawatha,* it was really named for ancient Rome's Acqua Felice aqueduct. When Pope Sixtus V completed the restoration of the aqueduct toward the end of the 16th century, Domenico Fontana was commissioned to design the commemorative fountain. As the story goes, a sculptor named Prospero da Brescia had the unhappy task of executing the central figure, which was to represent Moses (Sixtus liked to think of himself as, like Moses, having provided water for his thirsting population). The comparison with Michelangelo's magnificent *Moses* in the church of San Pietro in Vincoli was inevitable, and the largely disparaging criticism of Prospero's work is said to have driven him to his grave. Perhaps the most charming aspect of the fountain are the smug little lions spewing water in the foreground. ⊠ *Piazza San Bernardo.*

⑦ Galleria Nazionale d'Arte Antica (National Gallery of Art of Antiquity). The city's finest collection of paintings from the 13th to the 18th century is installed in Palazzo Barberini. Both Bernini and Borromini worked on this massive building, but the overall plan of Rome's most splendid 17th-century palace was produced by Carlo Maderno. Pope Urban VIII had acquired the property and given it to a nephew who was determined to build an edifice worthy of his generous uncle and the ever-more-powerful Barberini clan. You'll get an idea of the grandeur of the place as you visit the Gallery. The vast collections, formerly split between Palazzo Barberini and Palazzo Corsini, across the Tiber, are

88

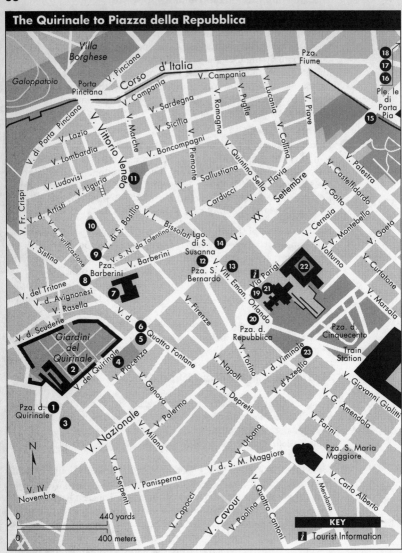

being united in refurbished quarters in Palazzo Barberini that will probably open before the end of 1999.

Entering the palace, you climb a broad marble staircase designed by Bernini. On the main floor (keep your ticket handy as you'll have to show it again upstairs) you'll find several magnificent paintings, including Raphael's *Fornarina*, a luminous portrait of one of the handsome artist's ladyloves, identified by later legend as a baker's daughter. A dramatic Caravaggio depicts a lovely young Judith regarding with some horror the neatly severed head of Holofernes. There's a Holbein portrait of Henry VIII in the finery he donned for his wedding with Anne of Cleves in 1540, and two small but striking El Grecos. The palace's large main salon is part of the gallery. It was decorated in the 1630s by Pietro da Cortona and is a spectacular and surprisingly early example of the Baroque practice of glorifying patrons by depicting them on the ceiling as part of the heavenly host. In this case, Pope Urban VIII appears as the agent of Divine Providence. Also prominent in this glowing vault are some huge Barberini bees, the heraldic symbol of the family. Upstairs you'll find an array of 17th- and 18th-century paintings, including some pretty little views of Rome by Vanvitelli, and four handsome Canalettos. Don't miss the stunning suite of rooms redecorated in 1728 for the marriage of a Barberini heiress to a scion of the Colonna family. ⊠ *Via delle Quattro Fontane 13,* ☎ *06/481–4591.* ▣ *8,000 lire.* ◷ *Mon.–Sat. 9–2, Sun. 9–1 (hrs may be extended in 1999).*

❻ Quattro Fontane (Four Fountains). The intersection takes its name from the four Baroque fountains—representing the Tiber (on the San Carlo corner), the Nile, Juno, and Diana—that constant heavy traffic fumes have managed to deface to the point of making them unrecognizable. Despite the traffic, take in the views from this point in all four directions: behind you, to the southwest as far as the obelisk in Piazza del Quirinale; to the northeast along Via Venti Settembre to the Porta Pia; to the northwest across Piazza Barberini to the obelisk of Trinità dei Monti; and to the southeast as far as the obelisk and apse of Santa Maria Maggiore. This extraordinary prospect is a highlight of Pope Sixtus V's campaign of urban beautification. ⊠ *Junction of Via delle Quattro Fontane, Via Quirinale, Via XX Settembre.*

❷ Palazzo del Quirinale (Quirinal Palace). Now official residence of the president of Italy, it is located atop the Quirinal Hill. The palace was begun in 1574 by Pope Gregory XIII, who planned to use it as a summer residence, choosing the site mainly for the superb view. However, as early as 1592 Pope Clement VIII decided to make the palace the permanent home of the papacy, at a safe elevation above the malarial miasmas shrouding the low-lying Vatican. It remained the official papal residence until 1870, in the process undergoing a series of enlargements and alterations by a succession of architects. When Italian troops under Garibaldi stormed the city in 1870, making it the capital of the newly united Italy, the popes moved back to the Vatican and the Quirinal became the official residence of the kings of Italy.

The palace isn't open to the public, but you get a fair idea of its splendor from the size of the building, especially the interminable flank of the palace on Via del Quirinale. Behind this wall are the palace gardens, which, like the gardens of Villa d'Este in Tivoli, were laid out by Cardinal Ippolito d'Este when he summered here. At 4 PM daily you can see the changing of the military guard, and occasionally you can glimpse the president's guards, the *corazzieri*. All extra-tall, they are a stirring sight in their magnificent crimson and blue uniforms, their knee-high boots glistening, and their embossed steel helmets adorned with flowing manes. ⊠ *Piazza del Quirinale.*

⓫ **Palazzo Margherita.** Built in 1890 as the residence of Italy's Queen Margherita, the white building is now the U.S. Embassy. American citizens on routine business (and that includes losing your passport) are directed to the big reddish consulate building next door. Embassy and consulate are part of a carefully guarded complex that includes U.S. Information Service offices and the American Library. ⊠ *Via Veneto 119,* ☎ *06/46741.*

㉓ **Palazzo Massimo alle Terme (Museo Nazionale Romano)** (Roman National Museum in Palazzo Massimo alle Terme). The enormous collections of the Roman National Museum—which range from stunning classical Roman sculptures and paintings to marble bric-à-brac and fragments picked up in excavations over the centuries—have been organized in four sections (Palazzo Massimo alle Terme, Palazzo Altemps, Aula Ottagona, and Terme di Diocleziano). Palazzo Massimo alle Terme holds the archaeological collection and the coin collection, as well as decorative stuccos and wall paintings found in the area of the Villa della Farnesina (in Trastevere) and the frescoes from Empress Livia's villa at Prima Porta, delightful depictions of a garden in bloom and an orchard alive with birds. Their colors are remarkably well preserved. These delicate decorations covered the walls of cool, sunken rooms in Livia's summer house outside the city. ⊠ *Piazza dei Cinquecento 68,* ☎ *06/489–03500.* ▣ *12,000 lire (ticket valid for Terme di Diocleziano).* ☉ *Tues.–Sun.* 9 AM–10 PM.

❸ **Palazzo Pallavicini Rospigliosi.** A patrician palace built for Cardinal Scipione Borghese, it is now the residence of another of Rome's aristocratic families. In the large garden enclosed by the wings of the palace, a summer pavilion has a famous ceiling fresco of Aurora painted by 17th-century artist Guido Reni. Once a month, when the family admits visitors to see the fresco, you can get a peek at the garden. ⊠ *Via XXIV Maggio 43,* ☎ *06/474–4019.* ▣ *Free.* ☉ *First day of month, 10–noon and 3–5.*

❽ **Piazza Barberini.** One of Rome's more modern quarters, the district was built during the late-19th-century construction boom on the site of the lush gardens of Villa Ludovisi, a patrician family's estate that had in turn been built over the celebrated ancient Roman gardens of Sallust. The piazza, a picturesque marketplace in the 17th and 18th centuries, has lost its original charm in the rush of progress. Undistinguished modern buildings overshadow the older ones, and traffic circles the Bernini **Fontana del Tritone** (Triton Fountain). Bernini's Baroque centerpiece in Piazza Barberini was created in 1637 for Pope Urban VIII, whose Barberini coat of arms is at the base of the large shell. The fountain's triton blows into his conch shell with gusto, sending an arc of water into the air. In a city of beautiful fountains, this is one of the most vivacious. ⊠ *Junction of Via del Tritone, Via Veneto, Via Quattro Fontane, Via Sistina.*

⓴ **Piazza della Repubblica.** This broad square was laid out in the late 1800s, and some suggested that the monument to Victor Emmanuel II be built here rather than in Piazza Venezia. The piazza owes its curved lines to the structures of the Baths of Diocletian; the curving, colonnaded neoclassic buildings on the southwest side trace the underlying form of the ancient baths. The exuberant **Fontana delle Naiadi** (Fountain of the Naiads), the pièce de résistance of Piazza della Repubblica, is draped with voluptuous bronze ladies wrestling happily with marine monsters. The nudes weren't there when the pope unveiled the fountain in 1870, sparing him any embarrassment. But when the figures were added in 1901 they caused a titillating scandal, for it's said that the sculptor, Rutelli, modeled them on the ample figures of two musical comedy stars

In case you want to see the world.

At American Express, we're here to make your journey a smooth one. So we have over 1,700 travel service locations in over 120 countries ready to help. What else would you expect from the world's largest travel agency?

do more.

Travel

In case you want to be welcomed there.

We're here to see that you're always welcomed at establishments everywhere. That's why millions of people carry the American Express® Card – for peace of mind, confidence, and security, around the world or just around the corner.

do more ®

Cards

In case you're running low.

We're here to help with more than 118,000 Express Cash locations around the world. In order to enroll, just call American Express before you start your vacation.

do more

Express Cash

And just in case.

We're here with American Express® Travelers Cheques and Cheques *for Two*.® They're the safest way to carry money on your vacation and the surest way to get a refund, practically anywhere, anytime.

Another way we help you...

do more®

Travelers Cheques

of the day. ⊠ *Junction of Via Nazionale, Via Vittorio Emanuele Orlando, Via delle Terme di Diocleziano.*

❶ Piazza del Quirinale. In this square, the **Fontana di Montecavallo** (Fountain of Montecavallo), or Fontana dei Dioscuri (Fountain of the Dioscuri), is composed of a huge Roman statuary group and an obelisk from the tomb of the emperor Augustus. The group of the Dioscuri trying to tame two massive marble steeds was found in the Baths of Constantine, which occupied part of the summit of the Quirinal Hill. Unlike just about every other ancient statue in Rome, this group survived the Dark Ages intact and accordingly became one of the great sights of Rome, especially during the Middle Ages. Next to the figures, the ancient obelisk from the Mausoleo di Augusto (Mausoleum of Augustus) was put here by Pope Pius VI at the end of the 18th century. In the 7th century BC this was the home of the Sabines, deadly enemies of the Romans, who lived on the Capitoline and Palatine Hills (all of half a mile away). Three sides of the piazza are surrounded by palaces, among them the **Palazzo del Quirinale** (☞ *above*). The facade of **Palazzo della Consulta,** on the east side of the piazza, is adorned with sculptures and richly decorated windows. This is where Italy's Constitutional Court meets. The open side of the piazza has a vista of rooftops and domes. ⊠ *Junction of Via del Quirinale and Via XXIV Aprile.*

⑮ Porta Pia. Named for Pope Pius IV, this is one of the principal city gates in the Aurelian walls. The emperor Aurelian ordered the walls built in the 3rd century, and they owe their survival for 16 centuries to the fact that the popes had to maintain them in good order to defend the Papal States from invaders. Porta Pia is also Michelangelo's last piece of architecture, completed in 1564. Nearby, a monument marks the breach in the walls created by Italian troops when they stormed into Rome in 1870 to claim the city from the pope for the new Italian state. ⊠ *Northeast end of Via Venti Settembre.*

❺ San Carlo alle Quattro Fontane. San Carlo (or San Carlino, as it is sometimes called because it is so diminutive) is one of Borromini's masterpieces. In a space no larger than the base of one of the piers of St. Peter's, he created a church that is an intricate exercise in geometric perfection, with a coffered dome that seems to float above the curves of the walls. Borromini's work is often bizarre, definitely intellectual, and intensely concerned with pure form. In San Carlo, he invented an original treatment of space that creates an effect of rippling movement, especially evident in the double-S curves of the facade. Characteristically, the interior decoration is subdued, in white stucco with no more than a few touches of gilding, so as not to distract from the form. Don't miss the **cloisters,** a tiny, understated Baroque jewel, with a graceful portico and loggia above echoing the lines of the church. ⊠ *Via del Quirinale 23.*

⑱ Santa Costanza. The main attraction of this little round church are the 4th-century mosaics on the vault of the unusual circular nave. The mosaics are among the oldest in Rome—and are perhaps also the most beautiful, with a grapevine motif, executed on a white ground, that seems more Bacchic than Christian. Unfortunately, what must have been similarly beautiful mosaics on the dome were destroyed in the 16th century to make way for the frescoes you see there now. The church was originally the tomb of Costantia, daughter of the emperor Constantine. Costantia probably built the first church over the tomb of St. Agnes (☞ Sant'Agnese, *below*), and her tomb in turn is one of the most important examples of early Christian architecture in Rome. It was circular, like the great tombs of Augustus and Cecilia Metella. Transformed into a baptistry, it was then consecrated as a church in 1254 and ded-

92

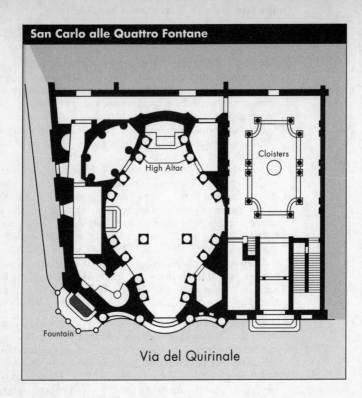

San Carlo alle Quattro Fontane

High Altar

Cloisters

Fountain

Via del Quirinale

icated to Constantia, whose sainthood had been recognized in the meantime. The figures on either side of the entrance probably represent Constantia and her husband. Opposite the entrance is a copy of the original heavy porphyry sarcophagus that is in the Vatican Museums. Its carved decorations are an adaptation of pagan symbols to Christian use, as in the sheep and the peacock, whose flesh was held to be incorruptible. Later mosaics in the niches date from the 6th and 7th centuries. ⊠ *Via di Sant'Agnese.* ▨ *Free (if you have not purchased a ticket to the catacomb, a tip is in order).*

17 Sant'Agnese. One of Rome's most revered early Christian sites, the church is of interest for its antique columns and 7th-century mosaics and as an example of how some of early Rome's churches grew up over catacombs. The body of St. Agnes, who is believed to have been martyred about AD 304 on the site marked by the church of the same name in Piazza Navona, was laid to rest in a Christian cemetery on the city's outskirts. Her cult spread quickly, and it was probably a member of Constantine's family who built a church over her tomb, sometime before AD 349. The entrance to the catacomb is on the left of the present church, built in the 7th century to replace the first. On January 21 each year, two flower-bedecked lambs are blessed before Agnes's altar. They are then carried to the pope, who blesses them again before they're sent to the nuns of St. Cecilia in Trastevere. The nuns use the lambs' wool to make the episcopal *pallia* kept in the casket in the niche of the *confessio* in St. Peter's. The custodian of the catacomb also acts as guide to the church of Santa Costanza (☞ *above*). ⊠ *Via di Sant'Agnese,* ☎ *06/862–05456.* ▨ *Catacomb: 8,000 lire.* ☉ *Mon. 9–noon, Tues.–Sat. 9–noon and 4–6, Sun. 4–6.*

21 Santa Maria degli Angeli. The curving brick facade on the northeast side of Piazza della Repubblica is one small remaining part of the colossal Baths of Diocletian (☞ Terme di Diocleziano, *below*), erected about AD 300 and the largest and most impressive of the baths of ancient Rome. The baths extended over what is now Piazza della Repubblica and covered much of this entire area. In 1561 Michelangelo was commissioned to convert the vast *tepidarium*, the central hall of the baths, into a church. His work was altered by Vanvitelli in the 18th century, but the huge transept, which formed the nave in Michelangelo's plan, has remained as he adapted it. The eight enormous monolithic columns of red granite that support the great beams are the original columns of the tepidarium, 45 feet high and more than five feet in diameter. The great hall is 92 feet high. Though the interior of the church is small in comparison with the vast baths Diocletian built here, it gives a better impression of the remarkable grandeur of ancient Rome's most imposing public buildings than any other edifice in the city. ⊠ *Piazza della Repubblica.*

⑩ Santa Maria della Concezione. This church built for the Capuchin monks in the 1600s holds one of Rome's oddest sights in the crypt below the church proper. Here are skeletons and assorted bones of 4,000 dead monks, artfully arranged in patterns in four chapels. This somewhat goulish practice was common in the 17th century and even later. (In a similar crypt in Palermo, Sicily, the skeletons are dressed in their finest clothes.) Upstairs in the church, the first chapel on the right contains Guido Reni's mid-17th-century *St. Michael Trampling the Devil*. The painting caused great scandal after an acute contemporary observer remarked that the face of the devil bore a surprising resemblance to the Pamphili Pope Innocent X, archenemy of Reni's Barberini patrons. Compare the devil with the bust of the pope that you saw in the Galleria Doria Pamphili and judge for yourself. ⊠ *Via Veneto 27,* ☎ *06/ 462–850.* 🎫 *Donation requested.* ☉ *Daily 9–12 and 3–6.*

⑭ Santa Maria della Vittoria. Like the church of Santa Susanna across Piazza San Bernardo, this church was designed by Carlo Maderno, but it's best known for Bernini's sumptuous Baroque decoration of the **Capella Cornaro** (Cornaro Chapel), on the left as you face the altar, and for his interpretation of heavenly ecstasy in the statue of St. Theresa. In the chapel Bernini produced an extraordinary fusion of architecture, painting, and sculpture, with *The Ecstasy of St. Theresa* as the focal point of the chapel. Your eye is drawn effortlessly from the frescoes on the ceiling down to the marble figures of the angel and the swooning saint, to the earthly figures of the Cornaros (the family that commissioned the chapel) to the two inlays of marble skeletons in the pavement, representing the hope and despair of souls in purgatory. As has been repeatedly pointed out, the out-and-out theatricality of the chapel is allied to a masterly fusion of the elements used by Bernini to make this one of the key examples of the mature Roman high Baroque: The members of the Cornaro family witnessing the scene are placed in what are, in effect, theater boxes, and they are turned to see the great moment of divine love being played out before them as though they were indeed actually at the theater. Notice the way the sculptor has carved the swooning saint's robes as though they are almost on fire, quivering with life. See, too, how the white marble group seems suspended in the heavens as golden rays illuminate the scene. An angel assists at the mystical moment of Theresa's vision as the saint abandons herself to the joys of divine love. In all, Bernini represented this mystical experience in what, to modern eyes, can seem very earthly terms. No matter what your reaction may be, you'll have to admit that it's great theater. ⊠ *Via Venti Settembre (Largo Santa Susanna).*

Sant'Andrea al Quirinale

High Altar

Sacristy →

Via del Quirinale

4 **Sant'Andrea al Quirinale.** This small but oddly imposing Baroque church was designed by Bernini. His son wrote that Bernini considered it one of his best works and that he used to come here occasionally just to sit and enjoy it. Bernini chose a simple oval plan, then gave it drama and movement in the decorations, which carry the story of St. Andrew's martyrdom and ascension into heaven, starting with the painting over the high altar, up past the figure of the saint over the chancel door, to the angels at the base of the lantern and the dove of the Holy Spirit that awaits on high. ⊠ *Via del Quirinale 29. Closed Tues.*

12 **Santa Susanna.** The building's foundations incorporate parts of a Roman house where Susanna was martyred, but the frescoes, carved ceiling, and stucco decorations all date from the late 16th century. Maderno's 1603 facade masterfully heralded the beginning of the Baroque era in Roman architecture. It is Rome's American Catholic church. ⊠ *Via Venti Settembre 14.*

22 **Terme di Diocleziano** (Baths of Diocletian). Though part of the ancient structure is now the church of Santa Maria degli Angeli (☞ *above*), and other parts were transformed into a Carthusian monastery or razed to make room for later urban development, a visit gives you an idea of the scale and grandeur of this ancient bathing establishment. The monastery cloister is strewn with classical serendipity, the lapidary collection of the Museo Nazionale Romano. ⊠ *Viale E. De Nicola 79,* ☎ *06/488–0530.* ⊡ *12,000 lire (valid for admission to Palazzo Massimo alle Terme).* ⊙ *Tues.–Sat. 10–2, Sun. 9–1.*

16 **Villa Torlonia.** Mussolini's residence as prime minister under Italy's king is now a public park. Long neglected, the park's vegetation and edifices are gradually being refurbished. The first of the buildings to be fully restored is now open to the public as a charming example of the art nouveau style of the early 1900s. In a gabled, fairytale-like cottage, the **Museo della Casina delle Civette** (Museum of the House of Owls) displays majolica and stained-glass decorations, including windows with owl motifs. ⊠ *Via Nomentana 70,* ☎ *06/442–50072.* ⊙ *Museum: Tues.–Sun., Apr.–Sept. 9–7, Oct.–Mar. 9–5.*

VILLA BORGHESE TO THE ARA PACIS

For visual excitement, this walk has few parallels in Rome, with Canova's sculpture of Paolina Borghese, the lush pines of Villa Borghese park, artistic masterpieces, and stunning urban vistas. You will be retracing various eras of the city's history as you make your way toward the Tiber. In ancient times, Rome's most lavish host, Lucullus, staged fabulous al fresco banquets in his terraced villa on the heights of the Pincian Hill. On the plain below, called the Campus Martius, by the banks of the Tiber, Augustus laid out a vast public garden, celebrating his own glory in his mausoleum and the Ara Pacis, and setting up an Egyptian obelisk that served as pointer in a huge sundial. Villa Borghese itself, the 17th-century pleasure gardens created by Cardinal Scipione Borghese, holds several treasures, none so precious as the Galleria Borghese, one of the finest and most beautiful museums in the city. On the other side of the park are Villa Giulia, a late-Renaissance papal summerhouse now containing a stunning collection of Etruscan art, and the Museo Nazionale d'Arte Moderna, with intriguingly varied collections of modern art in a vast neoclassical palace that has a fashionable terrace café. These are the three major museums in the area, but the past is also palpably preserved in the triangle that has its apex at Piazza del Popolo and extends to the Mausoleum of Augustus and the Spanish Steps. Here 17th-century buildings and churches are interspersed with art and antiques galleries and a plethora of boutiques. Together with the Via Condotti shopping area, this constitutes Rome's most abundant shopping district.

Numbers in the text and margin correspond to points of interest on the Villa Borghese to the Ara Pacis map.

A Good Walk

Start on Via Veneto if you want to begin with a cappuccino in one of this famous street's famous cafés. Via Veneto snakes upward from Piazza Barberini to the Porta Pinciana through the Ludovisi neighborhood, known for palatial hotels and stately residences that transformed patrician estates into commercial real estate in the 1880s. In the upper reaches of Via Veneto, near the flower vendors and big newsstands at the corner of Via Ludovisi is the Café de Paris, erstwhile hub of La Dolce Vita.

Past the big cafés, Via Veneto continues in a succession of more newsstands, boutiques, expensive shops, and a snack bar or two. If you intend to picnic in the Villa Borghese park (the entrance is at the top of the street), this is your chance to pick up some foodstuffs, whether ready-to-go from the snack bars or do-it-yourself from the *alimentari* stores on the side streets. (There are some mobile food carts in the park and a café in the Galleria Borghese.)

Porta Pinciana ① is one of the historic city gates in the Aurelian walls, built by emperor Aurelianus late in the 3rd century AD to protect Rome. Take care crossing the thoroughfares on either side of the gate: The traffic here comes hurtling in from all directions. Inside **Villa Borghese** ② park, first look to the left, across the Galoppatoio (riding ring). The handsome 16th-century palace that you can see across the lawns is **Villa Medici** ③, since 1804 the seat of the French Academy, where so many of France's great artists, from Ingres and David to Balthus, found inspiration. Head north on Viale del Museo Borghese to reach the Casino Borghese, which houses the **Galleria Borghese** ④. Once you've torn yourself away from Cardinal Scipione's collections, you can enjoy the vast park to your heart's content. On the right, as you leave the casino, you can continue along Viale dell'Uccelliera to the Rome zoo, currently being renovated and transformed into a "biopark." Alternatively, turn left, or south, onto Viale dei Pupazzi and head toward Piazza dei Cavalli Marini, with its sea-horse fountain. Continue straight ahead on Viale dei Pupazzi or turn right: Either way you'll come upon the **Piazza di Siena** ⑤, a grassy hippodrome shaded by tall pines. At the northwest end of Piazza di Siena, turn left onto Viale Canonica and you'll come to the entrance of the delightful Giardino del Lago.

If you want to take in one or both of the other museums on this walk, head northwest from the Giardino del Lago to Piazzale Paolina Borghese, at the head of a broad, monumental staircase that descends to Viale della Belle Arti and the **Galleria Nazionale d'Arte Moderna** ⑥. About ⅛ mile northwest on Viale delle Belle Arti is the **Museo Etrusco di Villa Giulia** ⑦. The entrance is at the far end of the building, on Piazza di Villa Giulia. Returning to the staircase, climb it to enter Villa Borghese again. Follow Via Bernadotte to Piazza del Fiocco and turn left onto Viale La Guardia.

At circular Piazza delle Canestre head west on Viale delle Magnolie. A bridge over heavily trafficked Viale del Muro Torto leads to the **Pincio** ⑧ gardens. After studying its layout from the Pincio terrace, which offers one of Rome's finest panoramas, descend the ramps and stairs to **Piazza del Popolo** ⑨ and **Porta del Popolo** ⑩. Stop in at the church of **Santa Maria del Popolo** ⑪ to see the art treasures inside. The churches of **Santa Maria in Montesanto** ⑫ and **Santa Maria dei Miracoli** ⑬ were part of a grand project carried out in the 1500s under several popes that urbanized this triangular area, previously uninhabited. Take Via di Ripetta, the most westerly of the three streets fanning out from Piazza del Popolo. On the left you pass the San Giacomo Hospital, and on the right is the horseshoe-shape, neoclassical building of the Academy of Fine Arts, usually covered with not-so-fine-art graffiti by student factions. The **Ara Pacis** ⑭ and the **Mausoleo di Augusto** ⑮ are on huge Piazza Augusto Imperatore, renovated and redesigned by American architect Richard Meier.

TIMING

This is a fair-weather walk, much of it in Villa Borghese park. The walk alone takes about two hours, plus at least 90 minutes for a visit to the Galleria Borghese. Advance reservations are mandatory for your visit to the Galleria. In addition to the Galleria Borghese, the walk includes two other major museums. If you intend to do justice to all three, it is advisable to skip the two on Viale delle Belle Arti during this walk, saving them for another day (or days). Both the Museo Nazionale Etrusco di Villa Giulia and the Galleria Nazionale di Arte Moderna are easily accessible from Via Flaminia. They are about 1 km (0.6 mi) from Piazza del Popolo. The 19 tram stops in front of both museums, and the 225 tram that runs along Via Flaminia stops at Piazza delle Belle Arti, about 350m (⅕ mile) from Villa Giulia's entrance. A visit to the Museo Nazionale Etrusco di Villa Giulia takes at least 90 minutes; for the Galleria Nazionale di Arte Moderna, allow at least an hour.

Sights to See

⑭ **Ara Pacis** (Altar of Augustan Peace). A simple classical altar, the Ara Pacis is noteworthy for the beautifully sculptured marble enclosure that surrounds it. The altar was erected in 13 BC by order of the Senate to celebrate the epoch of peace heralded by Augustus's victories in Gaul

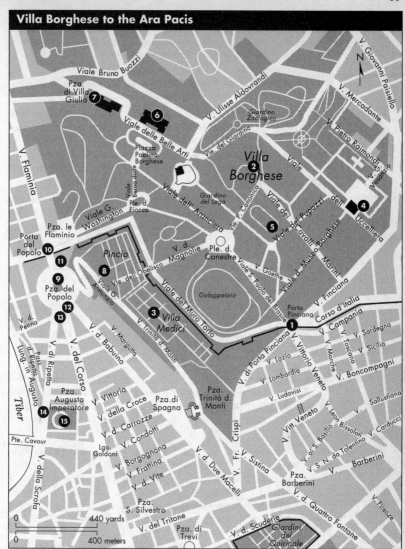

Villa Borghese to the Ara Pacis

and Spain. It was painstakingly reassembled and reconstructed here in 1938 after scholars spent years hunting for the dispersed fragments, some of them as far away as the Louvre. The marble altar enclosure bears magnificent reliefs. Most notable is *Aeneas's Sacrifice,* on the right of the main entrance, and the procession of historical figures, among them members of Augustus's family, on the sides. ⊠ *Via di Ripetta,* ☎ *06/671–0271.* ⊒ *3,750 lire.* ⊙ *Tues.–Sat. 9–5, Sun. 9–1:30.*

❹ **Galleria Borghese** (Borghese Gallery). Probably Rome's most beautiful museum, it is resplendent after extensive restorations. The **Casino Borghese,** as the building is known, was erected (from 1613) partly to house Cardinal Scipione Borghese's rich collections of painting and sculpture, partly as an elegant venue for summer parties and musical evenings. It was never intended to be, nor was it ever, lived in.

Like the gardens, the Casino and its collections have undergone many changes since the 17th century. Camillo Borghese, the husband of Napoléon's sister Pauline, was responsible for most of them. He sold off a substantial number of the paintings to Napoléon and swapped 200 of the classical sculptures for an estate in Piedmont, in northern Italy, also courtesy of Napoléon. These paintings and sculptures are all still in the Louvre in Paris. At the end of the 19th century a later member of the family, Francesco Borghese, replaced some of the gaps in the collections and also transferred to the casino the remaining works of art housed in Palazzo Borghese (☞ Toward the Spanish Steps and the Trevi Fountain, *above*). In 1902 the casino, its contents, and the park were sold to the Italian government.

The Caravaggio Room, to the left of the entrance, holds works by this hot-headed genius who died of malaria at age 37. The disquieting *Sick Bacchus* and charming *Boy with a Basket of Fruit* are naturalistic early works, bright and fresh compared with a dark *Madonna* and the *David and Goliath,* in which Goliath is believed to be a self-portrait of the artist.

The most famous work in the entire collection is Canova's sculpture of Pauline Borghese. It's technically known as *Venus Vincitrix,* but there has never been any doubt as to its real subject. Pauline reclines on a Roman sofa, bare-bosomed, her hips swathed in classical drapery, the very model of haughty detachment and sly come-hither. Surprisingly, Camillo Borghese seems to have been remarkably unconcerned that his wife had posed for this erotic masterpiece. Pauline, on the other hand, is known to have been shocked that her husband took such evident pleasure in showing off the work to guests. This coyness seems all the more curious given the reply Pauline is supposed to have made to a lady who asked her how she could have posed for the sculpture: "Oh, but the studio was heated." But then it was exactly this combination of aristocratic disdain and naïveté that is said to have made her so irresistible in the first place. At all events, and much to the dismay of Canova, following Camillo and Pauline's divorce, the statue was locked away for many years, though the artist was occasionally allowed to show it to a handpicked few. This he would do at night by the light of a single candle.

The next two rooms hold two key early Baroque sculptures: Bernini's *David* and *Apollo and Daphne.* Both illustrate the extraordinary technical facility of Bernini. As important, both also demonstrate the Baroque desire to invest sculpture with a living quality, to transform inert marble into living flesh. Where Renaissance sculptors wanted to capture the idealized beauty of the human form that they had discovered in ancient Greek and Roman sculptures, Baroque sculptors like Bernini wanted to make their work dramatic, too. They wanted movement and they wanted drama. The *Apollo and Daphne* shows the moment when, to escape the pursuing Apollo, Daphne is turned into a laurel tree. Leaves and twigs sprout from her fingertips as she stretches agonizingly away from Apollo, who instinctively recoils in terror and amazement. This is the stuff that makes the Baroque exciting. There are more Berninis to see in the collection, notably a very uncharacteristic work, a large unfinished figure called *Verità*, or Truth. Bernini had started work on this brooding figure after the death of his principal patron, Pope Urban VIII. His successor as pope, Innocent X, had little love for the ebullient Urban, and, as was the way in Rome, this meant that Bernini, too, was excluded from the new pope's favors. Bernini's towering genius was such, however, as to gain him the patronage of the new pope with almost indecent haste. The *Verità* was accordingly left incomplete.

In the Pinacoteca (Picture Gallery) on the first floor of the Casino, three Raphaels, a Botticelli, and a Pinturicchio are only a few of the paintings that the cardinal chose for his collection, which includes an incisive Cranach *Venus* and a shadowy Del Sarto *Madonna*. Probably the most famous painting in the gallery is Titian's allegorical *Sacred and Profane Love*, with a nude figure representing sacred love. ⊠ *Piazza Scipione Borghese 5,* ☎ *06/854–8577.* ⌨ *12,000 lire. Reservations required; book at least one week in advance by calling 06/328–101 or 06/842–4160.* ⊙ *Tues.–Sat. 9–10, Sun. 9–8.*

⑥ Galleria Nazionale d'Arte Moderna (National Gallery of Modern Art). This massive white beaux arts building looks anything but modern, yet it contains one of Italy's leading collections of 19th- and 20th-century works. A recent addition is an outstanding Dadaist collection. ⊠ *Via delle Belle Arti 131,* ☎ *06/322–981.* ⌨ *8,000 lire.* ⊙ *Tues.–Sat. 9–10, Sun. 9–8.*

NEED A
BREAK?

The **Caffè delle Arti** (⊠ Via Gramsci 73), attached to the Galleria d'Arte Moderna, has a pretty terrace and is a favorite all-day rendezvous for Romans and visitors to Villa Borghese park and its museums. This is the place to break up your walk with a gelato or lunch.

---

⑮ Mausoleo di Augusto (Mausoleum of Augustus). The mausoleum built by Augustus for himself and his family has had a checkered history. Like the emperor Hadrian's tomb across the Tiber, it was transformed into a fortress during the Middle Ages. There were further metamorphoses, however. At various times it was plundered for building material, planted with a vineyard, used as a hanging garden, and employed as an arena for such rousing public spectacles as bullfights and fireworks displays. In the early 1900s the large crypt at its core served as a concert hall (and was acclaimed for its perfect acoustics). The mausoleum was restored to its original form in 1936. Its Etruscan inspiration is evident, and it is quite similar to the marble-girded tumulus tombs at Cerveteri (☞ Chapter 8, Side Trips). Inside, a series of concentric corridors leads to the central crypt, where the funerary urns were kept. ⊠ *Piazza Augusto Imperatore.*

⑦ Museo Etrusco di Villa Giulia (Etruscan Museum of Villa Giulia). Even if you know nothing of the Etruscans, an ancient people who preceded the Romans and taught them a thing or two about refined living, visit this 16th-century villa to see just how gracious the Renaissance lifestyle could be. The world's outstanding collection of Etruscan art and artifacts is housed in Villa Giulia, built around 1551 for Pope Julius III (hence its name). Among the team called in to plan and construct the villa were Michelangelo and his fellow Florentine, Vasari. Most of the actual work, however, was done by Vignola and Ammanati. Though large enough to put up a sizable party of guests, the villa was never intended to be lived in, at least not by the pope. He came here for a day's distraction from the cares and intrigues of the Vatican, sailing up the Tiber on a boat. The villa's nymphaeum—or sunken sculpture garden— is a superb example of a refined late-Renaissance setting for princely pleasures. The building was set in a park planted with some 36,000 trees.

Today, the Villa Giulia houses one of the world's most important collections of Etruscan art. Be warned that though it's well arranged and displayed, it's overwhelming in size. Most of the exhibits come from sites in Etruria, the area north of Rome between the Tiber and the Arno that was once the Etruscan heartland. However, you'll also see fascinating objects from other parts of central Italy that were dominated by the Etruscans before the rise of Rome.

No one knows precisely where the Etruscans originated. Many scholars maintain that they came from Asia Minor, appearing in Italy about 1000 BC. Like the Egyptians, they buried their dead with everything that might be needed in the afterlife and painted their tombs with happy scenes of everyday activities. Thus, in death they have provided the present day with precious information about their life. There are countless artistic treasures in the Villa Giulia, and you'll find that even the tiniest gold earrings and brooches and the humblest bronze household implements display marvelous workmanship and joyful inventiveness. The most striking works are the terra-cotta statues. Some, like the *Apollo of Veio,* still retain traces of their original multicolored decoration; others, like the serenely beautiful *Sarcophagus of the Sposi,* are worn to a warm, glowing golden patina. There are rooms full of vases (most of them Greek); the Etruscans prided themselves on their refined taste for these handsome objects. In the garden in back of the museum building, a reconstruction of an Etruscan temple shows how this people used color in architecture, a model that was also followed in ancient Rome. ⊠ *Piazza di Villa Giulia 9,* ☎ *06/320–1951.* ▨ *8,000 lire.* ☉ *Wed. 9– 7:30, Tues. and Thurs.–Sat. 9–2, Sun. 9–1.*

❾ Piazza del Popolo. Decorative and immense, this square, with its obelisk and twin churches, is a Rome landmark. It owes its present appearance to architect Giuseppe Valadier, who designed it about 1820, also laying out the terraced approach to the Pincio and the Pincio's gardens (☞ *below*). It marks what was for centuries the northern entrance to the city, where all roads from the north converge and where visitors, many of them pilgrims, would get their first impression of the Eternal City. The desire to make this entrance to Rome something special had been a pet project of popes and their architects over three centuries. The piazza takes its name from the 15th-century church of ☞ **Santa Maria del Popolo,** huddled on the right side of the ☞ **Porta del Popolo,** or city gate. In the late 17th century, the twin churches of ☞ **Santa Maria in Montesanto** (on the left as you face them) and ☞ **Santa Maria del Miracoli** (on the right) were added to the piazza at the point where Via del Babuino, Via del Corso, and Via di Ripetta converge. The piazza has always served as something of a society meeting place, crowded with fashionable carriages and carnival revelers in the past, today a magnet for youngsters on flashy motorcycles and their blasé elders at café tables. At election time, it's the scene of huge political rallies, and on New Year's Eve Rome stages a mammoth al fresco party in the piazza. ⊠ *Junction of Via del Babuino, Via del Corso, Via di Ripetta.*

. . . .

NEED A
BREAK?

A café that has never gone out of style, **Rosati** (⊠ Piazza del Popolo 4) is a rendezvous of literati, artists, and actors. There's a sidewalk café, a tearoom, and an upstairs dining room for a more upscale lunch. Off Piazza del Popolo, on Via di Ripetta you'll find places where you can stop for sustenance. **Cose Fritte** (fried things; ✉ Via di Ripetta 3), specializes in rice croquettes, batter-fried vegetables, and other tasty snacks to take out. **PizzaRé** (✉ Via di Ripetta 14) offers a wide choice of toppings for pizza cooked in wood-burning ovens. **Buccone** (✉ Via di Ripetta 19) is a wine shop serving light snacks at lunch time and wine by the glass all day long.

⑤ Piazza di Siena. The piazza, actually an 18th-century replica of an ancient Roman amphitheater, was built for the Borghese family's games and named after the Tuscan city where the family originated. ✉ *Viale Canonica, Via dei Pupazzi.*

⑧ Pincio (Pincian hill and gardens). The view from the Pincio terrace is one of Rome's most celebrated, and the gardens are a favorite spot for strolling and enjoying occasional entertainment: Band concerts are held here on Sunday mornings at intervals during the year. The Pincio gardens occupy a corner of the Pincian Hill, one of the seven hills of ancient Rome, and they are separated from the southwest corner of Villa Borghese by a stretch of ancient walls. The gardens are laid out in the rather formal style of the early 19th century on the site of what must have been the far more elaborate terraced gardens of Lucullus, the Roman gourmand, whose banquets were legendary. Pathways are lined with white marble busts of Italian heroes. Along with the similar busts on the Janiculum Hill, these pose a constant problem. Since the busts first went up, a preferred sport of young Roman vandals has been a game that might be called "knock-nose," that is, knock the nose off the statue. Depending on the date of the last nose-knocking wave, you'll see the Pincio's busts forlornly noseless or in the throes of obvious plastic surgery.

From the balustraded Pincio terrace you can look down at Piazza del Popolo and beyond, surveying much of Rome. Across the Tiber, Via Cola di Rienzo cuts across the Prati district toward the heights of Monte Mario. That low, brownish building on top of the hill is the Rome Hilton. Off to the left are Castel Sant'Angelo and the dome of St. Peter's. In the foreground is the curve of the Tiber, embracing Old Rome, where the dark dome of the Pantheon emerges from a sea of russet-tiled rooftops and graceful cupolas. Southeast of the Pincio terrace is the **Casina Valadier,** a pretty neoclassic building that is owned by the city and functions as a café and restaurant on concession but is open only spottily. It is due for renovation and reopening before the year 2000. ✉ *Piazzale Napoleone I, Viale dell'Obelisco.*

⑩ Porta del Popolo (City Gate). The medieval gate in the Aurelian walls was replaced in 1561 by the present one, which was further embellished by Bernini in 1655 for the much-heralded arrival of Queen Christina of Sweden, who had abdicated her throne to become a Roman Catholic. ✉ *Piazza del Popolo, Piazzale Flaminio.*

❶ Porta Pinciana. Framed by two squat, circular towers, the gate was constructed in the 6th century. Here you can see just how well the Aurelian walls have been preserved and imagine hordes of Visigoths trying to break through them. Sturdy as the walls look, they couldn't keep out the Barbarians, and Rome was sacked three times in the 5th century alone. ✉ *Piazzale Basile, Via Veneto, Corso d'Italia.*

⑬ Santa Maria dei Miracoli. A twin to the church of Santa Maria in Montesanto (☞ *below*), the church was built in the 1670s by Carlo Fontana as an elegant frame for the entrance to Via del Corso from Piazza del Popolo. ✉ *Piazza del Popolo.*

⓫ Santa Maria del Popolo. Standing inconspicuously in a corner of the vast piazza, the church goes almost unnoticed, but it holds some treasures. Bramante enlarged the apse of the church, which had been rebuilt in the 15th century on the site of a much older place of worship. About 1513, the banker Agostino Chigi commissioned Raphael to build a chapel, known as the **Chigi Chapel** (the second on the left) after the donor, and in the mid-17th century another Chigi, Pope Alexander VII, commissioned Bernini to restore and decorate the building. Inside, in the first chapel on the right, you'll see some frescoes by Pinturicchio; the adjacent **Cybo Chapel** is a 17th-century exercise in marble decoration. The organ case of Bernini in the right transept bears the Della Rovere oak tree, part of the Chigi family's coat of arms. The **choir,** with vault frescoes by Pinturicchio, contains the handsome tombs of Ascanio Sforza and Girolamo delle Rovere, both designed by Andrea Sansovino. The **Cerasi Chapel,** to the left of the high altar on the side walls, has two stunning Caravaggios, both key early Baroque works. Compare their earthy realism and harshly dramatic lighting effects with the much more restrained and classically "pure" *Assumption of the Virgin* by Caravaggio's contemporary and rival, Annibale Carracci; it hangs over the altar of the chapel. Raphael provided the cartoons for the vault mosaic and the designs for the statues of Jonah and Elijah. More than a century later, Bernini added the oval medallions on the tombs and the statues of Daniel and Habakkuk. ⊠ *Piazza del Popolo.*

⓬ Santa Maria in Montesanto. Bernini supervised the construction of this church by his brilliant assistant, Carlo Fontana, and he may even have designed the saints' statues topping the facade. ⊠ *Piazza del Popolo.*

❷ Villa Borghese. The word *villa* means suburban estate, of the type developed by the ancient Romans and adopted by Renaissance nobles. Villa Borghese is in fact a park that was originally part of the pleasure gardens laid out in the early 17th century by Cardinal Scipione Borghese, a worldly and cultivated cleric and nephew of Pope Paul V. Today's gardens bear little resemblance to the originals. Not only do they cover a much smaller area—by 1630, the perimeter wall was almost three miles long—but they have also been almost entirely remodeled. This occurred at the end of the 18th century, when a Scottish painter, Jacob More, was employed to transform them into the style of the "cunningly natural" park so popular in 18th-century England. Hitherto, the park was probably the finest example of an Italian-style garden in the entire country. In contrast to the formal and rigidly symmetrical gardens of 17th-century France—that at Versailles is the best example—these Italian gardens had no overall symmetrical plan. Rather, they consisted of a series of small, interlinked formal gardens attached by paths and divided by meticulously trimmed hedges. Flowers—the Romans were particularly fond of tulips—statues, ponds, and small enclosures for animals (the more exotic the better; lions and peacocks were favorites) were scattered artfully around. Here, the cardinal and his friends strolled and discussed poetry, music, painting, and philosophy. Today the area immediately in front of the Casino (☞ Galleria Borghese, *above*) and the sunken open-air "dining room," a small stone pavilion close to the low wall along the Via di Porta Pinciana side of the park, are all that remain from the cardinal's original gorgeous park. Now the gardens are studded with neoclassical temples and statuary added to suit early 19th-century tastes. In addition to the gloriously restored Galleria Borghese museum, the highlights of the park are Piazza di Siena, a graceful amphitheater; the botanical garden on Via Canonica, where there is a pretty little lake, a neoclassical Temple of Aesculapius, a café under the trees, and the new **Giardino Zoologico,** (Zoo), currently being transformed into a biopark. The park has bike and skate rental concèssions and a children's movie theater (showing films for their elders in the evening). ✉ *Main entrances at Porta Pinciana, the Pincio, Piazzale Flaminio (Piazza del Popolo), Viale delle Belle Arti, and Via Mercadante.*

❸ Villa Medici. Purchased by Napoléon and today the home of the French Academy, the Villa Medici, otherwise closed to the public, stages prestigious art exhibits and music festivals. Check with the tourist office to see if anything is being scheduled during your stay or if the gardens are open to the public. ✉ *Viale Trinità dei Monti.*

TOWARD TRASTEVERE

The two separate communities of this route are both staunchly resisting the tides of change. The old ghetto, on the banks of the Tiber, is a neighborhood that has proudly retained its Jewish heritage. Right up to the end of the 19th century, this really was a ghetto, its dark buildings clinging to the sides of ancient ruins for support. Next to it is Tiberina Island, and beyond, Trastevere itself. Despite creeping gentrification, Trastevere remains about the most tightly knit community in Rome, its inhabitants proudly proclaiming descent—whether real or imagined—from the ancient Romans. As far back as the Middle Ages, Trastevere had a large foreign colony. Before they moved to the ghetto on the other side of the river, the Eastern Jews who came to Rome also settled here. Raphael's model and mistress, the dark-eyed Fornarina (literally, "the baker's daughter"), is believed to have been a Trasteverina. The artist reportedly took time off from painting the Vatican *Stanze* and the *Galatea* in Villa Farnesina to enjoy her favors.

Literally translated, Trastevere means "across the Tiber"; the Trasteverini have always been proud and combative, a breed apart. In the Middle Ages, Trastevere wasn't even considered part of Rome, and the "foreigners" who populated its maze of alleys and piazzas fought bitterly to obtain recognition for the neighborhood as a *rione,* or official district of the city. In the 14th century the Trasteverini won out and became full-fledged Romans. Since then they have stoutly maintained their separate identity, though in recent years popular tradition has been distorted into false folklore for the benefit of the tourists in the most-frequented locales. The real Trasteverini are still here, however, hearty and uninhibited, greatly annoyed at the reputation their quarter has justifiably acquired for purse-snatching and petty thievery and for its creeping gentrification. Countless boutiques, cafés, pizzerias, music clubs, and discos draw lively crowds, especially on weekend nights. For Romans and foreigners alike, Piazza Santa Maria is the meeting place of Trastevere, a sort of outdoor living room, open to all comers. The Janiculum Hill affords an overview of the neighborhood below and a marvelous vista of the entire city and the Castelli Romani.

Numbers in the text and margin correspond to points of interest on the Trastevere and the Janiculum map.

A Good Walk

To enjoy this walk and avoid worry about Trastevere's reputation for purse-snatching, don't carry a bag. Carry what you need in your pockets and if you have a camera, expensive or not, use it inconspicuously. Piazza Venezia (☞ Old Rome, *above*) is the starting point for touring the ancient Ghetto quarter of the city. From the piazza below the Campidoglio, take Via del Teatro Marcello and turn northwest, or right, onto Via Montanara and enter Piazza Campitelli, with its Baroque church and fountain. Take Via dei Funari at the northwest end of the piazza and follow it into Piazza Mattei, where one of Rome's loveliest fountains, the 16th-century **Fontana delle Tartarughe** ① is tucked away. A few steps down Via Caetani, off the north side of Piazza Mattei, you'll find a doorway into the public part of the old Palazzo Mattei, worth a peek for its sculpture-rich courtyard and staircase.

From Piazza Mattei go south on Via della Reginella into Via Portico d'Ottavia, heart of the Jewish ghetto. On the buildings, medieval inscriptions, ancient friezes, and half-buried classical columns attest to the venerable history of this neighborhood, a lively commercial quarter of old palaces and good restaurants. Here, warm weather brings family life out onto the streets: Tables and ill-assorted chairs appear in the piazzas toward evening, while steaming casseroles are carried down from cramped kitchens and the young and old of the clan prepare to enjoy an al fresco supper and a card game of *briscola* with the neighbors.

After **Sant'Angelo in Pescheria** ②, set within the remaining columns of the Portico d'Ottavia, you come to the **Teatro di Marcello** ③ on the left side of Via Portico d'Ottavia and the **Sinagoga** ④ on the right. Cross Ponte Fabricio, built in 62 BC and the oldest bridge in the city, onto the **Isola Tiberina** ⑤; then cross Ponte Cestio and head into Trastevere.

Begin your exploration of Trastevere at **Piazza in Piscinula** ⑥ (you will need a good street map to make your way around this intricate maze of winding side streets). Explore the little streets and piazzas around the Piazza. This was the site of Trastevere's port, Ripa Grande, the largest in Rome until it was destroyed early in the 20th century to make way for the modern embankments. Via del Porto gives you a fine view of the Aventine Hill across the Tiber. Piazza dei Mercanti is especially noted for its colorful, if touristy, restaurants.

Take Via dell'Arco dei Tolomei, one of the city's most picturesque byways, and cross Via dei Salumi, where the sausage-makers stored their goods, into tiny Vicolo dell'Atleta. It was in this minuscule alley, in 1849, that excavators discovered the statue *Apoxyomenos* (the athlete holding a *strigil,* or scraper) that is now in the Vatican Museum. Turn left onto Via dei Genovesi, then right into the piazza in front of the church of **Santa Cecilia in Trastevere** ⑦. Behind Santa Cecilia in Trastevere, on Via Anicia, the **Chiostro San Giovanni dei Genovesi** ⑧ is open on Tuesday and Thursday afternoons. Several blocks down Via Anicia at **San Francesco a Ripa** ⑨ is a famous Bernini sculpture. Go west on Via San Francesco a Ripa to Viale Trastevere. Take a detour east on Viale Trastevere to see the 13th-century mosaic pavements in the church of **San Crisogono** ⑩ on Piazza Sonnino. On the adjacent Piazza Belli the medieval Torre degli Anguillara (Tower of the Anguillara) is a typical fortified residence dating from the Middle Ages. Piazza Belli, by the way, is dedicated to the top-hatted 19th-century dialect poet whose bronze effigy watches over the square.

Follow Via San Francesco a Ripa or Via della Lungaretta west to the very heart of the rione, or district, of Trastevere. Piazza San Cosimato is the neighborhood's busy outdoor marketplace on weekday mornings, but **Piazza Santa Maria in Trastevere** ⑪ is the place where the neighborhood is at its best, embellished with the glowing mosaics on the church of **Santa Maria in Trastevere** ⑫ and with an octagonal fountain, as well as inviting sidewalk cafés.

Via Fonte dell'Olio, on the north side of the piazza, leads to Piazza dei Renzi. Bear right into Via della Pelliccia or Vicolo dei Renzi to Via del Moro and then proceed to Piazza Trilussa. Ponte Sisto links this part of Trastevere with ☞ **Old Rome,** across the Tiber. The bridge was built in the 15th century by Pope Sixtus IV to expedite commercial traffic in view of the upcoming Holy Year of 1475. On the north side of Piazza Trilussa stands a monument to the racy dialect poet Trilussa, beloved of Trasteverini. A neighborhood bag lady or two and occasional homeless brethren have elected him their protector. They doze in the little garden surrounding the statue and wash in the fountain. Both Via Benedetta and Via S. Dorotea lead north to Porta Settimiana. At the end of Via Corsini, off Via della Lungara, is the **Orto Botanico** ⑬. Walk north on Via della Lungara to visit **Villa Farnesina** ⑭, on the right, and, opposite, the section of the Galleria Nazionale d'Arte Antica that is housed in **Palazzo Corsini** ⑮ until it can be moved to Palazzo Barberini. Return to Porta Settimiana, and turn right into Via Garibaldi, which climbs to the Janiculum. Continue up Via Garibaldi to the church of **San Pietro in Montorio** ⑯ to see Bramante's architectural gem, the Tempietto. Be aware that stairs provide shortcuts up and down the Janiculum from various points in Trastevere; they save a lot of walking, but some are too seedy to be used by solitary walkers. As you continue your ascent of the Janiculum, you come upon the huge **Fontana dell'Acqua Paola** ⑰, an early 17th-century creation with a vast pool that can be tempting on a hot day. The fountain is near the entrance to the park at the summit of the **Gianicolo** (Janiculum) ⑱. Take in the views and then, if you're tired or pressed for time, ride the 870 bus north toward Corso Vittorio Emanuele, across the Tiber. You will pass a curious lighthouse, a gift of the Argentines in recognition of Garibaldi's efforts on behalf of their independence.

TIMING

This walk could take from four to five hours, but it is easily broken up into two parts—the Ghetto and Isola Tiberina, and Trastevere and the Janiculum—the first taking about two hours, and the second almost three hours, allowing time for detours into Trastevere's interesting shops and eating places. If you time your visit to Santa Cecilia in Trastevere for Tuesday or Thursday morning between 10 and noon, you can see a famous fresco. If it is not a clear day, end your walk at San Pietro in Montorio; the vistas are the rewards for the effort of making your way to the top of the Janiculum, so save this part of the walk for a day when visibility is good.

Sights to See

❽ **Chiostro San Giovanni dei Genovesi.** You have to ring for the custodian, who'll show you the 15th-century cloister of San Giovanni dei Genovesi, emanating the serene architectural harmony usually found in Florence and rarely in Rome. In fact, it is attributed to Florentine architect Bacio Pontelli. ⊠ *Via Anicia 12.* ▧ *Donation.* ☉ *Tues. and Thurs., May–Sept. 3–6, Oct.–Apr. 2–4.*

⑰ **Fontana dell'Acqua Paola** (Fountain of the Acqua Paola). With a facade inspired by ancient Rome's triumphal arches and worthy of an important church, this 17th-century fountain was commissioned by Pope Paul V to celebrate his renovation of Trajan's 1st-century AD aqueduct. This fountain has a namesake in the large but less imposing fountain that is the centerpiece in Piazza Trilussa, which was moved across the river from Via Giulia in 1898 when the Tiber's embankments were constructed. It, too, was built by Paul V. ⊠ *Via Garibaldi.*

❶ **Fontana delle Tartarughe**(Fountain of the Turtles). The 16th-century fountain is one of Rome's most charming, designed by Giacomo della Porta in 1581 and sculpted by Taddeo Landini. The focus of the fountain are four bronze boys, each grasping a dolphin that spouts water into marble shells. Bronze tortoises held in the boys' hands drink from the upper basin. The tortoises are the fountain's most brilliant feature, a 17th-century addition by, inevitably, Bernini. ⊠ *Piazza Mattei.*

Trastevere and the Janiculum

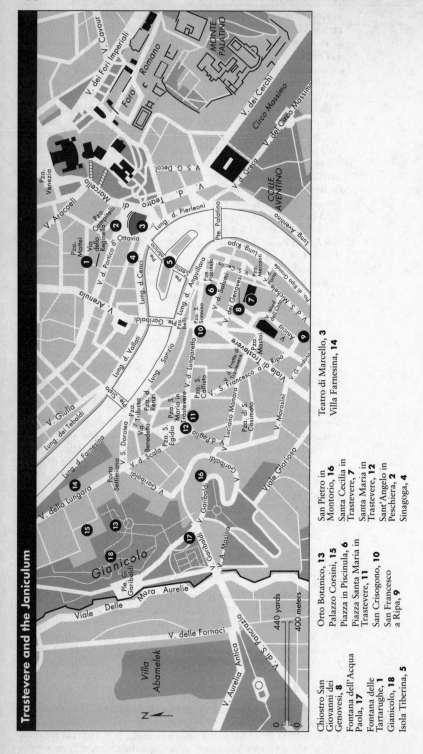

Chiostro San
Giovanni dei
Genovesi, **8**
Fontana dell'Acqua
Paola, **17**
Fontana delle
Tartarughe, **1**
Gianicolo, **18**
Isola Tiberina, **5**

Orto Botanico, **13**
Palazzo Corsini, **15**
Piazza in Piscinula, **6**
Piazza Santa Maria in
Trastevere, **11**
San Crisogono, **10**
San Francesco
a Ripa, **9**

San Pietro in
Montorio, **16**
Santa Cecilia in
Trastevere, **7**
Santa Maria in
Trastevere, **12**
Sant'Angelo in
Peschiera, **2**
Sinagoga, **4**

Teatro di Marcello, **3**
Villa Farnesina, **14**

⑱ Gianicolo (Janiculum). One of the seven hills of ancient Rome, the Janiculum is famous for splendid views of the city, a noontime cannon, Punch-and-Judy shows, statues of Giuseppe and Anita Garibaldi (Garibaldi was the guiding spirit behind the unification of Italy in the 19th century; Anita was his long-suffering wife), and, like the Pincio, noseless and bedaubed busts. ✉ *Via Garibaldi, Passeggiata del Gianicolo.*

❺ Isola Tiberina (Tiberina Island, or Island in the Tiber). On the little island in the Tiber River is the hospital of **Fatebenefratelli** (literally, "Do good, brothers"); though a city hospital, it belongs to the Franciscan Order. It continues a tradition that began in 291 BC when a temple to Aesculapius, with annexed infirmary, was erected here. Aesculapius—Asclepius to the Greeks—was the ancient god of healing and the son of the god Apollo. His symbol was the snake. The Romans adopted him as their god of healing in 293 BC during a terrible plague. A ship was sent to Epidaurus in Greece—heart of the cult of Aesculapius and a sort of Greek Lourdes—to obtain a statue of the god. As the ship sailed back up the Tiber, a great serpent was seen escaping from it and swimming to the island. This was taken as a sign that a temple to Aesculapius should be built there. Here the sick would come to bathe in the island's spring waters and to sleep in the temple, hoping that Aesculapius would visit them in their dreams to cure them. There's no trace of the temple now, but the island has been associated with medicine ever since—the present hospital was built on the site of a medieval hospital.

On the other end of the island is the church of **San Bartolomeo**, built at the end of the 10th century by the Holy Roman Emperor Otto III. Restorations and rebuilding down through the years have left precious little of Otto's original church. It's thought, however, that the little well-head on the chancel steps—the steps leading to the choir—is original, and that it stands on the site of the spring in the temple.

Seasonally, when the Tiber is in flood, the level of the river rises to within a few meters of the level of the piazza, and the island is half-submerged. If the waters are low, descend the steps from the piazza and explore the embankment, where Romans like to stroll on fair days and take the sun while listening to the rushing waters of the rapids. The Romans built a wall around the entire island and sheathed it with marble to make the island look like a ship, with the prow pointed downstream. Look for the few remnants of the travertine facing, with a figure of Aesculapius, on the downstream end opposite the left bank. ✉ *Ponte Fabricio, Lungotevere dei Pierleoni to Via Ponte Quattro Capi; Ponte Cestio, Lungotevere degli Anguillara to Piazza San Bartolomeo all'Isola.*

⑬ Orto Botanico (Botanical Garden). Behind ☞ **Palazzo Corsini** is an attractive oasis of greenery that was once part of the palace's extensive grounds. The garden is known for an impressive collection of orchids, ferns, and cacti. It seems odd, on the edge of Trastevere, to find faithful replicas of Californian and Mexican desert environments. ✉ *Largo Cristina di Svezia, end of Via Corsini,* ☎ *06/686–4193.* 🎟 *6,000 lire.* ◷ *Greenhouses Mon.–Sat. 9–12:30; garden May.–Sept., daily 9–6:30, Oct.–Apr. 9–5:30.*

⑮ Palazzo Corsini. A refined example of Baroque style, the palace currently houses the 17th- and 18th-century sections of the collection of the Galleria Nazionale d'Arte Antica until they can be moved to refurbished sections of Palazzo Barberini. Among the most famous paintings in this large, dark, and dull collection is Guido Reni's *Beatrice Cenci*. Stop in, if only to climb the 17th-century stone staircase, itself a drama of architectural shadows and sculptural voids. ✉ *Via della Lungara 10,* ☎ *06/688–02323.* 🎟 *8,000 lire.* ◷ *Tues.–Sat. 9–7, Sun. 9–1.*

⑥ Piazza in Piscinula. The square takes its name (*piscina* meaning *pool*) from some ancient Roman baths on the site. The tiny Church of **San Benedetto** on the piazza is the smallest church in the city and, despite its 18th-century facade, is much older that it looks, probably dating back to the 4th century AD. Opposite is the medieval **Casa dei Mattei** (Mattei House). Rich and powerful, the Mattei family lived here until the 16th century, when, after a series of murders on the premises, they decided to move out of the district entirely, crossing the river to build their magnificent palace in the ghetto. ⊠ *Via della Lungaretta, Piazza della Gensola, Via in Piscinula, Via Lungarina.*

⑪ Piazza Santa Maria in Trastevere. This piazza has seen the comings and goings of innumerable generations of tourists and travelers, intellectuals and artists, who come to lounge on the steps of the fountain or sip an espresso at a table in the sun. This is where neighborhood children kick a soccer ball around when school is out. Here the paths of the Trastevere's residents intersect repeatedly during the day; here they pause, gathering in clusters to talk animatedly in the broad accent of Rome or in a score of foreign languages. ⊠ *Via dela Lungaretta, Via della Paglia, Via San Cosimato.*

⑩ San Crisogono. Eagles and dragons, symbols of the Borghese family, crown the portico of this pretty church, an early Christian basilica that was done over in the Middle Ages and again in the 17th century. The medieval bell tower can best be seen from the little piazza flanking the church or from the other side of Viale Trastevere. Inside the church are a fine mosaic pavement by the medieval craftsmen of the Cosmati family and an imposing coffered wood ceiling. You can ask the custodian to show you the excavations of the early Christian church beneath the present one. San Crisogono is the religious focus of a lively festival honoring Trastevere's patron, the Madonna of Noantri, with a procession on July 15. ⊠ *Piazza Sonnino.*

....

NEED A
BREAK?

As its name suggests, the **Casa del Tramezzino** (House of Sandwiches; ⊠ Viale Trastevere 81) specializes in the earl of Sandwich's invention, offering a tantalizing variety over the counter.

....

⑨ San Francesco a Ripa. A Baroque church attached to a 13th-century Franciscan monastery, it is noted for one of Bernini's last works, a dramatically lighted statue of Blessed Ludovica Albertoni. ⊠ *Piazza San Francesco a Ripa.*

⑯ San Pietro in Montorio. The church was built by order of Ferdinand and Isabella of Spain in 1481 over the spot where, tradition says, St. Peter was crucified. A handsome and dignified edifice, the church contains a number of well-known works, including the *Flagellation* in the first chapel on the right, painted by the Venetian Sebastiano del Piombo from a design by Michelangelo, and the *St. Francis in Ecstasy,* in the next-to-last chapel on the left, in which Bernini made one of his earliest experiments with concealed lighting effects.

However, perhaps the most famous work here is the circular **Tempietto** (the Little Temple) in the monastery cloister next door. This sober little building—though tiny, holding only 10 people, it is actually a church in its own right—is one of the key Renaissance buildings in Rome. It was designed by Bramante, the original architect of the new St. Peter's, in 1502 and represents one of the earliest and most successful attempts to reproduce an entirely classical building; it is one in which the lessons of ancient Greek and Roman architecture are fully evident. The basic design was derived from a circular temple on the grounds of the Emperor Hadrian's great villa at Tivoli outside Rome. ⊠ *Piazza*

San Pietro in Montorio (Via Garibaldi); entrance to cloister and Tempietto at portal next to church. ☒ *Free.* ⊘ *9–12:30, 2–6 daily.*

❼ Santa Cecilia in Trastevere. This church commemorates one of ancient Rome's most celebrated early Christian martyrs, the aristocratic St. Cecilia, done to death by the emperor Diocletian around the year AD 300. After an abortive attempt to suffocate her in the baths of her own house (a favorite means of quietly disposing of aristocrats in Roman days), she was brought before the executioner. But not even three blows of the executioner's sword could dispatch the young girl. She lingered for several days, converting others to the Christian cause, before finally dying. A striking white marble statue of the saint languishing in martyrdom lies below the main altar. If you've timed your visit to the church for Tuesday or Thursday morning, between 10 and noon, you can enter the cloistered convent to see what remains of Pietro Cavallini's powerful and rich fresco *Last Judgment.* It is the only major fresco in existence known to have been painted by Cavallini, a forerunner of Giotto. The fresco dates from 1293. ☒ *Piazza Santa Cecilia in Trastevere.*

⓬ Santa Maria in Trastevere. Dazzling mosaics and a long history are the draws of this church. It is supposedly the first church in Rome to have been dedicated to the Virgin Mary. Originally built sometime before the 4th century, it certainly is one of the oldest churches in the city. The church was rebuilt in the 12th century, and the portico, which was added in the 19th century, seems to focus attention on the 800-year-old mosaics on the facade. The piazza is enhanced by their glow, especially at night, when the front of the church and its bell tower are illuminated. Additional mosaics of the 12th and 13th century light up the interior. In the representation of the *Life of the Virgin,* note the little building labeled "Taberna Meritoria" just under the figure of the Virgin in the Nativity scene, with a stream of oil flowing from it. It recalls the legend that on the day Christ was born, a stream of pure oil flowed from the earth on the site of the piazza, signifying the coming of the grace of God. Off the north side of the piazza, there's a little street called Via delle Fonte dell'Olio in honor of this miracle. ☒ *Piazza Santa Maria in Trastevere.*

❷ Sant'Angelo in Pescheria. The church was built right into the ruins of the Portico d'Ottavia, whose few surviving columns now frame it. The huge porticoed enclosure, named by Augustus in honor of his sister Octavia, was 119 meters wide and 132 meters long. It encompassed two temples, a meeting hall, and a library and served as a kind of grandiose entrance foyer for the adjacent ☞ **Teatro di Marcello.** The ruins of the portico became Rome's fish market in the Middle Ages. A stone plaque on a pillar, a relic of that time, admonishes in Latin that the head of any fish surpassing the length of the plaque was to be cut off "up to the first fin" and given to the city fathers or else the vendor was to pay a fine of 10 gold florins. The heads were used to make fish soup and were considered a great delicacy. ☒ *Via Portico d'Ottavia.*

| NEED A BREAK? | Stop in at bakery **Dolceroma** (☒ Via Portico d'Ottavia 20/b) and indulge in American and Austrian baked treats. |

❹ Sinagoga (Synagogue). The big, bronze-roofed synagogue is the city's largest temple and a Roman landmark. It contains a museum of precious ritual objects and other exhibits documenting the history of Rome's Jewish community. Until the 13th century the Jews were esteemed citizens of Rome. Among them were the bankers and physicians to the popes, who had themselves given permission for the construction of synagogues. But later popes of the Renaissance and

Counter-Reformation revoked this tolerance, confining the Jews to the ghetto and imposing a series of restrictions, some of which were enforced as late as 1870. The main synagogue was built in 1904; earlier, five smaller synagogues for communities of different national origin had existed on nearby Piazza delle Cinque Schole. ⊠ *Lungotevere Cenci,* ☎ *06/686–4648.* ☞ *8,000 lire.* ⊙ *Mon.–Thurs. 9:30–1 and 2–4:30, Fri. 9:30–1:30, Sun. 9:30–12:30.*

❸ **Teatro di Marcello** (Theater of Marcellus). Hardly recognizable as a theater today, it was originally a huge place, designed to hold 20,000 spectators. The theater was begun by Julius Caesar and completed by the emperor Augustus in AD 13. Like other Roman monuments, it was transformed into a fortress in the Middle Ages. Later, during the Renaissance, it was converted into a residence by the Savelli, one of the city's noble families. The archaeological zone of the theater is often used as an open-air concert venue. ⊠ *Via del Teatro di Marcello.*

⓮ **Villa Farnesina.** Money was no object to extravagant host Agostino Chigi, a banker from Siena who financed many a papal project. His munificence is evident in this elegant villa, built for him about 1511. He was especially proud of the delicate fresco decorations in the airy loggias, now glassed in to protect their artistic treasures. When Raphael could steal a little time from his work on the Vatican Stanze, he came over to execute some of the frescoes himself, notably a luminous *Galatea.* In his villa, host Agostino entertained the popes and princes of 16th-century Rome. He delighted in impressing his guests at al fresco suppers held in riverside pavilions by having his servants clear the table, casting the precious silver and gold dinnerware into the Tiber. His extravagance was not quite so boundless as he wished to make it appear, however: He had nets unfurled a foot or two under the water's surface to catch the valuable ware as it was flung into the river.

In the **Loggia of Psyche** on the ground floor, Giulio Romano and others worked from Raphael's designs. Raphael's lovely *Galatea* is in the adjacent room. On the floor above you can see the trompe l'oeil effects in the aptly named **Hall of Perspectives** by Peruzzi. Agostino Chigi's bedroom, next door, was frescoed by Il Sodoma with scenes from the life of Alexander the Great, notably the *Wedding of Alexander and Roxanne,* which is considered to be the artist's best work. The palace also houses the **Gabinetto Nazionale delle Stampe,** a treasure house of old prints and drawings. When the Tiber embankments were built in 1879, the remains of a classical villa were discovered under the Farnesina gardens, and their decorations are now in the Museo Nazionale Romano's collections in Palazzo Massimo alle Terme (☞ The Quirinale to Piazza della Repubblica, *above*). ⊠ *Via della Lungara 230,* ☎ *06/654–0565.* ☞ *6,000 lire.* ⊙ *Mon.–Sat. 9–1.*

THE AVENTINE TO ST. PAUL'S

The Aventine Hill, one of the seven hills on which the city was founded, basks in a serenity hard to find elsewhere in Rome. It is one of the city's quietest and greenest neighborhoods, an island on which ancient churches and gardens rise above streams of heavy traffic and the mundane goings-on in the Trastevere and Testaccio neighborhoods below. The approach from the Circus Maximus is worthy of the Aventine's august atmosphere. On the Aventine are a number of Rome's oldest and least-visited churches as well as one of the city's most surprising delights: the keyhole in the gate to the garden of the Knights of Malta. Beyond lies Testaccio, for traditional and inexpensive Roman food and an animated after-hours scene, and the Piramide di Caio Cestio, one of Rome's most distinctive and idiosyncratic landmarks: It's a tomb, built by an ancient Roman with more than half an eye on posterity. Not far away is one of the greatest pilgrimage churches in Italy, the medieval basilica of San Paolo fuori le Mura (St. Paul's outside the Walls).

Numbers in the text and margin correspond to points of interest on the Aventine to St. Paul's map.

A Good Walk

Start your walk at the southern end of Via del Teatro Marcello at the little church of **San Nicola in Carcere** ①. Follow Via Petroselli south, passing the Casa dei Crescenzi (Crescenzi House), on your right. This is one of only a handful of medieval houses in Rome to have survived almost intact. The inscription on its facade announces that the house was built by Nicolò di Crescenzio, and that in building it he wished— and you must at least admire his ambition—to re-create the glory of ancient Rome. To this end he incorporated various classical fragments in the facade. Far more important are the two small temples in front of you on Piazza Bocca della Verità. They are about 2,000 years old and remarkably well preserved for their age. The rectangular **Tempio della Fortuna Virilis** ② and the circular **Tempio di Vesta** ③ (also known as the Temple of Hercules), were both built about 100 BC. **Piazza della Bocca della Verità** ④ was the site of ancient Rome's cattle market. Cross the piazza to visit the church of **Santa Maria in Cosmedin** ⑤, like a Greek church inside, and famous for the Bocca della Verità (Mouth of Truth). Next, you head up the Aventine Hill. Take care crossing broad Via Greca—where cars pick up speed—and walk along the street, turning into the first street on the right, Clivo dei Publici. This skirts Valle Murcia, the city's rose garden; it's glorious in May and June. Where Clivo dei Publici veers off to the left, continue straight ahead on Via di Santa Sabina. You can see the church of Santa Sabina ahead, but just before you reach it, you can take a turn around the delightful walled park, Parco Savello, known for its orange trees and wonderful view of the Tiber and St. Peter's. Three of the Aventine's main attractions are lined up, one after another, on the right side of Via di Santa Sabina: the churches of **Santa Sabina** ⑥ and **Sant'Alessio** ⑦, and the famous keyhole on **Piazza Cavalieri di Malta** ⑧, the Square of the Knights of Malta. Via di Sant'Anselmo winds through the district's quiet residential streets. Cross busy Viale Aventino at Piazza Albania and climb the so-called Piccolo Aventino (Little Aventine) on Via di San Saba to the church of **San Saba** ⑨.

To explore the Testaccio neighborhood, return to Viale Aventino and head west, cutting across the park to Via Marmorata. The neighborhood has plain early 1900s housing, a down-to-earth working-class atmosphere, plenty of good trattorie where you can find traditional Roman food—and, of course, Monte Testaccio, a grassy knoll about 150 feet high. What makes this otherwise unremarkable-looking hill special is the fact that it's made from pottery shards—pieces of amphorae, large jars used in ancient times to transport oil, wheat, wine, and other goods. What began as a dump for the broken earthenware jars seemed in time to have taken on a life of its own, until by the Middle Ages the hill, growing even larger, had become a place of pilgrimage. Now clusters of converted warehouses around its base set the latest trends in Roman nightlife. Make your way to Piazza Testaccio, the marketplace, and prettier Piazza di Santa Maria Liberatrice. There are some quintessential Roman trattorie along Via Marmorata and near the Mattatoio, the former slaughterhouse.

Both Viale Aventino and Via Marmorata converge at **Porta San Paolo** ⑩, one of the ancient city gates in the 3rd-century AD Aurelian walls. You can't miss the big white **Piramide di Caio Cestio** ⑪. Behind it is the

Cimitero Acattolico/Cimitero Protestante ⑫. To reach the Church of **San Paolo fuori le Mura** ⑬, literally, St. Paul's outside the Walls, take a taxi or Metro line B (it's the second stop in the Laurentina direction) or bus 23. For most of 1999, the cream of the Capitoline Museums' collection of antiquities can be seen in **Centrale Montemartini** ⑭, a former power plant.

TIMING

The walk takes about 3½ hours, allowing 10 to 15 minutes for each church, and 30 minutes for the visit to San Paolo fuori le Mura. Additional time would be required for visiting the Cimitero Acattolico and the exhibition of ancient sculpture in the Centrale Montemartini on Via Ostiense.

Sights to See

⑭ **Centrale Montemartini.** Known officially as the Art Center ACEA, the former Montemartini power plant is the exhibition venue at least until 1999 of classical sculptures from the collections of the Capitoline Museums, currently undergoing restoration. Stunningly displayed, the sculptures are juxtaposed with the plant's massive machinery in an interesting confrontation between classical and industrial archaeology. ⊠ *Viale Ostiense 106,* ☎ *06/699–1191.* 🎫 *12,000 lire.* ☉ *Tues.-Fri. 10–6, Sat.–Sun. 10–7.*

⑫ **Cimitero Acattolico/Cimitero Protestante** (Non-Catholic Cemetery/ Protestant Cemetery). In a city whose great and not-so-great personages have taken such pride in their tombs over the centuries, the historic cemetery in the shadow of the Piramide is a tranquil understatement; the older sections are much like a country churchyard. The romantic melancholy of tall cypresses and ancient ruins among the headstones make it a fitting resting place for poets John Keats and Percy Shelley. The oldest tombstones date from 1738. ⊠ *Via Caio Cestio 6,* ☎ *06/ 574–1900.* 🎫 *Donation.* ☉ *Tues.–Sun. 9–6.*

❽ **Piazza Cavalieri di Malta.** This is the site of the keyhole with a view of the distant dome of St. Peter's. It is on the west side of the square, in the portal of the walled compound of the Knights of Malta. The Knights of Malta are members of the world's oldest and most exclusive order of chivalry, founded in the Holy Land in 1080. Though nominally tenders of the sick in those early days, a role that has since become the order's raison d'être, the knights amassed huge tracts of land in the Middle East and established themselves as a fearsome mercenary force. From 1530 they were based on the Mediterranean island of Malta, having been expelled from another Mediterranean stronghold, Rhodes, by the Turks in 1522. In 1798 Napoléon expelled them from Malta, and in 1834 they established themselves in Rome, with headquarters in Via Condotti. The compound here is the headquarters of the Italian branch of the order. The square itself, and the church and gardens inside the compound, were designed around 1765 by Piranesi, 18th-century Rome's foremost engraver (and not a bad architect, either). ⊠ *Via Santa Sabina, Via Porta Lavernale.*

❹ **Piazza della Bocca della Verità** (The Square of the Mouth of Truth). Originally the site of the Forum Boarium, ancient Rome's cattle market, it was later used for public executions. ⊠ *Via L. Petroselli, Via del Cherci, Lungotevere Aventino.*

⑪ **Piramide di Caio Cestio** (Pyramid of Gaius Cestius). The towering pyramid, reaching 120 feet into the sky, is a monumental tomb. Gaius, an immensely wealthy praetor, or magistrate, in Imperial Rome, had the tomb built for himself in 12 BC. Though he was an otherwise unremarkable figure, his desire for something approaching immortality

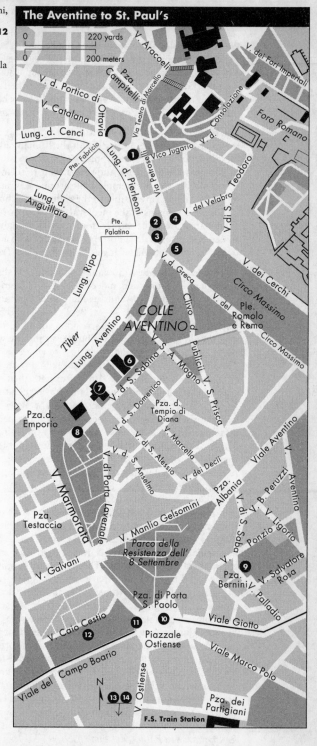

found concrete expression in this megalomaniac structure. ⊠ *Piazzale Ostiense.*

⑩ Porta San Paolo. This gate marked the beginning of the Via Ostiense, the city's vital overland link with the port city of Ostia Antica. Porta San Paolo, one of some 13 gates in the Aurelian walls, defended Rome's vital market area, including the Emporium—the riverside docks and warehouses through which supplies brought in by barge were funneled into the city. ⊠ *Viale Piramide Cestia, Via Marmorata, Via Ostiense.*

❶ San Nicola in Carcere. The interior of the church is unexceptional, but the exterior illustrates to perfection the Roman habit of building and rebuilding ancient sites, incorporating parts of existing buildings in new buildings, adding to them, and then adding to them again. The church stands on the site of a temple built around 250 BC, and some of the temple's columns are visible to the right of the church as you face it, beside what remains of the medieval campanile, or bell tower. The facade, dating from the mid-16th century, is thought to have been designed by Giacomo della Porta, the architect who completed the dome of St. Peter's after Michelangelo's death. ⊠ *Via Teatro di Marcello.*

⑬ San Paolo fuori le Mura (St. Paul's Outside the Walls). For all the dreariness of its location—and, indeed, for all of its exterior's dullness (19th-century British writer Augustus Hare said the church looked like "a very ugly railway station")—St. Paul's is one of the most historic and important churches in Rome, second in size only to St. Peter's. This is as it should be: As St. Peter's is built over the site where St. Peter was buried, so St. Paul's is built over the site where St. Paul was interred. The building has had a distinctly checkered past. It was built by the emperor Constantine in the 4th century AD, then rebuilt and considerably enlarged about a century later. It was then the largest church in Europe, larger by far than Constantine's St. Peter's. The church's location outside the city walls meant that it was especially vulnerable to attack, and indeed it was sacked by the rampaging Saracens in 846. The then pope, John VIII, took the precaution of fortifying it. Nevertheless, over the next 200 years, the church gradually declined in importance, especially once the marshes surrounding it became infected with malarial mosquitoes. Sheep wandered around the basilica, undisturbed by the few remaining monks, themselves largely sunk in a stupor of drunkenness and lethargy. This sorry state of affairs came to a sudden end in the middle of the 11th century with the arrival of a new abbot, Hildebrandt. He restored the building, recruited new monks, and made St. Paul's a revered center of pilgrimage once more. And such it remained until July 1823. Then, in a catastrophic fire, the church burned to the ground. All that remained, apart from a few mosaics, the sculptured ciborium (tabernacle) and other decorations, were the cloisters. Although the rebuilt St. Paul's has a sort of monumental grandeur, its columns stretching up the dusky nave, its 19th-century mosaics glinting dully, it's only in the cloisters that you get a real sense of what must have been the magnificence of the original building. The little columns supporting the arcades of the cloisters are remarkable for their variety and richness. Some are slim and straight, others corkscrew violently; some are carved in creamy marble, others are encrusted with mosaics. Look for the little animals carved in the spaces between the columns. The entrance to the cloisters is from the right transept, the "arm" of the church to your right as you face the altar. ⊠ *Piazzale San Paolo (Via Ostiense).*

❺ Santa Maria in Cosmedin. Though this is one of Rome's oldest churches, with an interesting, almost exotic interior, it plays second fiddle to the renowned artifact installed in the church portico. The **Bocca della Verità** (Mouth of Truth) attracts droves of tourists who line up to have their photos snapped with their hands in the grim marble mouth in the face of a river god—actually an ancient drain cover found, half-buried, during the Middle Ages. The legend that was quickly attached to it warns that anyone suspected of lying can be put to the test by having the person put a hand into the mouth. If the person is telling a lie, so the legend goes, the mouth will slam shut, severing the fingers.

The church was built in the 6th century for the city's burgeoning Greek population. Heavily restored at the end of the 19th century, the church has the typical basilica form, but it also has an altar screen, an element characteristic of Eastern churches. ⊠ *Piazza Santa Maria in Cosmedin.*

❾ **San Saba.** A medieval church with an almost rustic interior and Cosmateque mosaic pavement, San Saba harbors a hodgepodge of ancient marble pieces and, on the aisle on the left-hand side of the church, a curious fresco cycle painted by an unknown 13th-century artist. The most famous scene shows three young girls lying naked on a bed. Taken at face value, this apparently lewd scene seems unsuitable for a church; instead, it illustrates the good works of St. Nicholas, the prototype, as it were, for Santa Claus. The girls are the daughters of a highborn but impoverished father; that's him standing on the right of the bed, looking very unhappy. They are naked because the only future for them is prostitution, or so their despairing father thinks. Outside the window, however, is St. Nicholas, about to toss a bag of gold coins into the room to rescue the poor maidens from their lives of shame. ⊠ *Via San Saba.*

❼ **Sant'Alessio.** The church's entrance and Romanesque bell tower are on a medieval courtyard. As a whole, the church is the result of reconstructions and restorations over the centuries. Look for the curious marble sculpture at the head of the left nave. It commemorates St. Alexis, son of a wealthy patrician family of early Christian times. St. Alexis disdained the luxury to which he had been born and endured years of penitence and prayer before returning home so emaciated that no one recognized him. Ever humble and self-effacing, he elected to live anonymously, as a servant in his family's household, sleeping under the stairs for 17 years until his death. ⊠ *Via di Santa Sabina.*

❻ **Santa Sabina.** This early Christian basilica has the severe simplicity that was common to the other churches of its era. Here alterations and later decorations have been peeled away, leaving the essential form as Rome's Christians knew it in the 5th century. Once the church was bright with mosaics and frescoes, now lost. The beautifully carved and preserved wooden doors are the oldest of their kind in existence; they, too, date from the 5th century. ⊠ *Via di Santa Sabina.*

❷ **Tempio della Fortuna Virilis** (Temple of Manly Fortune). This rectangular temple from the 2nd century BC is built in the Greek style, as was the norm in Rome's early years. It owes its fine state of preservation, considering its venerable age, to the fact that is was consecrated and used as a Christian church. ⊠ *Piazza Bocca della Verità.*

❸ **Tempio di Vesta** (Temple of Vesta). All but one of the 20 original Corinthian columns in Rome's most evocative small ruin remain intact. Like the Tempio della Fortuna Virilis (☞ *above*), it was built in the 2nd century BC, considerably earlier than the Roman Forum. ⊠ *Piazza Bocca della Verità.*

THE CELIAN HILL AND
THE BATHS OF CARACALLA

Like the Aventine, the Celio (Celian Hill) seems aloof from the bustle of central Rome. On the slopes of the hill, paths and narrow streets wind through a public park and past walled gardens. Here are some of Rome's earliest churches, most of them with unfamiliar, Latin-sounding names, such as Santa Maria in Domnica, Santo Stefano Rotondo, Santi Quattro Coronati. Close by are the Baths of Caracalla, towering ruins of what must have been a spectacular bathing complex, though it does take some imagination to picture what they must have looked like in their prime. In contrast to the busier and noisier districts of the city, the Celio is pervaded with a quiet charm that encourages you to relax and reflect on some of the elements that make Rome so special: the grandeur of antiquity, the mystic power of religion, and the gentle blessings of nature.

Numbers in the text and margin correspond to points of interest on the Celian Hill and the Baths of Caracalla map.

A Good Walk

Start your walk at the Arco di Costantino (☞ Arco di Costantino and Colosseo *in* Ancient Rome, *above*)—it's right by the Colosseum—and walk south along Via di San Gregorio. To your right, on the slopes of the Palatine Hill, are all that remains of the great aqueduct built by the consul Appius Claudius about 300 BC. Stairs on the left lead to the **Antiquarium Comunale** ①, with archaeological exhibits. At the end of Via di San Gregorio, climb the shallow flight of stairs to visit the church of **San Gregorio Magno** ②. Then head up the hill on the Clivo di Scauro to the ancient church of **Santi Giovanni e Paolo** ③. The square in which it stands has been described as "one of the few spots in Rome that a medieval pilgrim would have little difficulty recognizing" (if there are no cars parked there, that is). Opposite the church, a gate marks one of the entrances to Villa Celimontana, a park still largely unknown to most visitors to the city. The gate is sometimes locked; if so, there's another entrance on Via San Paolo della Croce just around the corner. Keep to the left as you wander through the park to reach the main entrance on Via della Navicella, where there's a whimsical fountain topped with a Renaissance model in marble of an ancient Roman ship, in front of the church of **Santa Maria in Domnica** ④. This little church packs lavish decoration, including some vibrant mosaics, into a small space. Opposite, the round church of **Santo Stefano Rotondo** ⑤ is unusual for its circular plan and beamed ceiling.

Then head north into the large Piazza Celimontana. Passing the entrance to the military hospital, continue straight ahead into Via Celimontana. Turn right onto Via San Giovanni in Laterano, the route of papal processions between the basilicas of San Giovanni in Laterano and St. Peter's. The church of **San Clemente** ⑥ is sandwiched between Via San Giovanni in Laterano and Via Labicana. The ancient church is built on the site of even more ancient Roman buildings. From San Clemente walk uphill on Via Santi Quattro Coronati to the 12th-century church of **Santi Quattro Coronati** ⑦, part of a fortified abbey that provided refuge to early popes and emperors. Next, retrace your steps, returning to Piazza Celimontana. From Via della Navicella, follow Via Druso to huge Piazza Numa Pompilio, a busy crossroads. On the northwest side of Piazza Numa Pompilio, the little church of **Santi Nereo e Achilleo** ⑧ is worth a visit. The tall brick ruins of the **Terme de Caracalla** ⑨ dominate this side of the piazza. The present entrance to the Baths is at the northwest end.

On the south side of Piazza Numa Pompilio, Viale delle Terme di Caracalla leads to Via Cristoforo Colombo, a multi-lane boulevard linking the city and its EUR quarter with the sea at Castelfusano. Via Porta di San Sebastiano is a walled lane that channels fairly heavy city traffic southeast to Porta San Sebastiano and the beginning of the Via Appia Antica. To get an inside view of Porta San Sebastiano, one of the most imposing of the city gates in the Aurelian walls, and stroll along the battlements, make a detour to the **Museo delle Mura** ⑩. Passing cars can make the walk along Via Porta di San Sebastiano less than pleasant, but the sole bus, number 760, operates only on Sundays and holidays and returns toward the center of Rome on Via di Porta Latina; at other times, the alternative is to walk.

TIMING

The walk takes about 2½ hours, allowing for about 10 minutes in each church. Allow an additional 45 minutes for a visit to San Clemente's subterranean levels, and about the same to explore the Baths of Caracalla. Add another hour for a detour to the Museo delle Mura and the walk inside the Aurelian walls.

Sights to See

❶ **Antiquarium Comunale** (Municipal Antiquarium). The collection displays marble fragments and artifacts of daily life in ancient Rome. One exhibit has poignant appeal—an ivory doll, with delicate features and jointed limbs, that was buried with its owner, a young girl of Imperial Rome, and was found in her sarcophagus. ⊠ *Via del Parco del Celio 22,* ☎ *06/700–1569.* ▧ *3,750 lire.* ⊙ *Tues.–Sat. 9–7, Sun. 9–2.*

❿ **Museo delle Mura** (Museum of the Walls). The museum is housed in the twin towers of Porta San Sebastiano, the largest, most important and best preserved city gate in the walls built by the Emperor Aurelian to defend Rome from the barbarians. Begun in the 3rd century AD, the wall stretched for about 19 km (12 mi) around the city, encompassing the much earlier Servian wall. A century later, after a new wave of invasions, the walls were restored and doubled in height. The main attraction of the museum is the chance it offers to walk along a section of the wall comprising nine towers and a covered gallery that protected defenders. It has some unexpected views of the gardens and greenery that still exist within the walls. ⊠ *Via di Porta San Sebastiano 18,* ☎ *06/704–75284.* ▧ *3,750 lire.* ⊙ *Tues.–Sun. 9–7.*

❻ **San Clemente.** This church is one of the most extraordinary archaeological sites in Rome. San Clemente as it stands today is the third church built on this site. The first, a private home that was used as a place of Christian worship, was built in the 1st century AD. Little remains of it, but the second church, built in the 4th century, and over which today's church stands, has survived almost intact, perhaps because it was rediscovered only in the 19th century. Alongside these Christian churches you can also visit the remains of a 2nd-century AD temple to the god Mithras; it's buried deep under the second church.

San Clemente has one of the few complete medieval interiors in Rome. The most interesting features are near the altar. The marble panels in the choir were originally in the 4th-century church and were moved here when the present church was built. They are decorated with early Christian symbols: doves, vines, fish. In front of the altar is a sunken tomb containing the relics of St. Clement himself. The 16th-century canopy over the tomb is decorated with a large anchor, a reference to the martyrdom of St. Clement or, at any rate, to the legend of his martyrdom. St. Clement was the fourth pope and was reputedly banished to the Crimea in Russia by the emperor Trajan around the year 100. Here, chiefly as a result of his success in converting his fellow exiles,

The Celian Hill and the Baths of Caracalla

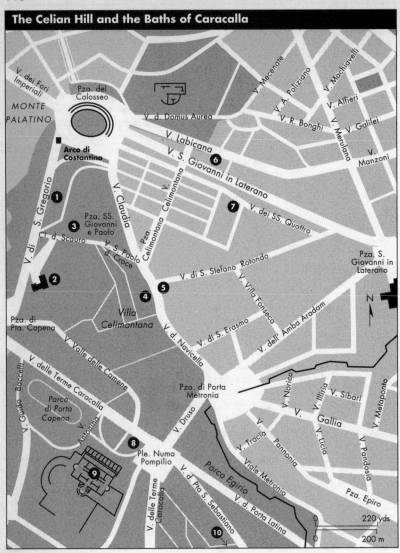

he was tied to an anchor and thrown into the sea. When, miraculously, the waters receded, his body was found in a tomb built by angels. At the beginning of the left nave, be sure to see the frescoes illustrating the life of St. Catherine of Alexandria, another early Christian martyr. Her story is memorable even by the standards of early Christian martyrs. She was born—no one seems to know when—in Alexandria in Egypt. Having publicly protested the worship of idols, she ensured the death of 50 pagan philosophers whose arguments against Christianity she had emphatically demolished; their punishment for failure was to be burned at the stake. Having then refused to marry the local governor, she was tied to a spiked wheel—hence the catherine wheel—which immediately disintegrated. This so impressed 200 watching Roman soldiers that they converted to Christianity on the spot. Eventually, however, she was beheaded, whereupon angels carried her soul to Mt. Sinai in the Holy Land. The frescoes were painted around 1400 by the Florentine artist Masolino, a key figure in the development of Italian painting from the two-dimensional decorative styles of the 14th century to the naturalism of the Renaissance.

The church is in the care of Irish Dominican priests, and a priest acts as your guide to the excavations. You descend into the remains of the 4th-century church. The entrance is in the right nave. A series of walls built along the nave of the 4th-century structure to support the newer church above make it hard to form a coherent picture of the layout. But though the gloomy interior is confusing, there are a number of areas that bring the building vividly to life. The most notable—not to mention bizarre—are the frescoes on the left wall of the nave illustrating scenes from the life of St. Clement, probably painted in the 11th century. Here in two panels, one above the other, Clement is shown getting the better of a wealthy Roman called Sisinnus. In the top panel, Sisinnus is struck deaf and dumb after having followed his wife Theodora, a Christian, to Clement's church. In the lower panel Clement cures Sisinnus, but the enraged Roman orders his servants to tie up the holy man and to carry him away. Due to the intervention of Divine Providence, the slaves and Sisinnus mistake some columns lying on the ground for Clement and his companions, and struggle furiously with ropes to strap them up. Perhaps the most unusual element of this farcical scene is the inscription under the lower panel in which Sisinnus bellows at his hapless slaves, "Go on, you sons of harlots, pull!"

From the apse at the end of the church, steps lead to the remains of the 1st-century AD house over which the 4th-century church stands. Only a few weighty stone blocks are left. Far more interesting are the remains of a "mithraeum," a shrine dedicated to the god Mithras. The shrine was installed on the first floor of a 2nd-century AD Roman apartment building (almost all ancient Romans, except the superrich, much like modern New Yorkers, lived in apartments or *insulae*). The cult of Mithras, which spread from Persia and gained a hold in Rome at about the time of the collapse of the Roman Republic, around 50 BC, is interesting mainly because it was the only pagan religion that offered the possibility of life after death. It was thus the only serious rival to Christianity at the time when Christianity was spreading across the Roman Empire. Moreover, it was the only pagan cult to continue to be practiced widely after the official "disestablishment" of paganism in favor of Christianity by the Romans in AD 382. Its rituals were always held in secret, generally in cavelike grottoes. Interestingly, the most complete part of the shrine left is the *triclinium,* a room used for religious banquets, the roof of which is studded with small rocks in imitation of a cave. Your visit is made all the more eerie by the sound of running water. The temple stands over an underground stream, and its gurgling and splashing provide a sinister accompaniment. ⊠ *Via San Giovanni in Laterano,* ☎ *06/704–51018.* ▭ *4,000 lire.* ☉ *Mon.– Sat. 9–12:30 and 3–6, Sun. 10–12:30 and 3–6.*

② **San Gregorio Magno.** The church, dedicated to St. Gregory the Great (590–604), was built about 750 by Pope Gregory II to commemorate his predecessor and namesake. It was from the monastery on this site that Pope Gregory the Great dispatched St. Augustine to Britain in 596 to convert the heathens there. The Church of San Gregorio itself appears to all intents and purposes to be a typical Baroque structure, the result of remodeling in the 17th and 18th centuries. But you can still see what's said to be the stone slab on which the pious Gregory the Great slept; it's in the far right-hand chapel. Outside are three chapels. The one on the left contains the simple table at which Gregory fed 12 poor men every day. A 13th appeared one day—an angel. The chapel in the center, dedicated to St. Andrew, contains two monumental frescoes showing scenes from the life of St. Andrew. They were painted at the beginning of the 17th century by Domenichino (*The Flagellation of St. Andrew*) and Guido Reni (*The Execution of St. Andrew*). It's a striking juxtaposition of the sturdy, if sometimes stiff, classicism of Domenichino with the more flamboyant and heroic Baroque manner of Guido Reni. ⊠ *Piazza San Gregorio.*

④ **Santa Maria in Domnica.** An early Christian structure, it was built over the house of a Roman martyr, St. Cyriaca, about whom little seems to be known other than that she was wealthy. The vibrantly colored 9th-century mosaics in the apse behind the altar are worth seeing. Notice the handkerchief carried by the Virgin: It is a *mappa,* a fashionable accoutrement in 9th-century Byzantium. ⊠ *Via della Navicella.*

③ **Santi Giovanni e Paolo.** The church has a fascinating history. It was built on the site of two ancient Roman houses around the year 370 by a Roman senator called Pammachius (who, following the death of his wife, gave away his money and saw out his days in monastic seclusion, dying in 410). Despite later rebuilding and remodeling, the church you see today is fundamentally the one built by Pammachius. The houses over which it was built belonged to SS John and Paul, not the Apostles of those names but a pair of aristocratic early Christian martyrs who had served as officers at the court of the Christian Emperor Constantine. Constantine's successor, Julian the Apostate, was the emperor who tried vainly to stem the rising tide of Christianity and to restore to Rome her pagan gods. John and Paul were early victims of his paganizing fervor; they were beheaded after having refused to serve as officers in Julian's court. A steep staircase in the far right-hand corner of the church leads down to the remains of their houses and their burial place. Frescoes, almost certainly dating from the same period, depict the beheading of two men and a woman; they are thought to have been early worshipers at the graves of John and Paul who, for their pains, received the same treatment at the hands of Julian. ⊠ *Piazza Ss Giovanni e Paolo.*

⑧ **Santi Nereo e Achilleo.** One of Rome's oldest churches, probably dating from the 4th century, it has accumulated treasures such as 8th-century mosaics, a medieval pulpit on a multicolored marble base from the Baths of Caracalla, a 13th-century mosaic choir, and a fine episcopal—or bishop's—throne. ⊠ *Viale delle Terme di Caracalla.*

⑦ **Santi Quattro Coronati.** The original 9th-century church was twice as large as the present one. The abbey was partially destroyed during the Normans' sack of Rome about 1085, but it was reconstructed about 30 years later. This explains the inordinate size of the apse in relation to the small nave. The apse frescoes are clearly Baroque, but the rest of the church is redolent of the Middle Ages. It's one of the most unusual and unexpected corners of Rome, a quiet citadel that has resisted the tide of time and traffic flowing below its ramparts. Don't miss the **cloister,** with its well-tended gardens and 12th-century fountain. The entrance is the door in the left nave; ring if it's not open.

There's another medieval gem hidden away off the courtyard at the church entrance: the **Chapel of San Silvestro.** (Enter the door marked "Monache Agostiniane" and ring the bell at the left for the nun; she will pass the key to the chapel through the wheel beside the grille.) The chapel has remained, for the most part, as it was when consecrated in 1246, decorated with marbles and frescoes. These tell the story of the Christian Emperor Constantine's recovery from leprosy thanks to Pope Sylvester I. Note, too, the delightful *Last Judgment* fresco above the door, in which the angel on the left neatly rolls up sky and stars like a backdrop, signaling the end of the world. When you leave, lock the door and return the key to the nun, with a voluntary admission fee if you like. ⊠ *Via Santi Quattro Coronati.*

⑤ Santo Stefano Rotondo. This 5th-century church was inspired perhaps by the design of the church of the Holy Sepulcher in Jerusalem. Its unusual round plan and timbered ceiling, in fact, set it apart from most other Roman churches. ⊠ *Via Santo Stefano Rotondo.*

⑨ Terme di Caracalla (Baths of Caracalla). These baths were not the largest in ancient Rome, but they seem to have been by far the most opulent. Begun in AD 206 by the emperor Septimius Severus and completed by his son, Caracalla, they could hold only 1,600 bathers, as compared to the 3,000 that the Baths of Diocletian, built a century later, could accommodate. The scale of the baths and the efficiency of their ingenious waterworks are amazing. The Roman baths were a remarkable social invention. For the Romans, the baths were much more than places to wash. It's true that bathing was the basic purpose of these establishments, but there were recital halls, art galleries, and libraries to improve the mind, and massage and exercise rooms and sports grounds to improve the body, in addition to gardens and areas just to sit in and talk in. Even the smallest public baths had at least some of these amenities. In the capital of the Roman Empire, they were provided on a lavish scale. But their functioning depended on the slaves who cared for the clients, checking their robes, rubbing them down, and seeing to their needs. Under the magnificent marble pavement of the stately halls, other slaves toiled in a warren of tiny rooms and passages, stoking the fires that heated the water.

Taking a bath was a long and complex process, though eminently understandable if you see it as a social activity first and foremost (and remember, too, that for all their sophistication the Romans didn't have soap). You began in the *sudatoria,* a series of small rooms resembling saunas. Here you sat and sweated. From these you moved to the *calidarium,* a large circular room that was humid rather than simply hot. This was where the actual business of washing went on. You used a *strigil,* or scraper, to get the dirt off; if you were rich your slave did this for you. Next you moved to the *tepidarium,* a warmish room, the purpose of which was to allow you to begin gradually to cool down. Finally, you splashed around in the *frigidarium,* the only actual "bath" in the place; in essence a shallow swimming pool filled with cold water. The rich might like to complete the process with a brisk rubdown with a scented towel. It was not unusual for a member of the opposite sex to perform this favor for you (the baths were open to men and women, though the times when they could use them were different). There was a nominal admission fee, often waived by officials and emperors wishing to curry favor with the plebeians. ⊠ *Via delle Terme di Caracalla,* ☎ *06/575–8626.* 🎫 *10,000 lire.* ☉ *Apr.–Sept., Tues.–Sat. 9–5, Sun.– Mon. 9–1; Oct.–Mar., Tues.–Sat. 9–3, Sun.–Mon. 9–1.*

THE CATACOMBS AND THE APPIAN WAY

In the swelling tide of urban development, a green belt of pastures and villas along Via Appia Antica has survived as an evocative remnant of the Roman Campagna (countryside). Strewn with classical ruins and dotted with grazing sheep, the Via Appia stirs images of chariots and legionnaires returning from imperial conquests, of barrel-shaped Roman carts transporting produce from the farms of Campania to the south, and of tearful families mourning at the tombs of their dead. Though time and vandals have taken their toll on the tombs along the Via Appia, what remains of them give you an idea of how Rome's important families made sure that their deceased members, and the family name, would be remembered by posterity. Known as "The Queen of Roads," the Via Appia was completed in 312 BC by Appius Claudius, who also built Rome's first aqueduct. He had it laid out to connect Rome with settlements in the south, in the direction of Naples: it was later extended to Brindisi, the port on the Adriatic. The dark, gloomy catacombs, the underground cemeteries that early Christians turned into places of worship, contrast with the fresh air, lush greenery, and classical ruins along the ancient road.

The catacombs aren't Rome's oldest cemeteries. Even before Christianity reached Rome, those citizens who couldn't afford a fine funeral monument along one of the consular roads were either cremated or buried in *necropolises* (cemeteries) outside the city gates. An imperial law prohibited burial within the city—except for deified emperors. During the 1st and 2nd centuries AD, Rome's Christians were buried together with their pagan brothers in these common burial grounds. Because the Christians had adopted the Hebrew tradition of burying their dead rather than cremating them, they soon required more space. They began to build cemeteries of their own, where they might also perform their religious rites. With the approval of the city fathers, they dug their cemeteries in the hilly slopes that lined the consular roads, usually on private land that the owner—often a Christian himself—granted for this purpose. As the need for space became more pressing, the cemeteries were extended in a series of galleries, often on two or more levels.

The general belief that the catacombs served as secret hiding places for the Christians during the persecutions that broke out during early Christian times is romantic but unrealistic. Rome's early Christians may have been a little odd in their ways, but they weren't stupid. The last place in the world they would have sought refuge would have been in the blind tunnels of the catacombs, whose location was common knowledge in Rome.

Between persecutions, the bodies of the martyrs who had fallen under the sword or had met death by fire, water, or wild beasts were interred in the catacombs. Their remains were given a place of honor, and their presence conferred great prestige on the underground cemetery in which they lay, attracting a stream of devout pilgrims. When this happened, the catacomb was embellished with frescoes, and existing staircases and galleries were enlarged to accommodate the faithful. Sometimes older parts of the cemetery were dug out to make room for underground basilicas. Here services in honor of the patron martyr were held, as at Sant'Agnese on Via Nomentana.

BONUS MILES MAKE GREAT SOUVENIRS.

Earn Miles With Your MCI Card.

Take the MCI Card along on this trip and start earning miles for the next one. You'll earn frequent flyer miles on all your calls and save with the low rates you've come to expect from MCI. Before you know it, you'll be on your way to some other international destination.

Sign up for MCI by calling 1-800-FLY-FREE

Earn Frequent Flyer Miles.

Is this a great time, or what? :-)

Easy To Call Home.

1. To use your MCI Card, just dial the WorldPhone access number of the country you're calling from.
2. Dial or give the operator your MCI Card number.
3. Dial or give the number you're calling.

# Austria (CC) ♦	022-903-012
# Belarus (CC)	
From Brest, Vitebsk, Grodno, Minsk	8-800-103
From Gomel and Mogilev regions	8-10-800-103
# Belgium (CC) ♦	0800-10012
# Bulgaria	00800-0001
# Croatia (CC) ★	0800-22-0112
# Czech Republic (CC) ♦	00-42-000112
# Denmark (CC) ♦	8001-0022
# Finland (CC) ♦	08001-102-80
# France (CC) ♦	0-800-99-0019
# Germany (CC)	0800-888-8000
# Greece (CC) ♦	00-800-1211
# Hungary (CC) ♦	00▼800-01411
# Iceland (CC) ♦	800-9002
# Ireland (CC)	1-800-55-1001
# Italy (CC) ♦	172-1022
# Kazakhstan (CC)	8-800-131-4321
# Liechtenstein (CC) ♦	0800-89-0222
# Luxembourg	0800-0112
# Monaco (CC) ♦	800-90-019
# Netherlands (CC) ♦	0800-022-9122
# Norway (CC) ♦	800-19912
# Poland (CC) ÷	00-800-111-21-22
# Portugal (CC) ÷	05-017-1234
Romania (CC) ÷	01-800-1800
# Russia (CC) ÷ ♦	
To call using ROSTELCOM ■	747-3322
For a Russian-speaking operator	747-3320
To call using SOVINTEL ■	960-2222
# San Marino (CC) ♦	172-1022
# Slovak Republic (CC)	00-421-00112
# Slovenia	080-8808
# Spain (CC)	900-99-0014
# Sweden (CC) ♦	020-795-922
# Switzerland (CC) ♦	0800-89-0222
# Turkey (CC) ♦	00-8001-1177
# Ukraine (CC) ÷	8▼10-013
# United Kingdom (CC)	
To call using BT ■	0800-89-0222
To call using C&W ■	0500-89-0222
# Vatican City (CC)	172-1022

CHASE

Flying to France on Friday? Get Francs from Chase on Thursday. Call Currency To Go at 935-9935 for overnight delivery.

CHASE CURRENCY TO GO 935-9935

r pounds for London. Or Deutschmarks for Düsseldorf. Or any of 75 foreign currencies. Call **Chase Currency To Go**[SM] **at 935-9935** in area codes 212, 718, 914, 516 and Rochester, N.Y.; all other area codes call 1-800-935-9935. We'll deliver directly to your door.* Overnight. And there are no exchange fees. Let Chase make your trip an easier one.

CHASE. The right relationship is everything.[SM]

You'll see a great variety of tombs and decorations in the catacombs. They range from a simple rectangular niche in the wall that was closed by bricks or marble slabs to a sarcophagus carved out of the wall and surmounted by a niche, to a freestanding sarcophagus in terra-cotta, marble, or lead. Off some of the galleries you'll see rooms lined with niches, where members of the same family or community were buried. Later, when space became scarce, tombs were dug in the pavement. Each tomb was distinguished by a particular mark or sign so that the deceased's relatives could recognize it among the rows of niches. Sometimes this was an object, such as a coin or oil lamp; sometimes it was an inscription. The wealthier families called in painters to decorate their tombs with frescoes and ordered sculptured sarcophagi from artisans' workshops.

After AD 313, when Constantine's edict put an end to the persecutions and granted full privileges to the Christians, the construction of the catacombs flourished; they were increasingly frequented by those who wished to honor their own dead and to venerate the tombs of the early martyrs. During the Dark Ages, invading armies made a habit of showing up at the gates of the city, devastating the countryside, and plundering from the living and the dead. When this part of the Campagna Romana became a malaria-infested wasteland, the popes prudently decreed that the remains of the martyrs be removed from the catacombs and laid to rest in the relative security of Rome's churches. With the loss of these holy relics and the appearance of the first cemeteries within the city walls, the catacombs fell into disuse and were abandoned and forgotten, with the sole exception of the Catacomb of San Sebastiano.

Numbers in the text and margin correspond to points of interest on the Catacombs and the Appian Way map.

A Good Walk

The initial stretch of the Via Appia Antica is not a pleasant place to walk, except on some Sundays, when all traffic is barred (check locally). There is heavy traffic and no sidewalk all the way from Porta San Sebastiano to the Catacomb of San Callisto. Also, the gardens and villas along this stretch are hidden behind walls, so there's really not much to see, with one exception. Not far beyond Porta San Sebastiano stands the little church of **Domine Quo Vadis** ①. To reach the catacombs and the prettier stretch of the Via Appia Antica, take bus 218 (which starts from San Giovanni in Laterano) at the stop near Porta San Sebastiano; the bus route follows Via Ardeatina, parallel to Via Appia Antica. You can get off at the stop nearer the **Catacombe di San Callisto** ②, or at Via San Sebastiano, which you take to reach Via Appia Antica, at the **Catacombe di San Sebastiano** ③, where you start your walk along Via Appia Antica. On Sundays you can take the 760 bus from Viale delle Terme di Caracalla; its route includes Via di Porta San Sebastiano and the initial tract of Via Appia Antica. Visit the catacomb of your choice, then walk south on Via Appia Antica. Opposite San Sebastiano are some Hebrew catacombs, not open to the public. Also on the left are the ruins of the round Mausoleo di Romolo, built by Emperor Maxentius as a tomb for his son, Romulus, and the entrance to the **Circo di Massenzio** ④. Continue south to the **Tomba di Cecilia Metella** ⑤, which marks the beginning of the most interesting and evocative stretch of Via Appia, lined with tombs and fragments of statuary. Cypresses and umbrella pines stand guard over the ruined sepulchers, and the occasional tracts of ancient paving stones are the same ones trod by Roman legions returning in triumph from southern conquests. In some stretches you can see the ruts worn in them by iron-clad cart wheels. Along the road are inconspicuous gateways to exclusive villas, residences of the

124

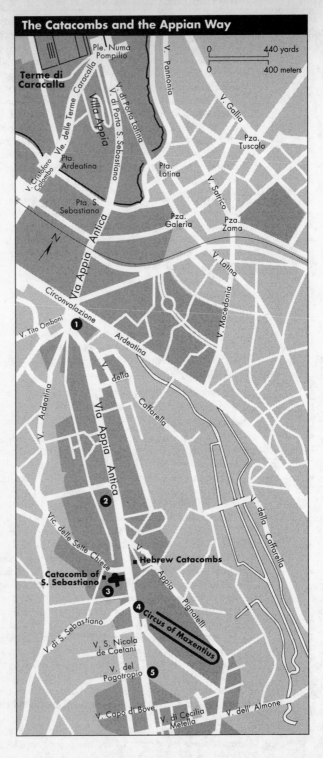

The Catacombs and the Appian Way

lucky few. Walk as far as you like along the road, but keep in mind that you have to retrace your steps to return to the bus stop. Among the more curious tombs here is a huge mass that seems balanced on a slender stem, and another tall mound on which a little house was built in a later age. You pass ruins of ancient villas, and to the left you can see the arches of an aqueduct.

TIMING

Weather is a determining factor, as the walk is almost entirely outdoors. There are no sidewalks along Via Appia Antica, so you will be walking mainly on beaten earth. Give a thought to carrying a picnic lunch or plan to dine at one of the pleasant restaurants near the catacombs. The walk takes about two hours, plus an hour for a visit to one of the catacombs, but allow another hour or so for the round-trip by bus as service is not frequent.

❷ **Catacombe di San Callisto** (Catacombs of St. Callistus). This is the oldest and one of the most important and best-preserved underground cemeteries, the burial place of many popes of the 3rd century. One of the friars who act as custodians of the catacomb will guide you through its crypts and galleries. ⊠ *Via Appia Antica 110,* ☎ *06/513–6725.* ☜ *8,000 lire.* ☉ *Thurs.–Tues., Apr.–Sept. 8:30–noon and 2:30–5:30, Oct.–Mar. 8:30–noon and 2:30–5.*

❸ **Catacombe di San Sebastiano** (Catacombs of St. Sebastian). The 4th-century church was named after the saint who was buried in the catacomb, which burrows underground on four different levels. This was the only early Christian cemetery to remain accessible during the Middle Ages. It was this cemetery from which the term *catacombs* is derived. It's located in a spot where the road dips into a hollow, known to the Romans as *catacumbas* (Greek for "near the hollow"). The Romans used the name to refer to the cemetery that had existed there since the 2nd century BC. The term came to be applied to all the underground cemeteries discovered in Rome in later centuries. ⊠ *Via Appia Antica 136,* ☎ *06/788–7035.* ☜ *8,000 lire.* ☉ *Fri.–Wed. 8:30–noon and 2:30–5.*

❹ **Circo di Massenzio** (Circus of Maxentius). The ruins of the Circus of Maxentius, built in AD 309, give you an idea of what the Roman circuses looked like. You can see the towers at the entrance; the *spina,* the wall that divided it down the center; and the vaults that supported the tiers of seating for the spectators. The obelisk in Piazza Navona was found here. The adjacent **Mausoleo di Romolo** is a huge tomb built by the emperor for his son, Romulus, who died young. Tomb and circus were on the grounds of the emperor's villa, much of which is yet to be excavated. ⊠ *Via Appia Antica 153,* ☎ *06/780–1324.* ☜ *3,750 lire.* ☉ *Apr.—Sept., Tues.–Sun. 9–7; Oct.–Mar., Tues.–Sat. 9–5.*

❶ **Domine Quo Vadis?** (Lord, Where Goest Thou?). This church was built on the spot where tradition says Christ appeared to St. Peter as the Apostle was fleeing Rome and persuaded him to return and face martyrdom. A paving stone in the church bears the imprint of what are said to be the feet of Christ. ⊠ Via Appia Antica at Via Ardeatina.

❺ **Tomba di Cecilia Metella** (Tomb of Cecilia Metella). Originally this round tomb was a smaller version of the Mausoleum of Augustus (☞ Villa Borghese to the Ara Pacis, *above*). It was the burial place of a Roman noblewoman, wife of Crassus, one of Julius Caesar's generals. The original decoration includes a frieze of bulls' skulls near the top. The travertine stone walls were made higher and the crenellations added when the tomb was transformed into a fortress by the Caetani family in the 14th century. ⊠ *Via Appia Antica 162,* ☎ *06/780–2465.* ☜ *Free.* ☉ *Tues.–Sat. 9–an hour before sunset; Sun.–Mon. 9–2.*

3 Dining

Romans have been known since ancient times for great feasts and banquets, and though the days of the triclinium and the saturnalia are long past, dining out is still all the night life most Romans need. Don't look for star chefs here, or the latest trends—with a few notable exceptions, the city's food scene is a bit like its historical sites, well-worn but still standing. But food-lovers nonetheless have much to look forward to; in fact, a lingering meal al fresco is one of Rome's great pleasures.

ROMAN COOKING IS PREDOMINANTLY SIMPLE; dishes rarely have more than a few ingredients, and meat and fish are most often baked or grilled. Although many traditional recipes are based on innards, you won't find much of that on the menu in restaurants in the center of town, with the exception of *trippa alla romana* (tripe stewed in tomatoes with wild mint).

The typical Roman fresh pasta is *fettuccine,* golden egg noodles that are at their classic best when laced with *ragú,* a thick, rich tomato and meat sauce. *Spaghetti alla carbonara* is tossed with a sauce of egg yolk, chunks of rendered *guanciale* (cured pork cheek), pecorino romano cheese, and lots of freshly ground black pepper. *Pasta all'amatriciana* has a sauce of tomato, guanciale, and onion. Potato gnocchi, served with tomato sauce and a sprinkling of Parmesan or Pecorino, are a Roman favorite for Thursday dinner. The best meat on the menu is often *abbacchio,* milk-fed lamb. Legs are usually roasted with rosemary and potatoes, and the chops are grilled *alla scottadito* ("burn your finger"— eaten hot off the grill with your fingers). Most Mediterranean fish are light yet flavorful, among them *spigola* (sea bass), *triglie* (red mullet), and *rombo* (turbot or flounder).

Local cheeses are made from sheep's milk; the best known is the aged, sharp Pecorino romano. Fresh ricotta is a treat all on its own, and finds its way into a number of dishes and desserts. Typical wines of Rome are those of the Castelli Romani, the towns in the hills to the southeast: Frascati, Colli Albani, Marino, and Velletri. Though the water in Rome is good to drink, restaurants will usually have you choose between bottled *gassata* (sparkling) or *liscia* (not sparkling) water.

Many restaurants make a specialty of the *fritto misto* (mixed fry) with whatever vegetables are in season. Rome is famous for artichokes (the season runs from November to April), traditionally prepared *alla romana* (stuffed with garlic and mint and braised), or *alla giudia* (fried whole, with each petal crisp). A special springtime treat is *vignarola,* a mixture of tender peas, fava beans, and artichokes, cooked with bits of guanciale.

One of the great joys of a meal in Italy is that most restaurants will not rush you out. Accordingly, service is often more relaxed than speedy, and the bill (*il conto*) will not be brought until you ask for it. Though the *pane e coperto* (bread and cover charge) has been officially eliminated, many restaurants still charge extra for bread. Unless otherwise written on the menu, service (*servizio*) is included; so don't pay for service twice. Locals customarily reward particularly good service with a just a few thousand lire per person. Almost all restaurants close one day a week (in many cases Sunday) and for at least two weeks in August.

Prices

CATEGORY	COST*
$$$$	over 100,000 lire
$$$	70,000–100,000 lire
$$	40,000–70,000 lire
$	under 40,000 lire

Prices are per person, for a three-course meal, including house wine and taxes.

Restaurants

Near Termini

$ ✕ **Fagianetto.** Massive wooden beams on high are as solid as the reputation of this family-run trattoria near Termini Station. It has a regular neighborhood clientele, but also satisfies tourists' appetites with a special menu for 25,000 lire. But you may well be tempted by à la carte offerings such as rigatoni *alla norcina* (with a sauce of crumbled sausage and cream) or osso buco *con funghi* (with mushrooms). Service is swift and courteous. ✉ *Via Filippo Turati 21,* ☎ 06/446–7306. *AE, DC, MC, V. Closed Mon. and 2–3 wks in Aug.*

$ ✕ **Pommidoro.** Mamma's in the kitchen and the rest of the family greets, serves, and keeps customers happy and well-fed at this popular trattoria near Rome's main university, a short cab ride east of Stazione Termini. The menu—not so well translated—offers especially good grilled meats and game birds and classic home-style *cucina.* You can dine outside in warm weather. ✉ *Piazza dei Sanniti 44,* ☎ 06/445–2692. *No credit cards. Closed Wed.*

Old Rome

$$$$ ✕ **El Toulà.** Rome's prestigious El Toulà—one of the many spin-offs of its namesake in Treviso—has the warm, welcoming comforts of a 19th-century country house, with white walls, antique furniture in dark wood, heavy silver serving dishes, and spectacular fruit and flower arrangements. In the cozy bar off the entrance you can sip a *prosecco* (Venetian semisparkling white wine), the aperitif best suited to the chef's Venetian specialties, such as *baccalà mantecato* (stockfish whipped with butter to a creamy consistency) or *fegato alla Veneziana* (sweet-and-sour liver with onions), which are always on offer, along with contemporary interpretations of Italian classics. ✉ *Via della Lupa 29/b,* ☎ 06/687–3750. *Reservations essential. Jacket and tie. AE, DC, MC, V. Closed Sun. and Aug. No lunch Sat.*

$$$$ ✕ **Il Convivio.** It's easy to walk right by this small restaurant where fake plants and wall posters of great paintings are hidden behind an unassuming facade on the corner of a narrow street just north of Piazza Navona. The food, however, is anything but anonymous. Cooking that begins with seasonal, traditional Italian dishes and fresh herbs ends up decidedly modern. Chef Angelo Troiani's inventions have long names, but they are tasty and well presented without being silly: *strudel di baccalà e broccoli con salsa di aglio dolce* (strudel with salt cod and broccoli rape in a sweet garlic sauce), *rollé d'agnello farcito con frittatine alle erbe con salsa di olive ascolane* (lamb roll stuffed with herb fritter in an olive sauce), and *soufflé di crema di mandorle e prugne, profumato d'arancia* (almond and prune soufflé, perfumed with orange). Brothers Massimo and Giuseppe manage the dining room and pour wine chosen from a vast cellar, one of the finest in town. ✉ *Via dell'Orso 44,* ☎ 06/686–9432. *Reservations essential. AE, DC, MC, V. Closed Sun.*

$$$$ ✕ **La Rosetta.** In 1992, chef/owner Massimo Riccioli took the nets and
★   fishing gear off the walls of his parents' trattoria to create what is widely known as *the* place to go in Rome to eat first-rate fish. The interior is simple elegance at its best, with warm wood paneling, fresh flowers, and a stunning display of fish at the entrance. Start with *ricci di mare* (sea urchins), *vongole veraci* (large, tasty sautéed clams), or a variety of delicately marinated fish. Pasta dishes are dressed with fish or seafood, alone or in combination with seasonal vegetables; particularly good are the *tonnarelli ai frutti di mare* (fresh spaghetti-like pasta with seafood) and penne *alla sarde* (with fresh sardines, pine nuts, raisins, and wild fennel). Second courses range from perfectly grilled fish and crustaceans to delicately poached fillets served on a bed of artichokes

or potatoes, sea bass with black truffle, and whole fish baked in salt. Desserts (made in-house) are worth saving room for. ⊠ *Via della Rosetta 9,* ☎ *06/686–1002. Dinner reservations essential. AE, DC, MC, V.*

$$$ ✕ **Al Ceppo.** Warm and well decorated with antiques and oil paintings, Al Ceppo has been the Sunday lunch favorite for a generation of Roman families. The ample selection of classic Italian dishes prepared with a creative flair changes daily but always includes a few specialties from the Marche region—where the owners come from—such as *olive ascolane* (large stuffed green olives, breaded and fried), *zuppa di ceci* (chickpea soup), and, on Fridays, *baccalà* (salt cod). Pasta is made fresh every day, and other hallmarks are *polpettine di melanzane al vapore* (steamed eggplant balls) and fried zucchini flowers stuffed with mozzarella cheese and anchovy. A wide selection of meats, fish, and vegetables grilled in the attractive fireplace in the front room rounds out the extensive menu. ⊠ *Via Panama 2,* ☎ *06/841–9696. AE, DC, MC, V. Closed Mon. and Aug.*

$$$ ✕ **Passetto.** Benefiting from a choice location near Piazza Navona, Passetto has been a favorite with Italians and tourists for many years: It's a place you can rely on for classic Italian food and gracious service. If you can, eat on the terrace—it's especially memorable at night; the mirrored dining room is more staid. Roman specialties, such as cannelloni and abbacchio, are featured. ⊠ *Via Zanardelli 14,* ☎ *06/ 688–06569. AE, DC, MC, V.*

$$$ ✕ **Piperno.** In the old Jewish ghetto next to historic Palazzo Cenci, Piperno has been in business for more than a century. It is *the* place to go for Rome's extraordinary *carciofi alla giudia* (fried whole artichokes). You eat in one of three small wood-paneled dining rooms or at one of a handful of tables outdoors. Try *filetti di baccalà* (fillet of cod), *pasta e ceci* (a thick soup of pasta tubes and chickpeas), and *fiori di zucca ripieni e fritti* (fried stuffed zucchini flowers). ⊠ *Monte dei Cenci 9,* ☎ *06/654–2772. AE, DC, MC, V. Closed Mon. and Aug. No dinner Sun.*

$$$ ✕ **Sangallo.** An intimate little restaurant not far from the Pantheon, Sangallo specializes in first-quality fish that is light, well-cooked, and invitingly presented in dishes such as *tagliolini con pomodorini, mazzancolle, e scaglie di pecorino* (fresh pasta with cherry tomatoes, shrimp, and scales of pecorino cheese) and *spigola in crosta di sale* (sea bass baked in a salt crust). The *menu degustazione* offers better value than the à la carte offerings. ⊠ *Vicolo della Vaccarella, 11/a,* ☎ *06/ 686–5549. AE, DC, MC, V. Closed Sun., 1 wk in Jan., and 2 wks in Aug. No lunch Mon.*

$$$ ✕ **Vecchia Roma.** Consistently good food, sure-handed service, and great
★ ambience make this restaurant long known to tourists and Romans still worthy of attention, even if prices are a bit exaggerated. With tables outside on a relatively quiet, narrow square close to the Campidoglio, Vecchia Roma is one of the best places in town to dine al fresco in summertime or on a not-too-cool winter evening (with radiating heaters). The tasteful interior is composed of several small rooms, some with floral frescoes, others with stucco panel reliefs. Unlike those of a great many "old Roman restaurants," the menu covers the classics without being stale. The wine list is sufficiently varied and fairly priced. ⊠ *Piazza Campitelli 18,* ☎ *06/686–4604. Reservations essential. AE, DC. Closed Wed. and mid-Aug.*

$$–$$$ ✕ **Dal Bolognese.** Long a haunt of the art crowd, this classic restaurant on Piazza del Popolo is a trendy choice for a leisurely lunch between sightseeing and shopping. An array of contemporary paintings decorates the dining room, but the real attraction is the lovely piazza—one of Rome's best for people-watching. As the name of the restaurant promises, the cooking here adheres to the hearty tradition of

130

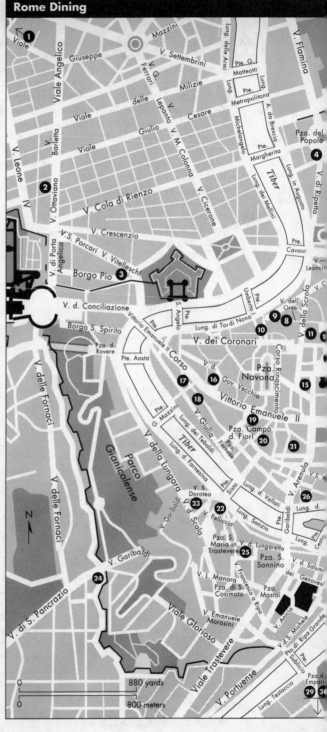

Rome Dining

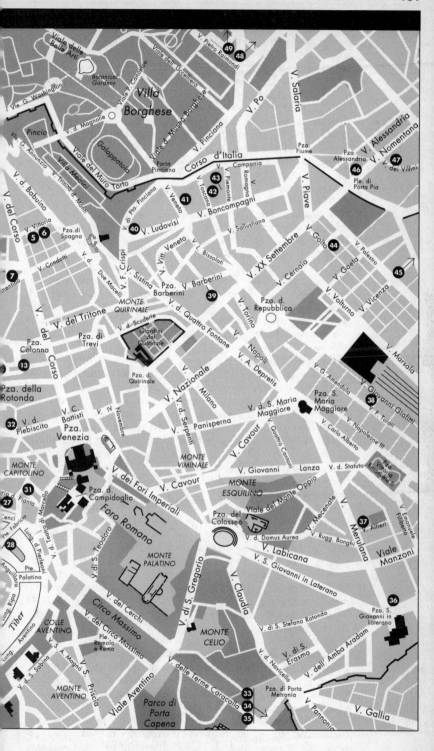

Viale delle Belle Arti

Botanical Gardens

V. P. Canonica

Viale dell' Uccelliera

V. Pietro Raimondi

49
48

V. Salaria

V. Po

Villa Borghese

Viale d. Museo Borghese

V. Pinciana

V. d. Magnolie

Vle. G. Washington

Pincio

Galoppatoio

Viale del Muro Torto

Villa Medici

V. G. Annunzio V. Trinità di Monti

Porta Pinciana

Pza. Fiume

Corso d'Italia

Pza. Alessandria

V. Alessandria

V. Nomentana

47
V. dei Villini

46
Ple. di Porta Pia

V. di Pza. Pinciana

V. Campania

V. Romagna

V. Piemonte

V. Toscana

43
42

V. Veneto

41

V. Boncompagni

V. d. Babuino

V. del Corso

V. Vittoria

5 6
Pza. di Spagna

V. Ludovisi

40

V. Sallustiana

V. Condotti

Vitt. Veneto

V. L. Bissolati

V. XX Settembre

V. Goito

44

V. Piave

V. Cernaia

V. Gaeta

V. Palestro

45

V. F. Crispi V. Sistina

Due Macelli

7

Pza. V. Barberini

Pza. Barberini

39

Pza. d. Repubblica

V. Volturno

V. Vicenza

MONTE QUIRINALE

V. del Tritone

V. d. Scuderie

V. d. Quattro Fontane

V. Torino

V. Marsala

del Corso

Pza. di Trevi

Giardini del Quirinale

Napoli

V. A. Depretis

V. G. Amendola

V. Giovanni Giolitti

38

Pza. Colonna

13

Pza. d. Quirinale

V. Nazionale

Milano

V. d. S. Maria Maggiore

Pza. S. Maria Maggiore

V. F. Turati

Pza. della Rotonda

V. C. Battisti

Pza. Venezia

V. IV Novembre

V. d. Serpenti

Panisperna

V. Carlo Alberto

V. Napoleone III

32
V. d. Plebiscito

MONTE CAPITOLINO

Pza. d. Campidoglio

V. dei Fori Imperiali

MONTE VIMINALE

V. Cavour

V. Giovanni

Lanza

V. d. Statuto

Pza. Vittorio Emanuele II

Emanuele Filiberto

d. Pianta

31
27

Foro Romano

V. Cavour

MONTE ESQUILINO

Viale del Monte Oppio

V. Mecenate

37

V. Altieri

Pte. Fabricio

V. di S. Teodoro

Pza. del Colosseo

V. d. Domus Aurea

V. Rugg. Bonghi

Merulana

28
Pte. Palatino

Lung. Ripa

Tiber

MONTE PALATINO

V. di S. Gregorio

V. Labicana

V. S. Giovanni in Laterano

Viale Manzoni

V. Claudia

36
Pza. S. Giovanni in Laterano

COLLE AVENTINO

Circo Massimo

V. del Circo Massimo

Ple. Romolo e Remo

MONTE CELIO

V. di S. Stefano Rotondo

V. dell' Amba Aradam

V. di S. Erasmo

V. d. S. Sabina

V. S. Prisca

V. delle Terme Caracalla

V. di S. Navicella

Esquilino

MONTE AVENTINO

Viale Aventino

Parco di Porta Capena

33
34
35

Pza. di Porta Metronia

V. Pannonia

V. Gallia

Bologna, with delicious homemade *tortellini in brodo* (filled pasta in broth), fresh pastas in creamy sauces, and steaming trays of boiled meats. Among the desserts, try the *dolce della mamma* (a concoction of gelato, zabaglione, and chocolate sauce) and the fruit-shaped gelato. ☒ *Piazza del Popolo 1,* ☎ *06/361–1426. AE, MC, V. Closed Mon. and Aug.*

$$ ✕ **Il Cardinale.** The serene little restaurant serves a fanciful, lightened-up version of traditional Roman fare, beautifully presented on king-size plates. Oil paintings and enlarged old photos of Roman landmarks hang against golden damask wall coverings; chairs and couches are covered in a pretty floral print. The menu always has a few suggestions from the chef but tends to include a selection of salads, vegetable soups, and pastas like *vermicelli cacio e pepe* (pasta with pecorino cheese and black pepper) or *ravioli di borragine* (ravioli filled with borage leaves), and various vegetable *sformati* (flans). ☒ *Via delle Carceri 6,* ☎ *06/686–9336. AE, DC, MC, V. Closed Sun.*

$$ ✕ **Le Maschere.** For a taste of southern Italian (Calabrian) fare, try this informal cellar restaurant hidden away between Largo Argentina and Piazza Campo dei Fiori—in summer, look for the planters and the few outdoor tables. Dark rustic walls are hung with everything from paper garlands to old utensils; there are pottery wine jugs and rush-seated chairs. To start, order spicy Calabria salami or hit the expansive antipasto table, and then go on to pizza or pasta with broccoli or with tomato and eggplant sauce. Grilled meat and seafood make up the list of second courses. Efficient service makes for a pleasant evening. ☒ *Via Monte della Farina 29,* ☎ *06/687–9444. DC, MC, V. Closed Mon. and Aug.*

$$ ✕ **Myosotis.** It may look brand new, but the Myosotis is the sequel to
★ a successful restaurant on the outskirts of town run by the Marsili family. Central location, extensive menu, and great value make Myosotis a place you might want to return to. The menu rides that delicate line between tradition and innovation, focusing more on the freshness and quality of the ingredients than on elaborate presentations. Fresh pasta gets special attention: it's rolled out by hand to order for the *stracci alla delizia di mare* (pasta with seafood). There's a wide choice of fish, meat, and seasonal veggies to choose from. The wine list is ample, the prices honest. ☒ *Via della Vaccarella 3/5,* ☎ *06/205–3943. Closed Mon. and 2 wks in Aug. AE, DC, MC, V.*

$$ ✕ **Otello alla Concordia.** The clientele in this popular spot—it's off a shopping street near Piazza di Spagna—is about evenly divided between tourists and workers from shops and offices in the area. The former like to sit outdoors in the courtyard in any weather; the latter have their regular tables in one of the inside dining rooms. The menu offers classic Roman and Italian dishes, and service is friendly and efficient. Since every tourist in Rome knows about it, and since the regulars won't relinquish their niches, you may have to wait for a table; go early. ☒ *Via della Croce 81,* ☎ *06/678–1454. Reservations not accepted. AE, DC. Closed Sun.*

$$ ✕ **Sora Lella.** What was once a simple trattoria ensconced on the Tiberina Island (great view from the bathroom) is now a monument to the late founder herself, a beloved example of true Roman warmth and personality. Inside are two small dining rooms lined with wood paneling and bottles of wine. Although prices are much higher than when Sora Lella presided over the cash desk, the cooking is still 100% Roman. Daily specials as well as menu standards are written on the chalkboard, but you'll usually find rigatoni all'amatriciana and *maialino all'antica roma* (suckling pig with prunes and baby onions). Leave room for the quintessential Roman ricotta cake. ☒ *Via Ponte Quattro Capi 16,* ☎ *06/686–1601. AE, DC, MC. Closed Sun. and Aug.*

$ $\times$ **Grappolo d'Oro.** This centrally located trattoria off Campo dei
★ Fiori has been afavorite for decades with locals and foreign residents.
This measure of notoriety has not induced the graying, courteous owners to change their two half-paneled dining rooms or menu, which features pasta all'amatriciana and scaloppine any way you want them.
Inquire about the day's special. ⊠ *Piazza della Cancelleria 80,* ☎ *06/
689–7080. AE, DC, MC, V. Closed Sun. and Aug.*

$ $\times$ **L'Eau Vive.** This is definitely a unique Roman dining experience, even
if the food isn't Italian. For the last 28 years the restaurant, which serves
(very good) classic French food, has been run by a society of French
missionary nuns. The atmosphere throughout is serene and soothing,
though rather plain (of course). Soft devotional music plays as the smiling sisters speedily bring plate after plate. They take a brief pause before dessert to sing "Ave Maria"—you are welcome to join in. The
upstairs rooms, reserved for non-smokers, have beautiful frescoes. ⊠
Via Monterone 85, ☎ *06/688–01095. AE, DC, MC, V. Closed Sun.
and Aug.*

$ $\times$ **Orso 80.** The good kind of tourist restaurant, this bright and bustling
trattoria near Piazza Navona is well known for its fabulous antipasto
table. Try the homemade egg pasta or the bucatini all'amatriciana; there's
plenty of seafood on the menu, too. For dessert, the ricotta cake, a genuine Roman specialty, is always good. ⊠ *Via dell'Orso 33,* ☎ *06/686–
4904. AE, DC, MC, V. Closed Mon. and Aug.*

$ $\times$ **Pierluigi.** This is a longtime favorite with foreign residents of Rome
and Italians in the entertainment field. On busy evenings tables are almost impossible to get, so make sure you reserve well in advance. Seafood
dominates (if you're in the mood to splurge, try the lobster), but traditional Roman dishes are offered, too, including fried zucchini blos-
soms and simple spaghetti. Eat in the pretty piazza in summer. ⊠
Piazza dei Ricci 144, ☎ *06/686–8717. AE, V. Closed Mon. and 2 wks
in Aug.*

$ $\times$ **Pollarola.** This typical Roman trattoria, near Piazza Navona and
Campo dei Fiori, has artificial flowers on the tables but—as a special
feature—it also has an ancient, authentic Roman column embedded
in the rear wall. Try a pasta specialty such as cannelloni with meat sauce,
or pollo *in porchetta* (with bacon and herbs). The house wines, white
or red, are good. You can eat outdoors in nice weather. ⊠ *Piazza della
Pollarola 24 (Campo dei Fiori),* ☎ *06/688–01654. AE, DC, V. Closed
Sun. and Aug.*

Trastevere/Testaccio

$$$ $\times$ **Checchino dal 1887.** Literally carved from a hillside composed of
potsherds from Roman times, Checchino serves the most traditional
Roman cuisine, carefully prepared and served without fanfare or dec-
oration, in a clean, sober environment. Though the slaughterhouses
of Rome's Testaccio quarter—a short cab ride from the city center—
are long gone, you can still try the variety meats that make up the soul
of Roman cooking: *trippa* (tripe), *testina* (head), *pajata* (intestine), *zampa*
(trotter), and *coratella* (sweetbreads and heart of beef). There are also
plenty of other dishes to choose from: house specialties include *coda
alla vaccinara* (stewed oxtail), a popular Roman dish; and *abbacchio
alla cacciatora* (braised milk-fed lamb) with seasonal vegetables. The
restaurant also has one of the city's best wine lists. ⊠ *Via di Monte
Testaccio 30,* ☎ *06/574–6318. AE, DC, MC, V. Closed Mon., Aug.,
and Christmas. No dinner Sun.*

$$$ $\times$ **Da Checco er Carettiere.** Maybe this is what all Italian restaurants
once looked like: an aging doorman, garlic braids hanging from the ceil-
ing, black-and-white photos in small frames lining the wood-paneled
walls. All the Roman standards are here, dependably prepared with

first-rate ingredients, plus plenty of local vegetables and an unusually good selection of fish. Family-run for three generations, Checco is a great place to soak up genuine Trastevere color and hospitality. ⊠ *Via Benedetta 10,* ☎ *06/581–7018. AE, DC, MC, V. Closed Mon. No dinner Sun.*

$$–$$$ ✕ **Paris.** On a small square just off Piazza Santa Maria in Trastevere, Paris (named after a former owner, not the city) has a reassuring, understated ambience, without the hokey flamboyance of so many eating places in this neighborhood. It also has a menu offering the best of classic Roman cuisine: homemade fettuccine, delicate fritto misto, and, of course, baccalà. In fair weather opt for tables on the piazza. ⊠ *Piazza San Callisto 7/a,* ☎ *06/581–5378. AE, DC, MC, V. Closed Mon. and 3 wks in Aug. No dinner Sun.*

$–$$ ✕ **Antico Arco.** Run by three friends with a passion for wine and fine
★   food, the Antico Arco has quickly won the hearts of Roman foodies with great invention and moderate prices. There are always 30 wines to choose from by the glass as well as an excellent list of Italian and French labels. Particularly good are starters like *sformato di finocchi in salsa d'arancia* (fennel flan with orange sauce) and second courses like *petto d'anatra con salsa di lamponi* (duck breast with raspberry sauce). Don't miss dessert; each is paired with an appropriate wine or spirit. ⊠ *Piazzale Aurelio 7,* ☎ *06/581–5274. AE, DC, MC, V. Closed Mon. No lunch Tues.–Sat.*

$ ✕ **Perilli.** A bastion of authentic Roman cooking and trattoria atmosphere since 1911 (the decor has changed very little), this is the place to go to try rigatoni *con pajata* (with veal's intestines)—if you're into that sort of thing. Otherwise the all'amatriciana and carbonara sauces are classics. The house wine is a golden nectar from the Castelli Romani. ⊠ *Via Marmorata 39,* ☎ *06/574–2415. No credit cards. Closed Wed.*

Parioli

$$$$ ✕ **Relais Le Jardin.** In the Parioli residential district, this restaurant draws a chichi crowd. It's in the exclusive Lord Byron hotel, itself a triumph of studied interior decoration. The menu is a tempting compendium of seasonal, newer-than-now nouvelle specialties. If on the menu, try the duck breast with balsamic vinegar or the sea bass in potato crust. ⊠ *Hotel Lord Byron, Via Giuseppe de Notaris 5,* ☎ *06/322–0404. Reservations essential. Jacket and tie. AE, DC, MC, V. Closed Sun. and Aug.*

Vatican

$$$$ ✕ **La Pergola.** High atop Monte Mario, the Cavalieri Hilton's rooftop
★   La Pergola restaurant offers a commanding view of the city below. Begin with an aperitif or a stroll out on the terrace before sitting down in the dining room, warmly elegant with trompe l'oeil ceilings, handsome wood paneling, and large windows. Amply spaced tables and low lighting create an intimate atmosphere not matched by other restaurants in town. Celebrated Wunder-chef Heinz Beck is a skilled technician and brings Rome its finest example of Mediterranean *alta cucina* (haute cuisine); dishes such as zucchini flowers stuffed with shrimp and fried or ravioli with potato and peas served in a sauce of lobster and saffron are balanced and light, and presentation is striking. The wine list and the cheese cart offer ample and interesting choices from Italy and France. ⊠ *Cavalieri Hilton, Via Cadlolo 101,* ☎ *06/350–9221. Reservations essential. Jacket and tie. AE, DC, MC, V. Closed Sun.–Mon. No lunch.*

$ ✕ **Dal Toscano.** This great family-run Tuscan trattoria near the Vati-
★   can has an open wood-fired grill and classic dishes such as *ribollita* (a thick bread-and-vegetable soup) and *pici* (fresh thick pasta, served with

a wild hare sauce). The glass-doored refrigerator opposite the entrance lets you know right away that the real attraction of the house is the prized *bistecca alla fiorentina*, a thick, bone-in steak, grilled but rare in the middle. Accompany it with a strong Chianti or a half-liter of the Tuscan house wine. Desserts such as pastry cream tarts, apple strudel, and *castagnaccio* (a tasty chestnut–and–pine nut treat) in wintertime are all homemade. Service is friendly and speedy. There's outside dining in good weather. ✉ *Via Germanico 58,* ☎ *06/397–25717. DC, MC, V. Closed Mon., Aug., and 2 wks in Dec.*

$ ✕ **Tre Pupazzi.** The "three puppets" after which the trattoria is named are the worn stone figures on a fragment of an ancient sarcophagus that embellishes the building. On a byway near the Vatican, the tavern, founded in 1625, wears its centuries lightly, upholding a tradition of good food, courteous service, and reasonable prices. The menu offers classic Roman and Abruzzese trattoria fare, including fettuccine and abbacchio, plus pizzas at lunchtime (a rarity in Rome) and well past midnight. ✉ *Via dei Tre Pupazzi at Borgo Pio,* ☎ *06/686–8371. AE, MC, V. Closed Sun.*

Veneto

$$$$ ✕ **La Terrazza dell'Eden.** The Hotel Eden's restaurant unfurls an un-
★ paralleled view of Rome's seven hills before your eyes, unfairly distracting you from some of the best food in the city. Modern yet simple Italian cuisine—high on flavor and herbs and low on butter and cream—has been the rule since the arrival of Chef Enrico Derflingher in 1994. Always on the prowl for superior fresh ingredients, he has taken the search to a new level: how many other restaurants have their own fishing boat (in this case named after the hotel), which reserves the best of the day's catch for the chef? In addition to the ever-changing à la carte selections, there are always set *romano* and macrobiotic menus. The restaurant is also open for breakfast (7AM–10 AM). A piano bar (with jazz 8 PM–1 AM) to the side, with a small outdoor terrace, shares the view. ✉ *Hotel Eden, Via Ludovisi 49,* ☎ *06/4781–2552. Dinner reservations essential. Jacket and tie. AE, DC, MC, V.*

$$$$ ✕ **Le Sans Souci.** All the glitz and glamour of the dolce vita days of Rome in the 1950s lives on in this overdecorated but superb subterranean sanctuary of gourmet delights. Impeccably dressed waiters slide over the carpeted floor, their gait reminiscent of Swiss walking lessons, their smiles captivating but discreet. An elaborate coffered ceiling, mirrors, and painted ceramics from Perugia decorate the main room, in which carved wooden busts of Roman emperors look at one another over tables set in the French fashion. Couples share couches rather than sitting opposite one another (so much easier to see the show) while a guitarist plays sentimental songs. The menu presents both French and Italian dishes, among them truffled terrine de foie gras and various sweet and savory soufflés. ✉ *Via Sicilia 20,* ☎ *06/482–1814. Reservations essential. Jacket and tie. AE, DC, MC, V. Closed Mon. and Aug. No lunch.*

$$$ ✕ **Coriolano.** The only tourists who find their way to this classic restaurant near Porta Pia are likely to be gourmets looking for quintessential Italian *cucina*—and that means market-fresh ingredients, especially seafood, light homemade pastas, and choice olive oil. The tables in the small antiques-filled dining room are set with immaculate white linen, sparkling crystal, and silver. Seafood dishes vary, but *tagliolini all'aragosta* (thin noodles with lobster sauce) is the house specialty; also order the seasonal porcini mushrooms (prepared with a secret recipe). The wine list is predominantly Italian, but includes some French and California choices. ✉ *Via Ancona 14,* ☎ *06/442–49863. AE, DC, MC, V. Closed Sun., Sat. in July, and 3 wks in Aug.*

$$ ✕ **Colline Emiliane.** A reliable, family-run neighborhood trattoria, it's not far from Piazza Barberini. Behind an opaque glass facade are a couple of plain dining rooms where you are served light, homemade pastas, *tortelli di zucca* (pumpkin-filled ravioli), and meats ranging from *bollito misto* (boiled beef) to *giambonetto di vitello* (roast veal) and *cotoletta alla bolognese* (fried veal cutlet with cheese and prosciutto). It's quiet and soothing—a good place to rest after a sightseeing stint. Service is cordial and discreet. ✉ *Via San Nicolò da Tolentino 26,* ☎ *06/481–8564. Reservations essential. AE, DC, MC, V. Closed Sun. and Aug.*

$$ ✕ **Mariano.** At this restaurant near Via Veneto, Mariano (who is actually Tonino, Mariano's son-in-law and successor) is an exponent of quality and tradition. Since he leaves flights of culinary fancy to others, you can be sure of finding authentic Roman and central Italian cuisine here, including delicate egg pastas, game, and abbacchio in season. ✉ *Via Piemonte 79,* ☎ *06/474–5256. AE, DC, MC, V. Closed Sun. No lunch Sat.*

$$ ✕ **Papá Baccus.** Italo Cipriani takes his meat as seriously as any Tus-
★ can. He even posts photocopies of the weekly invoice to show customers that he uses real Chianina beef, the prized breed traditionally used for the bistecca alla fiorentina, a house specialty. In this, Rome's best Tuscan restaurant, you can depend on the genuineness of the rest of the dishes, too. Cipriani brings many ingredients from his hometown in northern Tuscany. Try the sweet and delicate prosciutto from Pratomagno. The welcome is warm, the service excellent. ✉ *Via Toscana 36,* ☎ *06/427–42808. AE, DC, MC, V. Closed Sun., 2 wks in Aug., and Christmas. No lunch Sat.*

Via Appia Antica

$$ ✕ **Cecilia Metella.** From the entrance on Via Appia Antica, practically opposite the catacombs, you walk uphill to a low, sprawling construction designed for wedding feasts and banquets. There's a large terrace shaded by vines for outdoor dining. Although obviously geared to larger groups, Cecilia Metella also gives couples and small groups full attention, good service, and traditional Roman cuisine. The specialties are searing-hot *crespelle* (crepes), served in individual casseroles, and *pollo al Nerone* (chicken à la Nero; flambéed, of course). ✉ *Via Appia Antica 125,* ☎ *06/513–6743. AE, MC, V. Closed Mon. and last 2 wks in Aug.*

$$ ✕ **L'Archeologia.** In this farmhouse just beyond the catacombs, you dine indoors beside the fireplace in cool weather or in the garden under age-old vines in the summer. The atmosphere is friendly and intimate, and specialties include homemade pastas, abbacchio scottadito, and seafood. ✉ *Via Appia Antica 139,* ☎ *06/788–0494. AE, MC, V. Closed Thurs.*

Farther Afield

$$ ✕ **Cannavota.** On the square next to San Giovanni in Laterano, Cannavota has a large and faithful following and has fed generations of neighborhood families over the years. Seafood dominates, but carnivores are satisfied also. Try one of the pastas with seafood sauce—fettuccine with scampi is a good choice—and then go on to grilled fish or meat. The cheerful atmosphere and rustic decor make for an authentically Roman experience. ✉ *Piazza San Giovanni in Laterano 20,* ☎ *06/772–05007. AE, DC, MC, V. Closed Wed. and 3 wks in Aug.*

$$ ✕ **Tana del Grillo.** Near Santa Maria Maggiore, this family-run restaurant features the specialties of one of Italy's least-known regional cuisines—that of Ferrara. Sausages and salami of various types, gnocchi, and lasagna or *pasticcio di maccheroni* (pasta casserole) are typical dishes, but the pièce de résistance in the cooler months is the

bollito, a steaming cart laded with several types of boiled meat, which the waiter will carve to your order. In summer they make *vitello tonnato* (slices of veal in a tuna sauce). ⊠ *Via Alfieri 4*, ☎ *06/704–53517. AE, DC, MC, V. Closed Sun. No lunch Mon.*

Enoteche

It was not so long ago that wine in Rome (and other towns) was strictly local; you didn't have to walk far to find an osteria, where you could buy wine straight from the barrel or sit down to drink and nibble a bit, chat, or play cards. The tradition continues today, as many Roman wine shops are also open as *enoteche* (wine bars). The folding chairs and rickety tables have given way to designer interiors and chic ambience. Enormous barrels of Frascati have been replaced by shelves lined with hundreds of bottles from all over the country, representing the best in Italian wine-making. Behind the bar you'll find a serious wine enthusiast—maybe even a sommelier—with several bottles open to be tasted by the glass. And the food has changed, too. There are usually carefully selected cheeses and cured meats, and a short menu of simple dishes and desserts, making a stop in an enoteca a great alternative to yet another three-course restaurant meal.

Near Termini

$ ✕ **Trimani Il Winebar.** In a town where most restaurants don't unlock the door before 8 PM, Trimani opens for snacks and cold plates at 6 PM, serves hot food starting at 7:30, and stays open until 11:30. There's always a choice of a soup and a few pasta plates, as well as second courses, *torte salate* (savory tarts), and plenty to choose from to drink. The atmosphere here is modern and casually reserved. Around the corner is the wine shop of the same name—one of the oldest in Rome. Call about wine tastings and short courses (in Italian). ⊠ *Via Cernaia 37/b*, ☎ *06/446–9630. AE, D, MC, V. Closed Sun. and 2 wks in Aug. No lunch Sat.*

Old Rome

$ ✕ **Enoteca Corsi.** Very convenient to the historic center for lunch (no dinner) or an afternoon break, it looks like this little wine bar missed the revolution; prices and decor are *come una volta* (like once upon a time) when the shop sold—as the sign says—wine (red or white) and oil. The genuinely dated feel of the place has its charm: You can still get wine here by the liter, or choose from a good variety of fairly priced alternatives in bottles. There are also nicely prepared pastas and kind service. ⊠ *Via del Gesù 88*, ☎ *06/679–0821. AE, MC, V. Closed Sun. No dinner.*

$ ✕ **La Bottega del Vino di Anacleto Bleve.** This cozy wine shop in the Jewish ghetto sets out tables and opens up for lunch. Owner Anacleto Bleve and his sons make the rounds, proposing the latest cheese they have procured from the farthest reaches of Italy. Instead of a menu, there's mamma at the counter with a good selection of mixed salads, smoked fish, and sliced meats, as well as a few soups and *sformati* (thick flans). You point and she serves it up. There are always wines to drink by the glass, or you can choose from the several hundred bottles on the shelves that surround you. ⊠ *Via Santa Maria del Pianto*, ☎ *06/ 788–0494. AE, D, MC, V. Closed Thurs.*

$ ✕ **L'Osteria dell'Ingegno.** This is a perfect stop for a quick lunch or dinner after sightseeing or shopping. With its stylish decor and happening feel, the trendy wine bar seems almost out of place among the ruins of the old town. The short menu changes weekly, with simple dishes that emphasize fine ingredients. Service is fast. ⊠ *Piazza di Pietra 45*, ☎ *06/678–0662. Reservations not accepted. AE, D, MC, V. Closed Sun.*

Vatican

$ ✕ **Il Simposio di Costantini.** The classiest wine bar in town is wrapped in wrought-iron vines, wood paneling, and velvet. Choose from about 30 wines in *degustazione* (available by the glass) or order by the bottle from a list of over 1,000 Italian and foreign labels sold in the shop next door. Food is appropriately fancy; expect a multitude of marinated and smoked fish, composed salads, top-quality salami and cured meats (classical and wild), terrines and patés. If you are in the mood for hot food, there are always two soups on the menu, as well as several gussied-up vegetable and meat dishes. Equally vast is the best assortment of cheeses in the city—80 varieties, served in platters of 6 to 30 different selections grouped according to origin or type (French, goat, Italian, hard, herb-crusted). ✉ *Via Appia Antica 139,* ☎ *06/788–0494. AE, MC, V. Closed Thurs.*

Pizzerias

It may have been invented somewhere else, but in Rome it's hard to walk a block without passing pizza in one form or another. Pizza from a bakery is usually made without cheese—*pizza bianca* (just olive oil and salt) or *pizza rossa* (with tomato sauce). Many small shops specialize in pizza *a taglio* (by the slice), priced by the *etto* (100 grams, about ¼ lb.), according to the kind of topping. Both of these make a great snack any time of day. A few good addresses are: **Il Forno di Campo dei Fiori** (✉ Campo dei Fiori, ☎ 06/688–06662; closed Sun.) makes excellent pizza bianca and rossa all day. Just around the corner is **Pizza alla Pala**(✉ Via del Pellegrino 11, ☎ 06/686–5083; closed Sun.). **Zí Fenizia** (✉ Via Santa Maria del Pianto 65, ☎ 06/689–6976; closed Fri. eve., Sat., and Jewish holidays) makes kosher pizza in the old Jewish ghetto.

Don't leave Rome without having sat down to a Roman pizza in a pizzeria. Most are open only for dinner, usually from 8 PM to midnight. Look for a place with a *forno a legna* (wood-burning oven), a must for a good thin-crust, plate-size Roman pizza. Standard models are the *margherita* (tomato, mozzarella, and basil), *napoletana* (tomato, mozzarella, and anchovy), and the *capricciosa* (tomato, mozzarella, sausage, olives), but most pizzerias have a long list of additional options, including tasty *mozzarella di bufala* (buffalo-milk mozzarella). The wine at a pizzeria is worth skipping; Italians drink beer with pizza. There are sometimes other things to order on a pizzeria menu, but aside from *bruschetta* (grilled bread, usually topped with chopped fresh tomato, basil, garlic, and olive oil) and *crostini* (mozzarella toast), non-pizza items are often disappointing.

Near Termini

$ ✕ **La Soffitta.** You pay more, but hey, it's imported. This is Rome's hottest spot for classic Neapolitan pizza (thick, though crusty on the bottom, rather than paper-thin and crisp like the Roman kind) and the only pizzeria in town that has been certified by the Neapolitan Pizza Association to make the real thing. Desserts are brought in daily from Naples, of course. ✉ *Via dei Villini 1/e,* ☎ *06/440–4642. Reservations not accepted. No credit cards. Closed Sun. and Aug. No lunch.*

Old Rome

$$ ✕ **Baffetto.** Down a cobblestone street not far from Piazza Navona, this is Rome's best-known pizzeria and a summer favorite for outside dining. The plainly decorated interior is mostly given over to the ovens, but there's another room with more paper-covered tables. Turnover is fast; this is not the place to linger. ✉ *Via del Governo Vecchio 114,*

☎ 06/686–1617. *Reservations not accepted. No credit cards. Closed Sun. and Aug. No lunch.*

$ ✕ **Il Leoncino.** Lines out the door on weekends attest to the popularity of this florescent-lit pizzeria in the otherwise big-ticket neighborhood around Piazza di Spagna.It's one of the few pizzerie open for lunch as well as dinner. ⊠ *Via del Leoncino 28, near Corso,* ☎ 06/687–6306. *Reservations not accepted. No credit cards. Closed Sun. and Aug.*

Trastevere/Testaccio

$ ✕ **Dar Poeta.** Romans drive across town for great pizza from this neighborhood joint on a small street in Trastevere. Maybe it's the dough—the pizza is a bit cheaper than average, and made from a secret blend of flours that is reputed to be easier to digest than the competition. For dessert, there's an unusual calzone with Nutella chocolate-hazelnut spread and ricotta. ⊠ *Vicolo del Bologna 45,* ☎ *06/588–0516 Reservations not accepted. AE, MC, V. Closed Mon. No lunch.*

Caffès

As elsewhere in Italy, there is a caffè on nearly every corner in Rome. Locals usually stop in for a quickie at the bar, which is also much less expensive than the same drink taken at table. If you want your coffee without sugar, ask for it *amaro*. Pricey **Caffè Greco** (⊠ Via dei Condotti 86, ☎ 06/679–1700) is a national landmark; its red-velvet chairs and marble tables have hosted the likes of Byron, Shelley, Keats, Goethe, and Casanova. **Caffè Sant'Eustachio** (⊠ P. Sant'Eustachio 82, ☎ 06/86130), traditionally frequented by Rome's literati, has outstanding coffee. **Tazza d'Oro** (⊠ Via degli Orfani, near Pantheon, ☎ 06/583–5869) serves one of the city's best cups of coffee. You can sit yourself down and watch the world go by at **Rosati** (⊠ Piazza del Popolo 5, ☎ 06/322–5859). **Caffè della Pace** (⊠ Via della Pace 3, ☎ 06/686–1216) is on a quiet street near Piazza Navona. **Caffè Teichner** (⊠ Piazza San Lorenzo in Lucina 15/18, ☎ 06/687–1683) is just off the Corso.

Gelaterias and Pasticcerias

Gelato is more a snack for Italians than a serious dessert. **Il Gelato di San Crispino** (⊠ Via della Panetteria 54, near Trevi Fountain, ☎ 06/704–50412; closed Tues.) makes perhaps the most celebrated gelato in all of Italy, without artificial colors or flavors. It's worth crossing town for—nobody else makes flavors this balanced, ice cream this real. Other worthwhile addresses for gelato are **Fiocco di Neve** (⊠ Via del Pantheon 51, ☎ no phone; closed Sun.) and **Fonte della Salute** (⊠ Viale Trastevere, ☎ 06/589–7471; closed 4 wks at Christmas). **Cremeria Ottaviani** (⊠ Via Leone IV 83/85, ☎ 06/375–14774; closed Wed.) is an old-fashioned gelateria with an excellent *granita di caffè* (coffee ice slush).

Romans are not known for having a sweet tooth, and there are few pastry shops in town that distinguish themselves with particularly good examples of the few regional desserts. One exception is the **Forno del Ghetto** (⊠ Via del Portico d'Ottavia 20/b ☎ 06/687–8637; closed Fri. eve., Sat., and Jewish holidays). So maybe you didn't expect a Jewish bakery in Rome? This hole-in-the-wall—no sign, no tables, just a take-away counter—is an institution, preserving a tradition of Italian Jewish sweets that cannot be found anywhere else. The ricotta cake (with sour cherry jam or chocolate) is unforgettable. Just down the street is **Dolceroma** (⊠ Via del Portico d'Ottavia 20/b ☎ 06/689–2196; closed Mon. and 4 wks July–Aug.), where the specialties, alas, are not Roman: American pies and Austrian pastries.

4 Lodging

High-ceilinged rooms in Renaissance palazzi, sleek marble baths and plush carpets, and the thrill of opening your window to a view of the Pantheon's dome or a pretty Baroque church facade are some of the pleasures of staying in Rome's hotels. Even in budget hotels, where the rooms may be smaller, the furniture tackier, and the floors creakier, you may enjoy the same views and a sense of being in the heart of history. Rome has a wide range of hotels, most of them conveniently in the downtown area. Jubilee Year incentives have led many to upgrade their facilities, so there is no lack of satisfactory hotels in every category.

PALATIAL SETTINGS, luxurious comfort, spacious rooms, and high standards of service can be taken for granted in the city's top establishments, all in the very expensive price category. But in other categories, especially moderate and inexpensive, standards vary considerably. As a rule of thumb, in the moderate and inexpensive categories you have to expect to pay higher rates for less space and fewer comforts than you would for a hotel room in a comparable category in the United States. In renovated palazzi with a rigid structural scheme, space is at a premium; a few square feet of private bathroom space often has to be subtracted from the area of rooms that are not very big to start with.

International chains such as Hilton, Sheraton, Holiday Inn, and—as of 1999—Marriott, have luxury properties in Rome and maintain high standards of comfort. The Best Western group includes about eight moderately priced, independently owned and managed hotels in downtown Rome. Jolly hotels and Starhotels are Italy-based international chains with four-star hotels in Rome.

Hotels are graded on a five-star scale, with the five-star hotels at a deluxe level and one-star hotels at the opposite end of the scale. The stars are assigned by local boards on the basis of a complicated evaluation of facilities and services, but the system can be misleading. For tax purposes, hotels may prefer to have fewer stars than their amenities and services would warrant; as a result, their price-to-quality ratios may be excellent.

Five- and four-star hotels have all the amenities you would expect at top levels and rates, with full services, spacious lounges, bars, restaurants, and some fitness facilities. Three-star hotels may have fridge-bars and in-room safes and double glazing to keep out street noise. Two- and three-star hotels will have private bathrooms and in-room direct-dial telephone and television, and most will have air conditioning. In the less expensive places, you may have to pay extra for air-conditioning, and the shower may well be the drain-in-the-floor type that floods the bathroom. In one-star hotels you may have to share a bathroom and do without an elevator.

It can be hot in Rome from May through September. Always inquire about air-conditioning when booking a room for that time of year. Noise is also a concern in Rome. Romans are voluble—with or without cars and mopeds adding to the din. Rooms in all top hotels are soundproofed, but noise may be a problem in less expensive hotels anywhere in the city, especially in summer if there's no air-conditioning. Ask for an inside room if you're a light sleeper, but don't be surprised if it's on a dark courtyard. The old-fashioned Roman pensione ceased to exist long ago as an official category, but many smaller inexpensive and moderate hotels preserve the homey atmosphere that makes visitors prefer them, especially for longer stays.

The hotels listed below were selected according to criteria of quality, location, and character. Most of them are in downtown Rome, where you can find hotels in all categories. There are obvious advantages to staying in a hotel within easy walking distance of the main sights, particularly now that parts of downtown Rome are closed to traffic and are blessedly quieter than before. Stringent traffic and parking restrictions make a car a hindrance; if you have one, leave it in a garage and explore the city on foot. Staying in a central hotel means that you won't have to use crowded public transportation or take taxis all the time. The Termini station area has the highest hotel density, but accommodations vary widely from fine to seedy.

Rome Lodging

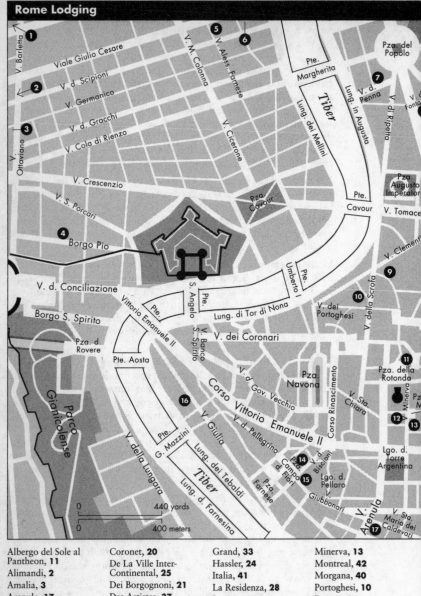

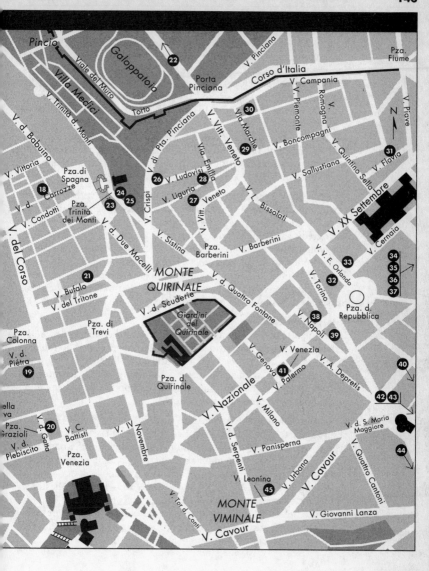

Always book in advance, even if only a few days ahead. Rome's religious importance makes it a year-round tourist destination, and there is never a period when Rome's hotels are predictably empty. However, July and August and late-January to February are generally slack months. Inquire about special rates at all times. If you do arrive without reservations, try **HR** (Hotel Reservation service; ☎ 06/699–1000), with desks at Leonardo da Vinci airport and Termini Station (an English-speaking operator is available daily 7 AM–10 PM). Municipal Information kiosks throughout the city can help you find accommodations free of charge. **CTS** (✉ Via Genova 16, ☎ 06/46791), a student travel agency, can help find rooms. Don't rely on official-looking men who approach tourists at Termini Station: They tout for the less desirable hotels around the train station.

You can book by telephoning and then following up with a letter or fax for confirmation. You will probably be asked to send a deposit, so get a statement from the hotel about its refund policy before releasing your credit card number or mailing a money order. Always insist on receiving written confirmation from the hotel with details of the duration of your stay, room rate, extras if any, and location and type of room (single or double, twin beds or double; with or without bath or shower). When corresponding with hotels, remember that mail in Italy can be exasperatingly slow; telephone, fax and E-mail are more effective.

Residence Hotels

If you plan to stay a month or more and want the independence offered by an apartment, consider staying in a residence hotel. Residence hotels have fully equipped kitchens and offer linens, laundry, and cleaning services. Most are available for monthly rentals; costs for an apartment for two range from about 2.5 million lire for a week to 5 million lire per month.

Residence Aldrovandi (✉ Via Aldrovandi 11, ☎ 06/322–1430) is in the toney Parioli residential district north of Villa Borghese park, where you have to take a taxi or tram to reach downtown Rome. It is furnished with distinction and has concierge and maid service; guests can use the pool of the adjacent Hotel Aldrovandi.

Residence Ripetta (✉ Via Ripetta 231, ☎ 06/323–1144), in the heart of the city, near Piazza del Popolo, is the most central of all of Rome's residence hotels. Its compact apartments are furnished in smart contemporary style, and it is well equipped for business travelers, with in-house meeting facilities.

Ratings

Room rates in Rome are on a par with those of most other major European capitals. Rates are always inclusive of service, but it is customary to tip porters, waiters, maids, and concierges. Taxes and breakfast are separate items in five-star hotels. In all other categories rates quoted for rooms generally include taxes, service, and breakfast, which may be Continental or buffet. The standard continental breakfast consists of coffee, cappuccino or tea, and a croissant or rolls, butter, and jam. Many hotels offer heartier buffet breakfasts, with cereals, yogurt, fresh fruit and juice, sometimes with bacon, eggs, and ham. In lower-priced hotels air-conditioning may add an extra charge of about 15–20,000 lire per day. All hotels are supposed to have rate cards on the room doors or inside the closet. These specify exactly what you have to pay and detail any extras. Rates in any given hotel can vary according to the location and amenities of individual rooms.

Unless otherwise stated, at the hotels reviewed there are elevators, TV (many with cable, including CNN) in the rooms, and telephones, and English is spoken. Few two-star hotels have minibars.

Highly recommended establishments are indicated by a star ★.

CATEGORY	COST*
$$$$	over 600,000 lire
$$$	350,000–450,000 lire
$$	250,000–350,000 lire
$	under 250,000 lire**

*for two people in a standard double room, including tax and service.

**The top rate is rarely applied; most hotels in this category charge 120,000–180,000 lire, depending on the season.

The Vatican

$$$$ ⊞ **Cavalieri Hilton.** Though the Cavalieri is outside the imaginary con-
★ fines of the city's center, distance has its advantages, one of them being the magnificent view from the hotel's hilltop site (ask for a room facing the city). This hotel is a stylish oasis of quiet and comfort, with good taste and a distinctive Italian flair. If you can tear yourself away from your balcony, the terraces, gardens, and swimming pool, you will find a courtesy shuttle bus leaving for the center of Rome every hour. Don't miss the deservedly acclaimed rooftop restaurant, La Pergola. (☞ Chapter 3, Dining). ⊠ *Via Cadlolo 101, 00136,* ☎ *06/35091,* FAX *06/350–92241. 358 rooms, 18 suites. EP. 2 restaurants, bar, indoor and outdoor pools, beauty salon, spa, fitness center. AE, DC, MC, V.*

$$$ ⊞ **Farnese.** A totally renovated turn-of-the-century mansion, the Far-
★ nese is two Metro stops from the Spanish Steps and within walking distance of St. Peter's. Furnished with great attention to detail in art deco style, it has an intimate atmosphere, dazzling modern baths, charming trompe l'oeil fresco decorations, and a roof garden. The ample sitting rooms on the main floor and the high-ceilinged bedrooms are soberly elegant, with lavish wainscoting and rich fabrics. Owner-run by the same family as the Giulio Cesare around the corner, it pampers guests with personalized attention. ⊠ *Via Alessandro Farnese 30, 00192,* ☎ *06/321–2553,* FAX *06/321–5129. 24 rooms. Bar, parking (fee). EP. AE, DC, MC, V.*

$$$ ⊞ **Giulio Cesare.** An aristocratic town house in the residential, but central, Prati district, the Giulio Cesare is a 10-minute walk across the Tiber from Piazza del Popolo. It's beautifully run, with a friendly staff and a quietly luxurious air. The rooms are elegantly furnished, with chandeliers, thick rugs, floor-length drapes, and rich damasks in soft colors. Public rooms have Oriental carpets, old prints and paintings, marble fireplaces, and a grand piano. The buffet breakfast is a veritable banquet. ⊠ *Via degli Scipioni 287, 00192,* ☎ *06/321–0751,* FAX *06/321–1736. 90 rooms. Bar. CP. AE, DC, MC, V.*

$$ ⊞ **Sant'Anna.** An example of the gentrification of the picturesque old Borgo neighborhood in the shadow of St. Peter's, this fashionable small hotel has ample, air-conditioned bedrooms in art deco style. The frescoes in the breakfast room and fountain in the courtyard are typical Roman touches. The spacious attic rooms have tiny terraces. ⊠ *Borgo Pio 134, 00193,* ☎ *06/688–01602,* FAX *06/683–8717. 20 rooms. Parking (fee). CP. AE, DC, MC, V.*

$ ⊞ **Alimandi.** On a side street only a block from the Vatican Museums,
★ this family-operated hotel offers excellent value in a neighborhood with moderately priced shops and restaurants. A spiffy lobby and ample lounges, a tavern for night owls, terraces, and roof gardens are some of the perks here. Rooms are spacious, airy, and well furnished; many can accommodate extra beds. Handy public transportation gets you to downtown Rome in 10 minutes or so. ⊠ *Via Tunisi 8, 00192,* ☎ *06/397–23948,* FAX *06/397–23943. 35 rooms. Parking (fee). EP. AE, DC, MC, V.*

$ 🏨 **Amalia.** Handy to St. Peter's, the Vatican, and the Cola di Rienzo shopping district, this small hotel is owned and operated by the Consoli family—Amalia and her brothers. On several floors of a 19th-century building, it has large, airy rooms with functional furnishings, TV sets, fridge-bars, pictures of angels on the walls, and gleaming marble bathrooms (hair dryers included). The Ottaviano stop of Metro A is a block away. ⊠ *Via Germanico 66, 00192,* ☎ *06/397–23356,* FAX *06/397–23365. 30 rooms, 25 with bath or shower. Parking (fee). CP. AE, MC, V.*

Old Rome

$$$$ 🏨 **Minerva.** The Holiday Inn Crowne Plaza Minerva is the very stylish reincarnation of the hostelry that occupied this 17th-century palazzo for centuries, hosting literati from Stendhal to Sartre and de Beauvoir. Entirely redone, with a stunning new stained-glass lobby skylight designed by architect Paolo Portoghesi, the Minerva has everything a guest could want in the way of comfort, all in an absolutely central location. And from the roof terrace, open for summer dining in fair weather, you can almost touch the immense, flattened dome of Hadrian's Pantheon. ⊠ *Piazza della Minerva 69, 00186,* ☎ *06/699–41888,* FAX *06/679–4165. 118 rooms, 16 suites. Restaurant, bar. EP. AE, DC, MC, V.*

$$$ 🏨 **Albergo del Sole al Pantheon.** This small hotel has stood opposite the Pantheon since the 15th century. Over the years, travelers have accepted the rather cramped quarters in exchange for the location on this historic square. The hotel has been tastefully decorated with a blend of modern and antique furnishings. Ceilings are high and floors are tiled in terra-cotta. Double glazing shuts out the din of the café scene below the windows. ⊠ *Piazza della Rotonda 63, 00186,* ☎ *06/678–0441,* FAX *06/699–40689. 25 rooms. Bar. CP. AE, DC, MC, V.*

$$$ 🏨 **Cardinal.** Staying at this hotel is like stepping inside a Renaissance painting—it was built by Bramante, first architect of St. Peter's, and is set on magnificent Via Giulia, whose vistas have scarcely changed since the 15th century. Cardinals would feel right at home: the lobby is pale and cool, while the rooms upstairs are almost ascetic. Serene, severe, and subdued, many of the rooms have antique engravings and Olympian-high ceilings. ⊠ *Via Giulia 62, 00186,* ☎ *06/688–02719,* FAX *06/678–6376. 73 rooms. Bar. CP. AE, DC, MC, V.*

$$ 🏨 **Cesari.** From the traffic-free street in front of this intimate and
★ quiet hotel in the center of Rome, you can see the columns of an ancient temple that were incorporated into the side of the stock exchange. The hotel's exterior is as it was when Stendhal and German historian Gregorovius stayed here in the 1800s, but the interior has been thoroughly renovated and redecorated, with cream-colored walls embellished with old prints of Rome and soft green drapes and bedspreads. A few rooms are furnished with antiques; all have smart two-tone blue marble bathrooms. ⊠ *Via di Pietra 89a, 00186,* ☎ *06/679–2386,* FAX *06/679–0882. 47 rooms. Parking (fee). CP. AE, DC, MC, V.*

$$ 🏨 **Portoghesi.** In the heart of Old Rome, the Portoghesi is a small hotel with big atmosphere and a truly European character. From a tiny lobby, an equally tiny elevator takes you to the quiet bedrooms, all decorated with floral prints and reproduction antique furniture. It has a charming roof garden with a view of the city's domes and rooftops. ⊠ *Via dei Portoghesi 1, 00186,* ☎ *06/686–4231,* FAX *06/687–6976. 22 rooms, 6 suites. CP. MC, V.*

$$ 🏨 **Santa Chiara.** Three historic buildings form this gracious hotel be-
★ hind the Pantheon. It has been in the same family for 200 years, and their personal attention shows in meticulously decorated and maintained

lounges and rooms. Though not all of the rooms are spacious, all have character and are quiet and well organized. Each has built-in oak headboards, a marble-topped desk, and an elegant travertine bath. Double-glazed front windows overlook Piazza della Minerva. The excellent location and low rates in this category give it a good quality-for-price ratio. The hotel also has three apartments, for two to five persons, with full kitchens. The topmost has beamed ceilings, a fireplace, and a huge terrace with a view of the Pantheon's dome. ⊠ *Via Santa Chiara 21, 00186,* ☎ *06/687–2979,* ℻ *06/687–3144. 100 rooms, 4 suites, 3 apartments. Bar. CP. AE, DC, MC, V.*

$$ 🏨 **Teatro di Pompeo.** Where else can you breakfast under the ancient stone vaults of Pompey's Theater, historic site of Julius Caesar's assassination? At this intimate and refined little hotel in the heart of Old Rome you are part of that history; the restored beamed ceilings of the bedrooms date from the days of Michelangelo. The tastefully furnished rooms offer comfort as well as charm. Book well in advance. ⊠ *Largo del Pallaro 8, 00186,* ☎ *06/683–00170,* ℻ *06/688–05531. 13 rooms. CP. AE, DC, MC, V.*

$ 🏨 **Campo dei Fiori.** Frescoes, exposed brickwork, and picturesque effects throughout this little hotel in Old Rome could well be the work of a set designer. There's an aura of fantasy and romanticism in the decoration, with the layout cleverly designed to make the most of limited space. A few rooms are so compact they're almost claustrophobic; others are larger, and all have some unusual decorative feature to remind you that you are in the heart of Rome. The hotel has no elevator, but the climb to the roof terrace rewards you with a marvelous view and a great area to relax. Rates for the best rooms exceed the range in this price category. ⊠ *Via del Biscione 6, 00186,* ☎ *06/688–06865,* ℻ *06/687–6003. 27 rooms, 14 with bath. EP. MC, V.*

$ 🏨 **Coronet.** You, too, can be a guest in the vast Palazzo Doria Pamphili off Piazza Venezia. This small hotel occupies part of a floor in one wing of the palace; seven interior rooms overlook the aristocratic family's lovely private garden court. Antique-style stuccoes and moldings in the carpeted halls and beamed ceilings in several rooms are in keeping with the historic surroundings. The good-sized rooms have oldish baths, some very small; several rooms can accommodate three or four beds. ⊠ *Piazza Grazioli 5, 00186,* ☎ *06/679–2341,* ℻ *06/699–22705. 13 rooms, 10 with bath. CP. AE, DC, MC, V.*

The Spanish Steps to Trevi

$$$$ 🏨 **De La Ville Inter-Continental.** For the well-heeled, this is a finely honed option just a stone's throw from the top of the Spanish Steps. Guests often ask for the rooms their great-grandparents favored; regulars are treated like family here—one reason the place is usually booked solid. Other lures include a lobby replete with marble and gilt furnishings; tastefully subdued guest rooms; and a staff high on initiative. Don't miss the morning meal or Sunday brunch served in La Piazzetta restaurant: Adorned with twinkling chandeliers, silky bergéres, and taffeta-draped French doors, it has to be the prettiest breakfast in Rome. ⊠ *Via Sistina 69, 00187,* ☎ *06/67331,* ℻ *06/678–4213. 192 rooms, 23 suites. EP. Bar, parking (fee). AE, DC, MC, V.*

$$$$ 🏨 **Hassler.** At the top of the Spanish Steps, the Hassler has sweeping ★ views of Rome from its front rooms and rooftop restaurant; other rooms overlook the gardens of Villa Medici. The hotel is run by the distinguished Wirth family of hoteliers, which assures a cordial atmosphere and imperial service from the well-trained staff, whose discretion is appreciated by the showbiz celebrities who are regular guests. The public rooms have an extravagant 1950s elegance—especially the clubby winter bar, the summer garden bar, and the glass-roofed lounge, with gold marble walls and a hand-painted tile floor. The comfortable guest rooms are decorated in a variety of classic styles, some with frescoed walls. The penthouse suite, resplendent with antiques, has a huge terrace. ⊠ *Piazza Trinità dei Monti 6, 00187,* ☎ *06/699–340,* FAX *06/ 678–991. 85 rooms, 15 suites. Restaurant, bar, beauty salon. EP. AE, DC, MC, V.*

$$$ 🏨 **Dei Borgognoni.** This quietly chic hotel is on a byway in the heart of the smart shopping district near Piazza San Silvestro. The centuries-old building has been remodeled to provide spacious lounges, a glassed-in garden, and stylishly furnished rooms that are cleverly arranged to create an illusion of space, though they are actually compact. Some rooms have balconies or terraces on an interior court. ⊠ *Via del Bufalo 126,* ☎ *06/699–41505,* FAX *06/699–41501. 50 rooms. Bar, business services, parking (fee). EP. AE, DC, MC, V.*

$$ 🏨 **Carriage.** The Carriage's location is what makes it special: it's just two blocks away from the Spanish Steps, in the heart of Rome. The stylish decor uses subdued Baroque accents and antique reproductions to give the hotel a touch of elegance. Though some of the rooms are pint-size, and a couple open onto an air shaft, several have little terraces, and all guests can use the roof garden. ⊠ *Via delle Carrozze 36, 00187,* ☎ *06/679–3312,* FAX *06/678–8279. 27 rooms. Bar. CP. AE, DC, MC, V.*

$$ 🏨 **Scalinata di Spagna.** An old-fashioned pensione that has hosted generations of romantics, this tiny hotel is booked solid for months—even years—ahead. Its location at the top of the Spanish Steps, inconspicuous little entrance, and view from the terrace where you breakfast make it seem like your own special, exclusive inn. And that's why rates for some rooms, all freshly renovated in 1998, go over the top of this category. ⊠ *Piazza Trinità dei Monti 17, 00187,* ☎ *06/679–3006,* FAX *06/ 699–40598. 16 rooms. Parking (fee). CP. AE, MC, V.*

$ 🏨 **Marcus.** The location, down the street from the Spanish Steps, is the premier feature of this small, homelike hotel occupying a large apartment on one floor of an 18th-century cardinal's palazzo. Many rooms have antique fireplaces but new bathrooms. The main living room has comfortable armchairs and a crystal chandelier. Double-glazed windows keep out most of the noise of central Rome. ⊠ *Via Clementina 94, 00184,* ☎ *06/683–00320,* FAX *06/683–00312. 15 rooms. CP. AE, MC, V.*

Trajan's Market to the Basilicas

$$ 🏨 **Duca d'Alba.** This elegant hotel has made a stylish contribution to
★   the ongoing gentrification of the Suburra, the neighborhood near the Colosseum and the Roman Forum. The tasteful neoclassic decor is in character, with ancient Roman motifs, custom-designed furnishings, and marble bathrooms. All rooms are entirely soundproofed; a few have tiny terraces. The four-bed suite with kitchenette is an excellent money-saving option for a family or a group of friends. This well-run establishment offers an exceptionally good value/price ratio. The attentive staff is another plus. ⊠ *Via Leonina 14, 00184,* ☎ *06/484–471,* FAX *06/488–4840. 27 rooms, 1 suite. CP. AE, DC, MC, V.*

$$ 🏨 **D'Este.** The fresh-looking decor in this distinguished 19th-century hotel evokes turn-of-the-century comfort, with brass bedsteads and lamps and dark-wood period furniture. Rooms are quiet, light, and spacious; many can accommodate family groups. The attentive owner-manager likes to have fresh flowers in the halls and sees that everything works. He encourages inquiries about special rates, particularly during the slack summer months. It's within hailing distance of Santa Maria Maggiore and close to Termini Station (you can arrange to be picked up there by the hotel car). ⊠ *Via Carlo Alberto 4b,* ☎ *06/446–5607,* ℻ *06/ 446–5601. 37 rooms. Bar. CP. AE, DC, MC, V.*

$$ 🔲 **Doria.** A convenient location and low rates in this category are the advantages of this compact hotel. Space is ingeniously exploited, from the minuscule elevator to the nicely furnished but smallish rooms. One of the hotel's most attractive features is the roof garden—again, not very large, but fine for enjoying an al fresco breakfast and an interesting view. The Doria has a clone, the Hotel Amalfi, across the street. Also owned by the courteous Nigro brothers, it has the same amenities and some larger rooms with three beds. ⊠ *Via Merulana 4, 00185,* ☎ *06/446–5888,* ℻ *06/446–5889. 20 rooms. Bar. CP. AE, DC, MC, V.*

$ 🔲 **Montreal.** This compact hotel stands across the square from Santa Maria Maggiore, only three blocks from Termini Station, with bus and subway lines close by. On three floors of an older building, it offers fresh-looking, though smallish, rooms. The owner-managers are pleasant and helpful, and the neighborhood has plenty of reasonably priced eating places. ⊠ *Via Carlo Alberto 4, 10085,* ☎ *06/445–7797,* ℻ *06/ 446–5522. 20 rooms. CP. AE, DC, MC, V.*

Quirinale to Piazza della Repubblica

$$$$ 🔲 **Grand.** A 100-year-old establishment of class and style, this hotel caters to an elite international clientele. It's only a few minutes from Via Veneto. Off the richly decorated, split-level main salon—where afternoon tea is served every day—is an intimate bar, a chic rendezvous. The guest rooms are decorated in gracious Empire style, with smooth fabrics and thick carpets in tones of blue and pale gold. Crystal chandeliers and marble baths add a luxurious note. The Grand also offers one of Italy's most beautiful dining rooms, called simply Le Restaurant. ⊠ *Via Vittorio Emanuele Orlando 3, 00185,* ☎ *06/47091,* ℻ *06/474–7307. 134 rooms, 36 suites. Restaurant, bar, free parking. EP. AE, DC, MC, V.*

$$$ 🔲 **Britannia.** This fine small hotel, with frescoed halls and a buffet-
★ breakfast room, is a very special place, offering superior quality at moderate rates. Its quiet but central location is one attraction; a caring management is another. Guests are coddled with English-language dailies and local weather reports delivered to their rooms each morning, with sybaritic marble bathrooms (some with Jacuzzis), and with well-furnished rooms (two with roof terraces). ⊠ *Via Napoli 64, 00184,* ☎ *06/488–3153,* ℻ *06/488–2343. 32 rooms, 1 suite. Free parking. CP. AE, DC, MC, V.*

$$$ 🔲 **Mascagni.** Outside is one of Rome's most central and busiest streets, but not a sound filters into the interior of this elegant establishment. It has a cheerful staff and the particular charm of the small hotel. Decorated in early 1920s style, it has handsome mahogany furnishings and coordinated fabrics. The intimate lounges and pleasant bar mirror the same decorating scheme, as does the breakfast room, where a lavish buffet is laid in the morning. ⊠ *Via Vittorio Emanuele Orlando 90, 00185,* ☎ *06/489–04040,* ℻ *06/481–7637. 40 rooms. Business services. CP. AE, DC, MC, V.*

$$ 🔲 **Morgana.** The dashingly marbled lobby, the antique accents in fully
★ carpeted halls, the cordial atmosphere, and soundproofed rooms decorated with fine fabrics make this an elegantly conceived hotel, with a luxury uncommon at this price level. It's also convenient to Termini Station. ⊠ *Via Filippo Turati 33, 00185,* ☎ *06/446–7230,* ℻ *06/446–9142. 100 rooms, 2 suites. Bar, parking (fee), airport shuttle. CP. AE, DC, MC, V.*

$ 🔲 **Italia.** Off Via Nazionale, this family-run hotel offers freshly painted, luminous rooms with big windows, desks, parquet floors, new baths with marble-look tiles, and attractive art on the walls, along with a generous buffet breakfast. Three rooms are triples. An eight-room annex across the street has high ceilings, double-glazed windows, and a slightly more upscale look. Ask for low August and winter rates. ⊠ *Via Venezia 18, 00184, ☎ 06/482–8355,* FAX *06/474–5550. 23 rooms. CP. AE, DC, MC, V.*

$ 🏨 **Miami.** Its location in a dignified 19th-century building on Rome's important Via Nazionale puts this hotel in a strategic spot for sightseeing, shopping, and getting around in general; it is on main bus lines and near Termini Station and the Metro. Winter rates from November through February are attractively low. The marble floors, chrome trim, and dark colors are brightened by the friendly family-style management. Rooms on the courtyard are quieter. ⊠ *Via Nazionale 230, 00184,* ☎ *06/481–7180,* FAX *06/484–562. 32 rooms, 2 suites. CP. AE, DC, MC, V.*

Northeast of Termini

$$ 🏨 **Siviglia.** You are transported back to a more opulent era in this freshly renovated 19th-century mansion in the quieter residential fringe of the Termini Station area. Like the several embassies in the neighborhood, it has bright flags flying at the entrance. Inside, Venetian glass chandeliers and reproduction antique furniture give the lounges considerable character; rooms are simpler, with a light, airy touch. ⊠ *Via Gaeta 12, 00185,* ☎ *06/444–1198,* FAX *06/444–1195. 42 rooms. Bar. CP. AE, MC, V.*

$ 🏨 **Des Artistes.** The three personable young Riccioni brothers are transforming their hotel into one of the best in the Termini Station neighborhood for quality/price ratio, lavishing it with paintings and handsome furnishings in mahogany, attractive fabrics, marble baths, and amenities such as air-conditioning and minibars. They promise that their rates won't go up and that they'll keep a floor with simpler rooms for travelers on a budget. ⊠ *Via Villafranca 20, 00185,* ☎ *06/445–4365,* FAX *06/446–2368. 40 rooms, 13 without bath. Bar, roof garden, in-room modem lines. CP. AE, DC, MC, V.*

$$ 🏨 **Art Deco.** This hotel's name tells all about its glamorous decor, attuned to the elegance and fancy of the 1920s, with whimsical accents in deco paintings and antiques. Underlying the style is reassuring technology: a fail-safe electrical system, air-conditioning, and whirlpool baths. The hotel is in a residential neighborhood 10 minutes from Termini Station and handy to public transport. Book through Best Western or directly for the best rates. ⊠ *Via Palestro 19,* ☎ *06/445–7588,* FAX *06/ 444–1483. 49 rooms. Restaurant, bar. CP. AE, DC, MC, V.*

$ 🏨 **Romae.** In the better part of the Termini Station neighborhood, the Romae has the advantages of a strategic location (within walking distance of many sights, and handy to bus and subway lines), a very friendly and helpful management, and good-size rooms that are clean and airy. The pictures of Rome in the small lobby and breakfast room, the luminous white walls and light-wood furniture in the rooms, and the bright little baths all have a fresh look. Amenities such as satellite TV, in-room safe, and hair dryer—not usual in this category—make this hotel a very good value. Families benefit from special rates and services. ⊠ *Via Palestro 49, 00185,* ☎ *06/446–3554,* FAX *06/446–3914. 20 rooms. CP. AE, DC, MC, V.*

Via Veneto to the Ara Pacis

$$$$ 🏨 **Eden.** A superlative hotel that combines dashing elegance and stun-
★   ning vistas of Rome with the warm charm of Italian hospitality, it has an intimate air and genuinely friendly staff. The Eden has been the pre-

ferred haunt of Hemingway, Ingrid Bergman, and Fellini, and of many celebrities before them. Precious antiques, sumptuous Italian fabrics, linen sheets, and marble baths exude understated elegance. The views from the rooftop bar and restaurant will take your breath away, and La Terrazza dell'Eden merits raves, too (☞ Chapter 3, Dining). ⊠ *Via Ludovisi 49, 00187,* ☎ *06/478–121,* ℻ *06/482–1584. 101 rooms, 12 suites. EP. Restaurant, bar, exercise room, free parking. AE, DC, MC.*

$$$$ ⊞ **Excelsior.** To Romans and many others, the white Victorian cupola of the Excelsior is a symbol of Rome at its most cosmopolitan. The hotel's porte cochere has long sheltered Europe's aristocrats and Hollywood's royalty as they alighted from their Rollses and Ferraris. They passed through polished doors that still open onto a world of luxury lavished with mirrors, carved moldings, Oriental rugs, crystal chandeliers, and huge, baroque floral arrangements. The theme of gracious living prevails throughout the hotel in splendidly appointed rooms and marble baths. ⊠ *Via Veneto 125, 00187,* ☎ *06/4708,* ℻ *06/482–6205. 282 rooms, 45 suites. Restaurant, bar, barbershop, beauty salon, parking. EP. AE, DC, MC, V.*

$$$$ ⊞ **Lord Byron.** This elegant hotel is a striking white art deco town house on the edge of Villa Borghese, the lush park in the center of Rome. It's a short taxi ride to the downtown area, a negligible inconvenience well compensated by the quiet setting. Inside, modern and antique styles are combined with flair in highly polished opulence. The downstairs bar—a magnificent piece of cabinetry—is a conversation piece, and the stylish restaurant is one of Rome's best. ⊠ *Via G. de Notaris 5,* ☎ *06/ 322–0404,* ℻ *06/322–0405. 28 rooms, 9 suites. Restaurant, bar, parking (fee). EP. AE, DC, MC, V.*

$$$$ ⊞ **Majestic.** In the 19th-century tradition of grand hotels, this establishment on Via Veneto offers sumptuous furnishings in turn-of-the-century style. The spacious rooms, swathed in fine fabrics, have opulent white marble bathrooms and are equipped with up-to-date accessories well concealed so as not to spoil the atmosphere. Many suites have whirlpool baths. There are authentic antiques in the public rooms. The excellent restaurant looks like a Victorian conservatory, with a terrace overlooking Via Veneto. The intimate Ninfa grill-café on street level serves light meals and drinks. ⊠ *Via Veneto 50,* ☎ *06/486–841,* ℻ *06/488–0984. 87 rooms, 8 suites. Restaurant, 2 bars, parking (fee). EP. AE, DC, MC, V.*

$$$ ⊞ **Victoria.** A 1950s luxury in the public rooms, solid comfort throughout at reasonable rates, and impeccable management are the main features of this hotel near Via Veneto. Oriental rugs, oil paintings, welcoming armchairs, and fresh flowers add charm to the public spaces, and the rooms are well furnished with armchairs and other amenities ignored by many modern decorators. American business travelers, who prize the hotel's personalized service and restful atmosphere, are frequent guests. Some upper rooms and the roof terrace overlook the majestic pines of Villa Borghese. ⊠ *Via Campania 41, 00187,* ☎ *06/ 473–931,* ℻ *06/487–1890. 108 rooms. Restaurant, bar. CP, FAP, MAP. AE, DC, MC, V.*

$$ ⊞ **La Residenza.** Mainly Americans frequent this hotel in a converted
★ town house near Via Veneto, with first-class comfort and a great atmosphere. The canopied entrance, spacious, well-furnished lounges, and the bar and terrace are of the type you would expect to find in a deluxe lodging. Rooms, done in aquamarine and beige with bentwood furniture, have large closets and heated towel racks; a few have balconies. Rates include a generous American-style buffet breakfast. ⊠ *Via Emilia 22, 00187,* ☎ *06/488–0789,* ℻ *06/485–721. 29 rooms. Bar. CP. AE, MC, V.*

$$ ⊡ **Locarno.** Art aficionados and people in the cinema have long appreciated this hotel's preserved fin de siècle charm, intimate feel, and central location off Piazza del Popolo. Wallpaper and fabric prints are coordinated in the rooms, and some have antiques. All is lovingly supervised by the owners, a mother-daughter duo. The buffet breakfast is ample; there's bar service on the panoramic roof garden and complimentary bicycles, if you dare pedal your way through traffic. ⊠ *Via della Penna 22, 00186,* ☎ *06/361–0841,* FAX *06/321–5249. 46 rooms, 2 suites. Bar, lobby lounge, garage (fee). CP. AE, DC, MC, V.*

$$ ⊡ **Marcella.** Known to connoisseurs as one of Rome's best midsize ho-
★   tels, with the feel of a smaller, more intimate establishment, this is 10 minutes from Via Veneto or Termini Station. Here you can do your sightseeing from the roof terrace, taking in the view while you breakfast. Many rooms also have good views, and they are all furnished with flair, showing a tasteful use of color, floral prints, and mirrored walls, echoing the elegant winter-garden decor of the lounges and bar. The spacious and flexible suites are ideal for families. ⊠ *Via Flavia 106, 00187,* ☎ *06/474–6451,* FAX *06/481–5832. 73 rooms, 2 suites. Bar. CP. AE, DC, MC, V.*

$ ⊡ **Margutta.** For location, good quality/price ratio, and friendly
★ owner/managers, the Margutta is outstanding. The lobby and halls in this small hotel are unassuming, but rooms are a pleasant surprise, with a clean and airy look, attractive wrought-iron bedsteads, and modern baths. Though it's in an old building, there is an elevator. It is well placed on a quiet side street between the Spanish Steps and Piazza del Popolo. ⊠ *Via Laurina 34, 00187,* ☎ *06/322–3674,* FAX *06/320–0395. 21 rooms. CP. AE, DC, MC, V.*

The Ghetto and Trastevere

$ ⊡ **Arenula.** This hotel—with a luminous and cheerful all-white interior—has a good quality/price ratio. Rooms have pale-wood furnishings and gleaming bathrooms, as well as double-glazed windows and air-conditioning (summer only; no help on warm spring or fall days). Two of the rooms accommodate four beds. The catch at the four-story Arenula is that the graceful oval staircase of white marble and wrought iron is the only way up—there is no elevator. The hotel stands on an age-worn byway off central Via Arenula, on the edge of the picturesque Ghetto neighborhood and just across the Tiber from Trastevere. ⊠ *Via Santa Maria dei Calderari 47, off Via Arenula, 00186,* ☎ *06/687–9454,* FAX *06/689–6188. 50 rooms. CP. DC, MC, V.*

5 Nightlife and The Arts

Rome is a magical city at night, its grandeur illuminated against the dark sky, its cafés and piazzas crowded with people watching people. Behind inconspicuous doors, the rites of the evening are celebrated in trendy music clubs, glamorous supper clubs, and grungy discos. When the late show at the cinema is over, the streets are suddenly as crowded as at midday. That's when the pizzerias do a booming business and traffic is more hectic than ever.

TO MANY PEOPLE, ROME ITSELF IS ENTERTAINMENT enough. The piazzas, fountains, and delicately colored palazzi make impressive backdrops for the living theater of vivacious Rome, with a *fortissimo* of motor vehicles. Rome has learned to make the most of its spectacular cityscape, transforming its most beautiful places into settings for performances of the arts, either outdoors in the summer or in splendid palaces and churches in the winter. Often the venue steals the show, as in the concerts at the Teatro di Marcello, Caracalla, or Palazzo Doria. Music is what Rome does best to entertain people until the wee hours, whether it be opera or jazz or disco. Theater, and especially the cinema, are a big draw for Italian-speakers, but late-night café-sitting in trendy spots is fun even if you don't speak the language.

THE ARTS

Though Romans used to take their culture rather distractedly, they are now showing a lively interest in the arts and in their new or refurbished museums, and they can't wait for the new concert hall designed by Renzo Piano to be finished (the site is near the Flaminio Stadium, north of Piazza del Popolo; promised for 1999, the opening may be delayed). The city offers an array of cultural events throughout the year, at outdoor venues during the warmer months. For all outdoor events in the evening, take a jacket or sweater and something to cover bare legs: despite the daytime heat of a Roman summer, the nights can be cool and damp. Events generally are poorly publicized; you can find out what's scheduled by keeping an eye on the posters announcing events and reading the lists in newspapers and specialized publications.

Schedules of events are published in the daily newspapers, in the *Trovaroma* Thursday supplement of *La Repubblica* newspaper, in the *Guest in Rome* booklet distributed free at hotel desks, and in flyers available at EPT offices and city tourist information kiosks. A fortnightly English-language periodical, *Wanted in Rome,* available at many newsstands, has good coverage of events in the arts. There are listings in English in the back of the weekly *Roma c'è* booklet, with a new edition at newsstands every Thursday. Look for posters outside churches announcing free concerts and recitals of religious music. The Europe Festival in June and July is a multivenue performing arts program.

Depending on the venue, concert tickets can cost anything from 15,000 to 50,000 lire. Often seating is open (that is, seats are not numbered, *posti non numerati*). Inquire about this when you buy the tickets; you may have to arrive early to get a good seat. Get opera and concert tickets in advance at the box office, or try just before the performance. **Roman Reference** (✉ Via de' Capocci 94, ☎ 06/489–03612) provides many types of personalized services for tourists, including ticket reservations for events in Rome and Italy. **Genti e Paesi** (✉ Via Adda 111, ☎ 06/853–01755) will book tickets for concerts, theaters, and museums.

Dance

The **Rome Opera Ballet** gives regular performances at the Teatro dell'Opera, often with leading international guest stars. Rome is regularly visited by ballet companies from all over the world; performances are at Teatro dell'Opera (☞ Opera, *below*), Teatro Olimpico (☞ *below*), or at one of the open-air venues in summer. The **Teatro Olimpico** (✉ Piazza Gentile da Fabriano 17, ☎ 06/323–4890) is the venue for contemporary dance companies. In addition, throughout the year, small dance companies from Italy and abroad give performances in various places; check entertainment listings for information.

Film

For programs and show times, see the entertainment pages of daily newspapers, *Roma c'è*, or Rome's English-language publications. Tickets are usually 12,000 lire. Rome has dozens of movie houses, but the only one to show exclusively English-language films in English is the **Pasquino** (⊠ Vicolo del Piede, just off Piazza Santa Maria in Trastevere, ☎ 06/580–3622), with two screens. The **Quirinetta** (⊠ Via Minghetti 4, ☎ 06/679–0012) has a policy of showing films in the original language, and they are often in English. The **Alcazar** (⊠ Via Merry del Val 14, ☎ 06/588–0099) has movies in the original language with Italian subtitles on Monday only.

Music

CLASSICAL

Despite the long-standing criticism that Rome doesn't have a central concert hall (a new one is currently under construction), the city hosts a wide variety of classical music concerts at various small venues throughout the city. This can make for memorable performances in smaller halls and churches whose ambience makes up for the less-grand space, particularly at Christmastime, an especially busy concert season in Rome. Of the larger companies, one principal concert series is organized year-round by the **Accademia di Santa Cecilia** (concert hall and box office: ⊠ Via della Conciliazione 4, ☎ 06/68801044). The **Accademia Filarmonica Romana** concerts are performed at the Teatro Olimpico (⊠ Piazza Gentile da Fabriano 17, ☎ 06/323–4890). Other good companies include **Istituzione Universitaria dei Concerti** (⊠ San Leone Magno auditorium, ⊠ Via Bolzano 38, ☎ 06/361–0051; ⊠ Aula Magna, Piazzale Aldo Moro 5, ☎ 06/361–0051). The internationally respected **Gonfalone** (⊠ Via del Gonfalone 32, ☎ 06/687–5952) series focuses on Baroque music. The **Concerti all'Orologio** (☎ 06/683–08735) performs chamber music. **Il Tempietto** (☎ 06/481–4800) organizes music festivals and concerts throughout the year. Depending on the venue, tickets run from about 15,000 to 50,000 lire.

In addition to the formal concert companies, many small concert groups perform in cultural centers and churches. Many concerts are free, including all those performed in Catholic churches, where a special ruling permits only concerts of religious music. Look for posters outside churches announcing free concerts, particularly at the church of **Sant'Ignazio** (⊠ Piazza Sant'Ignazio, near the Pantheon, ☎ 06/679–4506), which often hosts concerts in a spectacularly frescoed setting.

ROCK, POP, AND JAZZ

Rock, pop, and jazz concerts are frequent, especially in summer, although even performances by big-name stars may not be well advertised. Most of the bigger-name acts perform outside the center, so it's worth asking about transportation *before* you buy your tickets. Tickets for these performances are usually handled by **Orbis** (⊠ Piazza Esquilino 37, ☎ 06/474–4776). **Ricordi** music stores (⊠ Via del Corso 506, ☎ 06/361–2331; ⊠ Viale Giulio Cesare 88, ☎ 06/372–0216) also sell tickets.

Opera

Rome's opera season runs from November or December to May, and performances are staged in the **Teatro dell'Opera** (⊠ Piazza B. Gigl, ☎ 06/481–60255; 1670/166–665 toll-free in Italy). Tickets go on sale three days before a performance; the box office is open from 10 to 5. Prices range from about 30,000 to 150,000 lire for regular performances;

they can cost much more for special performances, such as an opening night or an internationally acclaimed guest singer. Standards may not always measure up to those set by Milan's fabled La Scala, but despite strikes and shortages of funds, most performances are respectable.

After the summer opera season was evicted from the ruins of the ancient **Terme di Caracalla** (☞ The Celian Hill and the Baths of Caracalla *in* Chapter 2), the debate over a permanent open-air venue continues. The most likely choice is **Villa Pepoli,** a parklike area adjacent to the ruins of the Baths.

NIGHTLIFE

After-hours entertainment in Rome consists mainly of late-night cafés, music clubs, and discos. Most spots, except the big discos, have a clubby atmosphere, with a regular clientele. The "in" places, especially the discos, change like the flavor of the month, and may fade into oblivion after a brief season of popularity. Many simply change name and decor from one year to the next. Hubs of after-dark activity are Piazza Navona and the Pantheon area, Trastevere, and Testaccio. The Spanish Steps are strictly for tourists.

The best sources for an up-to-date list of late-night spots and of who's playing what at the music clubs are the weekly entertainment guides, *Roma c'è* and *Trovaroma*.

Bars

There's a bar for every taste in Rome. The better hotel bars offer elegant surroundings and soft music, with drinks mixed by expert "barmen," as bartenders are called here. Their customers, too, are usually a mix of Italians and foreigners. Then there's a spate of informal, clubby cafés and wine bars catering to a fairly sophisticated crowd faithfully observing the Roman ritual of the evening aperitif (before-dinner drink) between 6:30 and 9. The most radical change in the bar scene in Rome over the past few years has been the opening of a plethora of quaintly named English and Irish pubs, complete with Guinness and darts and football on the TV. Italians love them.

ELEGANT

Harry's Bar (⊠ Via Veneto 150, ☎ 06/474–5832). Namesake of similar, separately owned operations in Venice and Florence, it is popular with American businessmen and journalists. The attached restaurant is pricey.

Jazz Café (⊠ Via Zanardelli 12, ☎ 06/686–1990). Though there's live music in the little room downstairs, it's the oval mahogany bar on street level that is the main attraction as a watering hole for well-dressed young Romans.

Le Bar (Grand Hotel, ⊠ Via Vittorio Emanuele Orlando 3, ☎ 06/482–931). Off the damask-hung lobby of this truly grand hotel, the bar is a perfect perch from which to watch the wealthy and powerful come and go.

PUBS

Birreria Marconi (⊠ Via di Santa Prassede 9c, ☎ 06/486–636). More a beer hall than pub, it occupies a corner overlooking Santa Maria Maggiore and has tables outdoors. Young Italians flock here for pizza and beer.

Birreria Santi Apostoli (⊠ Piazza Santi Apostoli 52, ☎ 06/678–8285). This pine-paneled beer hall near Piazza Venezia serves light meals and big steins of German beer.

La Briciola (⊠ Via della Lungaretta 81, ☎ 06/581–2260). Haunt of a young and multinational clientele, this beer hall in Trastevere serves

Austrian brews as well as pastas, salads, and more than 100 kinds of sandwiches.

Fiddler's Elbow (⊠ Via dell'Olmata 43, ☎ no phone). Near Santa Maria Maggiore, it's the oldest Irish pub in Rome, and its scruffy authenticity shows up the fancier usurpers that have opened all over town. Singing is encouraged.

Flann O'Brien(⊠ Via Napoli 29, ☎ 06/488–0418). Off Via Nazionale, this pub serves the usual Irish beverages but can also make a decent cappuccino.

Four Green Fields (⊠ Via Costantino Morin 42, off Via della Giuliana, ☎ 06/359–5091). The suitably dusky barroom is on street level; live music makes the lower level jump.

Trinity College (⊠ Via del Collegio Romano 6, ☎ 06/678–6472). Close to Piazza Venezia, this pub has two floors of classic Irish atmosphere and convivial music. It is open for breakfast, lunch, and dinner; the food, however, is Italian.

CAFÉS AND WINE BARS

Antica Enoteca (⊠ Via della Croce 76a, ☎ 06/679–0896). This enoteca occupies historic quarters on a corner near the Spanish Steps. Check out the menu on the stand outside the door; it may be the answer for a light lunch.

Antico Caffè della Pace (⊠ Via della Pace 3, ☎ 06/686–1216). Celebrities and literati hang out in this turn-of-the-century–style café near Piazza Navona. The atmosphere ranges from relaxed to electric, depending on who's in town. It's a cult coffeehouse with an upscale pizzeria annex next door.

Bar del Fico (⊠ Piazza del Fico 26, ☎ 06/686–5205). Once a modest neighborhood coffee bar, it's now a plastic-and-neon rendezvous for swingers who prefer the earthy to the intellectual; watch out for huge crowds on weekend and summer nights.

Cantiniere di Santa Dorotea (⊠ Via di Santa Dorotea 9, ☎ 06/581–91025). This bar in Trastevere has soft music and a friendly atmosphere that the neighborhood's sprinkling of English-speaking residents appreciate.

Cavour 313 (⊠ Via Cavour 313, ☎ 06/678–5496). Not far from the church of San Pietro in Vincoli, this establishment has dark-wood booths and wine shelves bearing bottles from Chile and Australia as well as Italy.

Cul de Sac (⊠ Piazza Pasquino 73, ☎ 06/688–01094). Close to Piazza Navona, the wineshop crams a counter and some wooden tables into a small space where you can sample good wines and snacks.

Il Piccolo (⊠ Via del Governo Vecchio 74, ☎ 06/688–01746). The name means "small," so don't expect much elbow room. Instead, you'll find *sangria* and rare *fragolino* wine, made with grapes that taste like strawberries.

Spiriti (⊠ Via Sant'Eustachio 5, ☎ 06/689–2499). Near the Pantheon, it is tiny, with limited seating and a few tables outdoors. Likewise, the wine list is limited but good, and light lunches and suppers are served.

Taverna del Campo (⊠ Piazza Campo dei Fiori 16, ☎ 06/6874402). This very friendly and popular place draws a young crowd; it features big barrels of peanuts and free nibbles at the bar (olives, cheese). There is also outdoor seating and a light food menu including delicious crostini.

Trimani Wine Bar (⊠ Via Cernaia 37b, ☎ 06/446–9630). With the resources of the huge Trimani wine shop behind it, this sophisticated, two-level spot assures you of the best in wine and tasty edibles to go with your choice, either at the counter or at tables upstairs or outdoors.

Vineria Reggio (⊠ Piazza Campo de Fiori 15, ☎ 06/688–03268). You never know who'll be here; the crowd ranges from aging beatnik poets to smartly turned out young executives, reflecting the heterogeneous character of this colorful market square.

Music Clubs

Jazz, folk, pop, and Latin-music clubs are flourishing in Rome, particularly in the picturesque Trastevere and more workaday Testaccio neighborhoods. Jazz clubs are especially popular at the moment, and talented local groups may be joined by visiting musicians from other countries. For admission, many clubs require that you buy a membership card (usually about 10,000–20,000 lire, which may or may not include one drink).

Alexanderplatz (⌧ Via Ostia 9, ☎ 06/372–9398). In the Trionfale district near the Vatican, Alexanderplatz has both a bar and a restaurant. It has jazz and blues live nightly, played by Italian and foreign musicians.

Berimbau (⌧ Via dei Fienaroli 30b, ☎ 06/581–3249). Latin rhythms are the specialty of this live Brazilian music club in the heart of Trastevere. There are usually two shows every evening, alternating with disco dancing.

Big Mama (⌧ Vicolo San Francesco a Ripa 18, ☎ 06/581–2551). For the best live music, including jazz, blues, rhythm-and-blues, African, and rock, come to Big Mama, an institution for great listening. There is also a bar and snack food.

Circolo degli Artisti (⌧ Via Lamarmora 28, ☎ 06/446–4968). An informal venue for live rock music, it has an underground disco open late. The clientele is mainly in the 20–30 age group.

Colosseum Jazz Live (⌧ Via P. Verri 17, ☎ 06/704–97412); open Wednesday–Saturday. On a side street off Via Labicana, between the Colosseum and San Giovanni in Laterano, this is one of the few clubs in Rome devoted solely to live jazz. There are no frills, but you hear great music from local and visiting jazzmen.

Edoardo II (⌧ Vicolo Margana 14, ☎ 06/699–42419); open Tuesday–Saturday. This music bar for gays has kitschy medieval castle decor, vaguely in keeping with the location in Old Rome, near Piazza Venezia.

Fonclea (⌧ Via Crescenzio 82a, ☎ 06/689–6302). Near Castel Sant'Angelo, it's a cellar with a publike atmosphere and live music ranging from jazz to Latin American to rhythm-and-blues, depending on who's in town. The kitchen provides Italian and Mexican food.

Four XXXX Pub (⌧ Via Galvani 29, ☎ 06/572–5091). This combination restaurant–beer hall–jazz club in the Testaccio neighborhood has live jazz groups and a nonsmoking section downstairs. The menu offers a mix of cuisines, including Latin American food.

Il Locale (⌧ Vicolo del Fico 3, ☎ 06/687–9075). In the heart of the after-hours scene near Piazza Navona, this little place is jammed with a lively young crowd that likes to listen to what's new in rock from both sides of the Atlantic, live or recorded.

Jam Session (⌧ Via del Cardello 13a, ☎ 06/474–5076). Live performances of jazz and soul by internationally known musicians alternate with disco in a funky cellar that was known as the St. Louis for 20 years.

Music Inn (⌧ Largo dei Fiorentini 3, ☎ 06/688–0220). In Old Rome, this is one of the city's historic jazz clubs. It puts on live music by Italian and international groups.

Spago (⌧ Via di Monte Testaccio 35, ☎ 06/574–4999). A sophisticated crowd comes here for cocktails and food until 2:30 AM. Canned music alternates with live, with a predilection for jazz.

Dance and Nightclubs

Most dance clubs open about 10:30 PM, but they really warm up only after midnight. They usually charge a cover of around 25,000–30,000 lire, which sometimes also includes the first drink. Subsequent drinks cost about 10,000–15,000 lire. Some clubs also open on Saturday and Sunday afternoons for the under-16s.

Alibi (✉ Via Monte Testaccio 40, ☎ 06/574–3448). The most famous gay disco in town is a rambling locale with a terrace facing Mount Testaccio that is open for dancing in the summer. Heteros like it too, but the crowd is predominantly gay and male. Events here are often organized by the Circolo Mario Mieli (☎ 06/541–3985), a gay advocacy group.

Bella Blu (✉ Via Luciani 21, ☎ 06/323–0490). The glitzy haunt of movers and shakers from the worlds of politics, commerce, and show biz, this spot is in the Parioli residential district. It's a supper club, with disco dancing and piano bar.

Black Out (✉ Via Saturnia 18, ☎ 06/704–96791). Stark, post-industrial decor leaves plenty of room for young rockers to enjoy themselves, and there's a separate "off-music" room for chilling out. Under various names and guises, this disco has hosted generations of Roman youth.

B-Side (✉ Via dei Funari 21a, ☎ 06/688–05024). This small and grungy downstairs disco in Old Rome is *in* with club kids who like to dance and drink until very late and don't mind doing it in cramped quarters.

Caffè Latino (✉ Via di Monte Testaccio 96, ☎ 06/572–88384). In the trendy Testaccio neighborhood, this club attracts a thirtyish crowd with dancing, an occasional live music performance and a separate video room and bar.

Gilda (✉ Via Mario dei Fiori 97, near Piazza di Spagna, ☎ 06/678–4838). This is the place to spot famous Italian actors and politicians. The sophisticated nightspot near the Spanish Steps has a piano bar as well as a restaurant and dance floors with live and disco music. Jackets are required.

Jackie O' (✉ Via Boncompagni 11, ☎ 06/428–85457). Show biz and sports personalities have no trouble getting past the doorman, but common mortals are advised to call in advance; this glamorous place is often taken over for PR events. There's a restaurant, piano bar, and disco, all dressy.

The Open Gate (✉ Via San Nicolo di Tolentino 4, near Via Veneto, ☎ 06/482–4464). The splashy disco swings to a Latin beat, with salsa and merengue lessons, and live music from Brazil. Sustenance is provided in the form of salads and pizza.

Piper (✉ Via Tagliamento 9, ☎ 06/841–4459). One of Rome's first discos, still hot and a magnet for young movers and shakers, it has dance music, live groups, pop videos, and Latin nights once a week. Occasionally, there's ballroom dancing for an older crowd, and Sunday afternoons it's open for teenagers.

Qube (✉ Via di Portonaccio 212, ☎ 06/438–1005). This is Rome's biggest underground disco, a veritable sea of young bodies dancing till they drop. The decor is minimal, but the lights are psychedelic and the decibels mind-blowing.

6 Outdoor Activities and Sports

If exercise is what you want, do as the gladiators did and run a lap or two around the Circus Maximus. Or play a set of tennis in the shade of ancient Roman walls. You can swim or ride or go golfing in Rome. But if that sounds too fatiguing, get a ticket to a sports event—soccer, anyone?—and see how the pros do it.

I N ROME, soccer, tennis, and horseback riding are the sports that draw the biggest crowds and generate the most hype. The national league soccer games at the Olympic Stadium from September to May and occasional international league games for the European championship are always an event; in May both the international tennis matches and the international horse show attract a mixed audience of bona fide sports fans and celebrities gleaming at the ubiquitous TV cameras. Roman fans are enthusiastic about basketball and volleyball, too, and international matches in both sports are usually sold out. If watching and cheering isn't enough, put on a sweat suit and get out there. Running is the easiest sport for a visitor in Rome, and if you plan your route and timing appropriately, you can get in some sightseeing while you exercise.

BEACHES

The beaches nearest Rome are crowded in summer. In built-up areas along the sea, beach-club concessions monopolize the sand. Patches of free town beaches are usually seedier and more littered. The best beach clubs offer attractive cabanas, restaurants, and beach facilities for which you can pay by the day, week, or month. The public beach at Castefusano is well maintained in season. For cleaner water and more of a resort atmosphere, you have to go farther afield. To the north of Rome, Santa Marinella offers shoals, sand, and seaside restaurants in what is primarily a residential resort. Santa Severa, also north of Rome, has a broad beach and a handsome castle on the sea sheltering a quaint hamlet within its walls. To the southeast of Rome are Sabaudia, San Felice Circeo, and Sperlonga, all with good beaches (☞ Chapter 8, Side Trips). Beaches and public transportation to them are likely to be crowded during July and August, especially on weekends.

Castelfusano is about 3 km (2 mi) southeast of Ostia and about 33 km (20 mi) from Rome. You can take a bus from Ostia to the south along the shore boulevard to Castelfusano, but the fastest and easiest way to reach the town from Rome is by Cotral train from the Magliana station on Metro line B. **Kursaal** (⊠ Lungomare Catullo 36, ☎ 06/562–1303) is one of the better beach clubs and has a swimming pool; it's strongly recommended as an alternative to the sometimes murky waters of the sea around Rome.

Castelporziano is a public beach area maintained by the city about 3 km (2 mi) southeast of Castelfusano. It is open only during the summer, when there is bus service from the Cristoforo Colombo stop at the end of the Cotral train line from the Magliana station on the Metro B line.

Fregene is a villa colony on the shore 37 km (23 mi) northwest of Rome. It can be reached from Rome by Cotral bus from the Via Lepanto stop of Metro Line A. The sand is pretty well monopolized by beach establishments, where you pay for changing cabins, cabanas, umbrellas, and such, and for the fact that the sand is kept clean and combed. Some establishments, such as **La Nave** (⊠ Via Porto Rose, ☎ 06/665–60703), are also known for their lively nightspots.

Ostia, officially called Lido di Ostia (*lido* means "beach"), is a busy urban center in its own right, a kind of satellite city 30 km (18 mi) southwest of Rome. You can reach it by Cotral train from the Ostiense Station and the Magliana station on Metro B line. However, the beach is badly eroded and the beach clubs rather seedy. This is the place to come out of season for a walk on the *pontile* (wharf), a shore dinner, or a gelato at **Sisto** (✉ Piazza Anco Marzio 7, ☎ 06/562–2982); closed Tuesday.

For simply sunning in the center of the city, barges on the Tiber are equipped with deck chairs, showers, and restaurants. Many are private; **Tonino Tulli** (✉ Lungotevere Prati, near Piazza Cavour, ☎ 706/686–1812), moored on the right bank of the Tiber between the Umberto I and Cavour bridges, is an institution and is open to the public.

PARTICIPANT SPORTS AND FITNESS

Biking

Pedaling through Villa Borghese, along the Tiber, and through the center of the city when traffic is light is a good way to see the sights. On smoggy days, wear a mask. Municipal bicycle paths have been laid out on mainly level ground. One of the longest starts at Viale Angelico, near the Vatican, and takes a northerly route to Foro Italico, where it turns away from the street to continue as a pleasant path along the Tiber. Another route goes through Villa Borghese. A 7-km (4-mi) path on the banks of the Tiber extends from Ponte Sublicio (connecting Porta Portese in Trastevere with Via Marmorata in Testaccio) to Ponte della Magliana, downstream.

There are bicycle rental concessions at the Piazza di Spagna and Piazza del Popolo Metro stops, at Largo San Silvestro, Largo Argentina, Viale della Pineta in Villa Borghese, and Viale del Bambino on the Pincio, among others. At concessions and the agencies below, bike rental costs about 4,000 lire per hour, about 7,000 lire for a mountain bike. Daily rates are convenient.

Collalti (✉ Via del Pellegrino 82, ☎ 06/688–01084), near Piazza Navona, can provide a regular or mountain bike, a tandem, and even a pedal-powered rickshaw.
Happy Rent (✉ Via Farini 3, ☎ 06/481–8185), near Santa Maria Maggiore, has a good choice of bikes and gives customers a free map of the city.
I Bike Rome (✉ underground parking lot, Section III, at Villa Borghese; entrance at Porta Pinciana, ☎ 06/322–52400) is open daily; rates are competitive and include helmet, chain, and padlock. The bikes are newish and in good condition.
St. Peter's Motor Rent (✉ Via di Porta Castello 43, ☎ 06/687–5714), close to the Vatican, offers regular and mountain bikes complete with helmets and locks.

Bowling

Rome has a hard core of bowling fans, most of them from the city's large foreign colony. Bowling has never really supplanted bocce in the hearts of Italians. (To see an intense and authentic game of bocce, go to a *bocciodromo*, as a bocce pitch is called. Among the most centrally located are those at Lungotevere Flaminio 39, at Via Austria in the Villaggio Olimpico development, and in Villa Ada park on Via Salaria.)

Bowling Roma (✉ Viale Regina Margherita 181, ☎ 06/855–1184), open 9AM–2AM, has 16 lanes and a snack bar. Shoe rental is included in the price per game, which starts at 3,000 lire on weekday mornings.

Fitness Facilities

Cavalieri Hilton (✉ Via Cadlolo 101, ☎ 06/35091)has a full-fledged fitness and beauty center, with sauna. There is a running path on the hotel's extensive grounds, as well as a stunning glass-domed pool, an outdoor pool, and two clay tennis courts, all open to non-guests.

Fitness Express (✉ Via dei Coronari 46, ☎ 06/686–4989), closed August, is a compact gym in Old Rome with a program of personal training directed by American Linda Foster that offers classic and low-impact aerobics, stretching, and step. Rates by the day are available.

Navona Health Center (✉ Via Banchi Nuovi 39, ☎ 06/689–6104), closed Sundays May–October, is a workout center in a historic palazzo in Old Rome, which offers aerobics, body-building, sauna, and turkish bath. The enrollment fee is waived for non-residents; a workout and use of the sauna costs about 20,000 lire.

Roman Sport Center (✉ Via del Galoppatoio 33, ☎ 06/320–1667; Parioli district, ✉ Largo Somalia 60, ☎ 06/862–12411) is the *in* place to work out. In vast underground premises adjacent to the Villa Borghese parking garage are two swimming pools, hydromassage, aerobic workout areas, gyms fully equipped for workouts and body-building, squash courts, turkish baths, and saunas. The basic daily rate is about 50,000 lire.

Sheraton Roma (✉ Viale del Pattinaggio, ☎ 06/5453) has a heated outdoor pool, a tennis court, two squash courts, a sauna, and a fitness center, all open to non-guests.

Golf

Formerly considered a sport for the elite, golf is definitely catching on in Italy. At these clubs, all with 18 holes, nonmembers are welcome but must show the membership cards of their home golf or country clubs.

Circolo del Golf Roma (✉ Via Acqua Santa 3, ☎ 06/780–3407) is the oldest and most prestigious golf club in Rome. Off the Via Appia Antica, near the tomb of Cecilia Metella, it is the course closest to downtown and is part of Rome's most aristocratic country club.

Country Club Castelgandolfo (✉ Via Santo Spirito 13, Castelgandolfo, ☎ 06/931–2301) is in the Castelli Romani zone, 25 km (15 mi) southeast of Rome. The Robert Trent Jones–designed course has a 17th-century villa as a clubhouse.

Marco Simone (✉ Guidonia Montecelio, ☎ 0774/366–469), 7 km (4 mi) east of the city, is one of Rome's newer courses. It is part of an upscale development adjacent to a medieval castle.

Olgiata Golf Club (✉ Largo Olgiata 15, on Via Cassia, ☎ 06/308–89141), 19 km (12 mi) from the center of Rome, hosts tournament play and is a favorite with residents of the upscale northern suburbs.

Parco de' Medici (✉ Viale Parco de' Medici 22, ☎ 06/655–3477), is only 4.5 km (less than 3 mi) west of Rome, close to the clusters of gleaming high-rise office buildings in the Parco de' Medici and EUR business centers.

Horseback Riding

Riding is a longstanding tradition in the country around Rome, where trails cover ground once inhabited by such ancient people as the Etruscans. Cross-country riding weekends can be arranged through local tourist offices and agritourism agencies. **Agriturist** (✉ Corso Vittorio Emanuele II 101, ☎ 06/685–2342) and the **Federazione Italiana Turismo Equestre** (Italian Federation of Equestrian Tourism; ✉ Via Ponte Castel Giubileo 27, ☎ 06/322–8060) can supply information.

Associazione Sportiva Villa Borghese (✉ Via del Galoppatoio 23, ☎ 06/322–6797), at the Galoppatoio riding track in Villa Borghese, is the most central riding club in the city.

Circolo Ippico Olgiata (⊠ Largo Olgiata 15, ☎ 06/378–8792), outside the city on the Via Cassia in the Olgiata suburb, has a riding ring and cross-country trails.

Running

The best bet for running in the inner city is the **Villa Borghese,** which offers the approximately ⅔-km (.4-mi) circuit of the Pincio gardens, among the marble statuary. A longer run in the park might include a loop around Piazza di Siena, a grass horse track measuring ¼ km (.4 mi). Although most traffic is barred from Villa Borghese, buses, taxis and official government and police cars speed through on the park's main roads. Be careful and stick to the sides of the roads. For a long run away from all traffic, try **Villa Ada** on Via Salaria and **Villa Doria Pamphili** on the Janiculum. On the other hand, if you really love history, you can run around the beaten-earth track of the old **Circus Maximus,** tracing the 1-km (.6-mi) oval circuit, or in the park along **Via delle Terme di Caracalla,** where many Romans run.

Swimming

Aldovrandi Hotel (⊠ Via Ulisse Aldovrandi 15, ☎ 06/322–3993), in the toney Parioli residential district, allows nonguests to use the pool, set in a walled garden studded with tall pine trees.
Cavalieri Hilton (⊠ Via Cadlolo 101, ☎ 06/35091) opens both its pools to nonguests. In fair weather you can lunch next to the outdoor pool, set in a lush oasis.
Piscina delle Rose (⊠ Viale America, ☎ 06/592–1862 in EUR) is a large Olympic pool open to the public from June to September.
Roman Sport Center (⊠ Via del Galoppatoio 33, ☎ 06/320–1667), in the heart of the city, has two Olympic swimming pools.
St. Peter's Holiday Inn (⊠ Via Aurelia Antica 415, ☎ 06/6642) opens its 25-meter pool and two tennis courts to nonguests.

Tennis

Increasingly popular with Italians, tennis is played in private clubs and on many public courts that can be rented by the hour. Your hotel *portiere* can direct you to the nearest courts and can book them for you. One of Rome's most prestigious private clubs is the **Tennis Club Parioli** (⊠ Largo de Morpurgo 2, Via Salaria, ☎ 06/862–00882), but you have to be invited by a member. **Federazione Italiana Tennis** (☎ 06/368–58510) has information about public courts.

SPECTATOR SPORTS

For schedules of sports events, buy the weekly *Roma C'è* booklet at newsstands or inquire at Municipal Information kiosks.

Basketball

Good pro teams, many starring players recruited from U.S. leagues, have boosted interest in basketball. In Rome, games are played at the **Palazzo dello Sport** (⊠ Piazzale dello Sport, ☎ 06/592–5107) in the EUR district.

Horseback Riding

The **Concorso Ippico Internazionale** (International Horse Show), held in May, draws a stylish crowd to the amphitheater of Piazza di Siena in Villa Borghese to witness the stiff competition. Every year the program includes a cavalry charge staged by the dashing mounted corps of the Carabinieri. For information call the **Italian Federation of Equestrian Sports** (⊠ Viale Tiziano 70, ☎ 06/323–3806).

Horse Racing

There's flat racing at the century-old **Capanelle** track (⊠ Via Appia Nuova 1245, ☎ 06/716–771), frequented by a chic crowd on big race days. The trotters meet at the **Tor di Valle** track (⊠ Via del Mare km 9.3, ☎ 06/529–0270).

Marathon

The Colosseum is the impressive starting point for the **Rome City Marathon** (☎ 06/301–83016 or 06/574–4246), run on the second Sunday in March, beginning at 9:30 AM. The route is 42 km (26 mi) long and passes through some of Rome's most beautiful squares, including Piazza di Spagna and Piazza Navona. There's also a 7-km (4-mi) route.

Soccer

Italy's favorite spectator sport stirs rabid enthusiasm among partisans. Games are usually held on Sunday afternoons throughout the September-to-May season; some are now played Saturday. Two teams—Roma and Lazio—play their home games in **Foro Italico**'s Olympic Stadium (⊠ Viale dei Gladiatori, ☎ 06/333–6316). Tickets are on sale at the box office before the games; your hotel *portiere* may be able to help you get tickets in advance. The so-called curve, the end sectors behind the goal, where the cheering is loudest, have the least expensive seats, costing about 30,000 lire. Be aware, though, that these tickets are not usually sold to visitors.

Tennis

Rome's Tennis Stadium at **Foro Italico** is scene of a world-class tennis tournament in May. For information, call the **Italian Tennis Federation** (⊠ Viale Tiziano 70, ☎ 06/368–58510).

7 Shopping

The smartest shops, the best buys, the most dazzling displays—they're all here. From Giorgio Armani to Ermenegildo Zegna, Rome is headquarters to many of the world's leading fashion names. Leather goods, silks, and knitwear are Rome's specialties, but there's much more to ogle or own in the city's plethora of shops, boutiques, and markets.

S HOPPING IN ROME is part of the fun, no matter what your budget. The Italian flair for transforming display windows into stunning artistic still-lifes and whimsical theatrical tableaux makes window-shopping an aesthetic experience. If you're bent on buying, you're sure to find something that suits your fancy *and* your pocketbook. If you have something specific in mind, like Missoni or Benetton knitwear or Bruno Magli shoes or Laura Biagiotti perfume, make a note of prices before you leave home, so you'll know whether you're getting a bargain by buying it in Italy. The best buys here are still leather goods of all kinds—from gloves to bags to jackets—and silk goods and knitwear. Boutique fashions may be slightly less expensive in Rome than in the United States. Some worthy old prints and minor antiques can be found in the city's interesting little shops, and full-fledged collectors can rely on the prestigious reputations of some of Italy's top antiques dealers. Genuine Italian handicrafts aren't so easy to find in these days of Asian imports, but some shops stock pottery and handwoven textiles made in Italy. Designer perfumes, from Versace to Armani to Moschino, may be a little cheaper here, but don't buy them in the designer boutiques; instead, look for them in the large *profumerie* (perfume and cosmetics stores), where you may be able to get a discount simply by asking for the *prezzo scontato* (discount price). Discounts are not generally given in other types of stores, though you can try to get one if you are making a large purchase in one store.

Italian sizes are not uniform, so always try on clothing before buying, and measure gift items. Children's sizes are all over the place, and though they usually go by age, they are calibrated to Italian children. Average size-per-age standards vary from one country to another. Check washing instruction labels on all garments, as many are not washable at all, and those that are washable may not be preshrunk. Glove sizes are universal. In any case, remember that Italian stores generally will *not* refund your purchases and that they often cannot exchange goods because of limited stock.

Credit Cards
Credit cards are widely accepted in Rome. Even some clothing vendors at outdoor markets honor them. Visa and MasterCard/CartaSì are the most common. Not all stores honor American Express or Diners Club cards, which are accepted, however, in department stores.

Duty-Free Shopping
Value-added tax (IVA) is 20% on clothing and luxury goods, but it is already included in the amount on the price tag of consumer goods. If you are not a resident of the EU, you may be eligible, under certain conditions, for a refund of this tax on good purchased here (☞ Taxes *in* the Gold Guide).

Counterfeits
The Prada, Gucci, Fendi, and Vuitton bags sold by sidewalk vendors are Italy's equivalent of fake Rolexes. An underground network organizes the illegal manufacture, distribution, and sale of these seemingly perfect counterfeits of stylish status symbols. Both manufacturers and vendors are always one jump ahead of the police. Be aware that any name brand bought on a sidewalk is surely a fake. If an incredibly good buy in a name brand product of any kind is proposed to you, examine the goods carefully. Reliable stores sell at the prices indicated by the manufacturers, so an enormous discount is suspect.

Rome Shopping

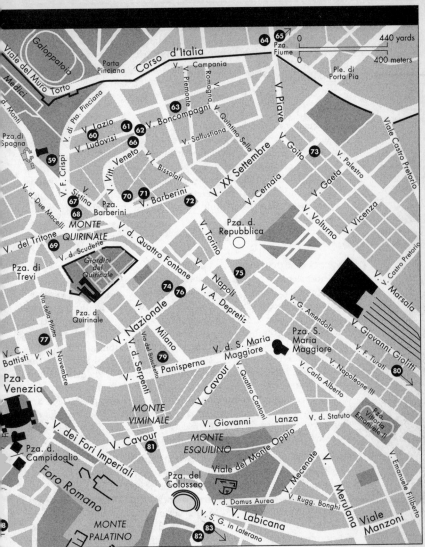

Sales

End-of-season sales (*saldi*) may mean real bargains in clothing and accessories. The main sales periods are in January (after January 6) and February, and mid-July to mid-September. Most stores adopt a no-exchange, no-return policy for sale goods. At other times of year, a *liquidazione* sign indicates a closing-out sale, but take a good hard look at the goods; they may be bottom-of-the-barrel.

Mailing Purchases Home

Always take your purchases with you: Having them shipped home from the shop may cause incomprehensible delays and unlimited grief. The mail is partly to blame; the cavalier attitude of some shop owners compounds the problem, especially if you have to correspond with them about delays. If circumstances are such that you can't take your goods with you, and if the shop seems reliable about shipping, get a detailed list of *what* is being shipped and a firm written statement of *when* and *how* your purchase will be sent.

Shopping Districts

Piazza di Spagna

The most elegant and expensive shops are concentrated in the area fanning out at the foot of the Spanish Steps. Via Condotti and Via Borgognona are lined with the boutiques of some of the leading names in high fashion: Armani, Versace, Prada, Mila Schon, and Gianfranco Ferre. Valentino has boutiques on Via Condotti and Via Bocca di Leone in addition to his palace-style headquarters and exhibition space on Piazza Mignanelli. From the bottom of the Spanish Steps and off to the right are Via Margutta, known for art galleries, and Via del Babuino, where the once-predominant antiques shops have had to make room for designer boutiques. Intersecting the top-price shopping streets are a number of streets, such as Via del Corso, Via Frattina, and Via del Gambero, that are lined with specialty shops and boutiques of all kinds where prices and goods are competitive.

Piazza Colonna and Piazza Barberini

The Rinascente department store, a large Rizzoli bookstore, and classic apparel shops for both sexes set a conservative tone for the lower edge of a hillside shopping district that takes in the more commercial areas of Via del Tritone and Via Barberini. The shopping atmosphere is more rarefied in the toney shops on Via Veneto. Shoes, bags, classic clothing, and leather apparel, at varying price levels, can be found throughout the area. One of Italy's most prestigious tailors and purveyors of classy men's ready-to-wear is Brioni, on Via Barberini. Via del Tritone has some medium-priced and a few expensive shops offering various goods. On Via Veneto are a scattering of high-priced boutiques and shoe stores, as well as newsstands selling English-language newspapers, magazines, and paperback books.

Via del Corso

Like a single-aisle shopping mall, this historic thoroughfare attracts droves of Romans and tourists who overflow the narrow sidewalks onto the street, dodging passing taxis and buses. Crowds are elbow-to-elbow in front of display windows chock-full of clothing and accessories. The stores adopt a what-you-see-is-what-you-get policy, putting most of their stock in the windows to help you make your selection even before you walk in the door. Young Rome comes here for jeans and inexpensive, trendy wear. Shoe shops have something for everyone. In the chic island of Piazza San Lorenzo in Lucina, smart and expensive specialty shops, such as the Profumeria Materozzoli, a 19th-century landmark, cater to the people from the patrician palaces

Via Condotti Shopping

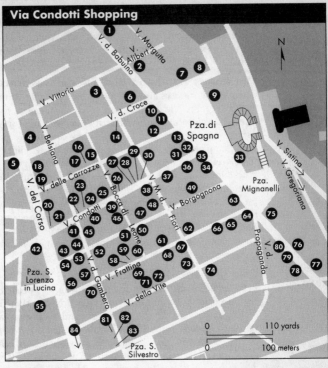

Alexander, **64**
Alinari, **2**
Amadei, **17**
Anglo American, **74**
Armani, **29**
Battistoni, **23**
Belfe e
Belfe, **82**
Laura
Biagiotti, **53**
Brighenti, **65**
Brioni, **39**
Buccellati, **40**
Bulgari, **37**
Mariella Burani, **15**
Campanile, **24**
Pier
Caranti, **75**
Castelli, **69**
Charles, **18**
Enzo Ceci, **72**
Chenzo, **73**
De Clerq e De Clerq, **12**
Demoiselle, **57**
Di Cori, **63**
Dolce e Gabanna, **13**
Fendi, **52**
Ferragamo Donna, **28**
Ferragamo Uomo, **25**

Ferre, **47**
Fiorucci, **3**
Sorelle
Fontana, **8**
Fratelli Rossetti, **49**
Frette, **7**
Furla, **9**
Galassia, **67**
Galleria San Carlo, **19**
Genny, **33**
Gherardini, **45**
Grimas, **81**
Gucci, **36**
Il Portone, **14**
Krizia, **11**
La Cicogna, **62**
La Perla, **30**
Le Sac, **71**
Mada Shoes, **4**
Bruno Magli, **20, 83**
Mariselaine, **27**
Merola, **43**
Messagerie Musicali, **5**
Elena Miro, **66**
Missoni, **32**
Eddy Monetty, **26**
Naj-Oleari, **1**
Onyx, **56**

Marisa Padovan, **16**
Pollini, **68**
Prada, **31**
Profumeria
Materozzoli, **55**
Red and Blue, **79**
Redwall, **22**
Renard, **80**
Roland's, **35**
Sergio Rossi, **10**
Roxy, **58**
Fausto Santini, **61**
Mila Schön, **21**
Emmanuel Schvili, **41**
Sermoneta, **34**
Skin, **77, 78**
Luisa
Spagnoli, **42, 60, 84**
Superga, **44**
Osvaldo Testa, **59**
Tod's, **54**
Valentino Donna, **46**
Valentino Uomo, **38**
Venier e Columbo, **70**
Versace, **50, 51**
Versari, **76**
Xandrine, **6**
Ermenegildo Zegna, **48**

in the area. Via Fontanella Borghese, between Via del Corso and the palace where Pauline Bonaparte Borghese lived, has a mix of boutiques and art and antiques galleries. Piazza della Fontanella Borghese, flanking the palace, is known for the permanent stalls selling prints and old books.

Old Rome: Pantheon and Via del Governo Vecchio

The narrow byways and gracious piazzas of Old Rome draw avant-garde shoppers. Via del Governo Vecchio is the place to browse in secondhand shops for the clothing of yesteryear and for hand-me-down Trifari jewelry. The secondhand shops on the streets are gradually being supplanted by minimalist boutiques known for trendy chic. True to its origins as a Roman circus, Piazza Navona has toy stores stocked with enormous stuffed animals. Around the Pantheon are reputable print and antiques stores. In May and October torches light the way on Via dei Coronari after dark, and shops are open late for the traditional antiques fair. Via Giulia and Via del Monserrato are also synonymous with art and antiques galleries. Romans shop Via dei Giubbonari for bargains in clothing, especially casual and funky young fashions, and household linens.

Cola di Rienzo

Between Piazza del Popolo and the Vatican, this broad avenue is lined with upscale shops that many Romans prefer to those around Piazza di Spagna because the wide sidewalks and big display windows make shopping easier. Clothing, housewares, gourmet foods, books, and, of course, shoes and bags, along with a Standa department store—Cola di Rienzo has it all, in a high-to-medium price range. Street-corner stands deal in bargain shoes and glassware. Near the Vatican at the west end of the avenue, off Piazza Risorgimento, a score of shops sell religious souvenirs, many of them on Via di Porta Angelica. Via Ottaviano, north of Piazza Risorgimento, has narrower sidewalks and lower priced goods than Via Cola di Rienzo.

Via Nazionale

The merchandise is mainstream and prices are generally moderate along this wide thoroughfare near Stazione Termini. A host of shoe stores, handbag and luggage retailers, and off-the-rack clothing stores line the avenue. There's a UPIM department store, too. The museum shop in Palazzo delle Esposizioni, the big neoclassical exhibition building in white marble about halfway along the street, has some interesting small objects that make good gifts or souvenirs.

Blitz Tours

With most of the best shopping in Rome crammed into the Piazza di Spagna–Via Condotti–Via del Corso areas, you can dive into one shop after another for stylish treasures, hardly taking time to come up for air. We have arranged these shopping itineraries by special interest, including addresses. For details, see the store listings below.

Handbags and Luggage

Survey the season's styles in bags from Italy's best-known manufacturers at **Sac Joli** (⊠ Via Tomacelli 154), near Largo Goldoni, then head into the heart of the Via Condotti shopping district. Swing north on Via del Corso, then turn east into Via delle Carrozze. On the left side of the street, between Via Belsiana and Via Bocca di Leone, you'll find **Amadei** (⊠ Via delle Carrozze 20) and its offbeat in-house styles. Continue up Via delle Carrozze to Piazza di Spagna to ogle the bags at **Furla** (⊠ Piazza di Spagna 22), then head down Via Condotti. Those tourists you see with the Gucci shopping bags have beat you to the multilevel **Gucci** store (⊠ Via Condotti 8) on the left. Stop at **Redwall** (⊠

Via Condotti 56), on the right, for a look at the latest trends in designer bags. Ahead, on the same side of the street, see what **Ferragamo** (⊠ Via Condotti 72) is showing in the way of emphatic elegance. Turn left off Via Condotti into Via Belsiana; that former church on the left is where **Gherardini** (⊠ Via Belsiana 48b) displays a good selection of handbags and soft luggage. By this time you may need an oversize tote to put all your purchases in. If you still don't want to say "Basta!" (Enough!) continue straight ahead into Via del Gambero and turn left onto Via Della Vite to **Le Sac** (⊠ Via della Vite 44), for casual styles.

Leather Clothing

If you're looking for leather clothing with fashion sense, see what **Roland's** (⊠ Piazza di Spagna 74) has to offer, then make a stop at **Renard** (⊠ Via Due Macelli 52). On the same street, check out the styles at both of the **Skin** stores (⊠ Via Due Macelli 59a, ⊠ Via Due Macelli 87). For good buys in casual and classic styles in leather, head uphill from Via Due Macelli by way of Via Capo le Case to **Crocco & Dille** (⊠ Via Francesco Crispi 77), a tiny factory outlet. For a much larger selection of classic leather fashions for men and women, return down Via Francesco Crispi, following it all the way to Largo Tritone, where **Virdel** (⊠ Via del Tritone 75) has wraparound display windows on the corner. For lower prices, or if you want something made to order, take a taxi or the Metro to Via Cavour, where **Very Pel** (⊠ Via Cavour 174) has a workshop and lower price tags than the boutiques in the fancier Piazza di Spagna area.

High Fashion Boutiques

Bring platinum credit cards. The stars of Italian couture shine in their shops and ateliers in the Piazza di Spagna–Via Borgognona area. Hard-to-pronounce Via Borgognona (Bore-go-nee-*owe*-na) is Rome's chicest shopping street. You don't even have to know how to say it if you can roll your tongue around the vowels in words like Versace, Ferre, and Fendi. Armani and Valentino stand slightly aloof from their colleagues, but you don't have to walk more than a block or two to find yourself in their refined realms. Starting from the Via del Corso end of Via Borgognona, you can bounce from the **Laura Biagiotti** boutique (⊠ Via Borgognona 43) to a **Fendi** boutique (⊠ Via Borgognona 36) to facing **Versace** boutiques (⊠ Via Borgognona 24, 34, and 33)—one for men and others for the Versace Versus line, **Ferre** (⊠ Via Borgognona 42b), and **Dolce e Gabbana** (⊠ Via Borgognona 7d). Just around the corner are **Valentino**'s Miss V ready-to-wear boutique (⊠ Via Bocca di Leone 15) and **Versace** Donna (⊠ Via Bocca di Leone 26). Follow Via Bocca di Leone to Via Condotti and browse at **Valentino**'s men's boutique (⊠ Via Condotti 13) and the **Armani** boutique for men and women (⊠ Via Condotti 77). Then you can pause at **Mila Schon** (⊠ Via Condotti 51) and **Prada** (⊠ Via Condotti 92) before making a sweep of the **boutiques on Piazza di Spagna**: Genny, Krizia, and Missoni among them. Wind down by heading north into Via del Babuino to investigate Valentino's **Oliver** boutique (⊠ Via Babuino 61), with casual wear for men and women, and the **Emporio Armani** (⊠ Via del Babuino 140).

Little Boutiques

For a strong fashion sense at prices much lower than Armani and friends, make the rounds of some boutiques where clothes are designed and made in-house. Start at **Mariella Burani** (⊠ Via Bocca di Leone 26), where the line between boutique fashion and designer ready-to-wear is a fine and very chic one. Then walk or take a taxi to **Dulce Vidoza** (⊠ Via dell'Orso 58) to consider the elegant pants suits in stunning fabrics. Take another taxi to **Le Tartarughe** (⊠ Via Piè di Marmo, near Piazza Venezia), and try on knit separates and spare little dresses that adapt to any occasion. For a change of fashion pace, take a taxi or walk, skirting the rear of the Pantheon and the west end of Piazza Navona, to **Maga Morgana** (⊠ Via del Governo Vecchio 27), where the in-house styles have a distinctly retro look.

Department Stores

Rome has few department stores. The classiest are the two Rinascente stores and the two Coin stores. They have welcome desks, multilingual guides, and Tax-Free Refund desks. They are open all day and may be open on Sunday, too.

The first of several shopping malls in Rome and the handiest to reach is **Cinecittà Due** (⊠ Piazza di Cinecittà, Viale Palmiro Togliatti, ☎ 06/722–0902); just take Metro A to the Subaugusta stop. The mall has 100 shops, including a Coin department store branch (☞ *below*), a big supermarket, snack bars, and cafés.

Coin (⊠ Piazzale Appio, ☎ 06/708–0020; ⊠ Via Mantova 1b, near Piazza Fiume, ☎ 06/841–6279; ⊠ Cinecittà shopping mall, ☎ 06/722–0931) is upscale, with merchandise arranged in well-spaced displays. The clothing ranges from classic and dressy to casual chic, with good separates and sportswear departments for men and women. The downstairs housewares department usually has a good stock of Italian ceramic ware.

La Rinascente (⊠ Piazza Colonna, ☎ 06/679–7691) was Rome's first department store, and the early-1900s building in which it opened makes a fine showcase for five floors of clothing and accessories. Perfumes and cosmetics share the main floor with bags, costume jewelry, fun hats, and beautiful silk scarves. Upstairs are mainstream styles, both casual and dressy, for men and women. The second **La Rinascente** (⊠ Piazza Fiume, ☎ 06/884–1231) has more floor space and a wider range of goods than the older store on Piazza Colonna. The basement is devoted to housewares, and the top floors have furniture, toys, and childrens' departments. In between, accessories and apparel for men and women replicate the goods at the other store.

Budget

The low-to-moderately priced Standa and Upim chains, with stores located throughout Rome, have fair-to-middling quality goods. They are the place to go for a pair of slippers, bathing suit, underwear, or the like, to see you through until you get home. In addition, they carry toiletries and first-aid needs. Most Standa and Upim stores have invaluable while-you-wait shoe repair counters.

Specialty Shops

Antiques and Prints

Antiques shopping in Rome can actually mean antiquities shopping; some shops showcase authentic ancient Roman works. Beyond those, the antiques scene is pretty much dominated by works and objects from the 17th century up to art deco. The stalls on Piazza Borghese are a happy hunting ground for old prints, postcards, and books at reasonable prices, and for the occasional rare edition or costly antique engraving. They are open all day, closed on Sunday, and do not accept credit cards.

Alinari (⊠ Via Aliberti 16/a, ☎ 06/679–2923) is Italy's equivalent of the Bettman Archive. Generations of the Alinari family have photographed Italy ever since the 1800s, starting in Florence but gradually extending their activity throughout the peninsula. In their gallery/store off Via del Babuino you can find early photographs of Rome and views of Italy that make interesting mementoes.

Daniela Bilenchi (✉ Via della Stelletta 17, ☎ O6/687–5222) restores chinaware and porcelain, but she also sells antique lamps and has a predilection for art nouveau and art deco styles.

Enrico Camponi (✉ Via della Stelletta 3, ☎ 06/686–5249) offers a collection of old and antique glass vases, many of them by Venetian masters. Antique vases from Barovier, Venini, and Seguso may cost hundreds of dollars, but pretty little Murano glass ashtrays dating from the 1940s and '50s are inexpensive.

Le Bateleur (✉ Via S. Simone 71, ☎ 06/654–4676), in a tiny 11th-century sacristy under a flight of stone steps, off Via dei Coronari, is what grandma used to call a curiosity shop. It's packed with a jumble of objects in styles from the 17th to the 20th century.

Nardecchia (✉ Piazza Navona 25, ☎ 06/686–9318) always has some of its large selection of beautiful prints of Rome in the big display window, vying for attention with the great Bernini fountain in the piazza. Romans consider Nardecchia one of the city's most reliable dealers.

Tanca (✉ Salita dei Crescenzi 10, near Pantheon, ☎ 06/687–5272) is a happy but cramped hunting ground for old prints. You can browse through piles and boxes to your heart's content in one of the three rather cluttered rooms; in another are showcases full of antique jewelry, old silver, and objets d'art.

Bookstores

Almost all of Rome's big bookstores have a few shelves of English-language books. The newsstands on Via Veneto also sell paperbacks in English, but the broadest selections are available in the specialized English-language stores listed below.

Anglo-American (✉ Via della Vite 102, ☎ 06/679–5222) carries books published in Britain and the States, including reference and scientific works. It also handles special orders. If you want to give an Italian friend a subscription to an English-language magazine, this is the place to arrange it.

Croce (✉ Corso Vittorio 156, ☎ 06/688–02269) has been a meeting place for literati and a showcase for their work for most of the 20th century. It has a now-dowdy 1950s look and large display windows featuring a host of titles; one is occupied by books on Rome, some of them in English.

Economy Book and Video Center (✉ Via Torino 136, ☎ 06/474–6877) has a regular clientele of Americans and Brits living in Rome who know they can find the latest in hardcover and paperbacks, calendars, greeting cards, and videos in English. The store is owned and run by Americans.

English Bookshop (✉ ViaRipetta 248, ☎ 06/320–3301), specializing in English literature, translations of Italian literature, and a truly exhaustive stock of books in English about Italy—including guidebooks—packs a lot of books into fairly small premises. There is a wide selection of postcards, greeting cards and calendars, and children's books and videos.

Feltrinelli (✉ Largo di Torre Argentina 5, ☎ 06/688–08160) is the marketing branch of one of Italy's major publishing houses. The several stores in Rome are all well organized and all stocked with English-language paperbacks.

Mondadori (✉ Piazza Cola di Rienzo 81, ☎ 06/321–0323) is big and modern, with a luminous open plan. Sections are well marked; one is devoted entirely to English-language books. There is an audio-video department and greeting cards, gadgets, and toys, too.

Rizzoli (✉ Largo Chigi 15, ☎ 06/679–6641) occupies two levels of the turn-of-the-century Galleria at Piazza Colonna. It stocks many books in English in addition to a wide selection of art books and cookbooks, some in English.

Ceramics
Artigianato Calabrese (✉ Via d'Ascanio 5, ☎ 06/687–7427) is a straightforward little store that sells a selection of typical Calabrian ceramics—heavy, no-nonsense pieces with the traditional bird motif. The store also carries hand-woven and embroidered goods.

Bottegantica (✉ Via San Simeone 141, ☎ 06/683–08909) is tucked away on a byway off Via dei Coronari. Along with solid Italian country furniture, it has a good collection of bright Sicilian ceramics: jugs, plates, cachepots, and vases by some of the island's most respected potters.

Marini e Polli (✉ Via del Pellegrino 85, ☎ 06/686–9698) used to be a housewares store but is gradually focusing on ceramics in the colorful Vietri style and in unglazed terra-cotta. The ware is unrefinedly rustic and prices are moderate.

Myricae (✉ Via Campo Marzio 11, ☎ 06/689–2485) is bright with multicolored ceramics. Large vases and cachepots make handsome decorating accessories. Many are one-of-a-kind pieces by Tuscan artists, with a hefty price tag.

Prestigio Interni (✉ Via del Governo Vecchio 38, ☎ 06/688–05134) has a mixed bag of country-style Apulian ceramics and more artistic pieces, in addition to a scattering of antiques. The store is open only in the afternoon from Monday to Friday and in the morning on Saturday.

Raku (✉ Via d'Ascanio 5, ☎ 06/580–3575) shows pottery in intriguing forms and colors with a distinctive, almost Oriental look, though it is made in Italy exclusively for this shop.

Children's Clothing
Shopping for the little ones is a delight here, where even kids' clothes have designer labels. But keep three things in mind. One, are the garments easy to care for? The prettiest things may not be washable, and cottons are not necessarily pre-shrunk. Two, are they practical? Features like gripper-fastened leg openings and neck openings are not widely adopted in children's fashions here. Three, will they fit? Sizes are totally different from U.S. kids' sizes, so take measurements before you leave home and bring along your tape measure.

Bonpoint (✉ Piazza San Lorenzo in Lucina 25, ☎ 06/687—1548) is a precious little emporium of French styles for children. They are expensive and exquisitely made, many embroidered and trimmed by hand. The Bonpoint look is picture-perfect.

Il Baule di Elianna (✉ Via dei Prefetti 17, ☎ 06/678–3744) is like an old-fashioned nursery. The shop, in the courtyard of an old palazzo, is a trove of handmade clothing for children from birth to age 10. The women who own it make and embroider each piece themselves, and the TLC shows in every stitch. Very special garments for that very special child, they are correspondingly costly.

La Cicogna (✉ Via Frattina 138, ☎ 06/679–1912; ✉ Via Cola di Rienzo 268, ☎ 06/689–6557), a nationwide chain, has several stores in Rome. Each is like a small department store of children's goods, from clothing to shoes, carriages, baby supplies and so forth, from birth to age 14. There's a maternity-wear department, too.

Naj-Oleari (✉ Via del Babuino 51, ☎ 06/321–8162) is a magnet for girls 8–18, who adore the accessories and gadgets made in Italy in cheery prints and vivacious colors. Naj-Oleari is a teen status symbol.

Emmanuel Schvili (✉ Via Frattina 71, ☎ 06/678–1687) features children's t-shirts and other styles for tots in the display windows on Via del Gambero, but the store also has men's and women's clothing. Children love the T-shirts and sweats, and even classic, puff-sleeved little girls' dresses printed with Mickey Mouse, Tweetie, and other cartoon characters.

Cosmetics/Beauty/Perfumes

Antica Officina di Santa Maria Novella (✉ Corso Rinascimento 47, ☎ 06/687–2446), like a 16th-century pharmacy, is wood-paneled and odorous of herbs and flowers and a very special potpourri. The essences, soaps, creams, and lotions sold here are based on antique, natural formulas devised centuries ago by the monks of Santa Maria Novella in Florence.

Castelli (✉ Via Frattina 54, ☎ 06/679–0339; ✉ Via Condotti 62, ☎ 06/679–5918; ✉ Via Oslavia 5, ☎ 06/372–8312) is a perfumed paradise offering everything imaginable in the way of beauty aids, cosmetics, and hair accessories, plus a dazzling selection of quality costume jewelry. The shop on Via Frattina has a beauty salon (☎ 06/678–0066), no kin to your neighborhood hairdresser in prices or atmosphere.

Materozzoli (✉ Piazza San Lorenzo in Lucina 5, ☎ 06/688–92686) is an antique herbalist's shop that has managed to preserve the old interior while modernizing its wares. There is a large selection of essences and naturally perfumed products, mainly English and French, and a good range of razors and brushes.

Fabrics

Italy is famous for silks and woolens. The country is one of the world's major textile manufacturers, so the choice is vast. You can find some real bargains when *scampoli* (remnants) are on sale.

Aston (✉ Via Buoncompagni 27, ☎ 06/428–71227) stocks couture-level fabrics for men and women. Though expensive, the goods cost much less here than at home.

Fratelli Bassetti (✉ Corso Vittorio Emanuele II 73, ☎ 06/689–2326) has a vast selection of world-famous Italian silks and fashion fabrics on several floors of a rambling palazzo.

Food and Delicacies

Ai Monasteri (✉ Piazza Cinque Lune 76, ☎ 06/688–02783) sells liqueurs, jams, and chocolate handmade by Cistercian monks in several monasteries in Italy.

Buccone (✉ Via di Ripetta 19, ☎ 06/361–2154) is a landmarked 1800s wineshop, with a vast selection of wines, sweets, and packaged candy. It serves light lunches, too.

Castroni (✉ Via Cola di Rienzo 196, ☎ 06/687–4383) has a vast and aromatic range of food products from all over the world. This is where members of the foreign colony come to find specialties from home, but you'll see plenty of Italian-made goodies on the shelves, too.

Enoteca al Parlamento (✉ Via dei Prefetti 15, ☎ 06/687–3446) is one of the city's traditional wineshops, a haunt of journalists and politicos who stop in for wine by the glass. The enoteca's prized bottle of Brunello di Montalcino, an early 1900s vintage, is defined as priceless.

Moriondo e Gariglio (✉ Via della Pilotta 2, ☎ 06/678–6662) is a tiny chocolate shop that has been catering to refined chocaholics' cravings for a century. Everything here is made in the store's own workshop.

Trimani (✉ Via Goito 20, ☎ 06/446–9661), one of Rome's best-stocked wine dealers, also has a broad selection of regional Italian delicacies.

Volpetti (✉ Via Marmorata 47, ☎ 06/574–6986) has the best cured meats in Rome, with a score of different salame. A vast selection of cheeses includes genuine buffalo-milk mozzarella. And the fresh pasta is heavenly.

Hats, Gloves, and Ties

Borsalino Boutique (✉ Piazza del Popolo 20, ☎ 06/326–50838) has hats for men and women in signature styles, dressy, casual, and always classic, including panama hats. The store also carries a line of shirts and ties.

Di Cori (⊠ Piazza di Spagna 43, ☎ 06/678–4140) packs a lot of gloves into a tiny space, offering every type of glove in every color imaginable. There is a limited selection of scarves and ties, too.

Merola (⊠ Via del Corso 143, ☎ 06/679–1961) has been purveying gloves to Romans for decades. It carries a line of expensive, top-quality gloves and scarves.

Roxy (⊠ Via Frattina 115, ☎ 06/678–6691; ⊠ Via Barberini 112, ☎ 06/488–3931; ⊠ Via Cola di Rienzo 313, ☎ 06/397–21003; ⊠ Piazza del Parlamento 31, ☎ 06/688–02465; ⊠ Via XX Settembre 58, ☎ 06/481–8510) has the best selection of moderately priced ties to be found in Rome. The choice is bewilderingly large, the stores relentlessly small and usually packed with customers.

Sermoneta (⊠ Piazza di Spagna 61, ☎ 06/679–1960) has a vast stock of gloves in rainbow hues or classic blacks, whites, and browns. The quality is reliable.

Jewelry

Buccellati (⊠ Via Condotti 31, ☎ 06/679–0329) is a tradition-rich Florentine jewelry house renowned for elaborately worked silver pieces and nostalgic jewelry recalling the days of grand decolletés and tiaras.

Bulgari (⊠ Via Condotti 10, ☎ 06/679–3876) dazzles with enticing doses of opulence in small display windows. You ring at the door to be admitted to the treasure trove of distinctly contemporary jewels within.

Maria Teresa Nitti Valentini (⊠ Via della Stelletta 3a, ☎ 06/683–08776) is known to connoisseurs for vintage jewelry (including some good costume jewelry), displayed along the narrow corridor that is the entrance to the minuscule shop.

Diego Percossipapi (⊠ Piazza Sant'Eustachio 16, ☎ 06/688–01466) is a tiny shop with an upscale clientele. Often based on ancient Roman models, the jewels show masterful technique and a knowing choice of stones.

Knitwear

Albertina (⊠ Via Lazio 20, ☎ 06/488–5876) elevates women's knitwear to the level of high fashion, imparting line and substance to creations for women that never go out of style. Coats, jackets, dresses, pants, and tops are made in exclusive wool, silk, or blended yarns.

De Clerq & De Clerq (⊠ Via delle Carrozze 50, ☎ 06/679–0988) caters to women's refined tastes and elevated budgets with exquisitely styled knitwear in cotton, silk, or wool.

Mariselaine (⊠ Via Condotti 70, ☎ 06/679–5817) is a small, elegant women's boutique showing knitwear in fashion yarns and colors; every piece has something that takes it out of the ordinary. In addition, Mariselaine has classy, classic day and afternoon wear.

Marisa Pignataro (⊠ Via dell'Anima 42, ☎ 06/689–3209) has handmade knitwear for women in unusual yarns, mainly silk and wool. The selection includes shawls, dresses, and pants, many made with an ample, easy-to-wear line. The prices here are consonant with the quality.

Luisa Spagnoli (⊠ Via del Corso 385, ☎ 06/679–8160; ⊠ Via Veneto 139, ☎ 06/420–11281; ⊠ Via Frattina 84b, ☎ 06/699–1706) is an internationally known name for women's knit fashions. The Spagnoli stores also carry a full range of ready-to-wear.

Leather Goods

BAGS

A fine Italian handbag in leather or stylish synthetic fabric is a worthwhile investment. Really good bags—the classic kind that you can carry for years—are not inexpensive. For styles that follow fashion, Redwall, Biasia, Evolution, The Bridge, and Zippo are names to look for.

Amadei (⊠ Via delle Carrozze 20, ☎ 06/678–33452) is a tiny shop with offbeat, trendy handbags for women. One of a kind, and made by Amedei, they are in leather or smart fabrics.

Furla (⊠ Piazza di Spagna 22, ☎ 06/692–00363) is the flagship store of a fleet with shops as far away as New York and Honolulu. They purvey chic bags and practical totes in bright colors, along with scarves and a selection of costume jewelry, all at moderate prices.

Gherardini (⊠ Via Belsiani 48b, ☎ 06/679–5501) has taken over a deconsecrated church and transformed it into a showplace for the Gherardini label, associated with casual, easy-to-carry bags in leather and logo-stamped synthetic material. It has leather totes and bags in bright colors and a line of soft luggage.

Gucci (⊠ Via Condotti 8, ☎ 06/678–9340), for all the revamping by designer Tom Ford, still has groups of eager customers lined up at the door waiting to get a chance at those perennial double-G logo bags and shoes.

Le Sac (⊠ Via della Vite 44, ☎ 06/679–4597) specializes in Italian-made handbags and luggage, as casual in style as the store's country-cabin decor. There are models for men and women, and the store carries a selection of Cerrutti and Zippo styles.

Mandarina Duck (⊠ Corso Vittorio Emanuele II 16, ☎ 06/678–9840) is the maker of soft bags and luggage in resistant synthetic fabrics, with the Mandarina Duck logo trim. Eminently practical in form and design (they can be folded up and slipped in a suitcase, and their capacity seems limitless), the bags are a boon to travelers.

Pier Caranti (⊠ Piazza di Spagna 43, ☎ 06/679–1621) displays a mountain of handbags in three big display windows. The store makes up in quantity and range of choice what it lacks in elegance. Clearly tourist-oriented, it has an Italian clientele, too.

Redwall (⊠ Via Condotti 56, ☎ 06/679–1973) is one of Italy's major handbag manufacturers, and it produces under license for several leading designers, among them Armani and Moschino. The company has its own label, too. The spare decor of this small store leaves the spotlight to the bags, well-made and hand-finished.

Sac Joli (⊠ Via Tomacelli 154, ☎ 06/687–8431) has one of the most comprehensive selections of leading makes in handbags to be found in central Rome. Ample display windows framed in 1970s-style stainless steel give you an idea of the range to be found inside; prices are as good as you'll find anywhere in the area.

Volterra (⊠ Via Barberini 102, ☎ 06/481–9315) has a good range of handbags from the best Italian manufacturers, and prices are competitive. The styles run the gamut from classy to casual.

LEATHER CLOTHING

Leather clothing for men and women is a good buy in Italy, where skins imported from many countries are cut and tailored in styles ranging from casual to elegant.

Crocco & Dille (⊠ Via Francesco Crispi 77, ☎ 06/678–5735) is so tiny you may easily pass it by. But this miniscule factory outlet is worth your attention if you're looking for a casual leather jacket.

Renard (⊠ Via Due Macelli 52, ☎ 06/679–7004) is a leather boutique, displaying a selection of styles in leather that are made exclusively in Italy. The store is large and airy, without the chock-full-of-goods look of sister stores.

Rock 'n Blue (⊠ Via Nazionale 223, ☎ 06/482–5510) is a jeans store that carries moderately priced young styles in leather, especially jackets to wear with jeans and the ever-popular aviator's jackets.

Roland's (⊠ Piazza di Spagna 74, ☎ 06/679–0391) has an extensive stock of good-quality leather fashions and accessories, as well as stylish casual wear in wool and silk.

Skin (⊠ Via Due Macelli 59a, ☎ 06/679–5856; ⊠ Via Due Macelli 87) is a double-barreled operation with sister stores across the street from one another. Both large, with big stocks, they have just about anything you could want in leather, and in any color, too. House styles are classic models of suits, skirts, jackets, and pants suits. They also show high-fashion styles by Missoni and other designers.

Versari (⊠ Via Due Macelli 115, ☎ 06/679–0539) has a limited selection of styles. The store's specialty is jackets and coats, but it offers a token choice of skirts, pants, and such.

Very Pel (⊠ Via Cavour 174, ☎ 06/4817640) is a small shop with a workroom on the premises. The ready-made and mainly casual jackets, skirts, and pants in leather and suede are made on the spot, so if you don't see anything you like, you can have it made to order. Prices are lower than at the fancier leather boutiques.

Virdel (⊠ Via del Tritone 75, ☎ 06/488–5883) occupies an entire corner of the busy intersection with Via Francesco Crispi. Much of the merchandise, including bags and belts, is on display, making choosing easy. This is the place for classic styles in leather suits and jackets for men and women; there is little that would appeal to younger, trendier dressers.

SHOES

Rome's shoe stores seem to be as numerous as the mopeds buzzing around downtown. They range from custom-made shoe boutiques to stores with huge displays of every model imaginable for men, women, and children. Most Italian shoes are made to a single, average width; if you need a narrower shoe you may have to try on many before you find the right fit. Valleverde and Melluso make wider, softer shoes for men and women.

Boccanera (⊠ Via Luca della Robbia 36, ☎ 06/575–0847), in the Testaccio neighborhood, is where the Romans go for great shoes, especially during sales, when the buys are terrific. The store hasn't changed much over the decades; it still has the relaxed elegance and courteous service once a tradition in Roman shops. Here you can find Prada, Tod's, Church, and other leading brands.

Bruno Magli (⊠ Via del Gambero 1, ☎ 06/679–3802) shows classy shoes in good-size corner display windows, but you will find many more styles inside, at high to moderate prices.

Campanile (⊠ Via Condotti 58, ☎ 06/678–3041) is the nonpareil name in classic Italian shoes for men and women. The shoes are costly but their quality is unbeatable.

Charles (⊠ Via del Corso 109, ☎ 06/679–2345) shows a host of styles in big display windows, offering practically all of the quality shoe labels, from Rossi to Rossetti. You choose your style in the window, then tell one of the bilingual clerks what you want. The store is clearly geared to tourists, but Romans come, too, for the wide selection and competitive prices.

Fausto Santini (⊠ Via Frattina 120, ☎ 06/678–8414) gives a hint of extravagance in minimally decorated, all-white show windows displaying surprising shoes that fashion mavens love. Santini's footwear for men and women is bright and trendy, sporting unusual forms, especially in heels. Coordinated bags and wallets add to the fun.

Ferragamo Donna (⊠ Via Condotti 72, ☎ 06/679–1565) has the ultimate in Italian fashion shoes for women, expensive and of excellent quality. Finding a bag or splashy Ferragamo scarf to match the shoes is no problem here.

Ferragamo Uomo (⊠ Via Condotti 64, ☎ 06/679–1130) shows classic styles in shoes for men, handcrafted in fine leather and in fabric for more sporty models.

Fratelli Rossetti (✉ Via Borgognona 5a, ☎ 06/678–2676) combines classic quality and good looks in men's and women's shoes with the telling detail that puts them high in fashion.

Mada Shoes (✉ Via della Croce 57, ☎ 06/679–8660) has a selection of classic, conservative shoe styles for women with attractive details that make them distinctive.

Nickol's (✉ Via Barberini 21, ☎ 06/474–1648) carries smart, classic styles for men and women but also offers frivolous dressy shoes for special occasions. It is one of the few stores in Rome that stocks shoes in American widths.

Pollini (✉ Via Frattina 23, ☎ 06/678–9028) is a his-and-hers store, divided down the middle into narrow but separate shops. Pollini styles for both sexes are classic, and prices are relatively high.

Sergio Rossi (✉ Piazza di Spagna 97, ☎ 06/678–3245) displays a discreet selection of classic men's and women's shoes in the windows of this store at the corner of Via della Croce. The styles are elegant and conservative.

Tod's (✉ Via Borgognona 45, ☎ 06/678–6828) has an English name, but the shoes are strictly Italian-designed and made in Italy. This exclusive Tod's store has every model of the manufacturer's signature button-soled moccasin, as well as other styles.

Lingerie and Linens

Brighenti (✉ Via Frattina 8, ☎ 06/679–1484) looks like what it is— a traditional Roman shop of a gentler era, with art nouveau light fixtures and sculptured wooden shelves. The women's lingerie, in silk and satin, is lavished with lace in the most classic and feminine styles. The store also carries stylish bathing suits.

Cesari (✉ Via Babuino 16, ☎ 06/361–1441) is a Roman institution for frothy lingerie, quality household linens, and sumptuous decorator fabrics, and it has less-expensive gift items such as aprons, beach towels, and place mats.

Demoiselle (✉ Via Frattina 93, ☎ 06/679–3752) is a chic shop at the corner of Via Belsiana, with high-fashion lingerie, including La Perla's luscious Italian-made sleepwear and undergarments. The shop has a good selection of Missoni bathing suits in season.

Frette (✉ Piazza di Spagna 10, ☎ 06/679–0673) shows lingerie for fabulous trousseaux and has a large range of household linens in stylish prints and colors.

La Perla (✉ Via Condotti 79, ☎ 06/699–41934), small and minimally decorated, offers a selection of high-quality lingerie and underwear for women and for men. See their sexy pajamas.

Lavori Artigianali Femminili (✉ Via Capo le Case 6, ☎ 06/678–1100) offers embroidered household linens, exquisitely embroidered layettes and christening dresses, hand-knitted suits for babies and small children, and women's blouses.

Marisa Padovan (✉ Via della Carrozze 81, ☎ 06/679–3846) is the place for exclusive, sometimes extravagant, lingerie in sexy, sumptuous styles, often trimmed with sequins and ostrich feathers.

Tebro (✉ Via dei Prefetti 52, ☎ 06/687–3441) has a long-estabished reputation for quality and courtesy in a large and classic Roman establishment. In fact, this is where the Roman establishment shops for lingerie and household linens.

Venier e Colombo (✉ Via Frattina 42, ☎ 06/679–2927) has a breathtaking selection of lace-trimmed lingerie and linens and also sells lace by the yard.

Men's and Women's Clothing

Battistoni (✉ Via Condotti 57, ☎ 06/678–6241) is a name that has been associated with smart, conservative style for generations. Classic Battistoni jackets, suits, shoes and accessories are staples in the wardrobe of Rome's elegant people.

Belfe & Belfe (⊠ Via del Gambero 9, ☎ 06/679–1725) stocks sportswear, including boat and golf shoes, as well as all-weather jackets, soft sweaters, and designer jogging suits.

Davide Cenci (⊠ Via Campo Marzio 1-7, ☎ 06/699–0681) is a Roman classic for quality clothing and accessories for every occasion, from a sailboat party to a formal wedding. Trench coats, cashmeres, and beautifully tailored ready-to-wear are Cenci specialties.

Degli Effetti (⊠ Piazza Capranica 93, ☎ 06/679–0202) has fashion on the cutting edge for men and women in separate stores on opposite sides of the piazza. This is the address of the women's store, which carries Miu Miu and Yoshi Yamamoto.

Red and Blue (⊠ Via Due Macelli 57, ☎ 06/679–1933) has sporty, casual wear for men and women, with a marked British accent. Burberry's is featured in the large display windows, but the store also carries such fine Italian brands as Loro Piana.

Superga (⊠ Via Borgognona 4/a, ☎ 06/678–8435) sells the sneakers that every Italian wears, in classic white or a rainbow of colors, and it now has a line of sportswear for men and women.

HIGH FASHION BOUTIQUES

Giorgio Armani (⊠ Via Condotti 77, ☎ 06/699–1460) is a showcase for the designer's inimitable styles for men and women.

Laura Biagiotti (⊠ Via Borgognona 43, ☎ 06/679–1205) shows her understated dresses, suits, separates, and line of women's sizes in her spacious, central boutique.

Dolce&Gabbana (⊠ Piazza di Spagna 82, ☎ 06/679–2294) is where these unconventional designers show their slightly extravagant styles and offbeat chic to Romans.

Fendi (⊠ Via Borgognona 36, ☎ 06/679–7641) is the fur and fashion emporium of this fashion dynasty; at their larger store (⊠ Via Fontanella Borghese 57, ☎ 06/687–6290) you can find bags and luggage and the Fendissime boutique, where price tags for fashion are relatively lower.

Genny (⊠ Piazza di Spagna 27, ☎ 06/679–6074) sells the classic but contemporary women's ready-to-wear fashions with a flair that are what Italian style is all about. Genny bags and shoes show the same dashing sense of style.

Krizia (⊠ Piazza di Spagna 87, ☎ 06/679–7625) shows her stunningly cut ready-to-wear line in an elegantly minimal setting.

Missoni (⊠ Piazza di Spagna 78, ☎ 06/679–2555) has samples of a magical way with knitwear in the display windows facing the Spanish Steps. There is plenty more for men and women inside.

Prada (⊠ Via Condotti 92, ☎ 06/679–0897), demonstrating that a good bag is just a starting point for a complete fashion statement, has raised the Prada name to status symbol.

Sorelle Fontana (⊠ Salita San Sebastianello 6, ☎ 06/679–8652) is the doyenne of Rome's high-fashion houses, where the legendary sisters dressed Audrey Hepburn, Ava Gardner, and other celebs in the *Dolce Vita* days. Now it shows ultra-classic clothes for the ultra-elegant woman.

Valentino Donna (⊠ Via Bocca di Leone, ☎ 06/679–5862) shows the designer's superlative ready-to-wear collections for women in an elegant boutique.

Valentino Uomo (⊠ Via Condotti 13, ☎ 06/678–3656) is the ineffable Italian designer's men's boutique, where expensive elegance reigns supreme. Quality fabrics and faultless tailoring, together with a genius for stlye, are Valentino's signature.

Versace (⊠ Via Bocca di Leone 26, ☎ 06/678–0521) has transformed a two-block area into Versaceville, with four other boutiques, three on Via Borgognona and one on Via Frattina.

Men's Clothing

Brioni (⊠ Via Barberini 79, ☎ 06/484–517) has a well-deserved reputation as one of Italy's top tailors: the list of customers reads like a *Who's Who* of the international elite. Brioni also has a ready-to-wear line that has the same impeccable look as his custom-made styles.

Chenzo (⊠ Via Mario dei Fiori 111, ☎ 06/678–6754) has two floors of everything from sportswear to classic suits with well-known labels, at moderate prices. The store is open on Sunday.

Eddy Monetty's (⊠ Via Condotti 63a, ☎ 06/679–4117) elegant store has the British look that Italians love, and Burberry's is a big seller. But there are plenty of Italian labels to choose from, and they don't come cheap.

Enzo Ceci (⊠ Via della Vite 52, ☎ 06/679–8882) caters to unconventional tastes, offering what Americans think Italian clothing should be: classic styles with a touch of extravagance, ties in flashy colors, wildly striped shirts, three-piece suits in pale colors.

Ermenegildo Zegna (⊠ Via Borgognona 7e, ☎ 06/678–9143), of the unpronounceable name, is one of Italy's finest manufacturers of men's clothing. Zegna's classic ready-to-wear line is made of the firm's premier fabrics (the clothing line is a spin-off of the family's century-old textile industry). For outdoor wear, Zegna has developed innovative fabrics for rain jackets and car coats.

Grimas (⊠ Via del Gambero 11a, ☎ 06/678–4423) is a favorite with Romans who want to dress well without spending a lot. Both the wood-paneled store and the merchandise are classics.

Il Portone (⊠ Via della Carrozze 71, ☎ 06/679–3355) embodies a tradition in custom shirtmaking. For decades, a man was a fashion nobody if he didn't have a few Portone shirts in his closet, identifiable by their cut and their signature stripes. The store also carries nightshirts and underwear.

Osvaldo Testa (⊠ Via Frattina 42, ☎ 06/678–5999) showcases Burberry's to attract Anglophile Italians, but it also has some fine Italian labels, including Cerrutti. If your suitcase has been lost, this is the place to come for everything from underwear to suits to shoes.

Music and Videos

Most video stores have a section with English and American movies in the original language, sometimes with Italian subtitles. Though mainly a bookstore, the Economy Book and Video Center (☞ Bookstores, *above*) has a large selection of English-language videos.

Blockbuster (⊠ Via Barberini 3, ☎ 06/487–1666) has invaded Italy. This is just one of a dozen stores in Rome stocked with a megaselection of videos.

Messagerie Musicali (⊠ Via del Corso 122, ☎ 06/679–8197) has central Rome's largest selections of tapes and CDs. It has a video department and sells sheet music and musical instruments, too.

Ricordi (⊠ Via Cesare Battisti 120, ☎ 06/679–8022) can provide any kind of music imaginable on tape or CD, from Italy's golden oldies to the latest on worldwide charts.

Rinascita (⊠ Via Botteghe Oscure 3, ☎ 06/679-7637) is in the building that houses the left-wing PDS (Partito Democratico della Sinistra, the former Communist Party). The floor below the big bookstore holds a music department with up-to-the-minute releases and a good choice of ethnic music.

Stationery

Pineider (⊠ Via della Fontanella Borghese 22, ☎ 06/687–8369) is where Rome's aristocratic families have their wedding invitations engraved and their stationery personalized. For stationery and desk accessories, hand-tooled in the best Florentine leather, it has no equals.

Teens' Clothing

Fiorucci (⊠ Via Mario dei Fiori 40c, ☎ 06/678–7877) displays Fiorucci's signature angels on T-shirts and delights adolescents with kitschy gadgets and accessories.

Onyx (⊠ Via Frattina 92, ☎ 06/679–1509) is a teenagers' hangout, complete with top-volume music, where girls can find the up-to-the-minute separates that they love, including minimal tops and miniskirts, at moderate prices.

Replay (⊠ Via della Rotonda 25, ☎ 06/683–3073) has the look of an American country store but sells youthful casual styles made in Italy. Prices are moderate.

Toys

Bertè (⊠ Piazza Navona 108, ☎ 06/688–01068) is Rome's version of FAO Schwarz, though only one-twentieth the size. Romans always include a stop at Bertè's display windows in a stroll around Pizza Navona. The doll population is astounding—from crying, eating, and talking dolls to lace- and ribbon-bedecked old-fashioned beauties. The menagerie of stuffed animals ranges from tiny kittens to enormous elephants and polar bears that you would be hard put to find room for in your suitcase. There's also a line of toys and supplies for infants.

Galleria San Carlo (⊠ Via del Corso 114, ☎ 06/679–0571) makes up in stock for what it lacks in decor. The store is basically composed of big display windows packed with toys; you show the clerks what you want and they will get it from stock. There's an ample selection of Italian-made dolls and a whole forest of wooden Pinocchios.

La Città del Sole (⊠ Via della Scrofa 65, ☎ 06/687–5404; ⊠ Piazza della Chiesa Nuova 18, Old Rome, ☎ 06/6878–2922) is the progressive parent's ideal store, chock-full of educational toys for all ages—even for adults (puzzles, tricks and gadgets). Shelves and floor space are crammed with toys in safe plastics and in wood and with games, puzzles, and children's books, mainly in Italian. You won't find a Barbie here.

Vintage Clothing

Cinzia (⊠ Via del Governo Vecchio 45, ☎ no phone) is known as a classic for vintage clothing, especially 1960s and 1970s styles, including leather jackets and Mary Quant sunglasses.

Le Gallinelle (⊠ Via del Boschetto 76, ☎ 05/488–1017) makes over vintage clothing, using old fabrics in new garments or reconditioning vintage dresses to look like new. This tiny shop even has a men's corner, with mainly overcoats and trousers. Prices are very reasonable.

Mado (⊠ Via del Governo Vecchio 89a, ☎ no phone) is like a trunk in grandma's attic, full of vintage clothing and costume jewelry, with ostrich plumes tickling your nose.

Women's Clothing

Alexander (⊠ Piazza di Spagna 49, ☎ 06/679–1351) brings the street right into the shop with continuous cobblestone paving and street-smart fashions and shoes for women who like trendy, aggressive styles.

Galassia (⊠ Via Frattina 21, ☎ 06/679–7896) has expensive, extreme, and extravagant women's styles by Gaultier, Westwood, and Yamamoto. This is the place for funky hats with ostrich plumes, feather boas, and flashy jewelry, at a price.

Wazoo (✉ Via dei Giubbonari 28, ☎ 06/686–9362) is one of Rome's trendiest boutiques for designer fashions for women, funky shoes, and very special dresses. Though small and divided into separate sections for shoes and clothing, the selection is wide and includes some of Vivienne Westwood's less outlandish styles.

BOUTIQUES

Dulce Vidoza (✉ Via dell'Orso 58, ☎ 06/689–3007) would be at home in New York's Soho; it's minimal and elegant. It takes classic pants suits out of the ordinary, using Nehru collars and unconventional fabrics and colors.

Elena Mirò (✉ Via Frattina 11, ☎ 06/678–4367) is an attractive shop with a selection of stylish casual and dressy wear in women's sizes. Fabrics and colors reflect fashion trends.

Lei (✉ Via dei Giubbonari 103, ☎ 06/687–5432) has young styles from this side of the cutting edge—up-to-the-minute but not futuristic. Dolce&Gabbana and Romeo Gigli are represented by ready-to-wear that is sweet or sexy, or both.

Le Tartarughe (✉ Via Piè di Marmo 17, ☎ 06/679–2249) makes a subtle fashion statement with a selection of versatile, easy-to-wear and easy-to-pack styles, many in knit fabrics, all designed in-house.

Maga Morgana (✉ Via del Governo Vecchio 27, ☎ 06/687–9995) shows faux vintage styles in bare little 1930s flowered dresses or with a folk look, as well as knitwear, all designed and made exclusively for the shop.

Mariella Burani (✉ Via Bocca di Leone 26, ☎ 06/679–0630) has classic chic with judiciously used high-fashion overtones. These clothes are ever wearable and never boring.

Xandrine (✉ Via della Croce 88, ☎ 06/678–6201) has dressy retro styles, in a choice of classic or extravagant, at moderate prices.

Markets

Flea Markets

There's a flea market on Sunday morning at **Porta Portese** (✉ Via di Porta Portese, access from Via Ippolito Nievo, off Viale Trastevere); it now offers mainly new or secondhand clothing, but there are still a few dealers in old furniture and sundry objects, much of it intriguing junk. Bargaining is the rule here, and it is imperative to take precautions against pickpockets. Though not strictly a flea market, the outdoor stalls at **Via Sannio** (✉ Near San Giovanni in Laterano), open weekdays 10–1 and Saturday 10–6, offer bargains in used clothing and army surplus. A plethora of flea markets, some charging admission, has sprung up in such places as the **Borghetto Flaminio** (✉ Via Flaminia, across from Ministry of the Navy) and in the garage on Via Ludovisi in the Via Veneto area. Look for schedules in the newpapers and in the *Roma C'è* magazine and inquire at tourist information kiosks.

Food Markets

Rome's biggest and most colorful outdoor food markets are at Campo dei Fiori (near Piazza Navona), Via Andrea Doria (in the Trionfale neighborhood, north of the Vatican), and Piazza Vittorio (near Termini station; this market is due to be moved from its traditional site skirting the piazza to another area close by). There are smaller outdoor markets in every neighborhood. All outdoor markets are open from early morning to about 2; some markets (among them, Trionfale and Piazza dell'Unita, on Via Cola di Rienzo) are open all day.

8 Side Trips

Ostia Antica; Cerveteri and Tarquinia; Viterbo, Bagnaia, Caprarola, and Bomarzo; Tivoli, Palestrina, and Subiaco; Sermoneta, Ninfa, and Sperlonga

In the background of Renaissance portraits of saints and princes lie dreamy landscapes sprinkled with medieval castles and quaint villages. You have to look closely to appreciate their beauty and wealth of detail, but your attention is rewarded with unexpected insight into a particular time and place. Rome is the undisputed prince of the Lazio region, dominating the foreground and monopolizing the attention, but, as in the paintings, a host of·charming sights and unexpected treasures sprinkle the countryside around it.

ABREATH OF COUNTRY AIR and a change of scenery can enhance your enjoyment of Rome and give you a new perspective on its disparate delights. For the greater part of 2,000 years, the grandeur and the glory of Rome have obscured the constellation of attractions in the region around it. Yet exploring Lazio (Latium, to the ancient Romans) is like applying a magnifying glass to an enormously complex painting replete with figures and action. By concentrating on one scene at a time, you get a much better understanding of the significance of the big picture.

by Barbara Walsh Angelillo

West of Rome by the sea, tall pines stand among the well-preserved ruins of Ostia Antica, the main port of ancient Rome and an archaeological site that rivals Pompeii. A visit to Ostia Antica tells you more about the way the ancient Romans lived than the Roman Forum does. (And it brings home just how close Islamic troops came to overrunning Rome, as they would have if the Turkish fleet had not been defeated off Ostia in 849.)

The rolling landscape of Lazio along the coast northwest of Rome was once Etruscan territory, and at Cerveteri and Tarquinia it holds some intriguing reminders of a people who taught the ancient Romans a thing or two about religion, art, and a pleasurable way of life. The Etruscan sites here give you a very concrete impression of the people whose art and artifacts are abstractly displayed in the Museum of Villa Giulia in Rome. Deep in the countryside north of Rome, Viterbo has an intact medieval core and historic traces of its days as a papal stronghold. Close by, the gardens of Villa Lante at Bagnaia and Palazzo Farnese at Caprarola give an inkling of how Renaissance cardinals took a break from their duties at the papal court. And at Bomarzo a 16th-century prince created one of the first theme parks in Europe.

East of Rome lie some of the region's star sites, which could be combined along a route that loops through the hills where ancient Romans built their summer resorts. At Tivoli, Hadrian's Villa shows you the scale of individual imperial Roman egos, while Villa d'Este demonstrates that Renaissance egos were no smaller. Eastward at Palestrina lies a vast sanctuary from ancient times. At Subiaco, St. Benedict founded the hermitage that gave rise to Western monasticism. Southeast of Rome are three romantic sites little known outside Italy: a castle at Sermoneta that once belonged to Cesare Borgia, a fairytale garden at Ninfa, and the seaside citadel of Sperlonga. In addition to rewarding you with a refreshing break from city sightseeing, Lazio's attractions offer the key to a fuller Roman experience.

Numbers in the margin correspond to numbers on the Side Trips and Ostia Antica maps.

Pleasures and Pastimes

Dining

A day in the country for the Romans traditionally includes a midday meal at a favorite trattoria or restaurant, so there's no lack of good places to eat in the Lazio region. Prices are generally a little lower than in the capital. Each town has culinary specialties that are worth trying, as is the local wine. Many towns are known for local cheese and also for their bread—crusty dark country bread that makes the ultimate *bruschetta* (toasted bread doused with extra virgin olive oil, sprinkled with salt, an optional rubbing of garlic, and topped with vine-ripe tomatoes). Restaurants on the coast, of course, usually have seafood specialties.

Side Trips from Rome

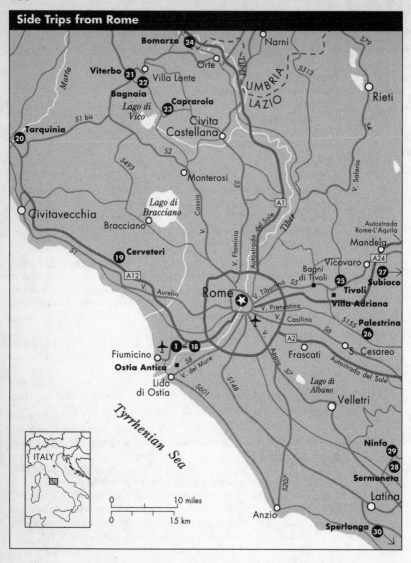

Bomarzo **24**

Narni

Viterbo **21**
Villa Lante
Orte

22

UMBRIA

Bagnaia
LAZIO
Caprarola **23**
Lago di
Vico
Civita
Castellana

Rieti

Tarquinia **20**

S1 bis

S493

S2

Monterosi

S3

A1

Lago di
Bracciano
Cassia

Tiber

Autostrada Rome-L'Aquila

Civitavecchia

Bracciano

V. Salaria

Mandela

A24

Cerveteri **19**

A12

Aurelia
V.

Vicovaro

Bagni
di Tivoli

25
Tivoli

Subiaco **27**

Rome
V. Tiburtina

S5

Villa Adriana

V. Prenestina

Palestrina **26**

Fiumicino **1** **18**

Ostia Antica

Lido
di Ostia

S8
V. del Mare

S601

S148

V. Casilina
A2
Appia
S7

Frascati

S6

S155

S. Cesareo

Autostrada del Sole

Lago di
Albano

Velletri

Tyrrhenian Sea

ITALY

Ninfa **29**

28

Sermoneta

Latina

0   10 miles
0   15 km

S207

Anzio

Sperlonga **30**

CATEGORY	COST
$$$	55,000–90,000 lire
$$	35,000–55,000 lire
$	under 35,000 lire

Lodging

With relatively few exceptions (hotels in beach and hill resorts and spas such as Fiuggi), accommodations throughout the region cater more to commercial travelers than to tourists. For this reason the public rooms and guest rooms tend to be functional and anonymous, though adequate for an overnight.

CATEGORY	COST
$$	150,000–200,000 lire
$	120,000–150,000 lire

OSTIA ANTICA: A PRETTIER POMPEII

Founded around the 4th century BC, Ostia Antica, 25 km (15½ mi) west of Rome, is reminiscent of Pompeii, but on a smaller scale and in a prettier, parklike setting. Fair weather and good walking shoes are requisites. On hot days, be there when the gates open or go late in the afternoon. A visit to the excavations takes two to three hours, including 15 to 20 minutes for the museum.

Ostia Antica was inhabited by a cosmopolitan population of rich businessmen, wily merchants, sailors, and slaves, and their respective families. The great *horrea* (warehouses) were built in the 2nd century AD to handle huge shipments of grain from Africa; the *insulae* (forerunners of the modern apartment building) provided housing for the growing population. Under the combined assaults of the barbarians and the *Anopheles* mosquito, and after the Tiber changed course, the port was eventually abandoned. Tidal mud and windblown sand covered the city, which lay buried until the beginning of the 20th century. Now it has been extensively excavated and is well maintained. The ad-

❶ mission charge to the **Scavi di Ostia Antica** (Ostia Antica excavations) includes entrance to the **Museo Ostiense** (☞ *below*), which is on the grounds. ⊠ *Via dei Romagnoli*, ☎ *06/565–0022.* ⊠ *8,000 lire.* ☉ *Excavations, daily 9 AM–1 hr before sunset; museum, daily 9–1:30.*

❷ The **Porta Romana,** one of the city's three gates, opens onto the Decumanus Maximus, the main thoroughfare crossing the city from end to end. Black-and-white mosaic pavements representing Neptune and

❸ Amphitrite decorate the **Terme di Nettuno** (Baths of Neptune). Directly behind the baths is the barracks of the fire department, which played an important role in a town with warehouses full of valuable goods and foodstuffs. ⊠ *North side of Decumanus Maximus.*

❹ On the north side of the Decumanus Maximus is the beautiful **Teatro** (theater), built by Augustus and completely restored by Septimius Severus in the 2nd century AD. In the vast Piazzale delle Corporazioni,

❺ where trade organizations similar to guilds had their offices, is the **Tempio de Cerere** (Temple of Ceres): this is appropriate for a town dealing in grain imports, as Ceres, who gave her name to cereal, was the

❻ goddess of agriculture. You can visit the **Domus di Apuleius** (House of Apuleius; ⊠ north side of Decumanus Maximus), built in the style of Pompeii's houses, which are lower and have fewer windows than most

❼ houses in Ostia. The **Mithraeum** (⊠ north side of Decumanus Maximus) has balconies and a hall decorated with symbols of the cult of Mithras. This men-only religion, imported from Persia, was especially popular with legionnaires.

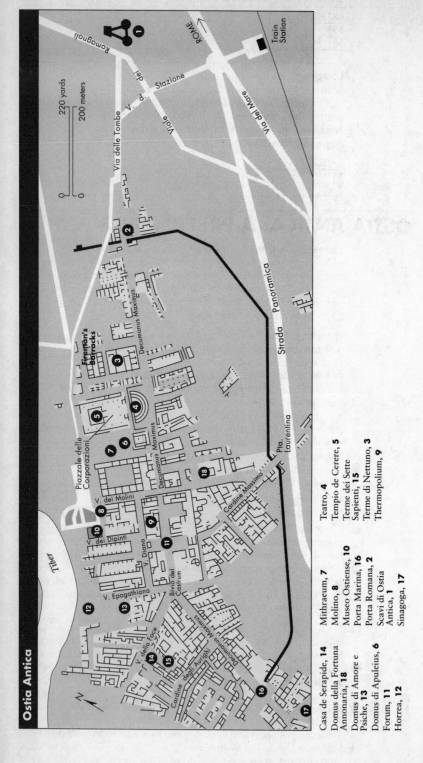

Ostia Antica

Casa de Serapide, **14**
Domus della Fortuna
Annonaria, **18**
Domus di Amore e
Psiche, **13**
Domus di Apuleius, **6**
Forum, **11**
Horrea, **12**

Mithraeum, **7**
Molino, **8**
Museo Ostiense, **10**
Porta Marina, **16**
Porta Romana, **2**
Scavi di Ostia
Antica, **1**
Sinagoga, **17**

Teatro, **4**
Tempio de Cerere, **5**
Terme dei Sette
Sapienti, **15**
Terme di Nettuno, **3**
Thermopolium, **9**

(8) On Via dei Molini you can see a **molino** (mill), where grain for the warehouses next door was ground with stones that are still here. Along Via

(9) di Diana you come upon a **thermopolium** (bar) with a marble counter and a fresco depicting the fruit and foodstuffs that were sold here. At

(10) the end of Via dei Dipinti is the **Museo Ostiense** (Ostia Museum), which displays some of the ancient sculptures and mosaics found among the ruins.

(11) The **Forum** (⊠ south side of Decumanus Maximus) holds the monumental remains of the city's most important temple, dedicated to Jupiter, Juno, and Minerva; other ruins of baths; a basilica (in Roman times a basilica served as a secular hall of justice); and smaller temples.

(12) Via Epagathiana leads toward the Tiber, where there are large **horrea** (warehouses), erected in the 2nd century AD to receive the enormous amounts of grain imported into Rome during that period, the height of the Empire.

(13) The **Domus di Amore e Psiche** (House of Cupid and Psyche; ⊠ west of Via Epagathiana), a residence, was named for a statue found here; you can see what remains of a large pool in an enclosed garden decorated with marble and mosaic motifs. Even in ancient times a premium was placed on water views: the house faces the shore, which would

(14) have been only about ⅓ km (¼ mi) away. The **Casa de Serapide** (House of Serapis; ⊠ Via della Foce) is a 2nd-century multilevel dwelling; another apartment building stands nearby on Cardo degli Aurighi. The

(15) **Termi dei Sette Sapienti** (Baths of the Seven Wise Men; ⊠ Via della Foce) are named for a fresco found here.

(16) The **Porta Marina** leads to what used to be the seashore. In the vicin-
(17) ity are the ruins of the **sinagoga** (synagogue), one of the oldest in the
(18) Western world. On Via Semita dei Cippi you can see the **Domus della Fortuna Annonaria** (House of Fortuna Annonaria), the richly decorated residence of a wealthy Ostian, which displays the skill of the mosaic artists of the period. One of the rooms opens onto a secluded garden.

Dining

$$ ✕ **Monumento.** Handily located near the entrance to the excavations, this trattoria serves Roman specialties and seafood. ⊠ *Piazza Umberto I,* ☎ *06/565–0021. AE, DC, MC, V. Closed Mon. and Aug. 20–Sept. 7.*

Ostia Antica A to Z

Arriving and Departing

BY CAR

Follow Via del Mare southwest, which leads directly from Rome to Ostia (a 30- to 40-minute trip).

BY TRAIN

Regular train service links the Ostia Antica station with Rome's Ostiense train station, near Porta San Paolo; the ride takes about 30 minutes. A long walkway goes from Ostiense station to the Piramide stop on Metro B; save steps by making connections with the train from Ostiense at the Magliana stop on Metro B. Trains from Ostiense run every half hour. Call ☎ 1478/88088 for toll-free train information.

CERVETERI AND TARQUINIA: ETRUSCAN LANDSCAPES

Northwest of Rome lie Etruscan (☞ Villa Giulia *in* Chapter 2,) sites on hills near the sea. The Etruscans were an apparently peaceable and pleasure-loving people who held sway over a vast territory north of

Rome before the rise of the Roman Republic. They loved life and they were sure that they would enjoy the afterlife, too. The Etruscan necropolis, or "city of the dead," was a cemetery faithfully reproducing the homes and lifestyles of the living.

Beyond Rome's city limits, the countryside is green with pastures and endless fields of artichokes. To the west, by the sea, the coast is dotted with suburban developments. Because the beaches in this area are popular with Romans, highways and public transportation can be uncomfortably crowded on weekends from spring to fall. The Etruscan sites are laced with uneven stairways and rough dirt paths.

At Cerveteri, the principal Etruscan site closest to Rome, in the necropolis of the Banditaccia, the mossy stones and variously shaped monuments, memorials to revered ancestors, stand in a sylvan setting. Tarquinia is close to Civitavecchia, the principal port of Rome. The port installations, which include a fort designed by Michelangelo, are visible from the highway or train. The low mountains to the east are the Tolfa range, where the Etruscans mined metals for export to ancient Mediterranean markets.

Cerveteri

⑲ *42 km (26 mi) northwest of Rome.*

The nucleus of the town, in the shadow of a medieval castle, stands on a spur of tufo rock that was the site of the Etruscan city of Caere, a thriving commercial center in the 6th century BC. The necropolis is about a mile on foot or by taxi from Cerveteri's main piazza.

In the **Necropoli della Banditaccia** (Banditaccia Necropolis), a monumental complex of tombs set in parklike grounds, the Etruscan residents of Caere laid their relatives to rest, some in simple graves, others in burial chambers that are replicas of Etruscan dwellings. In the round tumulus tombs you can recognize the prototypes of Rome's tombs of Augustus and Hadrian (in the Mausoleo di Augusto and Castel Sant' Angelo; ☞ Chapter 2) and the Tomb of Cecilia Metella on the Via Appia (☞ Chapter 2). Important tombs are open on a rotating basis, so you may not be able to enter all of them on a given day. Look for the **Tomba dei Capitelli**, with carved capitals; the **Tomba dei Rilievi**, its walls carved with reliefs of household objects; and the similar **Tombe degli Scudi e delle Sedie**. The **Tomba Moretti** has a little vestibule with columns. Some tombs have several chambers. ☞ *8,000 lire.* ☉ *Tues.–Sun. 9–1 hr before sunset.*

In Cerveteri's medieval castle, the **Museo Nazionale Cerite** is a small archaeological museum with some of the finds, mostly pottery, from the various Etruscan cemeteries that have been located in the area. The more important objects found in the tombs are in Rome's Museo Nazionale di Villa Giulia and the Musei Vaticani (☞ Chapter 2). ☒ *Piazza del Castello.* ☞ *Free.* ☉ *Tues.–Sun. 9–7.*

Dining

$ **Da Mimma.** About ½ km (⅓ mi) from the entrance to the Banditaccia necropolis, on the road leading to the site, this country trattoria offers simple and satisfying home-style food, especially handmade fettuccine and locally grown artichokes served in various ways. Tables are set outdoors in fair weather. ☒ *Via della Necropoli Etrusca. No credit cards. Closed Mon.*

Tarquinia

 About 90 km (55 mi) northwest of Rome; 50 km (30 mi) northwest of Cerveteri; 20 km (12 mi) north of Civitavecchia.

Tarquinia sprawls on a hill overlooking the sea. Once a powerful Etruscan city, its medieval core shows that it was a major center in the Middle Ages, too. Though it lacks the harmony of better-preserved medieval towns, Tarquinia offers unexpected visual pleasures, among them views of narrow medieval streets opening onto quaint squares dominated by palaces and churches, and the sight of the majestic, solitary church of Santa Maria di Castello, encircled by medieval walls and towers. For Tarquinia's Etruscan heritage, visit the museum in Palazzo Vitelleschi, and then see the frescoed underground tombs, in the fields east of the city. You can walk to the necropolis from town. From Piazza Matteotti, the town's main square, take Via Porta Tarquinia south past the church of San Francesco; go through the Porta Tarquinia (also known as Porta Clementina) gate and continue south on Via Ripagrotta. At the intersection with Via delle Croci, head east on the main road to reach the necropolis. There is very sketchy bus service from Piazza Cavour to the necropolis, with only a couple of morning and afternoon departures.

The **Museo Nazionale Tarquiniense** (National Museum of Tarquinia) is housed in Palazzo Vitelleschi, a splendid 15th-century building that contains a wealth of Etruscan treasures. Even if pottery vases and endless ranks of stone sarcophagi leave you cold, what makes a visit here memorable are the horses. A pair of marvelous golden terra-cotta winged horses gleam warmly against the gray stone wall on which they have been mounted in the main hall. They are from a frieze that once decorated an Etruscan temple, and they are strikingly vibrant proof of the degree of artistry attained by the Etruscans in the 4th century BC. The museum and its stately courtyard are crammed with sarcophagi from the tombs found beneath the meadows surrounding the town. The figures of the deceased recline casually on their stone couches, mouths curved in enigmatic smiles. Upstairs are vases and other Etruscan artifacts, together with some of the more precious frescoes from the tombs, removed to keep them from deteriorating. ⊠ *Piazza Cavour.* 🎫 *8,000 lire.* ⊙ *Tues.–Sun. 9-7.*

The **Necropoli** (Necropolis), the Etruscan city of the dead, is the main reason for a visit to Tarquinia. The entrance to the necropoli is about 800 m (½ mi) outside the town walls. Frequent, regularly scheduled 90-minute guided tours leave from the ticket office, visiting about 10 of the 100 most interesting tombs, on a rotating basis. The tombs, dating from the 7th to the 2nd century BC, were painted with lively scenes of Etruscan life. The colors are amazingly fresh in some tombs, and the scenes show the vitality and highly civilized life-style of this ancient people.

Of the thousands of tombs that exist throughout the territory of Etruria (there are 40,000 in the vicinity of Tarquinia alone), only a small percentage have been excavated scientifically. Many more have been found and plundered by "expẻrts" called *tombaroli*, who dig illegally, usually at night. The tombaroli are able to pinpoint many of the countless tombs that archaeologists know about but lack the means to protect. By pillaging the site, tossing aside what they don't want, they do irreparable damage. Their illicit finds are channeled into a thriving clandestine market with global outlets. What the tombaroli can't find, they make. Counterfeit copies of Etruscan antiquities that have come out of secret workshops in the area have been known to fool the experts—even in museums. The tombs in the Tarquinia necropolis are bare except for the paintings; the only evidences of their original function are the stone platforms on which the sarcophagi rested. ⊠ *Monterozzi, on the Strada Provinciale 1b (Tarquinia-Viterbo).* ⌑ *8,000 lire.* ⊙ *9–1 hr before sunset.*

Dining and Lodging

$$ ✕⌂ **San Marco.** In a centuries-old former monastery across the square from the entrance to Tarquinia's archaeological museum, the restaurant caters to visitors who need sustenance after trudging through rooms of sarcophagi. The menu of classic Italian food is diversified with seasonal offerings, such as wild mushrooms. Tables are set outdoors in fair weather. The San Marco also has simple guest rooms. ⊠ *Piazza Cavour 18,* ☎ *0766/842–234. 16 rooms. Restaurant. AE, DC, MC, V. Closed Mon. Sept.–May.*

$$ ✕⌂ **Tarconte.** This modern hotel with wraparound windows is in a panoramic position just outside the center of town, about 600 m (⅓ mi) south of the museum. It attracts business meetings and small conventions, but is also a haven for visitors who want to spend more than a day exploring Etruscan country. The hotel's Solengo Restaurant serves hearty pastas and *agnello scottadito* (grilled lamb chops), a local specialty. ⊠ *Via della Tuscia 19,* ☎ *0766/856–141. 53 rooms. AE, DC, MC, V.*

Cerveteri and Tarquinia A to Z

Arriving and Departing

BY BUS
COTRAL buses leave for **Cerveteri** from the Lepanto stop of Metro A, with service every 40 minutes or so during the day. The ride takes about 70 minutes. Also from the Lepanto stop, COTRAL buses depart for Civitavecchia, where you have to change to another COTRAL bus to **Tarquinia.** The trip takes about 2 hours.

BY CAR
For **Cerveteri,** take either the A12 Rome–Civitavecchia toll highway to the Cerveteri-Ladispoli exit, or take the Via Aurelia. The trip takes about 40 minutes. To get to **Tarquinia,** take the A12 Rome–Civitavecchia highway all the way to the end, where you continue on the Via Aurelia to Tarquinia. The trip takes about 60 minutes.

BY TRAIN
From Termini, Ostiense, and Trastevere stations in Rome, FS and Metropolitana suburban trains take you to the Cerveteri-Ladispoli station, where you can get a bus for **Cerveteri.** The train takes 30 minutes; the bus ride takes 15 minutes. To get to **Tarquinia,** take an FS train (Rome–Genoa line) from Rome or from Cerveteri to the Tarquinia station, then a local bus from the station up to the hilltop town. The trip takes about 75 minutes.

Visitor Information
Cerveteri (Piazza del Castello, 06/994–1354). **Tarquinia** (Piazza Cavour 1, 0766/856–384).

VITERBO, BAGNAIA, CAPRAROLA, AND BOMARZO: WHERE POPES AND PRELATES TOOK THEIR EASE

The Viterbo region, north of the capital, is rich in history embodied in cameo scenes of dark medieval stone, dappled light on wooded paths, a prelate's palace worthy of Rome itself, and another prelate's pleasure garden, where splashing fountains were aquatic jokes played on unsuspecting guests. From Viterbo and Bagnaia to Caprarola and Villa Lante, this region has a concentration of first-rate attractions—with the surprising Renaissance theme park at Bomarzo thrown in for good measure. The city of Viterbo, which overshadowed Rome as a center of papal power for a time during the middle ages, lies in the heart of Tuscia, the modern name for the Etruscan domain of Etruria, a landscape of dramatic beauty punctuated by thickly forested hills and deep, rocky gorges. The farmland east of Viterbo conceals small quarries of the dark, volcanic peperino stone that shows up in the walls of so many buildings here, as well as in portals and monumental fireplaces. Lake Bracciano is an extinct crater, and the sulfur springs still bubbling up in Viterbo's spa were used by the ancient Romans.

Bagnaia is the site of Villa Lante, where there are Italian gardens and a vast park, and at Caprarola are the huge Renaissance palace and gardens designed for the Farnese family. Both were the work of the virtuoso architect Vignola. He rearranged the little town of Caprarola, too, to enhance the palazzo's setting.

The ideal way to explore this region is by car, making Bomarzo your first stop. By train, you can start at Viterbo and get to Bagnaia by local bus. If you're traveling by train and/or bus, you will have to check schedules carefully, and you may have to allow for an overnight if you want to see all four attractions.

Viterbo

㉑ *104 km (64 mi) north of Rome.*

Viterbo's moment of glory was in the 13th century, when it became the seat of the papal court. The medieval core of the city still nestles within 12th-century walls. Its old buildings, their windows bright with geraniums, are made of dark peperino, the local stone that colors the medieval part of Viterbo a dark gray, contrasting here and there with the golden tufa rock of walls and towers. Peperino is also used in the characteristic and typically medieval exterior staircases that you see throughout the old town. Viterbo's San Pellegrino district is a place to get the feel of the Middle Ages, seeing how daily life is carried on in a setting that has remained practically unchanged over the centuries. The Palazzo Papale and the cathedral enhance the effect.

The Gothic **Palazzo Papale** (Papal Palace) was built in the 13th century as a residence for the popes who chose to sojourn here. At that time Rome was a notoriously unhealthy place, ridden with malaria and plague and rampaging factions of rival barons. In 1271 the palace was the scene of a novel type of rebellion. A conclave held here to elect a new pope had dragged on for months, apparently making no progress. The people of Viterbo were exceedingly exasperated by the delay, especially as custom decreed that they had to provide for the cardinals' board and lodging for the duration of the conclave. So they tore the roof off the great hall where the cardinals were meeting, and put them on bread and water. Sure enough, a new pope—Gregory X—was elected in short order. The interior is not always open, but you can climb the stairs to what was once the loggia. ⊠ *Piazza San Lorenzo.*

The facade and interior of the **cattedrale, Chiesa di San Lorenzo** (cathedral, Church of St. Lawrence) date from the Middle Ages. On the ancient columns inside the church you can see the chips that an exploding bomb took out of the stone during World War II. ⊠ *Piazza San Lorenzo.*

The medieval district of **San Pellegrino** is one of the best preserved in Italy. It has charming vistas of arches, vaults, towers, exterior staircases, worn wooden doors on great iron hinges, and tiny hanging gardens. You pass many an antiques shop as you explore the little squares and byways. The **Fontana Grande** in the piazza of the same name is the largest and most extravagant of Viterbo's authentic Gothic fountains. ⊠ *Via San Pellegrino.*

Dining

$$ ✕ **Enoteca La Torre.** Though *enoteca* means wine shop, you'll find a wide range of dishes here, from delicate vegetarian antipastos such as fennel custard to *ossobuco* (sautéed veal shin), served in the dining room. ⊠ *Via della Torre 5,,* ☎ *0761/226–467. AE, DC, MC, V. Sun.*

Bagnaia

㉒ *5 km (3 mi) east of Viterbo.*

The village of Bagnaia is the site of a cardinal's summer retreat where small twin residences are but an excuse for the hillside garden and park that surround them, designed by Vignola for a member of the papal court.

Villa Lante is a terraced extravaganza, the handiwork of virtuoso architect Giacomo Barozzi (ca. 1535–ca. 1584), known as Vignola, who later worked with Michelangelo on St. Peter's. On the lowest terrace a delightful Italian garden has a centerpiece fountain fed by water channeled down the hillside. On another, higher terrace a stream of water runs through a groove carved in a long stone table where the cardinal entertained his friends al fresco, chilling wine in the running water. And that is only one of the most evident and innocent of the whimsical water games that were devised for the cardinal. The symmetry of the formal gardens contrasts with the wild, untamed park adjacent to it, reflecting the paradoxes of nature and artifice that are the theme of this pleasure garden. ⊠ *Via J Barozzi 71.* 🖭 *4,000 lire.* ☉ *Open Tues.–Sun. 9–1 hr before sunset.*

Caprarola

㉓ *19 km (12 mi) south of Viterbo.*

The wealthy and powerful Farnese family took over this sleepy village in the 1500s and endowed it with a palace that rivals the great residences of Rome.

The massive, magnificent, 400-year-old Palazzo Farnese, built on an unusual pentagonal plan, has an ingenious system of ramps and terraces designed by Vignola (☞ Villa Lante, *above*) that leads right up to the main portal. This nicely allowed carriages and mounts to arrive directly in front of the door. Though the salons are unfurnished, the palace's grandeur is still manifest. An artificial grotto decorates one wall, the ceilings are covered with frescoes unabashedly glorifying the splendors of the Farnese family, and an entire room is frescoed with maps of the world as it was known to 16th-century cartographers. From the windows you can glimpse the Italian garden, which can be visited only by special permission. ⊠ *Via Nicolai.* ☎ *0761/646–052.* 🖭 *4,000 lire.* ☉ *Tues.–Sun. 9–1 hr before sunset.*

Bomarzo

㉔ *15 km (9 mi) east of Viterbo.*

The eerie 16th-century **Parco dei Mostri** (Monster Park) is populated by weird and fantastic sculptures of mythical creatures and eccentric architecture. It was created by Prince Vicino Orsini for his wife Giulia Farnese, who is said to have taken one look at the park and died of heart failure. No one really knows why the prince had the sculptures carved in outcroppings of stone in a dusky wood on his estate, but it probably has something to do with the artifices that were an artistic conceit of his time. Children usually love it, and there are photo ops galore. ⊠ *1.5 km (1 mi) west of town.* ✆ *15,000 lire.* ☉ *Daily 8:30–1 hr before sunset.*

Viterbo, Bagnaia, Caprarola, Bomarzo A to Z

Arriving and Departing

BY BUS

COTRAL buses for **Viterbo** depart from the Saxa Rubra stop of the Ferrovie COTRAL train. The *diretta* (direct) bus takes about 75 minutes. Other buses are slower. Bus schedules will probably change by 1999 when a new Rome–Viterbo train line is completed. **Bagnaia** can be reached from Viterbo by local city bus. For **Caprarola,** COTRAL buses leave from the Saxa Rubra station on the Ferrovie COTRAL line.

BY CAR

Head out of Rome on the A1 autostrada, exiting at Attigliano. **Bomarzo** is only 3 km (2 mi) from the autostrada. The trip takes 60 minutes. It takes about 20 minutes to get to **Viterbo** from Bomarzo. **Bagnaia,** just east of Viterbo, can be visited before entering Viterbo. For **Caprarola,** head south on the Via Cimina; the ride takes 30 minutes.

BY TRAIN

The new Rome–**Viterbo** train line should be operating by 1999 and should make travel between the two cities faster and easier. Trains also stop at **Bagnaia.** For schedules and information, contact **Ferrovie CO-TRAL** (⊠ Piazzale Flaminio, ✆ 167431784.

Guided Tours

For Viterbo, authorized guides are available through the APT office (☞ *below*).

Visitor Information

APT Viterbo (⊠ Piazza San Carluccio, ✆ 0761/304–795).

TIVOLI, PALESTRINA, AND SUBIACO: FOUNTAINS, VILLAS, AND HERMITAGES

In this region east of Rome are two of the area's most attractive sights—Villa Adriana (Hadrian's Villa) and the Villa d'Este in Tivoli—and two less-conspicuous attractions in the mountains. The road from Rome to Tivoli passes through some uninspiring industrial areas and burgeoning suburbs that used to be lush countryside. You'll know you're close to Tivoli when you see vast quarries of travertine marble and smell the sulfurous vapors of the little spa, Bagni di Tivoli. Both of the sites in Tivoli are outdoors and entail walking.

With a car, you can loop through the mountains east of Rome, taking in two very different sights that are both focused on religion. The ancient pagan sanctuary at Palestrina is set on the slopes of Mt. Ginestro, from which it commands a sweeping view of the green plain and distant mountains. Subiaco, the cradle of Western monasticism, is tucked away in the mountains above Tivoli and Palestrina. If you want to take in all three towns, plan an overnight stop along the way unless you start out very early and have plenty of stamina.

Tivoli

㉕ *36 km (22 mi) east of Rome.*

Villa Adriana (Hadrian's Villa), 3 km (2 mi) south of Tivoli, should be visited first, especially in summer, to take advantage of cool mornings. Hadrian's Villa was an emperor's theme park, an exclusive retreat where the marvels of the classical world were reproduced for a ruler's pleasure. Hadrian, who succeeded Trajan as emperor in AD 117, was a man of genius and intellectual curiosity. Fascinated by the accomplishments of the Hellenistic world, he decided to re-create it for his own enjoyment by building this villa over a vast tract of land below the ancient settlement of Tibur. From AD 118 to 130, architects, laborers, and artists worked on the villa, periodically spurred on by the emperor himself when he returned from another voyage full of ideas for even more daring constructions. After his death in AD 138, the fortunes of his villa declined. It was sacked by barbarians and Romans alike; by the time of the Renaissance, many of his statues and decorations had ended up in the Villa d'Este (☞ *below*).

The exhibits in the visitors' center at the entrance and the scale model in the building adjacent to the bar help you make sense out of what can otherwise seem a maze of ruins. It's not the single elements but the peaceful and harmonious effect of the whole that makes Hadrian's Villa such a treat. Oleanders, pines, and cypresses growing among the ruins heighten the visual impact. A visit here should take about two hours, more if you like to savor antiquity slowly. ⊠ *Bivio di Villa Adriana, off Via Tiburtina, 6 km (3½) mi southwest of town.* ☒ *8,000 lire.* ☉ *Daily 9 AM–90 min before sunset.*

Villa d'Este is Tivoli's main attraction, though it is rundown and bereft of what was once a magical view of the countryside, which is now blanketed with ugly urban sprawl. Ippolito d'Este, active in the political intrigues of mid-16th-century Italy, was also a cardinal, thanks to his grandfather, Alexander VI—the infamous Borgia pope. To console himself at a time when he saw his political star in decline, Ippolito tore down part of a Franciscan monastery that occupied the hillside site he had chosen for his villa. Then the determined prelate diverted the Aniene River into a channel to run under the town and provide water for the Villa d'Este's fountains. Big, small, noisy, quiet, rushing, and running, the fountains create a late-Renaissance playground. Though time is beginning to take its toll, and the fountains and gardens aren't as well kept as they were in the cardinal's day, it is easy to see why many travelers of the past considered Villa d'Este one of the most beautiful spots in Italy. A tour of Villa d'Este requires stair climbing and walking and takes about an hour. ⊠ *Piazza Trento 1.* ☒ *8,000 lire.* ☉ *Tues.–Sun. 9 AM–90 min before sunset.*

Dining

$$$ ✕ **Adriano.** At the entrance to Hadrian's Villa, this restaurant is a handy though pricey place to have lunch before heading up the hill to the Villa d'Este. The food is Italian with a gourmet touch, as in risotto *ai fiori di zucchine* (with zucchini flowers) or grilled porcini mushrooms in season. The atmosphere is relaxing. ⊠ *Via di Villa Adriana 194,* ☎ *0774/ 382–235. AE, DC, MC, V. No dinner Sun.*

$ ✕ **Del Falcone.** A central location—on Tivoli's main street leading off Largo Garibaldi—means that this restaurant is popular and often crowded. In the ample and rustic dining rooms, you can try homemade fettuccine and cannelloni. Country-style grilled meats are excellent. ⊠ *Via Trevio 34,* ☎ *0774/312–358. No credit cards. Closed Tues.*

Palestrina

㉖ *27 km (17 mi) south of Tivoli on S636; 37 km (23 mi) east of Rome along Via Prenestina.*

Palestrina is surprisingly little known outside Italy, except to students of ancient history and music lovers. Its most famous native son, Giovanni Pierluigi da Palestrina, born here in 1525, was the renowned composer of 105 masses, as well as madrigals, magnificats, and motets. But the town was celebrated long before the composer's lifetime.

Ancient Praeneste (modern Palestrina) was founded much earlier than Rome. It was the site of the Temple of Fortuna Primigenia, which dates from the beginning of the 2nd century BC. This was one of the largest, richest, and most frequented temple complexes in all antiquity. People came from far and wide to consult its famous oracle. In modern times, however, no one had any idea of the extent of the complex until World War II bombings exposed ancient foundations that stretched far out into the plain below the town. It has since become clear that the temple area was larger than the town of Palestrina is today. Now you can make out the four superimposed terraces that formed the main part of the temple; they were built up on great arches and were linked by broad flights of stairs. The whole town sits on top of what was once the main part of the temple.

Large arches and terraces scale the hillside up to the **Palazzo Barberini,** built in the 17th century along the semicircular lines of the original temple. It's now a museum containing material found on the site, some dating back to the 4th century BC. The collection of splendid engraved bronze urns, plundered by thieves in 1991 and later recovered, takes second place to the chief attraction, a 1st-century BC mosaic representing the Nile in flood. This delightful work—a large-scale composition in which form, color, and innumerable details captivate the eye—is alone worth the trip to Palestrina. But there's more: a model of the temple as it was in ancient times, which will help you appreciate the immensity of the original construction. ✉ *Museo Nazionale Archeologico, Palazzo Barberini, Palestrina,* ☎ *06/953–8100.* ✉ *4,000 lire.* ☉ *Daily, Apr.–June and Oct. 9–6, July–Aug. 9–7:30, Nov.–Mar. 9–4.*

Dining and Lodging

$ ✕▦ **Hotel Stella** In the dining room ($$) of this small, centrally located hotel in Palestrina's public garden, you'll find simple decor, a cordial welcome, local dishes such as light and freshly made fettuccine served with a choice of sauces, and more unusual items such as *pasta e fagioli con frutti di mare* (pasta and bean soup with shellfish). The rooms are acceptable for an overnight. ✉ *Piazzale Liberazione,* ☎ *06/953–8172. 28 rooms. AE, DC, MC, V.*

Subiaco

㉗ *54 km (33 mi) east of Rome.*

Tucked in among wooded mountains in the deep and narrow valley of the Aniene River, which empties into the Tiber in Rome, Subiaco is a modern town built over World War II rubble. It is chiefly important (aside from being the birthplace of Gina Lollobrigida, whose family name is common in these parts) as the site of the monastery where St. Benedict devised his rule of communal religious life in the 6th century, founding the order that was so important in transmitting learning through the ages. Even earlier, the place was a refuge of Nero, who built himself a villa here, said to have rivaled that of Hadrian at Tivoli, damming the river to create three lakes and a series of waterfalls. The road to the monastery passes the ruins of the emperor's villa.

Between the town and St. Benedict's hermitage on the mountainside is the **Convento di Santa Scolastica** (Convent of St. Scholastica), the only one of the hermitages founded by St. Benedict to have survived the Lombard invasion of Italy in the 9th century. It has three cloisters; the oldest dates from the 13th century. The library, which is not open to visitors, contains some precious volumes; this was the site of the first print shop in Italy, set up in 1474. ⊠ *Road to Jenne and Vallepietra, 2.6 km (1½) mi east of town.* ☎ *Free.* ☉ *Daily 9–12:30 and 4–7.*

The 6th-century **Monastero di San Benedetto** (Monastery of St. Benedict) is a landmark of Western monasticism. It was built over the grotto where the saint lived and meditated. Clinging to the cliff on nine great arches, it has resisted the assaults of humans for almost 800 years. Over the little wooden veranda at the entrance, a Latin inscription wishes PEACE TO THOSE WHO ENTER. Every inch of the upper church is covered with frescoes by Umbrian and Sienese artists of the 14th century. In front of the main altar, a stairway leads down to the lower church, carved out of the rock, with yet another stairway leading down to the grotto where Benedict lived as a hermit for three years. The frescoes here are even earlier than those above; look for the portrait of St. Francis of Assisi, painted from life in 1210, in the **Cappella di San Gregorio** (Chapel of St. Gregory), and for the oldest fresco in the monastery, in the **Grotta dei Pastori** (Shepherds' Grotto). ☎ *Free.* ☉ *Daily 9–12:30 and 3–6.*

Dining and Lodging

$ ✕ **Mariuccia.** This modern, barnlike restaurant close to the monasteries caters to wedding parties and other groups but is calm enough on weekdays. There's a large garden and a good view from the picture windows. House specialties are homemade fettuccine with porcini mushrooms and *scaloppe al tartufo* (truffled veal scallops). In the summer you dine outdoors under bright umbrellas. ⊠ *Via Sublacense,* ☎ *0774/84851. No credit cards. Closed Mon. and Nov.*

$ ✕🏨 **Belvedere.** This small hotel on the road between the town and the monasteries is equipped to feed crowds of skiers from the slopes of nearby Mt. Livata, as well as pilgrims on their way to St. Benedict's hermitage. The atmosphere is homey and cordial. Specialties include homemade fettuccine with a tasty ragù (sauce) and grilled meats and sausages. Adequate for an overnight, the rooms are simply furnished. ⊠ *Via dei Monasteri 33,* ☎ *0774/85531. 20 rooms. No credit cards.*

Tivoli, Palestrina, and Subiaco A to Z

Arriving and Departing

BY BUS

COTRAL buses (☎ 167431784 toll free) serve the region. Buses leave Rome for **Tivoli** every 15 minutes from the terminal at the Rebbibia stop on Metro B, but not all take the route that passes near Hadrian's Villa. Inquire which bus passes closest to Villa Adriana and tell the driver to let you off there. The ride takes about 60 minutes. From Rome to **Palestrina**, take the COTRAL bus from the Anagnina stop on Metro A. From Rome to **Subiaco**, take the COTRAL bus from the Rebbibia stop on Metro B; buses leave every 40 minutes; the circuitous trip takes one hour and 45 minutes.

BY CAR

For **Tivoli**, take Via Tiburtina or the Rome–L'Aquila autostrada (A24). To get to **Palestrina** directly from Rome, take either Via Prenestina or

Via Casilina or take the Autostrada del Sole (A2) to the San Cesareo exit and follow signs for Palestrina; this trip takes about one hour. From Rome to **Subiaco,** take S155 east for about 40 km (25 mi) before turning left onto S411 for the remaining 25 km (15 mi) to Subiaco; the trip takes about 70 minutes.

BY TRAIN

FS trains connect Rome's Termini and Tiburtina stations with **Tivoli** in about 30 minutes; Villa d'Este is about a 20-minute walk from the station in Tivoli. The FS train from Stazione Termini to **Palestrina** takes about 40 minutes; you can then board a bus from the train station to the center of town.

Getting Around

BY BUS

Bus service links Tivoli and Palestrina; check schedules locally.

BY CAR

From Tivoli to **Palestrina,** follow signs for Via Prenestina and Palestrina. To get to **Subiaco** from either Tivoli or Palestrina, take the autostrada for L'Aquila (A24) to the Vicovaro-Mandela exit, then follow the local road to Subiaco.

Guided Tours

CIT (☎ 06/47941) has half-day excursions to Villa d'Este in Tivoli. **American Express** (☎ 06/67641) has tours to Hadrian's Villa. **Appian Line** (☎ 06/488–4151) has excursions to Hadrian's Villa. **Carrani Tours** (☎ 06/482–4194) has tours that include Hadrian's Villa.

Visitor Information

Palestrina(⊠ Piazza Santa Maria degli Angeli, ☎ 06/957–3176. **Subiaco** (⊠ Via Cadorna 59, ☎ 0774/822–013). **Tivoli** (⊠ Largo Garibaldi, ☎ 0774/334-522).

SERMONETA, NINFA, AND SPERLONGA: PICTURESQUE TOWNS AND ROMANTIC RUINS

A trio of romantic places south of Rome, set in a landscape defined by low mountains and a broad coastal plain, lure you into a past that seems centuries away from the city's bustle. Sermoneta is a castle town. Ninfa, nearby, is a noble family's fairytale garden that is open to the public only at certain times. Both are on the eastern fringe of the Pontine Plain, once a malaria-infested marshland that was ultimately reclaimed for agriculture by one of the most successful projects of Mussolini's regime. Several new towns were built here in the 1930s, among them Latina and Pontinia. Sperlonga is a fishing village perched above the sea and site of one of emperor Tiberius's most fabulous villas. You really need a car to see them all in a day or so, and to get to Ninfa. But Sermoneta and Sperlonga are accessible by public transportation.

Sermoneta

㉘ *80 km (50 mi) southeast of Rome.*

In Sermoneta, the town and castle are one. Within concentric rings of walls, in medieval times, townspeople lived and farmers came to take shelter from marauders. The lords—in this case the Caetani family—held a last line of defense in the tall tower, where if necessary they could cut themselves off by pulling up the drawbridge.

The **Castello Caetani** (Caetani Castle) dates from the 1200s. In the 15th century, having won it by ruse from the Caetanis, Borgia Pope Alexander VI transformed it into a formidable fortress and handed it over to his son Cesare. The chiaroscuro of dark and light stone, the quiet of the narrow streets, and the bastions that hint at siege and battle take you back in time. ⊠ *Via della Fortezza.* 🎟 *5,000 lire. Guided tours only.* ⊗ *Open Apr.–Sept., Fri.–Wed. 10–11, 3–4, 5–6; Nov.–Mar., Fri.–Wed. 10–11:30, 2–3, 4–5.*

Ninfa

㉙ *5 km (3 mi) north of Sermoneta.*

In the Middle Ages Ninfa was a thriving village, part of the Caetani family's vast landholdings around Sermoneta. It was abandoned when malaria-carrying mosquitoes infested the plain, and it fell into ruin. Now it is a place of rare beauty, a dream garden of romantic ruins and rushing waters, of exotic species and fragrant blooms. Ninfa is part of a WWF Oasis, managed in collaboration with the Caetani heirs. Preceding generations of the Caetani family, including English and American spouses and gardening buffs, created the garden over the course of the 20th century. ⊠ *Via Ninfina, Doganella di Ninfa,* 🕾 *0773/695–407 (APT Latina/Provincial Tourist Office).* 🎟 *12,000 lire. Guided tours only.* ⊗ *Apr.–June, call for designated days; July–Sept., 1st weekend of month 9–12 and 2:30–6. Closed Nov.–Mar.*

Sperlonga

㉚ *127 km (79 mi) southeast of Rome.*

Sperlonga is a labyrinth of whitewashed alleys, arches, and little houses, like a casbah wrapped around a hilltop overlooking the sea, with broad, sandy beaches on either side. Long a favorite haunt of artists and artisans in flight from Rome's quick pace, the town has ancient origins. The medieval town gates, twisting alleys, and watchtower were vital to its defense when pirate ships came into sight. Now they simply make this former fishing town even more picturesque.

Under a cliff on the shore only 1 km (0.6 mi) south of Sperlonga are the ruins of a grandiose villa built for Roman emperor Tiberius and known as the **Grotta di Tiberio** (Grotto of Tiberius). The villa incorporated several natural grottoes, in one of which Tiberius dined with guests on an artificial island. The various courses were served on little boats that floated across the shallow seawater pool to the emperor's table. Showpieces of the villa were the colossal sculpture groups embellishing the grotto. The **Museo Nazionale** (National Museum) was built on the site especially to hold the fragments of these sculptures, discovered by chance by an amateur archaeologist. The huge statues had been smashed to pieces centuries earlier by Byzantine monks unsympathetic to pagan images. For decades the subject and appearance of the originals remained a mystery, and the museum was a work in progress as scholars there tried to put together the 7,000 pieces of this giant puzzle. Their achievement, the immense Scylla group, largest of the sculptures, is on view here. ⊠ *Via Flacca.* 🎟 *4,000 lire.* ⊗ *Daily 9–1 hr before sunset.*

Dining

$$–$$$ ✕ **Gli Archi.** Tucked away in a corner of Old Sperlonga, this attractive restaurant has brick-arched interiors and a courtyard for fair-weather dining. A touch of refinement puts it a cut above the establishments closer to the beach, and its owners take pride in serving quality ingredients exalted by culinary simplicity. Seafood, including pasta with seafood

sauces, predominates on the menu, but there are a few meat courses, too. ⊠ *Via Ottaviano 17,* ☎ *0771/54300. AE, DC, MC, V. Closed Wed. and Jan.*

$–$$ ✕ **La Bisaccia.** A favorite with locals, it is popular with seasonal residents, too. La Bisaccia is near the beach in the newer ·part of town, and you can walk to it in about 10 to 15 minutes from the center of Old Sperlonga. Book a table for lunch on weekends and in summer. Seafood comes just about any way you want it, from pasta with scampi to fried, baked, or grilled fish. And if you don't want fish, the menu has some basic meat dishes and a local specialty, creamy buffalo-milk mozzarella. ⊠ *Via Romita 19,* ☎ *0771/54576. AE, DC, MC, V. Closed Tues. (except mid-June–Sept.) and Nov.*

Sermoneta, Ninfa, and Sperlonga A to Z

Arriving and Departing

BY BUS

COTRAL buses for **Sermoneta** leave Rome from the EUR Fermi stop of Metro B. The ride takes about 60 minutes. For **Sperlonga,** COTRAL buses leave from the same stop. The trip takes about 90 minutes.

BY CAR

The fastest route south is the Via Pontina, an expressway. An alternative is the Via Appia. For **Sermoneta,** turn east at Latina. The trip takes about 50 minutes. For out-of-the-way **Ninfa,** proceed as for Sermoneta, but before reaching Sermoneta, follow the signs for Doganella/Ninfa. An alternative is to follow the Via Appia to Cisterna and then look for signs for Doganella/Ninfa. The trip takes about 60 minutes. For **Sperlonga,** take the Via Pontina to Latina, then the Via Appia to Terracina and Sperlonga. The trip takes about 90 minutes.

BY TRAIN

FS trains on the Rome–Formia–Naples line stop at Latina Scalo, where you can get a local bus to **Sermoneta,** though service is sketchy. Traveling time is about 60 minutes. For **Sperlonga,** on the same line, get off at the Itri station, from which buses leave for Sperlonga. The trip takes about 90 minutes.

Visitor Information

APT Latina (⊠ Via Duca del Mare 19, Latina, ☎ 0773/695–407).

9 Portraits of Rome

Rome dazzles, bewitches, irks. It has the grandeur of antiquity, the splendors of the Renaissance and Baroque ages, the panache of the present. Rome has great art, great style, and great food—and piques the visitor with some annoying inefficiencies. Rome wasn't made in a day, but just what does make Rome what it is today? Here are some insights into the Eternal City.

ROME AT A GLANCE: A CHRONOLOGY

c. 1000 bc Estruscans settle in central Italy.

753 Legendary founding of Rome by Romulus.

600 Latin script develops. Rome becomes urban center.

510 Last of the Etruscan kings—Tarquin the proud—expelled from Rome; Republic founded, headed by two annually elected consuls. First Temple of Jupiter on the Capitol built.

471 First plebeian magistrate is elected.

390 Rome sacked by Celts.

380 Servian wall built to defend city.

312 Appius Claudius begins construction of Appian Way and Acqua Appia, Rome's first aqueduct.

280–275 War against Pyrrhus, King of Epirus.

260–241 First Punic War: Rome struggles with Carthage in North Africa for control of central Mediterranean; gains Sicily.

250 Rome completes conquest of Italy.

220 Flaminian Way between Rome and Rimini completed.

219–202 Second Punic War: Hannibal invades Italy and destroys Roman army in 216; Scipio Africanus carries war back to Spain and to Carthage; in 206 Rome gains control of Spain; in 203, Hannibal defeated by Scipio.

168 Rome begins colonization of Greece and defeats Macedonia.

149–146 Third Punic War: Carthage is laid waste for good.

146 Rome completes conquest of Greece.

133 Rome rules entire Mediterranean basin except for Egypt.

102–101 Gaius Marius defeats Germanic tribes invading from north.

86 Civil war: Sulla defeats Marius.

82 Sulla becomes dictator of Roman Empire.

71 Slaves revolt under Spartacus.

66–63 Pompey colonizes Syria and Palestine.

49 Gallic War: Julius Caesar defeats Gaul.

47–45 Civil War: Julius Caesar becomes ruler of Rome.

46 Julian calendar introduced.

44 Julius Caesar assassinated.

31 Octavian (later Augustus) defeats Antony and Cleopatra in the battle of Actium and becomes sole ruler of Rome.

27 Octavian becomes Emperor Augustus: Imperial Age begins. Augustan Age (31 bc–ad 14) is celebrated in the works of Virgil (70 bc–ad 19), Ovid (43 bc–ad 17), Livy (59 bc–ad 17), Horace (65 bc–ad 27).

42 Building of harbor at Ostia Antica begins.

43 Emperor Claudius (ad 41–54) invades Britain.

50 Population of Rome reaches 1 million; city is largest in world.

64 Rome burns; Nero (54–68) begins rebuilding city.

79 Emperor Titus (79–81) completes Colosseum.

90–120 Silver age of Latin literature: Tacitus (c. 55–120), Juvenal (c. 55–140), Martial (c. 38–102).

98–117 Emperor Trajan builds the Baths of Trajan and Trajan's Market.

100 Roman army reaches peak, with 300,000 soldiers.

116 Conquest of Mesopotamia.

117 Roman Empire at its apex.

125 Emperor Hadrian (117–138) rebuilds Pantheon and begins construction of his mausoleum (now Castel Sant'Angelo).

161–180 Rule of Marcus Aurelius, philosopher-emperor.

165 Smallpox ravages empire.

211–217 Rule of psychopath Caracalla; he begins Baths of Caracalla.

284–305 Rule of Diocletian; empire divided between West and East.

312–337 Rule of Constantine; reunites empire but transfers capital to Constantinople (later Byzantium, today Istanbul).

313 Edict of Milan recognizes Christianity; Constantine begins construction of St. Peter's and San Giovanni in Laterano basilicas.

370 Huns appear in Europe.

380 Christianity made state religion.

406 Vandals lay waste Gaul and Spain.

410 Visigoths under Alaric invade Italy and take Rome; Western Empire collapses.

452 Huns invade northern Italy.

455 Rome sacked by Vandals.

488 Ostrogoths invade Italy; in 493 Theodoric proclaimed ruler of Gothic Kingdom of Italy.

536–40 Justinian, Byzantine emperor, invades Italy.

553 Italy reincorporated into Roman Empire.

570 Lombards gain control of Rome.

590–604 Pope Gregory the Great reinforces power of papacy.

609 Pantheon consecrated as a church.

610 Eastern Empire separated from Rome for good and continues (until 1453) as Byzantine Empire.

800 Charlemagne crowned Holy Roman Emperor in Rome.

1073 Gregory VII elected pope; his rule sees start of struggle for supremacy between papacy and Germanic Holy Roman Empire. Rome sinks into stagnation and ruin for five centuries.

1309 Papacy moves to Avignon in southern France.

1347 Cola di Rienzo, adventurer and dreamer, tries to restore the Roman Republic; he is hanged six months later.

1377 Pope returns to Rome; Gregory XI makes Vatican the papal residence.

c. 1500 Renaissance spreads to Rome—still little more than a malarial ruin—chiefly in persons of Bramante (1444–1514), Michelangelo (1475–1564), and Raphael (1483–1520).

1503–1513 Reign of Pope Julius II; begins rebuilding St. Peter's and commissions Raphael to decorate his apartments (*stanze*) and Michelangelo to paint the Sistine Chapel.

1527 Sack of Rome: Confidence of High Renaissance evaporates as troops of Holy Roman Empire ravage city.

1534 Michelangelo begins *Last Judgment* in Sistine Chapel.

1546 Michelangelo commissioned to complete rebuilding of St. Peter's.

1568 Church of the Gesù begun.

1595 Annibale Carracci begins painting *salone* of Palazzo Farnese, ushering in Baroque Age. Architects Bernini (1598–1680) and Borromini (1599–1667) build churches, palaces, and fountains, largely under ecclesiastical patronage, transforming face of Rome. Leading painters include Caravaggio (1571–1610), Guido Reni (1575–1642), and Pietro da Cortona (1596–1669).

1626 St. Peter's completed.

1656–1667 St. Peter's Square built.

1735 Spanish Steps laid out.

1797 Napoléon captures Rome and proclaims a new republic; Pope Pius VI expelled from city.

1808 Pope Pius VII prisoner in Quirinale.

1814 Pope Pius VII reinstated as ruler of Rome.

1870 Italian nationalists storm Rome and make it capital of united Italy; in protest, pope withdraws into voluntary confinement in Vatican.

1885 Monument to Vittorio Emanuele II begun (completed 1911).

1922 Fascists under Mussolini march on Rome.

1929 Lateran Treaty establishes formal relations between pope and state; Via del Fiori Imperiali begun (completed 1933).

1936 Via della Conciliazione begun (completed 1950).

1944 Rome liberated from German occupation.

1957 Treaty of Rome establishes European Economic Community.

1960 Rome hosts Olympic Games.

1962 Pope John XXIII convenes the Second Vatican Council, culmination of his efforts to promote ecumenism and give new vitality to the Roman Catholic Church.1978   Pope John Paul II, first Polish pope, elected. Extremist political activity in Italy reaches climax with kidnapping and murder of Premier Aldo Moro.

1981 Attempted assassination of Pope John Paul II. Cleaning of Michelangelo's frescoes on ceiling of Sistine Chapel in Vatican begins.

1990 Cleaning of Sistine Chapel ceiling completed. Work begins on cleaning Michelangelo's *Last Judgment* on wall over altar. Italian government passes so-called Law for Rome Capital, allotting funds and energy to a wave of major urban projects, including conservation and infrastructure.

1991   Rome's first mosque opens.

1997   Countdown toward replacement of the lira with the euro, the new European currency, begins, with the lira due to be phased out entirely by 2002. A copy of the statue of Roman emperor Marcus Aurelius is mounted on the pedestal of the original on the Campidoglio as a symbol of Rome's historic grandeur.

1998   Public works and restorations in preparation for the Jubilee Year 2000 under way throughout Rome. Several 1st-century AD frescoes discovered in excavations of Nero's Domus Aurea on the Colle Oppio, including one cityscape that is the first of its kind ever found.

CREATIVE ROME: GLIMPSES OF GLORY

FOR THE LOVER OF ART, Rome remains the richest city in the world, its accumulated treasures inexhaustible despite centuries of plundering and decay. The epic time span of its art and architecture is immediately apparent when you arrive at the train station: While still under the daring modern sweep of its curving forecourt roof (finished in 1950) you can see to the right imposing fragments of the first city walls (of the 4th century BC, but traditionally ascribed to the 6th-century BC King Servius Tullius), and a walk across the piazza leads to Michelangelo's brilliant adaptation for Christian use in the 1560s of the last of the great imperial Roman baths (finished by Diocletian in AD 306). In fact, the idlest stroll in town still offers a succession of subtle or dramatic pleasures for the eye.

Conservation and export regulations give some protection to the city against property developers and rapacious collectors, and the biggest threat to the city's marble monuments since the barbarians and the Barberini now comes from the automobile, whose exhaust fumes cause rain to fall as corrosive sulfuric acid on triumphal arches and ancient columns. Even the Colosseum may have to be given a protective covering until scientists or politicians come up with a solution—or the world's oil runs out.

Given Rome's reputation as an artistic center and source of inspiration, it is surprising, but significant, that it has almost never had a native school of art, most of the distinguished works to be seen being imports, copies, or the work of outsiders in the service of kings, consuls, emperors, or popes. Servius Tullius was the successor of an Etruscan king (and of Romulus, whose legendary foundation of the city is set at 753 BC), and the story of the earliest Roman art is that of domination by the neighboring Etruscans (and, through them, by the colonizing Greeks). The first great temple—that of Jupiter, Juno, and Minerva on the Campidoglio (Capitol)—was built for Servius's successor, Tarquin the Proud, by "workmen summoned from every part

of Etruria," among them the first named artist to work in Rome, sculptor Vulca from Veii. Only the blocks of the temple's base survive—a large portion of which came to light in 1998 under the pavement of Palazzo Caffarelli, on the Campidoglio—but its lively, colored terra-cotta ornament can be judged from the engagingly grinning faces on antefixes preserved in museums, especially in the Etruscan Museum in Villa Giulia.

From the Etruscans, the Romans adopted the habit of making graven images of their gods and probably also of casting statues in bronze. There are reports of bronzes made at the time of the first kings, but among the earliest and most numerous to survive is the Capitoline Wolf, vigilantly offering her teats to the infants Romulus and Remus, who, perhaps like the legend itself, are of later date. Etruscan, too, is the practice that was to prevail throughout antiquity of setting up commemorative portrait statues in public—of kings and of women but, principally, of military heroes. The victorious Republican, Spurius Carvilius, used the enemy armor he captured in 293 BC to have a giant figure of Jupiter made; and, from the filings left over after the chasing, a statue of himself was cast—as triumphator—one of the many precursors of the splendid marble Augustus now in the Vatican. In 158 BC the Forum had become so crowded with portrait statues that the consuls removed those that had not been authorized. Portraits were also commonly made for family reasons. Wax masks of the dead, which could be worn by the living so that a man's ancestors could be present at his funeral, and images, along with triumphal spoils, might be displayed on the lintels of the family house. Portraits were frequent also on the later marble coffins, or sarcophagi, in which even freed slaves might be buried, and although neither sarcophagi nor portraits were invented by the Romans, their eventual mastery (and occasional monotony) of portraiture is legendary; the early bronze bust of "Brutus" on the Campidoglio is a noble example.

EVEN THE ORNAMENT on everyday objects produced in early Rome is Etruscan in style; witness the mirrors and the cylindrical copper toiletry box, known as the cista Ficoroni, in Villa Giulia, its elegantly incised figures showing how strongly the Etruscans had been influenced by the Greeks.

Elegance was in general a marked feature of early Roman taste. But the expulsion of the Etruscans and the kings, and the expansion in the last centuries BC of the republican state that was to dominate Italy, and eventually the whole Mediterranean, brought with them a massive influx into the capital city of foreign booty; not just captured weapons but captured gods and works of art, carried in the triumphal processions of returning generals along with (presumably newly commissioned) paintings of their exploits and set up later as public ornaments. "Prior to this," says Pliny, "Rome knew nothing of these exquisite and refined things . . . rather it was full of barbaric weapons and bloody spoils; and though it was garlanded with memorials and trophies of triumphs there was no sight which was joyful to refined spectators." As the old-fashioned Cato is reported to have said, "Now I hear far too many people praising and marveling at the ornaments of Corinth and Athens, and laughing at our terra-cotta antefixes of the Roman gods."

Rome was thus exposed to a much more direct contact with Greek art, and the new conquests brought Greek artists and materials as well as booty. Temples retained some traditional Etruscan features in plan but began to look more Greek, such as those in Largo Argentina or the 2nd-century BC Temple of Fortuna Virilis by the Tiber, built of rough local tufa and travertine. The nearby circular Temple of Vesta (originally the Temple of Hercules, as an inscription discovered in the 20th century has shown), which dates from the next century, is made of the more "luxurious" material of marble. Not all old-style macho Romans welcomed this, and when Lucius Crassus used foreign marble for his house on the Palatine he was dubbed "the Palatine Venus." The great orator Cicero was not unusual in collecting examples of Greek art for his villa (a practice he called "my voluptuous pleasure"). Similarly, public art galleries were set up. Masterpieces of Greek sculpture were indeed in such demand that war booty did not suffice and many works were mechanically copied by the "pointing" process (invented by the Greeks and now used for the first time on a large scale)—so many in fact that a great proportion of the surviving antique statues in Rome's museums, even the Belvedere Apollo in the Vatican, are Roman copies or adaptations of Greek originals.

ART IN REPUBLICAN ROME was not entirely the consequence of plunder or imported labor. There were some exceptional native artists, principally in the more socially acceptable field of painting, in which a noble, Fabius Pictor, worked as early as the 4th century BC and later emperors such as Nero and Hadrian are reported to have excelled. Mural painting is also a genre in which one can speak of a distinctively Roman contribution. Compared with Pompeii, however, sadly little ancient painting or interior decoration survives in Rome, particularly from the early period. A noteworthy find, made in 1998, is a large bird's-eye view of a city that may be Rome itself, painted in Nero's time on a wall of the emperor's fabulous Golden House (Domus Aurea). There are some very fine examples of 1st-century BC painting and stucco—the charming landscape garden of Livia's villa and the "picture gallery" decor of the Farnesina House—in the Museo Nazionale Romano in Palazzo Massimo alle Terme and on the Palatine.

The transition from a republican to an imperial form of government in the late 1st century BC was achieved gradually, by stealth as well as force. Subtly as well as extensively, Julius Caesar and Augustus used public art as propaganda to buttress their positions. Famously, this involved big building projects and the claim that Augustus "found Rome brick and left it marble." Marble had of course been introduced earlier, but the forum Augustus built contains a greater variety of foreign colored marbles imported from the subject provinces of the Mediterranean than had been used before. Similarly, he was responsible for the introduction to Rome of the first Egyptian obelisks, which came to play such a distinctive role in the urban fabric (that at Montecitorio was originally used as a giant sundial).

The triple-bayed triumphal arch built for him in the Forum (whose fragments helped to build St. Peter's) also prefigures a characteristically Roman form, but Augustus's patronage was not overwhelmingly self-promoting. He was responsible for, but did not give his name to, the Theater of Marcellus and other buildings and built a temple in honor of the deified Julius Caesar, but he would not allow temples to be dedicated to himself unless they were also dedicated to Rome. The most attractive and best-preserved monument from his day is the Ara Pacis (Altar of Augustan Peace), reconstructed near his mausoleum in this century. Its sophisticated carving is interesting as a revival of classical Greek style, though the use of historical imagery, with its portrait scenes, allegories, and episodes from the early history of the city, is characteristically Roman.

AUGUSTUS'S SUCCESSORS did not need to be so circumspect. While Tiberius followed in his footsteps and left little personal mark on the city, and Claudius busied himself more with practical matters such as the aqueducts (most imposingly represented by the Porta Maggiore), Caligula and Nero were notorious megalomaniacs—Nero wanted to rename the city Neropolis. Many of Nero's public buildings—the Circus and the first great public baths—and the city planning undertaken after the great fire of AD 64 benefited the city as a whole, but the most extensive project of his reign was the enormous Golden House (the Domus Aurea) he built for himself, an engineering marvel set in parklike surroundings. When it was finished he said he was "at last beginning to live like a human being." The revolving ivory ceilings of the dining rooms are gone, but its dark ruins are still brightened by the paintings of the fastidious Famulus, who always wore a toga at work.

The succeeding Flavian emperors erased the traces of Nero's work. Nero's Colossus (a 115-foot gilt statue of him) was converted into an image of the Sun, and an amphitheater was built by Vespasian nearby on the site of the Domus Aurea's ornamental lake. This was the Colosseum, most famous of all Rome's buildings and scene of the grisly spectacles with which all classes of the Roman welfare state, including the slaves, were kept amused. It is also a distinguished piece of engineering, embodying another of the comparatively few architectural forms invented by the Romans—the amphitheater. Not that the Flavians were against self-advertisement. They continued to use the triumphal arch as a billboard to boast of their victories and assert their divinity (a notable survivor is the Arch of Titus, where the emperor is carried to heaven by an eagle) and the style of their sculpture was more robust and confidently ornamental than ever before.

Under the Spaniard Trajan (AD 98–117) the empire reached its widest extent. He was the last to add to the series of Imperial Fora (its adjacent market is still fairly intact). The largest forum to date, his was financed by the booty from his campaigns against the Dacians in what is modern-day Romania. Trajan's exploits are immortalized in the continuous sculpted narrative that spirals round the innovative 120-foot column, which still dominates the area.

Trajan's ward Hadrian (117–138)—the first bearded emperor, a keen hunter, singer, and devotee of the arts, and nicknamed "the little Greek"—was perhaps less concerned with his own fame, but no less active in embellishing the city. To him we owe the rebuilding of the Pantheon, a masterpiece of mathematical proportion and the only surviving building in which we can appreciate the full spectacular impression created by the Romans' increasing use of cladding in colored marbles from the imperial provinces. (Most of the marbles from the other ancient buildings, like the great baths, have long since been stripped off and now adorn the churches and palaces of Christian Rome.) Hadrian was an enthusiastic builder and frequenter of public baths, which, besides offering exercise and hygiene for the body, pleased the eye with their marble and mosaic decorations and their collections of sculpture (the Farnese Hercules, now in Naples, was found in the Baths of Caracalla), and nourished the mind with the literature kept in their libraries.

HAVING MADE PLANS for the most elaborate mausoleum in the city (which was later converted into the fortress of Castel Sant' Angelo), Hadrian in fact spent his last years almost exclusively at his sumptuous villa at Tivoli a few miles outside the city. This complex is notable both for the variety and beauty of its experimental architecture, with its references to famous sites in the Hellenistic world that Hadrian knew so well, and for the classical Greek revival sculpture that has been found there, including the Erechtheum caryatids beside the Canopus canal and the figure of his beautiful Syrian friend Antinoös, now in the Capitoline Museum (one of the many statues of him, sometimes in the guise of a god, which Hadrian caused to be set up throughout the Empire).

The Greek tradition dominated most Roman art till the time of Hadrian, but with his successors other ideals emerge, the change being particularly evident in the differing styles of the two sculpted panels of the base of the column of Anoninus Pius (c. 161), now in the Vatican, in the Arch of Septimius Severus (203), and, later, in the magnificent, if highly eclectic, Arch of Constantine (c. 315). On this arch, reliefs and statues from earlier monuments of Trajan, Hadrian, and Marcus Aurelius are juxtaposed, perhaps with a deliberate programmatic intention, with Constantinian reliefs, which are striking in their formality, severity, frontality, and, it must be said, crudity. The first two of these characteristics are often connected with the increasing absolutism of the Imperial Court.

The age of Constantine was a great turning point in the history of Rome and its art. The city was no longer the center of the empire (Diocletian had spent most of his time in Italy in Milan) and was not safe from external attack (as Aurelian had judged in 270, when he began building the massive walls that still ring the city). Constantine himself is famous for having founded the "New Rome" of Constantinople (later Byzantium and today Istanbul) in 330, but he did make a notable impact on the old city. Primarily this involved the discreet promotion, with imperial backing, of his adopted religion, Christianity, and the building of impressive churches for Christian worship and the privilege of burial. But this did not mean immediately abandoning all the old values, and indeed one of his principal achievements as emperor was the completion of what is now the dominant structure in the Forum, the Basilica, which had been begun by, and retains the name of, his rival, Maxentius. In its apse was placed for veneration a

gigantic seated figure of the emperor, whose scale can be judged from the fragments of head, hand, and foot in the courtyard of Palazzo dei Conservatori on the Campidoglio.

For his Christian churches Constantine adopted a form that had long served a variety of functions in Roman secular life and was to remain a standard church design for hundreds of years: the colonnaded basilica, with a flat roof and semicircular apse (a barnlike structure with two rows of pillars down its length and one rounded end). The principal ones, San Giovanni in Laterano and old St. Peter's, were on a massive scale, but it is worth noting that Constantine's churches were rather plain externally and placed on the outskirts of the city on imperial property. They were not assertively imposed on its civic and religious heart.

SAN GIOVANNI IN LATERANO and St. Peter's have since been remodeled or rebuilt, but a Constantinian interior, though smaller in scale and circular in plan, may be seen at Santa Costanza, the mausoleum built for the emperor's daughter, who was buried in an awe-inspiring imperial porphyry sarcophagus, now in the Vatican. Here the artistic continuity between pagan and Christian Rome is neatly exemplified. The column capitals are not all of the same type and, like so much of the building material used for subsequent churches, were clearly taken from earlier buildings, while the grape-crushing putti in the mosaics (and on the sarcophagus) had long been popular as a Bacchic motif and were now adopted by Christians as an allusion to the Eucharist.

No paintings survive in the early Christian basilicas, but paintings can be seen in the many catacombs, such as those of Sant' Agnese, near Santa Costanza. (The catacombs had, in fact, been used for Christian burials not from fear of persecution or as hiding places but because land for burial was expensive.) In these paintings, too, we see a similar transfer of pagan forms to Christian uses.

After Constantine, no emperor returned to reside permanently in Rome and the next century saw a struggle by the early church to assert itself in the face of old-established pagan power. Churches were built closer to the center, such as the original San Marco, near the Campidoglio, and the impressively Roman authority of Christian imagery can be seen in the apse mosaics of Santa Pudenziana (c. 400), where the Apostles wear togas.

By 408 imperial edicts had forbidden the use of pagan temples (or any other place) for pagan worship (though it was not till 609 that the Pantheon became the first pagan temple to be used as a Christian church). The sack of Rome in 410 by the Visigoths (the first major military disaster for the city in 1,000 years) was traumatic but did not prevent the emergence of the church as the unrivaled heir to the grand cultural dominance exercised previously by the now absent emperor. This is visibly expressed in the large 5th-century churches of Santa Maria Maggiore, where the well-preserved mosaics on the triumphal arch show the Virgin Mary as an empress with a jeweled crown, and Santa Sabina, restored in the 1930s as the most graceful and perfect example of an early Christian basilica, its 20 Corinthian columns taken from classical buildings.

BUT THE CENTURIES OF DECLINE had already begun. The city was sacked again—by the Vandals in 455—and taken over by the Goths. When Gregory the Great became pope in 590, it had been for years a mere outpost of Byzantium, its population shrunk and its urban fabric reduced to a skeleton by decades of war and natural disasters. The Byzantine commander, when cornered in Hadrian's mausoleum, had repelled besieging Goths by having its statues smashed and the pieces catapulted at them. The erection of new churches had not entirely stopped: In the 520s the city prefect's audience hall in the Forum was converted into the church of Santi Cosma e Damiano and given mosaics in the more formal and abstract Byzantine style—and the administration of the city increasingly fell into the hands of the church. But the future was bleak.

In the eight turbulent centuries that followed, the city's prosperity—and art—depended on the patchy success with which the pope could maintain his claim to temporal and spiritual power in the "western"

world, keeping the marauding Lombards, Saracens, and Normans at bay and the population of Rome in order. A major revival was signaled in 800, when the German Emperor Charlemagne, who saw himself as a new Constantine, acknowledged the supreme authority of the pope in the West by receiving his crown from Leo III in St. Peter's. Impressive new basilicas such as San Prassede were built and, not surprisingly, given Charlemagne's revivalist ideology, their form and mosaic decoration owed more to the art of Constantine's early church in Rome than to contemporary Byzantium.

But the revival was short-lived, not to be matched until the early 12th century, which saw a crop of new churches. In basic form they are almost monotonously traditional basilicas, innocent of developments taking place elsewhere in Europe, but they have attractive extras: tall brick bell towers (Santa Maria in Trastevere); cool colonnaded cloisters (Santi Quattro Coronati) and porticoes (San Lorenzo fuori le Mura); and lavish ancient marble fittings and pavements of the kind the Cosmati family were to specialize in, as well as mosaics (San Clemente). At San Clemente in particular, the charming still-life details and lush acanthus scrolls of the mosaics show a renewed interest in the pagan ingredients of early Christian art. But these ingredients had of course long been absorbed into Christian culture, and the examples of purely pagan art that survived had, to judge from pilgrim guidebooks, acquired superstitious, magical connotations—like the ancient marble mask installed in the portico of Santa Maria in Cosmedin, reputed to bite the hands of liars.

FURTHER REVIVALS occurred in the 13th century, not so much in architecture—despite Rome's one concession to the Gothic, the now transformed Santa Maria sopra Minerva—as in painting and mosaic. In the 1290s, and especially in Cavallini's mosaics of the Life of the Virgin in Santa Maria in Trastevere, methods changed so that pictures of people, buildings, and whole stories became more lifelike than before, changes that later helped Giotto revolutionize pictorial narrative. Giotto himself worked in Rome, painting the triptych for the high altar of the old St. Peter's, now in the

Vatican museum. But development in Rome suddenly ground to a halt, as the popes moved to Avignon (1305), and for 100 years the city became a backwater. Petrarch lamented the state of "widowed Rome," cows wandered in the Forum, and the only artistic event of note was the building of the massive stairs up to Aracoeli, part of the populist Cola di Rienzo's fantasy of reviving the ancient Roman Republic on the Campidoglio.

The schism caused by the move of the popes to Avignon ended with the emergence of Martin V, a Roman, as undisputed pope (1417–31). He began the long process of restoration and renewal that, over the next three centuries, eventually resulted in spectacular and successful attempts to rival and surpass the achievements of the ancients.

To begin with, this involved the restoration of civil order and much repair work, but Martin V and his successors lived at a time of artistic resurgence in the rest of Italy, particularly in Florence, and they were able to import distinguished talent from outside. The great Florentine painter Masaccio came to Rome in the 1420s; his colleague Masolino's attractive frescoes survive at San Clemente as the first example of the new, more naturalistic style in painting with its mathematical perspective, while other Florentines—Donatello and Filarete—produced idiosyncratic but impressive sculpture for St. Peter's. All these artists were stimulated by what they could see of ancient Rome, and their patrons by what they could read of its literature. In particular, Nicholas V (1447–55) was a classical scholar and, convinced that the only way of impressing the authority of the Church on the feeble perceptions of the illiterate was by means of "outstanding sights . . . great buildings . . . and divine monuments," he produced an ambitious plan of building and decoration for Rome in general and the Vatican in particular, doubtless with the help of his friend and fellow scholar, the artist Alberti.

HIS SUCCESSOR PIUS II (1458–64) remarked that if the projects "had been completed, they would have yielded to none of the ancient emperors in magnificence," but little progress was in fact made. A rare exception was the decoration of the chapel of Nicholas V in the 1440s by Fra Angelico, with, for him, extraordinarily monumental frescoes. More substantial results were achieved by the Franciscan Sixtus IV (1471–84), who built a new bridge across the Tiber—only two had survived from antiquity, at the island and at Castel Sant'Angelo—and a large up-to-date hospital (Santo Spirito) near the Vatican, both designed to accommodate the pilgrims who flocked to Rome in jubilee years. Churches, such as Santa Maria del Popolo, and palaces for cardinals, such as the enormous Cancelleria, were begun in new styles that paid increasing if still limited attention to ancient example. Property development was encouraged by new legislation. Although he was something of a philistine in his artistic taste, Sixtus did choose to import such outsiders as Botticelli and Perugino to decorate his large new chapel in the Vatican, and tried to organize painters in Rome by setting up a guild. Although he was not especially interested in classical culture, and, like all the popes of his period, continued to use the ancient ruins as quarries, he performed an important service by setting up on the Campidoglio the first modern public museum of antique sculpture.

Such at this point was the enthusiasm, and excavation, for antique sculpture that his nephew Julius II (1503–13) was quickly able to stock the sculpture garden that he in turn set up in the Vatican Belvedere with the choicest pieces, such as the Laocoön group, dug up in 1506. And it is partly due to the presence in Rome of these rediscovered and revalued treasures that the artists he employed, notably Raphael and Michelangelo, were inspired to evolve their grand styles of painting and sculpture, which we may think of as specifically Roman, even though their art owed so much to Florence.

They must also have been responding to the imperial vision of their employer, the aggressive warrior-pope, who, in his determined efforts to continue his uncle's policy for the city, ordered the demolition of Constantine's St. Peter's, to be replaced by an audacious structure planned by his architect Bramante, nicknamed "the Wrecker," which would, in scale and design, have "placed the dome of the Pantheon on the vaults of the Temple of Peace." For Julius, although he identified with previous popes in the dramatic propaganda decoration which Raphael painted in the Stanza of Heliodorus in the Vatican, also compared himself with Trajan in murals painted in his castle at Ostia. On his return from an expedition in 1507 a copy of the Arch of Constantine, depicting a history of his own exploits, was erected at the Vatican. Michelangelo's decoration of the Sistine Ceiling, with its grand ensemble of sculptural figures, medallions, and reliefs, is clearly an imaginative exercise in this imperial genre, and his original design for the pope's tomb (which is in San Pietro in Vincoli) "surpassed every ancient and imperial tomb ever made . . . in its beauty and magnificence, wealth of ornament and richness" (Vasari).

THE LUXURY-LOVING MEDICI pope, Leo X (1513–21), who followed, asked Raphael to decorate the largest room in the papal apartments with scenes from the life of Constantine, but he also borrowed jokes from Augustus and is reported to have said, "Since God has given us the papacy, let us enjoy it." There is plenty to enjoy in the long private loggia that Raphael and his pupils decorated next door, where tiny scenes from the Bible are overwhelmed by hundreds of painted and stucco images, mimicking ancient cameos and the kind of ancient fantasy painting to be seen in what had become the grottoes of Nero's Golden House when it was rediscovered in the 1480s. Hence the name "grotesque" for the style of painting that was to become enormously popular in Roman and, with the spread of engravings, European interior decorations in subsequent years. It was also used in Raphael's saucy decoration of the nearby (but not visitable) bathroom of Cardinal Bibbiena and on a grand scale in the imposing unfinished villa that Raphael designed for Leo's cousin, Villa Madama. This is hard to visit, too, but other attractive villas of the day exist—the Farnesina, also decorated by Raphael, and the later Villa Giulia.

Villa Madama was a conscious re-creation of the ancient Roman villa as described by Pliny, and contemporary palaces tried to re-create the ancient-Roman house with its atrium and courtyards, as described by the Roman architect Vitruvius. Palazzo Farnese, finished by Michelangelo, is a stunning example, while Peruzzi's Palazzo Massimo is on a smaller scale but no less impressive. The courtyards of Palazzo Massimo alle Colonne and Palazzo Mattei also show how contemporaries displayed their prize antique sculptures—by setting them in the wall as decorations. Many less wealthy Romans imitated this fashion by having monochrome sculpturelike frescoes on their facades. A lonely survivor is Palazzo Ricci in Via di Monserrato.

But in 1527 the fun had to stop when German soldiers sacked the city, giving a glimpse of Purgatory and causing an exodus of artists (with further diffusion of their ideas) and, it is often believed, a change of heart in the city's art. Certainly Michelangelo's Last Judgment in the Sistine Chapel is a tremendous warning to the wicked, but artists such as Salviati and Perino del Vaga continued to paint in the most exuberant and deliciously witty styles, for example at Castel Sant'Angelo.

The Church did attempt to reform itself from inside, however, and among the churches built for the new religious orders after the Council of Trent (1545–63) were the Gesù for the Jesuits, originally rather severe inside, and the Chiesa Nuova for the Oratorians, one of the many churches to be influenced by the design of the Gesù, with a broad nave for preaching to large congregations. Here, St. Philip Neri, the founder of the Oratorians, was frequently found in a state of ecstasy in front of the painting of the Visitation by Barocci, his (and many others') favorite artist.

SPIRITUAL EXCITEMENT and intensity, theatrically presented, were to become dominant themes in the next century's art—most obviously in Bernini's chapel in Santa Maria della Vittoria, where members of the Cornaro family look out from their boxes at an ethereal vision of the ecstasy of St. Teresa, bathed in light, the whole executed in the most splendid ancient and modern marbles and materials. Not all artists, though, looked so resolutely to heaven, and the most brilliant and influential painter in the period after Barocci was the passionate criminal Caravaggio, whose dramatically illuminated and controversial work ranged from luscious homosexual pornography for clerics to profound but distinctly earthy religious subjects—notice the obtrusively dirty feet of the adoring peasant in his St. Agostino altarpiece. Other distinguished painters of the day were more traditional—indeed, Annibale Carracci and his relatives pioneered a revival and extension of the styles of Raphael and Michelangelo, notably the opulent Galleria in Palazzo Farnese (c. 1600). Their work can be compared (and contrasted) with that of Caravaggio in Santa Maria del Popolo.

Humble details such as Caravaggio's dirty feet may have moved the lower orders, but art was still effectively commanded by popes and cardinals: If Julius II's artistic propaganda had been grandiose, it was almost eclipsed by the whopping stories put out for the 17th-century Church. In painting this means, among others, the extraordinary achievements of Pietro da Cortona, who extended the powerful language of Michelangelo's decorations with a Venetian fluency and sense of color in his exaltation of the Barberini family on the ceiling of their palace's salone. But the most spectacularly theatrical effects were created in public architecture, both on a large scale in Bernini's piazza for St. Peter's, for example, where hundreds of huge travertine columns provide encircling porticoes, and on a smaller scale in innumerable projects such as Pietro da Cortona's brilliant scenographic setting for Santa Maria della Pace. Perhaps the most gifted and inventive of these architects was Borromini, a difficult (and in the end suicidal) person who did not get the biggest commissions. But his San Carlo and Sant'Ivo show how he could convert a restricted site into a tight ensemble of exhilarating power.

WHILE THIS ARCHITECTURE was designed to impress, attempts were also afoot to make the city more comfortable. Bernini's porticoes not only broadcast the fame of Alexander VII but protected pilgrims from rain and sun. From the 16th century on, popes had striven to create straighter, wider streets, making it easier to visit the principal basilicas and speeding the progress of carriages. They also restored some of the ancient Roman aqueducts. The latter provided increasingly necessary water for the populace and supplied the impressive sculpted fountains that, from Bernini's Four Rivers Fountain in Piazza Navona to Salvi's Trevi Fountain, continue to delight and refresh the populace.

The Trevi Fountain, the Spanish Steps, and Galilei's facade for San Giovanni in Laterano were among the last great spectacles of the late 17th and early 18th centuries. The artistic importance of 18th-century Rome lay not so much in what was done for the city, as in what the city did for its many visitors. These were now the foreign artists studying the history paintings of Raphael and the religious works of Michelangelo in Rome's academies and the grand tourists, rather than the pilgrims of old. Piranesi's prints, fighting a magnificent rear-guard action for the grandeur of Rome against the growing popularity of a different—more purely Greek—view of antiquity, provided souvenirs for them; Batoni elegantly painted their portraits; and most of Canova's cool poetic sculptures were produced for export. The most distinguished building commissioned by the Vatican in this period was a museum—the Museo Pio-Clementino.

The power of the popes, and the city's art, continued to decline in importance in the 19th century, as Rome emerged as the secular capital of the modern Italian state. Large but creaking and empty edifices were erected to its ideals—the monument to King Vittorio Emanuele and the Palace of Justice. The city was besieged by suburbs, and the river embanked to cope with flooding and traffic, but it survived remarkably well even the ambitions of Mussolini. His attempts to re-create something of the glory of the Roman Empire produced monotonous boulevards through the Forum and at St. Peter's, spoiling the effect of Bernini's piazza. But his grandiosity also gave birth to the striking architecture of the suburb of EUR.

Nor, in modern times, has Rome been an international center of the musical and theatrical arts, though ancient theaters and triumphal arches testify to the early Roman love of spectacle—even emperors performed and sang. Nero, who made his operatic debut with a group of sycophants in Naples, put his stage clothes on and sang (not fiddled) to a select audience while Rome burned. Opera-lovers can recapture something of this experience at open-air performances of Verdi's *Aïda,* traditionally staged each summer with great gusto.

At the summer-long, outdoor, multiscreen movie festival one can see what gives Rome its claim to modern preeminence in the arts—the cinema. Successive generations of filmmakers working in the city and at Cinecittà since World War II—Rossellini, Pasolini, and Fellini—have created an enduring art, perceptively chronicling and imaginatively exploring the inside and the outside of modern life, and particularly, and most endearingly, of Roman society.

—Roger Jones

FEASTING AT ROME'S TABLES

THERE IS NO SUCH THING AS Italian cuisine. The Italian food that almost everybody loves to eat is really regional cooking. Lasagna and tortellini come from Bologna, veal cutlet and creamy risotto from Milan, pasta e fagioli and tiramisù from Venice, pizza or spaghetti with tomato sauce from Naples. Rome, too, has its very own culinary specialties, drawn from a tradition that goes back to the days when ancient Romans bought their groceries in the brand-new market that Emperor Hadrian had built. Yet Roman cooking seems to have had few ambassadors abroad.

Even in Rome, genuine Roman cooking is not easy to find. Restaurants and trattorias serve the cooking of other regions and other countries, catering to an increasingly heterogeneous population. The "Romans of Rome," a distinction that can be claimed only by those who have seven generations of Rome-born ancestors, are outnumbered by the "new" Romans—Italians from other regions and foreign residents, including legal and illegal immigrants from Asia, Africa, and Eastern Europe. Creeping mediocrity among Rome's eating places is making it increasingly difficult to get a really good taste of authentic Roman cooking.

The merit of Roman cooking is based on local ingredients, many of which are at their best only at certain times of year—milk-fed lamb, glorious globe artichokes from the sandy coastal plains, fresh vegetables from the farms of the Campagna Romana, as the countryside around Rome has been called since the time of the Caesars. Now, thanks to technology and imports from faraway continents, most ingredients are available year-round. But die-hard Roman cooks know there's no substitute for the real thing—food that nature has made ready for eating, not for traveling.

Simple, hearty, and redolent of herbs, genuine Roman cooking comprises the economical dishes of the carters, shopkeepers, and artisans of Old Rome along with the refined and elaborate specialties concocted in the kitchens of popes, emperors, and kings. In the 1st century Juvenal wrote of

dining on "a kid from the Agro Tiburtino, tenderest of the flock, who had not yet tasted grass and had more milk than blood in its veins." Martial, writing in the same era, sings the praises of the "lettuce, leeks, mint and dandelion greens, joys of the garden" brought to him by a farmer's wife. True to Roman tradition, he includes in his menu a baby lamb, "saved from the wolf's cruel jaws" only to meet a similar fate on Martial's table.

Celery, the indispensable ingredient of today's oxtail stew and bean soup, was covered with honey in ancient Rome and served as a dessert. Fish has also been a Roman choice through the centuries. In Trajan's time, slaves selected their master's favorite fish live from large tanks in the market, choosing between fresh- and saltwater varieties. At the entrance to the church of Sant'Angelo, at Portico d'Ottavia in the Ghetto, site of the old fish market, a curious plaque with a Latin inscription warns that the head of any fish surpassing the length of the plaque is to be cut off "up to the first fin" and given to the Conservators of the Capitol under pain of a fine of 10 gold florins. The heads were used to make a superb soup and were considered a great delicacy.

Eating habits have changed rapidly in Rome over the past few decades. Breakfasts are still sketchy: People usually start their day with a cappuccino and *cornetto* (brioche) at a neighborhood bar. Then, when mid-morning hunger pangs strike, they go to the nearest bakery for a square of crisp pizza *all'olio,* also known as pizza bianca (baked pizza dough, salt and olive oil) hot from the oven. Romans love to eat it slathered with fresh ricotta cheese or dotted with sliced fresh figs. Pizza recurs throughout the day as a quick snack or fast meal; you can find it in bakeries and from morning to evening in the ubiquitous *pizza rustica* places where you can buy squares of crusty pizza with all kinds of toppings to take out or eat standing up. Pizzerias keep restaurant hours and serve classic round pizzas that are made to order and served at your table. Pizzerias also offer *bruschetta* (toasted garlic bread, often topped with sliced tomatoes) and *crostini* (rounds of toasted bread topped with grilled mozzarella and prosciutto or anchovies).

On their coffee breaks Romans have an espresso. Like all Italians they consider the cappuccino, half coffee and half frothy milk, strictly a morning drink, like *caffè latte* (much more milk than coffee)—they would never order it after a meal. If they want their coffee diluted, they'll ask for *caffè lungo*, made with a little more water, or *caffè macchiato* (espresso with a splash of milk added at the counter). Many bars serve what they call *caffè americano*, a cup of American-style coffee. Caffè Hag is the best-known brand of decaffeinated coffee. *Caffè freddo* has little in common with iced coffee; it's more like coffee syrup and is served cold, not iced. *Granità di caffè* is frozen coffee slush that is sweetened and usually served with whipped cream. *Thè freddo* is presweetened tea served cold but not iced. It may be served *alla pesca* (with peach flavoring) or *al limone* (with lemon flavoring). Ice is something the Italians use little of, except in a granità. Except in top hotels and restaurants, if you ask for ice in Rome you're likely to get only a few small pieces served on the side. It's for your own good, the Italians would say; iced drinks are harmful, they upset the all-important digestion and can cause collapse. It's not easy to get a really cold beer, either. But you can try: Ask for whatever you want *molto freddo* (very cold), and emphasize the molto!

In theory, the main midday meal consists of several courses. However, problems of time and distance have forced Rome's working population to accept the idea of a light lunch, especially since offices and even stores have done away with the three-hour lunch break. As a result more and more places have sprung up in the city where you can find one-course meals, salads and such, with table or cafeteria-style service. Some restaurants also offer lunch menus.

A classic full Roman meal starts with an antipasto (hors d'oeuvre). In its simplest form, antipasto usually consists of a few slices of salami and prosciutto with olives and pickled vegetables and a butter curl (butter isn't served with bread anywhere in Italy, except in the most tourist-conscious places). A summertime delicacy is *melone* (chilled melon) or *fichi* (fresh figs) with prosciutto. *Antipasto di mare* is a seafood salad, usually already dressed with a citronette or vinaigrette sauce. Some restaurants are famed for their antipasto tables. This poses the question of how to order. As a rule of thumb, consider the antipasto the equivalent of one course. Throughout Italy pasta or soup is considered a first course; that's why these dishes are called *primi* (first). A normal meal would include a primo and a *secondo* (a main meat or seafood course). A basic restaurant or trattoria meal thus consists of two courses, with antipasto, vegetables and/or salad and dessert as individually priced optionals. To have only the antipasto is to snub the kitchen and to cut into the proprietor's cost/profit ratio. If you want to do as the Romans do, have one other course before or after the antipasto, perhaps a pasta or a second course or even a vegetable (a *carciofo*, or artichoke, nicely substitutes for a first or main course).

Though you'll find all sorts of primi on the menu, from the tortellini of the Emilia Romagna region to the risotto of northern Italy, remember that the truly Roman pasta is fettuccine: light golden ribbons of egg pasta cooked al dente and served with a savory meat sauce (*al ragù*) or *alla papalina*, in a delicate sauce of butter, ham, and mushrooms (sometimes with peas, too). Fettuccine may also be served with seasonal vegetables such as artichokes and porcini mushrooms.

You'll hear several versions of the origin of spaghetti alla carbonara, served piping hot with raw egg, chunks of *guanciale* (unsmoked bacon), and lots of freshly ground black pepper. The one holding that the flecks of pepper evoke the image of a carbonara (one of the sturdy women who sold coal on the streets of Old Rome) is as good as any. Another Roman favorite is pasta *all'amatriciana*, served with a sauce of tomato, unsmoked bacon, and a bit of hot chili pepper, with a generous dusting of pecorino (sheep's milk cheese). Pasta *alla gricia*, dressed with hot oil, unsmoked bacon, and plenty of black pepper, also is typically Roman, though it's not found on many menus. For an utterly simple and delicious summer dish, try *pasta alla checcha*, steaming hot pasta that is tossed with fresh, uncooked chopped tomatoes, garlic, olive oil, and basil. "Giovedì gnocchi!" (Thursday gnocchi), traditional Thursday fare in Roman restaurants and trattorias, gnocchi are tiny dumplings of semolina or potatoes, served as a first course with tomato sauce and lots of cheese.

The truly Roman soup is *stracciatella,* steaming chicken broth with a beaten egg stirred into it together with parmigiano cheese and a dash of nutmeg. The egg cooks as it's carried to the table.

Among the main courses, *abbacchio,* the baby lamb mentioned by Martial, is a classic choice. Spring is the best time for this dish. It is either roasted or served *al scottadito*—that is, grilled in the form of tiny chops that may burn your fingers (scotta dito) as you pick them up, a practice quite acceptable here.

On the menu, in addition to the usual *bistecca* (steak; with the exception of Tuscan meat, beef tends to be tough) and *cotoletta* (cutlet), you'll probably find *saltimbocca alla romana* (tender veal cutlets with sage and prosciutto) and *straccetti* (paper-thin slices of beef sautéed in oil). *Involtini* are little meat rolls, and *polpette* are meat balls. *Pollo alla diavola,* grilled chicken with a touch of lemon, is a simple main course. Many varieties of seafood are offered, from scampi (large shrimp) to *dentice or orata* (types of bream) and *rombo* (turbot). Though seafood dishes are generally more expensive, they are in great demand, so many Rome restaurants make seafood a specialty. "He's a baccalà" the Romans say, meaning that a person is stupid, perhaps unjustly maligning the *baccalà,* or codfish, which they otherwise esteem, especially in the form of crunchy hot fillets fried in batter.

The Roman way with innards is a story in itself. Centuries ago the men who cleaned and tanned the hides of the animals butchered in Rome were given the animals' innards to take home as a bonus. Ingenious housewives used these humble ingredients to create numerous dishes that have become staples of authentic Roman cooking. The most famous is *coda alla vaccinara,* oxtail simmered for hours in a tomato and celery stew. *Trippa* (tripe) is another favorite and a tradition on Saturday. *Coratella* (sautéed lamb's innards) and *pagliata* (baby lamb's intestines, usually served with rigatoni pasta) are still specialties of the restaurants and trattorias of Testaccio, where the slaughterhouses used to be.

Fritto misto alla romana consists of batter-fried tidbits of artichokes or zucchini, ricotta, apples, brains, and sweetbreads. Roman trattorias may also serve *fagioli con le cotiche,* beans with pork rind.

Green vegetables are good in Rome. You'll see them on open-air market stalls in the morning and in the gastronomic still lifes that greet you in restaurants. Order *piselli e prosciutto* (peas and ham) in the spring, green salads, *cipolline in agrodolce* (baby onions in a sweet-sour sauce) and by all means try *puntarelle,* a truly Roman specialty, a variety of tender chickory curled in ice water and served with a garlicky anchovy dressing. It's usually available only in winter and spring.

The queen of Roman vegetables is the globe artichoke (*carciofo romanesco*), grown mainly in the iron-rich fields of the coastal plain north of Rome. It is particularly delicate when prepared *alla giudia,* the Jewish way, just as it originated in the kitchens of the Ghetto. Tender young artichokes are deep-fried and opened out to take the form of a flower, with each petal crisp and light enough to melt in your mouth. *Carciofo alla romana* is sautéed whole with garlic and parsley or mint.

As in most of Italy, Romans like to finish off their meal with fresh fruit or *macedonia* (fruit cup). Tiramisù is popular, as is *panna cotta,* milk custard that may be served with berries. *Gelato* (ice cream) is usually available and may be served *affogato* (literally, "drowned," with whisky). *Torta di ricotta* is the Roman version of cheesecake, made with ricotta, similar to cottage cheese. The local cheeses are mild caciotta and sharp, hard pecorino. You may be offered a liqueur by your host, and it will probably be *limoncello,* the popular lemon liqueur.

The ideal accompaniment to Roman food is the wine produced in the nearby hill towns known as the Castelli Romani and in the wineries around Lake Bolsena, a bit farther afield. Among the Castelli Romani wines, Frascati is a dry, fruity white; when it's good it's very, very good, but too often the stuff served in carafes as Frascati is a poor substitute for the real thing. When in doubt, ask for a bottled wine. Colli Albani is quite similar to Frascati. Lanuvio is dry, golden-yellow and rather robust. Marino may be either dry (*secco*) or slightly sweet (*abboccato*); it is either white or red. Velletri also produces a dry white and a red that ranges in color from pale to ruby red. The dry white Est Est Est of Montefiascone, on Lake Bolsena, turns up on Roman tables, as do some unpretentious but good whites from Capena and Cerveteri and whites and reds from Vignanello, near Viterbo.

Not many Romans indulge in the full banquet anymore, except on special occasions, mainly family get-togethers. But Romans do consider eating an essential component of traditional conviviality. With fast-food chains encroaching and the pace of life quickening, they defend their sociable and relaxed lifestyle by seizing every opportunity to gather in noisy family groups to enjoy good food and wine and congenial company.

—Barbara Walsh Angelillo

ROME IN BOOKS AND ON FILM

Books

The Italians, by Luigi Barzini, is a comprehensive, lively analysis of the Italian national character, still worth reading although published in 1964 (Atheneum). Though the Italian way of life has changed considerably since he wrote the book, his analysis provides insight into some immutable traits. More recent musings on Italian life include *Italian Days,* by Barbara Grizzuti Harrison (Ticknor & Fields), and *That Fine Italian Hand,* by Paul Hoffman (Henry Holt), for many years *New York Times* bureau chief in Rome. In *Rome The Biography of a City* (Penguin), Christopher Hibbert provides a well-written and informative view of the city's eminent past and complex present. *When in Rome* (Robson Books) is a humorous anthology of whimsical passages about Rome written by such famous authors as Dickens. Classics of the travel essay genre include Elizabeth Bowen's *A Time in Rome* (Penguin) and James Lee Milne's *Roman Mornings* (New Amsterdam). Historic musings about Italy are offered in Henry James's perceptive *Italian Hours* (offered in many editions, including *Traveling in Italy with Henry James: Essays,* William Morrow), and in Edith Wharton's *Italian Backgrounds and Italian Villas and their Gardens* (Ecco Press).

For historical background, Edward Gibbon's *Decline and Fall of the Roman Empire* is available in three volumes (Modern Library). Consult Giorgio Vasari's *Lives of the Artists* and *The Autobiography of Benvenuto Cellini* (both available in Penguin Classics) for eyewitness accounts of the 16th century. An enlightening study of the complexities of Italy's contemporary history is offered by Paul Ginsborg's *A History of Contemporary Italy: Society and Politics 1943–1988* (Penguin).

A comprehensive introduction to Italian art is Frederick Hartt's *History of Italian Renaissance Art* (Abrams). For aficionados of Rome's artistic treasures, Georgina Masson's *Companion Guide to Rome* (Univ. of Rochester Press) is available in a new, updated edition.

For lively historical fiction, pick up *I Claudius* and *Claudius the God* by Robert Graves, available in a single edition (Penguin). Irving Stone's *The Agony and the Ecstasy* (NAL), relates a fictionalized version of the life of Michelangelo. Rome's inhabitants are portrayed during and after World War II in *History: A Novel* by Elsa Morante (Vintage Aventura).

Videos

Set in a Rome that was recovering from World War II, Roberto Rossellini's *Rome, Open City* (1946), and Vittorio De Sica's *Shoeshine* (1946) and *Bicycle Thieves* (1948) are classics of the postwar cinema's neorealism. The delightful *Roman Holiday* (1953), in which a princess plays hooky from her royal entourage to go slumming with Gregory Peck, won Audrey Hepburn an Oscar. Federico Fellini's *La Dolce Vita* (1961), with Marcello Mastroianni discovering the decadence of high society in Rome, gave its name to an era. Fellini's *Roma* (1972) is the director's exuberant paean to the city.

ITALIAN VOCABULARY

	English	Italian	Pronunciation
Basics			
	Yes/no	Sí/No	see/no
	Please	Per favore	pear fa-**vo**-ray
	Thank you	Grazie	**grah**-tsee-ay
	You're welcome	Prego	**pray**-go
	Excuse me, sorry	Scusi	**skoo**-zee
	Good morning/afternoon	Buon giorno	bwohn **jor**-no
	Good evening	Buona sera	**bwoh**-na **say**-ra
	Good bye	Arrivederci	a-ree-vah-**dare**-chee
	Mr. (Sir)	Signore	see **nyo**-ray
	Mrs. (Ma'am)	Signora	see-**nyo**-ra
	Miss	Signorina	sey-nyo-**ree**-na
	Pleased to meet you	Piacere	pee-ah-**chair**-ray
	How are you?	Come sta?	**ko**-may **stah**
	Very well, thanks	Bene, grazie	**ben**-ay **grah**-tsee-ay
	And you?	E lei?	ay **lay**-ee
Numbers			
	one	uno	**oo**-no
	two	due	**doo**-ay
	three	tre	tray
	four	quattro	**kwah**-tro
	five	cinque	**cheen**-kway
	six	sei	say
	seven	sette	**set**-ay
	eight	otto	**oh**-to
	nine	nove	**no**-vay
	ten	dieci	dee-**eh**-chee
Useful Phrases			
	Do you speak English?	Parla inglese?	**par**-la een-**glay**-zay
	I don't understand	Non capisco	non ka-**peess**-ko
	Slowly!	Lentamente!	**len**-ta-men-tay
	I don't know	Non lo so	noan lo **so**
	I'm American/British	Sono americano(a)	**so**-no a-may-ree-**kah**-no(a)
		Sono inglese	**so**-no een-**glay**-zay
	What's your name?	Come si chiama?	**ko**-may see kee-**ah**-ma
	My name is . . .	Mi chiamoo . . .	mee kee-**ah**-mo
	What time is it?	Che ore sono?	kay **o**-ray **so**-no?
	Yesterday/today/tomorrow	Ieri/oggi/domani	**yer**-ee/**o**-jee/do-**mah**-nee

This morning/ afternoon	Stamattina/Oggi pomeriggio	sta-ma-**tee**-na/**o**-jee po-mer-**ee**-jo
Tonight	Stasera	sta-**ser**-a
Where is . . . the bus stop?	Dov'è . . . la fermata dell'autobus?	doe-**veh** la fer-**mah**-ta del ow-toe-**booss**
the train station?	la stazione?	la sta-tsee-**oh**-nay
the subway station?	la metropolitana?	la may-tro-po-lee-**tah**-na
the post office?	l'ufficio postale?	loo-**fee**-cho po-**stah**-lay
the bank?	la banca?	la **bahn**-ka
the . . . hotel?	l'hotel . . . ?	lo-**tel**
the store?	il negozio?	ell nay-**go**-tsee-o
the . . . museum?	il museo . . . ?	eel moo-**zay**-o
the hospital?	l'ospedale?	lo-spay-**dah**-lay
a telephone?	un telefono?	oon tay-**lay**-fo-no
Where are the restrooms?	Dov'è il bagno?	do-**vay** eel **bahn**-yo
Here/there	Qui/là	kwee-la
Left/right	A sinistra/a destra	a see-**neess**-tra/ a **des**-tra
Straight ahead	Avanti dritto	a-**vahn**-tee **dree**-to
Is it near/far?	È vicino/lontano?	ay vee-**chee**-no/ lon-**tah**-no
I'd like . . . a room the key a stamp	Vorrei . . . una camera la chiave un francobollo	vo-**ray** **oo**-na **kah**-may-ra la kee-**ah**-vay oon-frahn-ko-**bo**-lo
I'd like to buy . . . some soap a city plan a postcard	Vorrei comprare . . . una saponetta una pianta della città una cartolina	vo-**ray** kom-**prah**-ray **oo**-na sa-po-**net**-a **oo**-na **pyahn**-ta day-la chee-**tah** **oo**-na car-toe-**lee**-na
How much is it?	Quanto costa?	**kwahn**-toe **coast**-a
It's expensive/ cheap	È caro/economico	ay **car**-o/ay-ko- **no**-mee-ko
A little/a lot	Poco/tanto	**po**-ko-**tahn**-to
More/less	Più/meno	pee-**oo**/**may**-no
I am sick	Sto male	sto **mah**-lay
Please call a doctor	Chiami un dottore	kee-**ah**-mee oon doe-**toe**-ray
Help!	Aiuto!	a-**yoo**-toe
Stop!	Alt!	ahlt
Fire!	Al fuoco!	ahl **fwo**-ko
Caution/Look out!	Attenzione!	a-ten-**syon**-ay

INDEX

Fodor's
ESCAPE

One-of-a-kind Italian experiences

The perfect companions to **Fodor's** Gold Guides, these exquisite full-color guidebooks will inspire you with their unique vacation ideas, help you plan with detailed contact information, and safeguard your memories with their gorgeous photographs.

WHEREVER YOU TRAVEL, HELP IS NEVER FAR AWAY.

From planning your trip to

providing travel assistance along

the way, American Express®

Travel Service Offices are

always there to help

you do more.

do more AMERICAN EXPRESS

Travel

www.americanexpress.com/travel

American Express Travel Service Offices
are located throughout Rome.